PROPS+©

Probabilistic and Optimization Spreadsheets
Plus What-If-Solver™

Limited Warranty

Addison-Wesley warrants that PROPS⁺ ("the program") will substantially conform to the published specifications and to the documentation during the period of 90 days from the date of original purchase, provided that it is used on the computer hardware and with the operating system for which it was designed. Addison-Wesley also warrants that the magnetic media on which the program is distributed and the documentation are free from defects in materials and workmanship during the period of 90 days from the date of original purchase. Addison-Wesley will replace defective media or documentation or correct substantial program errors at no charge, provided you return the item with dated proof of purchase to Addison-Wesley within 90 days of the date of original purchase. If Addison-Wesley is unable to replace defective media or documentation or correct substantial program errors, your license fee will be refunded. These are your sole remedies for any breach of warranty.

Except as specifically provided above, Addison-Wesley makes no warranty or representation, either express or implied, with respect to this program, documentation or media, including their quality, performance, merchantability, or fitness for a particular purpose.

Because programs are inherently complex and may not be completely free of errors, you are advised to verify your work. **In no event will Addison-Wesley or PS be liable for direct, indirect, special, incidental, or consequential damages arising out of the use of or inability to use the program, documentation, or media,** even if advised of the possibility of such damages. Specifically, neither Addison-Wesley nor PS is responsible for any costs including, but not limited to, those incurred as a result of lost profits or revenue (in any case, the program must be used only for educational purposes, as required by your license), loss of use of the computer program, loss of data, the costs of recovering such programs or data, the cost of any substitute program, claims by third parties, or for other similar costs. In no case shall the liability of Addison-Wesley or PS exceed the amount of the license fee.

The warranty and remedies set forth above are exclusive and in lieu of all others, oral or written, express or implied. No Addison-Wesley dealer, distributor, agent, or employee is authorized to make any modification or addition to this warranty.

Some statutes do not allow the exclusion of implied warranties; if any implied warranties are found to exist, they are hereby limited in duration to the 90-day life of the express warranties given above. Some states do not allow the exclusion or limitation of incidental or consequential damages, nor any limitation on how long implied warranties last, so these limitations may not apply to you. This warranty gives you specific legal rights and you may also have other rights which vary from state to state.

To obtain performance of this warranty, return the item with dated proof of purchase within 90 days of the purchase date to: Addison-Wesley Publishing Company, Inc., Business and Economics, Jacob Way, Reading, MA 01867.

PROPS+©

Probabilistic and Optimization Spreadsheets
Plus What-If-Solver™

E. R. Petersen
Queen's University

A. J. Taylor
Queen's University

Addison-Wesley Publishing Company

Reading, Massachusetts ▪ Menlo Park, California ▪ New York
Don Mills, Ontario ▪ Wokingham, England ▪ Amsterdam ▪ Bonn
Sydney ▪ Singapore ▪ Tokyo ▪ Madrid ▪ San Juan ▪ Milan ▪ Paris

PROPS[+] is published by Addison-Wesley Publishing Company, Inc. Contributors
include:

Julia G. Berrisford, Mac Mendelsohn *Sponsoring Editors*
Kim T.M. Kramer *Associate Editor*
Barbara Ames *Production Coordinator*
Trish Gordon *Manufacturing Media Manager*
Eileen Hoff *Cover Design*
Galley Graphics, Ltd. *Composition*

0-201-53813-X (manual)
0-201-58808-0 ($5\frac{1}{4}''$ format)
0-201-58809-9 ($3\frac{1}{2}''$ format)

1 2 3 4 5 6 7 8 9 10-MU-97969594

Preface

Over the last decade, spreadsheet programs have made a dramatic change in the analysis of business situations. Originally, spreadsheet systems were used primarily as financial modeling tools. As they became more commonplace, their potential for analyzing alternative scenarios for a wide variety of problems was recognized, and a number of "fixed templates" useful for analyzing specific cases and problems emerged.

The original PROPS, published in 1988 by Alwington Press, took a different approach by integrating general decision models directly into the spreadsheet. The PROPS models retained the capabilities of the spreadsheet for data input, output, and manipulation while providing the user with a range of sophisticated modeling techniques. PROPS+ extends this philosophy by offering an increased range of models, and it includes the What-If Solver from Frontline Systems, an optimization package for spreadsheet systems. PROPS+ thus combines the flexible and familiar modeling environment of a spreadsheet with the speed and power of the Solver to permit the analysis of a wide range of operations research, management science, and operations management models.

All PROPS+ commands take the form of spreadsheet menus, called up with one common key sequence, [Alt M], which have the look and feel of normal spreadsheet commands. All of the capabilities and power of the spreadsheet system are retained and are used to input data and to analyze, print, and graph the model results. You do not have to learn a new language or system.

The real power of PROPS+ is embodied in the parallel structure of data entry and analysis. That is, once a problem is defined, data may be entered in any order, and no predefined sequence must be followed. This parallel structure has three major implications:

- You can return to any cell during data entry and alter data as desired, so input errors are easily corrected.
- Data can be entered using the spreadsheet system to define cell contents through formulas, rather than by direct entry of numeric values. Cost functions or other relationships need not be determined through subroutines or elsewhere but can be defined within the spreadsheet itself. Spreadsheet utilities, such as Copy and Move commands, assist you in setting up problem data quickly.

• The recalculation capability of a spreadsheet allows you to examine the current solution to the problem and to easily modify the data to explore the sensitivity of the solution to any variation in input data.

In addition, integration into the spreadsheet means that you are no longer restricted to a fixed output format. In many applied problems, the results of models become inputs for further problem analysis and study. For example, queueing models usually calculate statistics that form the input to a subsequent cost/benefit analysis. PROPS⁺ allows you to set up the cost relationships in the spreadsheet and then to carry out sensitivity analysis on the impacts on costs of changing assumptions in the queueing model directly.

PROPS⁺ is organized into the following modules, each of which runs independently of the others:

Linear, Integer, and		Production Planning	(Chapter 9)
Nonlinear Prog.	(Chapter 2)*	Queueing	(Chapter 10)
Transportation/Assign.	(Chapter 3)*	Simulation	(Chapter 11)
Transshipment	(Chapter 4)*	Probability Distrib.	(Chapter 12)
Networks	(Chapter 5)	Decision Analysis	(Chapter 13)
Project Management	(Chapter 6)*	Markov Chains	(Chapter 14)
Forecasting	(Chapter 7)*	Dynamic Programming	(Chapter 15)
Inventory	(Chapter 8)	Stochastic Dynamic	
		Programming	(Chapter 16)

* indicates that some of the component models in these modules use the What-If Solver.

The Menu Map immediately following this preface illustrates the internal organization of the modules and will give you a more complete overview of the types of problems PROPS⁺ solves.

PROPS⁺ can be used at many different levels. The most basic level involves setting up a problem and entering data to obtain a solution. This use is appropriate for beginners in modeling and requires minimal knowledge of spreadsheets. A more advanced level shows the real value of PROPS⁺, when the user learns to experiment with the data and thus develops an understanding of how the model results change with variations in assumptions. We have found that the fast response of PROPS⁺ to parameter changes and the ability to store results in the worksheet encourage insights into how models function and how they enhance understanding of the underlying problem.

PROPS⁺ is also a valuable tool for the operations research professional, because it offers a fast and flexible system for creating prototypes for complex problems and provides a platform for more specialized analyses. Information on the PROPS⁺ Professional version can be obtained from

PROPS Systems
74 Alwington Avenue
Kingston, Ontario, Canada K7L 4R3

Each chapter of this manual begins with a general description of the models, including a mathematical description of both the model and the solution method. (These descriptions are included for reference and are not required for effective use of PROPS⁺.) A small example showing you how to set up problems and follow the PROPS⁺ output comes next. We then show how to use PROPS⁺ to analyze the models and carry out sensitivity analysis. Finally, some more difficult examples are analyzed to illustrate the power of the PROPS⁺ system in solving complex problems.

PROPS⁺ is written as Lotus 1-2-3 macro programs. These macros will run on all Lotus Releases from 2.01 onwards (full or student versions) and will also run on Quattro Pro and Excel for Windows. The What-If Solver is an add-in for Lotus 1-2-3 Releases 2.2, 2.3, and 2.4. However, Lotus does not have compatibility for add-ins between 1-2-3 Release 2.x and Release 3.x, nor for Lotus 1-2-3 for Windows; the modules using the Solver will not run on these host systems. (Quattro Pro Version 4.0 and Excel for Windows have a built-in version of the Solver, and a version of PROPS⁺ is being developed for these systems.) This manual is written with the assumption that the host spreadsheet system is Lotus 1-2-3 Release 2.3.

The manual provides a summary of the description and solution of each model but does not attempt to *teach* the underlying techniques. There are many good text-books, and we suggest that you refer to these for a full explanation of the models and techniques. The following table provides cross-references to the appropriate chapters in several of the major textbooks.

Operations Research Textbooks

ASW: Anderson, D.R., D.J. Sweeney, and T.A. Williams. *An Introduction to Management Science*. 6th ed. St. Paul: West Publishing, 1991.

Wi: Winston, W.L. *Operations Research: Applications and Algorithms*. 2d ed. Boston: PWS-Kent, 1991.

HL: Hillier, F.S. and G.J. Lieberman. *Introduction to Operations Research*. 5th ed. New York: McGraw-Hill, 1990.

T : Taha, H. *Operations Research*. 5th ed. New York: MacMillan, 1992.

Wa: Wagner, H.M. *Principles of Operations Research*. 2d ed. Englewood Cliffs: Prentice-Hall, 1975.

S : Shogan, A.W. *Management Science*. Englewood Cliffs: Prentice-Hall, 1988.

Model	ASW	Wi	HL	T	Wa	S
Linear Programming	3-6	3-6	3-6	2-5, 7	2-5	2-7
Integer Programming	8	9	13	9	13	9
Nonlinear Programming	19	12	14	20	14	-
Transportation/Assignment	7	7	7	6	6	4.5
Transshipment	7.3	7.6	7.3	6.4	6.3	4.6
Networks	9	8	10	8	7	8
Project Management	10	8.4	10.8	13	7.5	10, 11
Forecasting	16	24	19	11	-	-
Inventory	11	16	18	14	19	15
Production Planning	11	16	18	14	9	14
Queueing	12	2	16	15	20	16
Simulation	13	23	23	17	21	17
Decision Analysis	14	13	22	12	-	12, 13
Markov Chains	17	19	15	18.6	18	-
Dynamic Programming	18	20	11	10	8, 9	-
Stochastic Dynamic Prog.	-	17, 21	20	18	17	15

Note: The notation 4.5 indicates Chapter 4, Section 5.

The authors gratefully acknowledge support from the Natural Science and Engineering Research Council of Canada. The technical and programming skills provided by Mr. Gordon D. Thompson have been invaluable. We also owe a debt of gratitude for the insights, assistance, and encouragement of Professor Jack Yurkiewicz of Pace University and to Mr. Dan Fylstra of Frontline Systems. Finally, we offer a general thank you to the many others who have made encouraging suggestions since the first release of this software (as "PROPS"). Of course, all errors and omissions remain our sole responsibility.

E. R. P.
A. J. T.

PROPS⁺ Menu Maps

```
┌─────────────────┐
│ 1.  Quit        │
└─────────────────┘


┌──────────────────────────────────────────────────┐
│ 2.  Linear, Integer & Nonlinear programming        │
└──────────────────────────────────────────────────┘
    ┌──────────────────────────────────────────────────────────────┐
    │ Solve   Edit   Bound_defn   Integer_defn   Nonlinear_defn     │
    └──────────────────────────────────────────────────────────────┘
          ┌──────────────────────────────────────────────────┐
          │ Add_constr  Del_constr  Add_var  Del_var          │
          └──────────────────────────────────────────────────┘
       ┌──────────────────────────────────┐
       │ LP    IP    NLP    Tableau_LP     │
       └──────────────────────────────────┘


    ┌──────────────────────────────────────┐
    │ 3.  Transportation/Assignment         │
    └──────────────────────────────────────┘
          ┌──────────────────┐
          │ Solve    Edit     │
          └──────────────────┘
             ┌───────────────────────────────────────────────┐
             │ Add_origin  Del_origin  Add_Dest  Del_Dest     │
             └───────────────────────────────────────────────┘


    ┌──────────────────────┐
    │ 4.  Transshipment     │
    └──────────────────────┘
    ┌───────────────────────────────────────────────┐
    │ Solve  Edit  Capacity_defn  Nonlinear_defn     │
    └───────────────────────────────────────────────┘
           ┌───────────────────────────────────┐
           │ Add_arc   Del_arc   Add_node       │
           └───────────────────────────────────┘
    ┌───────────────────────────┐
    │ Linear    Nonlinear        │
    └───────────────────────────┘
    ┌───────────────────────────────────┐
    │ Unconstrained    Constrained       │
    └───────────────────────────────────┘


    ┌──────────────┐
    │ 5.  Networks  │
    └──────────────┘
    ┌──────────────────────────────────────────────────────────┐
    │ Shortest_path  Maximum_flow  Minimum_span   Edit          │
    └──────────────────────────────────────────────────────────┘
                      ┌──────────────────────────┐
                      │ Add_arc   Del_arc         │
                      └──────────────────────────┘


    ┌──────────────────────────────┐
    │ 6. Project Management          │
    └──────────────────────────────┘
       ┌──────────────────────────────────────────────┐
       │ Solve   Edit   Crash_data   PERT_data         │
       └──────────────────────────────────────────────┘
            ┌──────────────────────────────────┐
            │ Add_activity   Del_activity       │
            └──────────────────────────────────┘
       ┌──────────────────────────────────────────────┐
       │ CPM   Crash_CPM   PERT   PERT_Simulation      │
       └──────────────────────────────────────────────┘
```

x

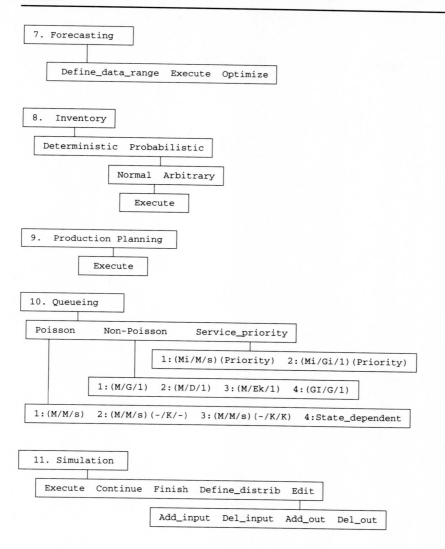

7. Forecasting

Define_data_range Execute Optimize

8. Inventory

Deterministic Probabilistic

Normal Arbitrary

Execute

9. Production Planning

Execute

10. Queueing

Poisson   Non-Poisson   Service_priority

1:(Mi/M/s)(Priority) 2:(Mi/Gi/1)(Priority)

1:(M/G/1) 2:(M/D/1) 3:(M/Ek/1) 4:(GI/G/1)

1:(M/M/s) 2:(M/M/s)(-/K/-) 3:(M/M/s)(-/K/K) 4:State_dependent

11. Simulation

Execute Continue Finish Define_distrib Edit

Add_input Del_input Add_out Del_out

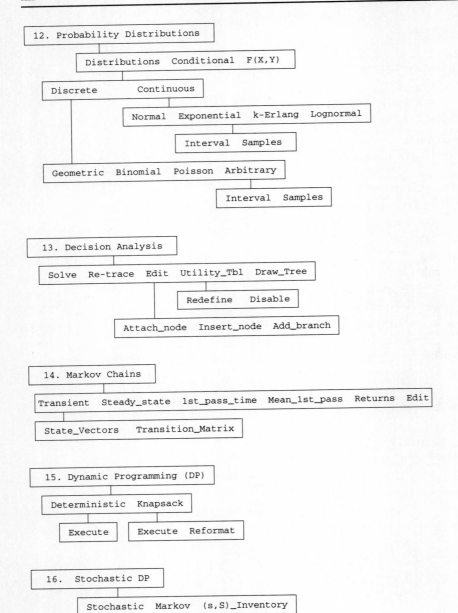

12. Probability Distributions

Distributions Conditional F(X,Y)

Discrete   Continuous

Normal Exponential k-Erlang Lognormal

Interval Samples

Geometric Binomial Poisson Arbitrary

Interval Samples

13. Decision Analysis

Solve Re-trace Edit Utility_Tbl Draw_Tree

Redefine   Disable

Attach_node Insert_node Add_branch

14. Markov Chains

Transient Steady_state 1st_pass_time Mean_1st_pass Returns Edit

State_Vectors   Transition_Matrix

15. Dynamic Programming (DP)

Deterministic Knapsack

Execute   Execute Reformat

16. Stochastic DP

Stochastic Markov (s,S)_Inventory

Execute Continue   Execute Continue

Execute

Table of Contents

List of Example Problems

Chapter 1. Getting Started

PROPS⁺ is a system of computer modules designed to solve the most important decision models in management science, operations management, and operations research. This chapter will get you up and running in PROPS⁺.

Checking Your Package

Your PROPS⁺ package should contain
- the PROPS⁺ manual and
- one disk (5¼ or 3½ inch format) that contains the following files:

    install.exe   install.dat
    pplus001.exe   pplus002.exe   pplus003.exe

These are compressed files containing the PROPS⁺ spreadsheet modules and the What-If Solver Add-Ins.

PROPS⁺ is a copyrighted program. You are authorized to make backup copies for your own use. Any other copying is an infringement of copyright law.

The Spreadsheet System

PROPS⁺ and the What-If Solver are designed to run under LOTUS 1-2-3 Release 2.2, 2.3, or 2.4 (either the full version or the student version). The PROPS⁺ macros themselves (excluding the What-If Solver) will run under Quattro Pro Version 4.0 and Excel Version 4.0a for Windows. These latter systems have their own internal solvers, and a compatible PROPS⁺ version is under development. In this manual the assumption is that the host system is 1-2-3. The last section of this chapter reviews the fundamentals of 1-2-3, and we recommend that you read this section even if you are familiar with Lotus 1-2-3.

For a hard disk system:

Make sure that the directory containing the LOTUS 1-2-3 program files is in the PATH. Type the DOS command

        path   [Enter]

You will see a list of the directories in the path. If the 1-2-3 directory is not in the path, edit the AUTOEXEC.BAT file in your hard disk root directory to add the 1-2-3 directory to the path. See your DOS manual for details.

For a floppy disk system:

If you choose to use a two-disk system, the a: drive will be used for the 1-2-3 system and the b: drive will be used for the PROPS⁺ program files. If you have only one disk drive, you will have to insert the correct disk in your single drive when we refer to the logical drives A: and B:.

Installing PROPS⁺

The install program on the PROPS⁺ disk will unpack the PROPS⁺ files and copy these files either to a directory on a hard disk or to a formatted floppy disk. Note that if your computer uses only double-density 5¼" floppy disks with a maximum of 360K bytes each, you will need two formatted disks.

Follow Step 1 through Step 6 to install the PROPS⁺ system.

Step 1: Install

Insert the original PROPS⁺ disk into drive A: and run the install program by typing

A: install [Enter]

The install program will
-ask you for your name (your name will appear on all the worksheets), and
-ask if you have a hard drive.

If you have a hard drive, the install routine will
-check the location of the 1-2-3 program files (if this directory is not in the path as just described, the installation will be terminated), and
-ask for the directory where you want the PROPS⁺ program files to be located. If you press [Enter], it will create the directory C:\PROPS\ and copy all files into it. You can specify any other directory by typing another name here. The program will verify that the name is correct before proceeding.

If you have only floppy disk drives, the install routine will
-ask whether you have one or two floppy drives,
-ask for the disk capacity, and
-direct you when to change or insert disks.

When these steps are completed the install routine will unpack the files and copy them into a directory on the hard disk or onto one or more floppy disks. (This may require several minutes to complete, depending on the speed of your computer.) It will then

-create the file PROPS.BAT and copy it to the directory or disk containing the 1-2-3 program files.

-copy the file 123.CNF from the directory or disk containing the 1-2-3 files to the PROPS⁺ program disk or directory. This step sets up a particular configuration for 1-2-3 for PROPS⁺. The 1-2-3 configuration that you set up for PROPS⁺ will not affect the configuration for other 1-2-3 programs.

-set the attribute of the PROPS⁺ worksheet files to "read-only" to prevent accidental erasure.

Step 2: Set the Default Directory

Make sure that you are pointing to the directory or disk that contains PROPS⁺. (When you leave the install program, you will be pointing to the correct directory. With a hard disk installation, you will see the prompt C:\PROPS>.) Run LOTUS 1-2-3 by typing

123 [Enter]

You will see a blank screen similar to this:

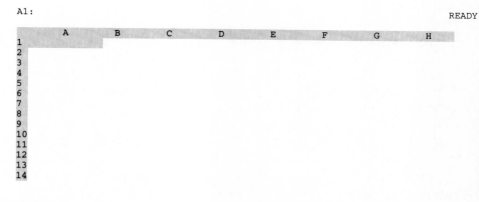

Then type

/**Worksheet Global Default Directory**

followed by the name of the drive and the directory containing the PROPS$^+$ program files. For example, type

C:\PROPS [Enter]

if that is the directory on your hard disk or

B: [Enter]

if you have a floppy drive system. Save these options by selecting **Update** and **Quit** from the successive menus.

Step 3: Auto-attach the What-If Solver Add-Ins

You need to set up 1-2-3 to attach the What-If Solver Add-Ins automatically whenever PROPS$^+$ is run. The Auto-attach Add-Ins are specified as Worksheet Global Defaults. From your worksheet in READY mode, make the following selections:

/Worksheet **G**lobal **D**efault **O**ther **A**dd-In

You will see the following menu:

```
A1:                                                                                      MENU
Set  Cancel  Quit
Specify an add-in to be attached automatically, and attach it
┌─────────────────────────────── Default Settings ───────────────────────────┐
1  │                                                                           │
2  │     Directory: [C:\PROPS\·······]                    ┌─Clock─────────┐    │
3  │                                                       │ (*) Standard  │    │
4  │     [x] Auto-execute Macros on                        │ ( ) International │ │
5  │     [ ] Instant access to Help file                   │ ( ) None      │    │
6  │     [ ] Undo on                                       │ ( ) File name │    │
7  │     [ ] Enhanced expanded memory on                   └───────────────┘    │
8  │     [x] Computer Bell on                                                   │
9  │                                                                           │
10 │   ┌─Auto-attach add-ins──────────────┐              ┌─Add-in Keys───────┐ │
11 │   │ 1: [········]   5: [········]     │              │ ALT-F7:           │ │
12 │   │ 2: [········]   6: [········]  Invoke:           │ ALT-F8:           │ │
13 │   │ 3: [········]   7: [········]     │              │ ALT-F9:           │ │
14 │   │ 4: [········]   8: [········]     │              │ ALT-F10:          │ │
15 │   └──────────────────────────────────┘              └───────────────────┘ │
```

Use the **C**ancel option to delete other Add-Ins if they are attached. We recommend that you avoid other Add-Ins while using PROPS$^+$ as they may conflict with the WHATSOLV and PRODUCT Add-Ins. Make sure the "Auto-execute Macros on" option is set, as shown in row 4. If not, use the **W**orksheet **G**lobal **D**efault **A**utoexec **Y**es **Q**uit command (**/WGDAYQ**) to turn the option on.

Use the **S**et option to specify WHATSOLV.ADN and PRODUCT.ADN as the Auto-attach Add-Ins. Press [Enter] to select **S**et, and you will see the following menu:

```
A1:
1  2  3  4  5  6  7  8                                                    MENU
Select auto-attach add-in setting
```

Select **1** and you will see

```
  List
  Enter name of add-in: C:\PROPS\*.ADN                                    FILES
  PRODUCT.ADN        WHATSOLV.ADN
```

Select PRODUCT.ADN by pressing [Enter]. You will be returned to the menu:

```
A1:
Set  Cancel  Quit                                                        MENU
Specify an add-in to be attached automatically, and attach it
```

Select **S**et and select **2** and WHATSOLV.ADN from the successive menus, and you will see

```
                                                                         MENU
No-Key  7  8  9  10
Do not assign add-in to a key
```

Press [Enter] to select the **N**o-Key option, and you will see

```
A1:                                                                      MENU
No  Yes
Automatically invoke this add-in whenever you start 1-2-3?
```

Press [Enter] so that WHATSOLV is *not* automatically invoked when it is loaded.

To save these options, first select **Q**uit, then **U**pdate, and finally **Q**uit. (These changes will be saved in the 123.CNF file in the PROPS⁺ directory or disk.)

Step 4: Disable the UNDO Feature

The UNDO feature of 1-2-3 Release 2.2 and later allows you to reverse or "undo" changes you have made to the spreadsheet. If this feature is enabled, it sharply reduces the memory available. Hence it is essential to turn off or "disable" the UNDO feature. If the UNDO feature is enabled, the letters UNDO will appear in the status line at the bottom of your screen. If you see these letters, disable UNDO by starting in the READY mode and making the following selections from the successive menus:

/Worksheet Global Default Other Undo Disable

From the menu that appears, select Update and then Quit to save these changes.

Step 5: Back-up Copy

PROPS⁺ is not write protected!

Make a back-up copy of the files contained in the PROPS⁺ program directory. You can use the DOS command **copy *.* a:** if you have a hard disk or else the DOS command **diskcopy** to make a copy of the PROPS⁺ program disks. Store this copy and the original disk in a safe place.

The PROPS⁺ files have been stored as "read-only" files. If you want to remove or modify the files later, you will have to cancel their read-only status by issuing the DOS command

attrib -r *.wk1

Running PROPS⁺

To run PROPS⁺, simply type

props [Enter]

You should see both the 1-2-3 screen and the What-If Solver screen flash as the system is loaded. If this does not occur, the What-If Solver has not been attached. Return to the section "Auto-attach the What-If Solver Add-Ins" on page 4, and follow the instructions.

When PROPS⁺ is loaded, you will see

```
A9: [W36] '' 1. Quit                                              READY
```

```
                        A                                B
 1                                             Copyright (C)
 2            PROPS+    v1.00            E.R.Petersen & A.J.Taylor
 3      Probabilistic and Optimization    Queen's University at Kingston
 4            Spreadsheets                  programmed by G.D.Thompson
 5      ==============================    ==============================
 6
 7           Move cursor to the desired menu item and press [Enter]
 8
 9       1. Quit                        11. Simulation
10       2. LP, IP and NLP             12. Probability Distributions
11       3. Transportation/Assignment  13. Decision Analysis
12       4. Transshipment              14. Markov Chains
13       5. Networks                   15. Dynamic Programming (DP)
14       6. Project Management         16. Stochastic DP
15       7. Forecasting
16       8. Inventory
17       9. Production planning
18      10. Queueing
19
20
```

Use the up/down and right/left arrow keys to move the cursor to the module you wish to use, and press [Enter] to make your selection. PROPS⁺ will look in the default directory for the corresponding worksheet and will present an initial screen and menu for that module. Each chapter in this manual describes how to use one module.

If you have already run a PROPS⁺ model and you wish to retrieve a different module, use the **F**ile **R**etrieve command (**/FR**) and select the worksheet called ACCESS.WK1 (the first in the list at the top of the screen) by pressing the [Enter] key. These steps will redisplay the initial screen, from which you can select a different module.

Modes of Operation

PROPS⁺ has two modes of operation, PROMPT and READY. PROMPT mode is indicated by the highlighted letters **CMD** at the bottom of the screen, indicating that PROPS⁺ is waiting for data. In this mode, you will see a question or statement on the screen indicating what PROPS⁺ is expecting, and the cursor will be resting on the cell in which the data will be stored. To respond, type in the required information and press the [Enter] key. (Note that you can move the cursor away from that cell to look at other parts of the spreadsheet before continuing, but you *must* bring the cursor back to that cell before typing in your response.) The PROMPT mode is always used to enter data describing the size of the problem to the PROPS⁺ system.

In READY mode, the word **READY** appears in the upper right corner of the screen, and the **CMD** indicator does not show at the bottom of the screen. In this mode, normal spreadsheet usage applies. That is, you can carry out all the usual activities: entering data into cells, performing calculations, creating graphs, or printing results. In each PROPS⁺ model, once the problem size is described, PROPS⁺ constructs a data input area and returns you to READY mode to complete the data entry. You are always in READY mode when PROPS⁺ has finished solving the current problem.

Correcting Data Input

When you are in PROMPT mode, if you make an error in typing a response to a question from PROPS⁺ and have not pressed [Enter], you can simply backspace and retype the correct response. You could also press the [Esc] key to clear your entry and retype the whole response.

> **Remember, when you are in PROMPT mode, always check what you have typed before you press [Enter].**

If you make a typing error in READY mode, you can simply go back to the cell with the error and change the entry by typing in the correct input.

PROPS⁺ Output

PROPS⁺ does not have any special print features. Rather, you are encouraged to make full use of the print features of 1-2-3 to obtain hard copy (including graphs). These features are described in the review of Lotus 1-2-3 beginning on page 11.

To save a problem analysis, it is simplest to save the whole worksheet in a file using the 1-2-3 **F**ile **S**ave command (**/FS**). See page 20 for guidelines to follow in saving files.

Changing between Modules

If you have completed a problem analysis in PROPS⁺ and wish to go to a different module, you can access the PROPS⁺ system with the **F**ile **R**etrieve command (**/FR**) and select the worksheet called ACCESS.WK1 (the first in the list at the top of the screen) by pressing the [Enter] key.

> **Remember that this will erase your current worksheet, so be sure to save it before pressing /FR.**

PROPS⁺ Worksheet Layout

The PROPS⁺ program instructions are always situated in the far right side of the spreadsheet. The PROPS⁺ introductory screen is in the top left corner of the spreadsheet. Models are constructed along the left-hand side of the spreadsheet, starting from this screen and continuing down. Their width depends on the number of variables in the problem. A scratch work area in the range of cells [I1..P20] is always available. In addition, each worksheet within PROPS⁺ will have other blank areas for additional scratch work or data storage that you can locate by inspection.

What-If Solver Error Messages

Each time you initiate PROPS⁺, the 1-2-3 system is loaded and the What-If Add-Ins are automatically attached. You should see both the 1-2-3 screen and the What-If Solver screen flash as the system loads. If you do not see the What-If screen flash, it has not been attached. Go to the section "Auto-attach the What-If Solver Add-Ins" on page 4, and follow the instructions. If an error occurs during loading, an ERROR message will appear. The following list contains the most common errors, and a suggested corrective action is shown for each.

Add-in initialization error

While trying to load or attach an add-in, 1-2-3 detected an error. This message often occurs because the file 123.DYN either is missing or does not match the version number of your 1-2-3 program.

No .DYN file found

The file 123.DYN, found on your 1-2-3 PrintGraph diskette, must be present in your 1-2-3 program directory. Copy the 123.DYN file to your 1-2-3 program directory from the original diskette.

Cannot load overlay file WHATSOLV.OVL

The add-in WHATSOLV.ADN loads additional program code from the overlay file WHATSOLV.OVL when it is first attached. This message appears if the overlay file is not found or if a disk error occurs while reading the file.

Insufficient memory to load Solver

The What-If Solver allocates memory for program code from the overlay file WHATSOLV.OVL when it is first attached. This message occurs if there is not enough conventional memory available to hold the overlay code. To use the Solver, you will need to detach other add-ins or remove "terminate-and-stay-resident" programs (TSRs) and buffers to free up approximately 52K bytes of RAM for the overlay program. To detach other add-ins, see the section "Auto-attach the What-If Solver Add-Ins" on page 4, and follow the instructions. See your DOS manual for changing buffers and removing TSRs.

Out of memory

If this message appears when you are loading the system, it means that memory is severely limited in your system; about 70K additional bytes of RAM are needed to load the What-If Solver program code and allocate space for the optimization problem. You will need to detach other add-ins or remove TSRs and buffers to free up memory. Make sure that UNDO is disabled.

When PROPS[+] has been installed properly with the What-If Solver Add-Ins, the macros in PROPS[+] that need the Solver will set up the data and call the Solver into action. If the Solver is not present when called by PROPS[+], you will see the 1-2-3 ERROR message

"File Does Not Exist"

Save the worksheet, return to the section "Auto-attach the What-If Solver Add-Ins" on page 4, and follow the instructions.

Once PROPS[+] passes control to the Solver program, it may display the following run-time error messages:

Constraint RHS negative in Simplex method

The right-hand side of a constraint is negative for a problem for which the Solver is using the simplex method. The simplex method requires nonnegative right-hand sides. To work around this limitation, create an equivalent constraint by changing the direction of the constraint and multiplying the coefficients on both sides by -1.

Out of memory

If this message appears at run time, it means that memory is severely limited in your system. You will need to detach other add-ins or remove any TSRs and buffers to make more memory available to the Solver. Also ensure that you have disabled the UNDO feature of 1-2-3 (see page 5).

What-If Solver Completion Messages

When the Solver has completed its solution, it will beep and you will see one of the following completion messages at the top of your screen:

Results within tolerance
Successive Whatifs close
Max. iterations reached
Values do not converge
Feasible point not found
Result value is ERR or NA

The program will pause. Press [Enter] to continue. If a solution has been found, PROPS⁺ will save the results in an output table. If a solution cannot be found, PROPS⁺ will display an error message in the output table.

Review of Lotus 1-2-3

PROPS⁺ has been designed to take maximum advantage of the filing, data manipulation, and graphing features provided by the 1-2-3 spreadsheet system. This section reviews the fundamental spreadsheet operations and describes some of their features and powerful facilities. Even if you are familiar with 1-2-3, we recommend that you skim through this material; some of it may be new to you.

In essence, Lotus 1-2-3 provides a large grid of cells (256 columns by 8192 rows), and each cell of this grid can contain alphabetic labels, numbers, or formulas that act on the values contained in other cells. In addition, 1-2-3 comes with a built-in menu to allow you to carry out filing, printing, graphing, and other chores. Once you have started the 1-2-3 program by typing **123** or **LOTUS** from the DOS prompt, you will see the following screen:

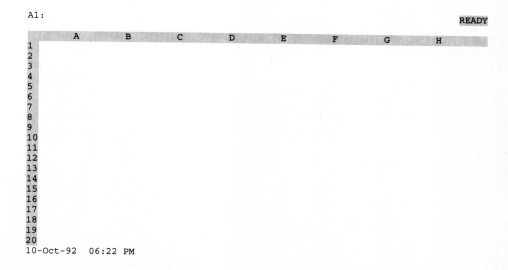

Each cell has an address denoted by the column letter and the row number. Cell B5 is the cell in column B, row 5.

Moving around the Spreadsheet

When you begin a 1-2-3 session, the cursor is resting on cell A1 in the spreadsheet and the READY message appears in the upper right corner of your screen. Note that the upper left corner shows the symbol A1:, indicating that you are pointing at cell A1 and that it is currently empty. The arrow keys on your number pad will shift the cursor one cell in any direction on the spreadsheet. The [PgUp] and [PgDn] keys shift the cursor up and down one whole screen (20 lines on a standard display). Simultaneously pressing the control key [Ctrl] and the right or left arrow shifts the display to the right or left one whole screen (8 columns on a standard display). The [Home] key always returns the cursor to cell A1.

From any starting cell, pressing the [End] key followed by an arrow key does one of three things:

-if the starting cell is empty, the cursor moves to the *first* nonempty cell in the indicated direction or to the edge of the spreadsheet, whichever occurs first;

-if the starting cell is not empty and the adjacent cell in the direction of the arrow is empty, the cursor moves to the *first* nonempty cell in that direction or to the edge of the worksheet if there are no nonempty cells;

-if the starting cell is not empty and the adjacent cell in the arrow's direction is also not empty, the cursor moves to the *last* nonempty cell in that direction.

Although the different effects of the [End][arrow] key sequence may seem confusing, they are very useful for modeling within spreadsheets and will soon be familiar to you.

Entering Data

Cells can contain alphabetic information (a "label"), numeric values, or formulas. An example of each follows. The right-hand figure shows the actual contents of each cell and the left-hand figure shows the appearance of the worksheet on your screen. Note that labels are indicated by one of the three prefix marks (' ^ or ") that indicate left, center, or right justification. Labels can be up to 240 characters and will be displayed in full on the screen if the cells to the right are empty. If the cell immediately to the right contains any data, the label will be truncated to the column width.

	A	B
1	A Column Title	
2		12
3		34
4		46
5		

	A	B
1	'A Column Title	
2		12
3		34
4		+A2+A3
5		

Appearance of Screen   Actual Cell Contents

Formulas generally describe arithmetic operations on cell contents, as in cell A4 in the example. The standard operations include addition (+), subtraction (−), multiplication (*), division (/), and exponentiation (^). The order of operation conforms to standard usage, so exponentiation is done first, then multiplication and division, and finally addition or subtraction. If B5 contains the formula

$$+B1+B2*B3\wedge B4$$

the spreadsheet would raise the contents of B3 to the power of the contents of B4, multiply the result by the contents of B2, add the contents of B1, and store the results in B5. You can confirm this order of operations with the following example:

```
B5: +B1+B2*B3^B4
```

	A	B	C	D	E
1		5			
2		4			
3		3			
4		2			
5		41			

We recommend the liberal use of parentheses to ensure that the order of operation is clear. For clarity, the above formula could be written as

$$+B1+(B2*(B3\wedge B4))$$

Formulas can be entered by simply typing the symbols *with no blanks between any entries*. A better method is using the 1-2-3 POINT feature: first type an arithmetic symbol and move the cursor to the first cell address referred to in the formula, then type the next arithmetic symbol and move the cursor to the second address, and so on until the formula is complete. Then press [Enter]. You can edit the contents of a cell by moving the cursor to that cell and pressing the function key [F2]. Note that the upper right-hand corner of the screen shows **EDIT**, indicating you are in cell edit mode. You can use the backspace and delete keys and type in any new additions to the cell contents. Press [Enter] to leave cell edit mode.

The spreadsheet has a default column width of 9 characters. If you enter a decimal value that has more decimal digits than this, the decimal will appear to be truncated on your screen: only the first 9 digits will be seen. (The complete number is still there, and what you see is *not* rounded off.) If you enter a very large number, it may be rounded off and expressed in exponential notation: 2,700,000 may appear as 3E06.

If you wish to see more columns on your screen, you can change the width of all of the columns using the **Worksheet Global Column-width** command (**/WGC**). When you enter this sequence, the current column width will be displayed in the upper left corner of your screen. You can type in a new width for all of the columns, followed by [Enter]; or you can use the left and right arrow keys to change the current value. You can also change the width of any particular column, leaving the other columns unchanged, by moving the cursor to the column you wish to change and using the **Worksheet Column Set-width** command (**/WCS**), which prompts you for a new column width for that column.

Lotus 1-2-3 allows designated cells to be "protected," meaning that you cannot alter the cell contents, while other cells are unprotected. Protected cell contents appear as bold characters on monochrome monitors and in a different color on color screens.

The 1-2-3 Menu
The 1-2-3 system provides a menu of special functions to modify the appearance and contents of the worksheet. This menu can be accessed by pressing the "forward slash key" (*/*). You will see the following menu at the top of your worksheet (note that the upper right-hand corner of your screen shows the indicator **MENU**):

```
A1:                                                                 MENU
Worksheet  Range   Copy    Move  File  Print  Graph  Data  System  Add-In  Quit
Global     Insert  Delete  Column  Erase  Titles  Window  Status  Page  Learn
       A          B          C         D         E          F        G        H
1
```

Note that the cursor is resting on the first item of the menu, **Worksheet**. Pressing the [Enter] key will execute that menu item. You can select a different menu item either by moving the cursor to that item and pressing [Enter] or by pressing the letter corresponding to the first letter of the menu item (e.g., press **F** to select and execute the **F**ile menu item). Selecting **F**ile yields another menu:

```
A1:                                                                 MENU
Retrieve  Save  Combine  Xtract  Erase  List  Import  Directory  Admin
Erase the current worksheet from memory and display the selected worksheet
       A          B          C         D         E          F        G        H
1
```

If you press **R** (or simply press [Enter]), you will initiate the file retrieval operation. In this book, we will refer to this sequence of keystrokes as the **File Retrieve** command (**/FR**). You can use either uppercase or lowercase letters in 1-2-3.

Working with Data

Many operations in 1-2-3 act on rectangular blocks of cells called "ranges", denoted by specifying the cell in the upper left corner, two periods, and the cell in the lower right corner of the block. Thus, the range [A2..B4] includes the six cells A2, A3, A4, B2, B3, and B4. The range [A2..A2] is composed of a single cell, since the upper left and lower right cells are identical. When commands involving ranges are given, the default range is the cell on which the cursor is currently positioned. For instance, if the cursor is resting on cell A2 and you give the **Copy** command (/C), you will see the following message at the top of your screen:

```
A2: 5                                                                    POINT
Enter range to copy FROM: A2..A2
          A         B         C         D         E         F         G         H
1
```

The upper left corner of the range is called the "anchor cell." For example, moving the cursor to B4 will cause the range A2 to B4 to be highlighted, and the range at the top of the screen will appear as [A2..B4]. Now, suppose that after entering the **Copy** command (/C) as above with the cursor on A2, you realized that you want to copy only the range [B1..B3]. To change the anchor cell, first press the [Esc] key. The top of the screen shows

```
        Enter range to copy FROM: A2
```

As you move the cursor, the anchor cell changes. Move to cell B1, and the top of the screen shows

```
        Enter range to copy FROM: B1
```

Press the period key [.] to anchor the range at B1. The top of the screen now shows

```
        Enter range to copy FROM: B1..B1
```

Move the cursor down to B3 and the range will adjust to follow the cursor movement. Some data manipulation commands that are useful in conjunction with PROPS[+] models are summarized on the following pages.

Copying a range   The function of the **Copy** command has been discussed in the description of ranges in 1-2-3. However, you must be careful using this command when cells contain formulas. Suppose that cell A4 contains the formula +A2+A3. If cell A4 is copied to D6, for example, the contents of D6 will be +D4+D5. Cell addresses expressed in this way in a formula are *relative* to the position of the cell containing the formula. If you want the formula to refer to a particular cell, even if the formula is copied elsewhere, you should preface each address element with a $ sign. For example, suppose A4 contained the formula +$A$2+A3, which is copied to D6. The contents of D6 would then be +$A$2+D5. An address with $ signs is called *absolute*. **Hint:** When you are entering or editing a formula, pressing the special function key [F4] will convert a cell address from relative to absolute form.

Moving data You can move data with the **Move** command (**/M**), which is exactly like the **Copy** command except that the source range is erased. All formulas that refer to a cell that is being moved will immediately be adjusted to refer to the new location. You must use this command with caution when using PROPS⁺ because once data areas are defined through the PROPS⁺ set-up procedures, the system expects to find data in the designated areas. You can move data freely within data input areas, however, as long as the structure of the input area itself is not altered.

Erasing data Cell contents are erased with the **Range Erase** command (**/RE**). The default range is the single cell on which the cursor rests when the command is issued, and the range can be adjusted as described earlier.

Copying results of computations If you wish to copy the *current values* (as distinct from the cell contents, which may be formulas) in a range of cells to another location, use the **Range Value** command (**/RV**). This procedure follows the same steps as the **Copy** command.

Filling a range with a sequence of numbers Often it is desirable to fill a range with a set of numbers in sequence with a constant interval between each. For example, you may wish to create a set of values for the x-axis for a graph. The 1-2-3 command to use is the **Data Fill** command (**/DF**). To fill the range [A20..A30] with the sequence starting at 100 and going to 200 in steps of 10, move the cursor to A20 and press **/DF**. The message at the top of the screen is

```
A20:                                                          POINT
Enter fill range: A20
```

	A	B	C	D	E	F	G	H

Press the period key [.] to anchor the range on A20, and move the cursor to A30, highlighting the range [A20..A30]. Then press [Enter]. The screen now appears as follows:

```
A20:
Enter fill range: A20..A30                                           EDIT
Start: 0
```
	A	B	C	D	E	F	G	H

The cursor is blinking on the Start value default of 0. Type the digits **100** and press [Enter]. You are asked for the size of the Step:, so type **10** [Enter]. Finally you are asked for the value at which to Stop: with a default value of 8192. The range will be filled until either the end of the range or this stopping value is reached, so you can either simply press [Enter] or type the value **200**. The range [A20..A30] is then filled with the values 100, 110, 120, ..., 200.

The Data Table command. An interesting question in spreadsheet models is how sensitive the end result of a series of computations is to a particular cell's value. The **Data Table 1** command (**/DT1**) is a powerful facility provided by 1-2-3 to answer this question. We will illustrate using one of the PROPS$^+$ queueing model spreadsheets. The screen that follows shows the spreadsheet for a standard queueing situation with a Poisson arrival rate (an average of 1 customer every 2 minutes) and an exponential service time (an average of 1 minute per customer) for a single server queue.

	A	B	C	D	E	F	G	H
24	INPUT DATA:							
25		Mean Arrival Rate		0.5	("lambda")			
26		Mean Service Rate		1	("mu")			
27		Number of Servers		1	("s")			
28								
29	MOMENTS:							
30		Traffic Intensity		0.5	("rho")			
31						Queue	System	
32		Expected Number of Customers				0.5	1	
33		Expected Waiting Time per Customer				1	2	

What happens to the expected waiting time per customer in the system (in cell G33) as the customer arrival rate increases? To find out, we can use the **Data Fill** command just described to create a range of values for the arrival rate in an unused area of the spreadsheet, shown in Step 1. Then move the cursor to the cell immediately to the right, and up one, from the first entry in the data filled table; insert the formula +G33 (this is the cell address containing the quantity we are interested in). The actual cell contents are shown in Step 2. Next move the cursor to the blank cell immediately above the data-filled range, as shown in Step 3.

	A	B
53		
54		
55	0.5	
56	0.55	
57	0.6	
58	0.65	
59	0.7	
60	0.75	
61	0.8	
62	0.85	
63	0.9	
64	0.95	
65	1	

	A	B
53		
54		+G33
55	0.5	
56	0.55	
57	0.6	
58	0.65	
59	0.7	
60	0.75	
61	0.8	
62	0.85	
63	0.9	
64	0.95	
65	1	

	A	B
53		
54		+G33
55	0.5	
56	0.55	
57	0.6	
58	0.65	
59	0.7	
60	0.75	
61	0.8	
62	0.85	
63	0.9	
64	0.95	
65	1	

| Step 1 | Step 2 | Step 3 |

Now call the **Data Table** command by pressing **/DT**, and you will see the following at the top of your screen:

```
A54:
1  2  Reset
One input cell, one or more dependent formulas
        A       B       C       D       E       F
53
54
```

Press [Enter] to select **1**, and you will be asked for a range for the table. Include both the column that has been data-filled and the adjacent column in this table, as follows:

```
B65:
Enter table range: A54..B65
        A       B       C       D       E       F
53
54              +G33
55      0.5
56      0.55
57      0.6
58      0.65
59      0.7
60      0.75
61      0.8
62      0.85
63      0.9
64      0.95
65      1
66
```

> In this example, for demonstration purposes, we are showing the actual contents of cell B54 and not the numeric value that appears on your screen.

Now press [Enter] and you will be asked for the input cell, which is the cell you are varying. In this case we are varying the arrival rate, which is contained in cell D25. Type **D25** and press [Enter]; the following table will be created:

	A	B	C
53			
54		+G33	
55	0.5	2	
56	0.55	2.222222	
57	0.6	2.5	
58	0.65	2.857142	
59	0.7	3.333333	
60	0.75	4	
61	0.8	5	
62	0.85	6.666666	
63	0.9	10	
64	0.95	20	
65	1	ERR	

You can now put titles in cells A53 and B53 if you wish. Column A contains alternative arrival rates, and column B contains the expected time in the system for each arrival rate. Note that when the arrival rate is 1 (equal to the service rate), the expected waiting time becomes infinite, which is shown as ERR in 1-2-3.

Built-in functions 1-2-3 has a number of predefined built-in functions for some common operations. These are known as "at-functions" because they are preceded by the @ symbol. For instance, the following operations can be carried out using at-functions.

@**sum**(*range*) adds up the cell values in the specified range,
@**npv**(*interest,range*) computes the net present value of the cash flows in the specified range, discounted at the specified interest rate per period,
@**max**(*range*) finds the maximum value in the indicated range,
@**if**(*condition,cell_A,cell_B*) tests the specified condition. If it is true, the contents of cell A appear; if not, the contents of cell B appear. For example, the statement @**if(A4>6,C5,D5)** tests to see if the value of cell A4 is more than 6. If this is true, the contents of C5 appear in the cell containing this formula; if it is false, the contents of D5 appear.

A variety of other @ functions are summarized in your 1-2-3 manual.

Working with Files

When you set up your PROPS⁺ files as described in the Installing PROPS⁺ section of this chapter, the default directory is the PROPS⁺ directory c:\PROPS. We recommend that you do *not* change the default directory through the 1-2-3 File Directory command, since the PROPS⁺ access system will search for PROPS⁺ files on the \PROPS directory. Use the following commands to save data on another directory.

To save data or models created in PROPS⁺ for future use, you can use the 1-2-3 **File Save** (**/FS**) command. When you issue this command, 1-2-3 assumes that you will want to save your file under the same name as that which you retrieved. **Be careful here!** If you press [Enter], your original PROPS⁺ file will be overwritten with your model spreadsheet, and you will have to reinstall PROPS⁺ to return it to its original format. *You should rename files when you save them.* We recommend that you use the DOS command **M**ake **D**irectory to create a subdirectory to contain problem worksheets, such as C:\PROPS\PROBLEMS. For example, suppose you have created an inventory model and wish to save it; pressing the **/FS** key sequence displays the following at the top of your screen:

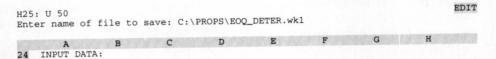

```
H25: U 50                                                          EDIT
Enter name of file to save: C:\PROPS\EOQ_DETER.wk1
        A       B       C       D       E       F       G       H
24  INPUT DATA:
```

At this point you can simply begin typing the new name under which you will file the new sheet, including its subdirectory path. You might simply type a name such as PROBLEMS\WIDGET1.WK1. (You can also press the escape key [Esc] until the file name area is clear of default names, allowing you to type a whole new path, including a new drive letter, if desired.)

This procedure also saves a copy of the PROPS⁺ program as well as the problem data in the new file. Hence, to rerun the model, you need only retrieve the saved file and press [Alt M] to call up the PROPS⁺ menu in the normal fashion. (To ensure that the What-If Solver Add-In is attached, always start 1-2-3 from the PROPS⁺ default directory or start by typing PROPS.) **Hint:** You will find that it is tidy to create separate directories in which to store your own models, and only keep PROPS⁺ files on the **\PROPS** directory. **Remember:** If you have retrieved a PROPS⁺ file, change the file name before saving or the original file will be lost.

The **F**ile **R**etrieve command (**/FR**) works the same way as the **F**ile **S**ave command. When you are in **READY** mode and type the key sequence **/FR**, you will see a message like this at the top of your screen:

```
A1:                                                               FILES
Name of file to retrieve: C:\PROPS\*.wk?
ACCESS.WK1      AUTO123.WK1     CPM_PERT.WK1    DECISION.WK1    DP_DETER.WK1
        A       B       C       D       E       F       G       H
1
```

The system is pointing to the default directory (C:\PROPS in this case) and presents a list of the Lotus files in this directory. To select a file from a subdirectory of \PROPS, you can type the subdirectory name or highlight it with the cursor and press [Enter]. If you want a file from another directory, press [Esc] to clear the defaults until the following appears at the top of the screen:

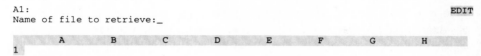

```
A1:                                                                    EDIT
Name of file to retrieve:_
```
```
        A        B        C        D        E        F        G        H
1
```

Now you can type the path and file name of the file you wish to recall, such as A:\PROBLEMS\WIDGET.WK1. Press [Enter] and the designated file will be retrieved. **Caution:** When you retrieve a file, the current contents of your spreadsheet will be erased. Save your worksheet contents if you will ever need them again.

You can copy portions of one worksheet into another, similar to using the **Copy** command for a range *between* worksheets instead of within a worksheet, by using the **File eXtract** command (**/FX**) in conjunction with the **File Combine** command (**/FC**). The **/FX** command copies a source range (you specify either formulas or values) into a new worksheet file. You can incorporate this new file into the target worksheet range with the **/FC** command. The following example shows a typical use of these commands.

Suppose you have set up a Linear Programming model in a worksheet and wish to copy the data area containing the variable names, objective function coefficient, and absorption coefficients to another worksheet. Place the cursor in the upper left corner of the range you wish to copy and press the key sequence **/FX**. Your screen appears as follows:

```
A30: [W10] "Row                                                        MENU
Formulas  Values
Save data including formulas
        A        B        C        D        E        F        G        H
21                Analyst Name      Your_name
22                Problem Name      demo
23
24                Number of Variables          3
25                Number of Constraints        3
26                Problem type (max or min)    max
27
28 INPUT DATA -- Press [Alt M] after entering coefficients
29                Variables:
30        Row      X1        X2        X3    Rel'n    RHS
31 -------------------------------------------------------
32 LP Obj Fn      20        25        18    (n/a)
33  Rows: 1)       3         2         4    <=       18
34        2)       1         1         1    <=       12
35        3)       1        -2         0    =         0
36 -------------------------------------------------------
```

At this point, the cursor is resting on cell A30, which is the upper left corner of the range to be extracted from this worksheet and saved. The menu at the top of the screen asks whether you would like to transfer any formulas in cells within the range (similar to the **/C**opy command) or simply transfer the current values of the cell contents (similar to the **/R**ange **V**alue command). Here, the **V**alues choice is appropriate, so move the cursor to the right and press [Enter] (or press **V**). You are then asked for the name of a file in which to store the extracted range. 1-2-3 assumes you want to store in the default directory, and provides you with a list of the current files in the directory:

```
A30: [W10] "Row                                                    FILES
Enter name of file to extract to: C:\PROPS\*.wk1
ACCESS.WK1       AUTO123.WK1     CPM_PERT.WK1    DECISION.WK1    DP_DETER.WK1
         A           B         C         D         E         F       G       H
21                   Analyst Name        Your_name
```

If you wish to store the extracted range in the current directory, you can simply type a new file name in which the range will be stored. To select a different directory, press [Esc] until the defaults disappear, type in the path name of the file that will contain the extracted range (say, C:\PROBLEMS\LP_DATA.WK1), and press [Enter]. 1-2-3 will create the new file automatically. You are then asked to specify the range to be extracted:

```
A30: [W10] "Row                                                    POINT
Enter extract range: A30..A30

         A           B         C         D         E         F       G       H
21                   Analyst Name        Your_name
```

Move the cursor to F35 to define the range [A30..F35] and press [Enter]. The range is extracted and stored in the file you have indicated.

      To retrieve these stored values into another worksheet using the **File Combine** command, move your cursor to the upper left corner of the target range and press **/FC**. You will see:

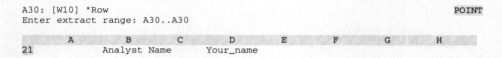

```
A39: [W10]                                                         MENU
Copy   Add   Subtract
Copy data from a file on disk to the worksheet
         A           B         C         D         E         F       G       H
```

Select **C**opy. You will then see:

```
A39: [W10]                                                         MENU
Entire-File   Named/Specified-Range
Incorporate entire file into worksheet
         A           B         C         D         E         F       G       H
```

Select Entire-File. Finally, you are asked for the name of the file you extracted to. 1-2-3 assumes you have stored it in the default directory. If so, you can highlight the file name and press [Enter]. Otherwise, press the escape key [Esc] to clear the default file names and directory, type in the path name of the file, and press [Enter]. The range is immediately retrieved into your current worksheet.

Printing Results

The **P**rint command (**/P**) on the main 1-2-3 menu allows you to print ranges from your worksheet either directly to a printer or to a file for subsequent word processing. Issuing the command **/P** calls up the following menu:

```
A60: 500                                                          MENU
Printer  File
Send print output directly to a printer
      A         B         C         D         E      F      G      H
```

Select **P**rinter to send the output directly to a printer. Selecting **F**ile will cause the system to prompt you for a file in which to store this output. In either case, you then see the following print menu:

```
A60: 500                                                          MENU
Range  Line  Page  Options  Clear  Align  Go  Quit
Specify a range to print
      A         B         C         D         E      F      G      H
```

Select **R**ange, and describe the range of cells you wish to print in the usual way. Then select **G**o to print the range. **P**age advances the printer to the next page, and **A**lign resets the printer to start at the top of the page. **O**ptions allow you to reset the number of lines per page, the print font, the margins, and so on. See your 1-2-3 manual for a description of each of these options.

Working with Graphs

One of the major advantages of PROPS$^+$ is that it makes sensitivity analysis easy, and the results are often best shown through a graph. This section describes the basics of creating and printing a graph in 1-2-3. Suppose you have created a table in your worksheet for an inventory control problem that computes the total cost of inventory control over a range of order sizes, such as:

	A	B	C
59	Order Q	T.Cost	
60	500	750	
61	525	738.6904	
62	550	729.5454	
63	575	722.2826	
64	600	716.6666	
65	625	712.5	
66	650	709.6153	
67	675	707.8703	
68	700	707.1428	
69	725	707.3275	
70	750	708.3333	
71	775	710.0806	
72	800	712.5	
73	825	715.5303	
74	850	719.1176	
75			

Move the cursor to the start of the x-axis column as shown, and use the **Graph** command (**/G**) to call up the following 1-2-3 graph creation menu:

```
A60: 500                                                                          MENU
Type  X  A  B  C  D  E  F  Reset  View  Save  Options  Name  Group  Quit
Line  Bar  XY  Stack-Bar  Pie
         A          B          C       D        E         F        G        H
```

Type selects the type of graph to create. In this example, an **XY** graph is most appropriate, so press [Enter] and select **XY** from the menu. To specify the range of values for the horizontal axis, select **X** from the graph menu and indicate the range [A60..A74] in the usual way (see the range discussion on page 15). 1-2-3 allows for six different series to be plotted on any graph, indicated by the letters A through F on the menu. Here we have only one series to plot, so select **A**, and indicate the range [B60..B74] in the usual way. You can preview the graph by selecting **V**iew from the graph menu. In this case, the following graph appears:

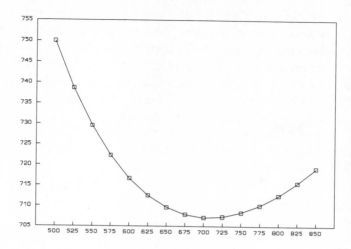

Press the spacebar to return to the graph menu. **Note:** To view the graph, your computer must have a graphics capability, and you must have specified the type of graphics system during the 1-2-3 installation procedure. If your screen blanks when you select **View**, press the spacebar to return to the menu. It is likely that your installation of 1-2-3 did not included a graphic display device. You can install one by returning to DOS and following the 1-2-3 install procedure, using the Change Selected Equipment option, to include a Graphics Display in your monitor description.

   The **O**ptions item in this menu allows you to rescale axes, insert titles, and change the appearance of your graph. For instance, if you want a simple line graph without a marker for each observation as in the view above, select the following sequence from the successive menus:

Options **F**ormat **G**raph **L**ines

Pressing [Esc] takes you back through the menu sequence to return to the original graph menu. See your 1-2-3 manual for other graph appearance options.

Printing graphs is a two-step process. First, the current graph image must be saved in a file. Select the graph menu item **S**ave and provide a file name *without an extension* when prompted. 1-2-3 will automatically add the file extension .PIC to this name to indicate that it is a graph image file. The file can be printed by leaving 1-2-3 and using the separate PrintGraph program (your \123 directory should contain a program called PGRAPH.EXE for this purpose). See the Lotus manual for directions on using PrintGraph. You can also import the graph image file into many standard word processing systems, such as WordPerfect, through the word processor's graphics features. In WordPerfect, for example, use the sequence [Alt F9] **F**igure **C**reate **F**ilename, followed by the full name of the graph image file (including the .PIC extension) to import the graph. Other WordPerfect graph options can reposition and resize the graph as you wish, and the result can be printed using the standard word processing format.

Warnings on Using 1-2-3 and PROPS⁺

1. When a PROPS⁺ model is being executed, you can abort it by simultaneously pressing the keys [Ctrl] and [Break]. The screen will show an ERROR indicator in the top right-hand corner. Press [Esc] to return the system to READY mode. Now, since the program was interrupted, it may not know where it is to restart. You can try rerunning the model, but if this is not successful, you will have to save the data and re-initialize PROPS⁺.

    Whenever [Ctrl Break] is used, a break flag is set in the Solver. The next time the Solver is called, a "BREAK ERROR" will occur. Pressing [Enter] clears the error and allows you to solve the problem.

2. Use caution with the 1-2-3 commands to **M**ove (**/M**) and **C**opy (**/C**) ranges, since these commands overwrite any cell entries in the target ranges. Copying data within a data entry area of a PROPS⁺ model is always permissible and is often useful for rapid, accurate data entry. You can also copy data from a scratch area elsewhere in the worksheet into the data entry area in any PROPS⁺ model.

3. *Never* use **W**orksheet **I**nsert (**/WI**) or **W**orksheet **D**elete (**/WD**) columns or rows in a PROPS⁺ worksheet. The likely effect will be to amend the logic flow in the program, and PROPS⁺ will no longer function properly.

4. Use caution with the **R**ange **E**rase command (**/RE**). This is a useful command for cleaning up a worksheet and removing unwanted analysis. Ensure, however, that there is no PROPS⁺ program information (or data you don't recognize) in the range you are erasing, or PROPS⁺ may not function properly after the erasure.

Technical Support

Neither Addison-Wesley nor PROPS Systems provides phone assistance to students. Phone assistance is provided to registered instructors adopting PROPS[+].

If you have to ask your instructor for assistance, describe your question or problem in detail. Write down what you were doing (the steps or procedures you followed) when the problem occurred. Also, write down the exact error message, if any.

Features

1. Linear Programming

- calculates the optimal solution and reduced costs.

- calculates the dual price for each constraint.

- calculates sensitivity analysis ranges for objective function coefficients and right-hand sides.

- calculates simplex method tableaux, if desired.

- makes problem editing easy (e.g., adding or deleting constraints or variables).

- permits lower- and upper-bound constraints on variables.

2. Mixed Integer Programming

- uses the branch-and-bound solution procedure for general, 0-1, and mixed integer problems.

- permits bounded variables.

3. Nonlinear Programming

- calculates the optimal solution for a convex objective function, subject to linear constraints.

- permits bounded variables.

- uses a generalized reduced gradient method.

Chapter 2. Linear, Integer, and Nonlinear Programming

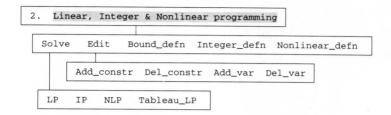

Linear programming (LP) is the most important method developed for solving resource allocation problems. Typically, these problems involve allocating limited resources among competing activities in the best possible way: that is, so that profits are maximized or costs minimized. The adjective "linear" means that all the mathematical functions in the model are linear. The word "programming" does not mean computer programming, but planning. Thus, a programming problem means the planning of activities to obtain an optimal result.

Integer programming (IP) is a special form of linear programming problem in which all or some of the variables may be required to assume only integer values. If all the variables are required to be integral, we have a pure integer programming problem; if some are integers and the others may take on non-integral values, the problem is called a mixed integer program.

Nonlinear programming (NLP) refers to allocation problems in which the objective function and constraints may be nonlinear. The model included in PROPS⁺ allows for nonlinear objective functions, but requires all constraints to be linear. This type of model is important, for example, in cases of diminishing marginal returns or for problems with increasing marginal costs.

Linear Programming

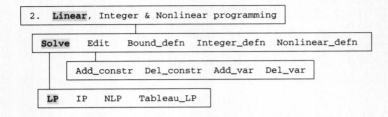

The Model:

$$\max \sum_{j=1}^{n} c_j x_j \quad \text{(or min)}$$

subject to

$$\sum_{j=1}^{n} a_{ij} x_j \ (\le, \ =, \ \ge) \ b_i, \qquad\qquad i = 1, 2, \ldots, m$$

$$x_j \ge 0, \qquad\qquad\qquad\qquad j = 1, 2, \ldots, n$$

Computation: PROPS⁺ solves for the optimum using the simplex method in the What-If Solver. (Integer values or nonlinear objective functions that may have been defined are ignored.) The shadow price is the improvement in the objective if the right-hand side value is increased by one unit.

Limitations: Problem size is limited to 120 variables and 120 constraints. The right-hand side must be nonnegative.

Example: The Car-Truck Problem

An automobile plant can make cars and trucks, and produces a single type of each. It can sell all that it produces in one month. The incremental contributions to profits and overhead are $400 for a truck and $300 for a car. There are, however, some restraining factors on production.

(a) The metal body stamping portion of the firm can produce a maximum of 8000 bodies (car or truck) per month;

(b) The engine assembly facility can assemble at most 10,000 car engines per month (one truck engine requires the time of two car engines);

(c) There is a maximum of 12,000 worker-hours per month available for truck assembly and each truck requires three worker-hours;

(d) Car assembly has available a maximum of 14,000 worker-hours per month and each car requires two worker-hours.

You might be interested in the following questions:

i)   What is the optimal mix of car and truck production each month?

ii)   What is the value of the resources used?

The car-truck problem can be formulated as the following LP problem:

$$\max \quad 400\,x_1 + 300\,x_2$$

subject to

$$
\begin{aligned}
x_1 + x_2 &\le 8{,}000 \\
2x_1 + x_2 &\le 10{,}000 \\
3x_1 &\le 12{,}000 \\
2x_2 &\le 14{,}000 \\
x_1, x_2 &\ge 0
\end{aligned}
$$

where x_1 is the number of trucks and x_2 the number of cars produced each month. There are two variables and four constraints. (The nonnegativity requirements on variables are not counted as constraints.)

You can solve for the optimal production schedule in the car-truck problem using PROPS$^+$. Begin by typing

props [Enter]

You should see both the 1-2-3 screen and the What-If Solver screen flash as the system is loaded. If you do not see the What-If screen flash, it has not been attached. Go to the section "Auto-attach the What-If Solver Add-Ins" (page 4) and follow the instructions. If you were already in 1-2-3, you can start PROPS$^+$ using the File Retrieve command (**/FR**) and selecting the worksheet called ACCESS.WK1 (the first in the list at the top of the screen). When the system is loaded, you will see the following screen:

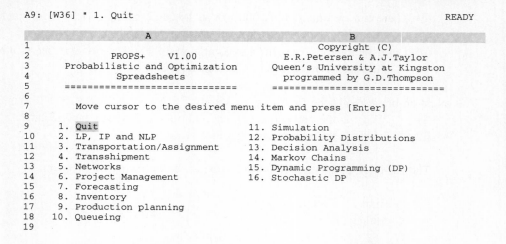

```
A9: [W36] " 1. Quit                                                      READY

         A                                          B
1                                           Copyright (C)
2            PROPS+    V1.00               E.R.Petersen & A.J.Taylor
3       Probabilistic and Optimization     Queen's University at Kingston
4              Spreadsheets                programmed by G.D.Thompson
5       ==============================     ==============================
6
7        Move cursor to the desired menu item and press [Enter]
8
9     1. Quit                              11. Simulation
10    2. LP, IP and NLP                    12. Probability Distributions
11    3. Transportation/Assignment         13. Decision Analysis
12    4. Transshipment                     14. Markov Chains
13    5. Networks                          15. Dynamic Programming (DP)
14    6. Project Management                16. Stochastic DP
15    7. Forecasting
16    8. Inventory
17    9. Production planning
18   10. Queueing
19
```

Select **2. LP, IP and NLP** by moving the cursor down one cell using the down arrow key
and pressing [Enter]. You will see the following screen:

```
         A        B        C        D        E        F        G
1     ==============================
2                PROPS+                 LINEAR, INTEGER and NONLINEAR
3                                       PROGRAMMING SPREADSHEET
4              Copyright (C)            -LP simplex solution
5              PROPS SYSTEMS              tableaux, sensitivity analysis
6                                       -bounded variables, interior
7              12/29/91 12:51 PM          point method
8     ==============================    -integer and mixed integer
9                                       -nonlinear objective function
10   Instructions:
11           -Enter number of variables, number of constraints
12                   and problem type (max or min) when prompted. An
13                   appropriate data-input area will be constructed.
14           -Enter coefficients for the objective function and
15                   constraints. The variables "X" and constraints
16                   "Rows:" may be renamed (optional).
17           -Press [Alt M] for the command menu.
18        PROMPT mode when CMD is on. Type response, press [ENTER].
19
```

Pressing [Enter] initiates a sequence of questions. Note that you are in the
spreadsheet PROMPT mode (the letters CMD are lit at the bottom of the screen), and so
you must follow each response with the [Enter] key. Remember, if you make a typing
mistake before you press [Enter], you can use the backspace key to delete characters, or
press the [Esc] key and re-type your whole response. If you recognize a mistake in the
set-up portion of data entry (which describes the problem size and type) *after* pressing
[Enter], it is best to simply start over, using the **File Retrieve** command (**/FR**) to recall
the ACCESS worksheet.

You are asked for the problem name, "car-truck"; the number of variables, "2"; the number of constraints, "4"; and finally the problem type, "max". After you have answered the questions, the screen will look like this:

	A	B	C	D	E	F	G
21		Analyst Name		Your_name			
22		Problem Name		car-truck			
23							
24		Number of Variables			2		
25		Number of Constraints			4		
26		Problem type (max or min)			max		

After you enter **max**, PROPS[+] will construct the input data area for a general problem with the dimensions you have just provided. In this case, the input data area appears as follows:

	A	B	C	D	E	F	G
27							
28	INPUT DATA -- Press [Alt M] after entering coefficients						
29		Variables:					
30	Row	X1	X2	Rel'n	RHS		
31	--						
32	LP Obj Fn	0	0	(n/a)			
33	Rows: 1)	0	0	<=	0		
34	2)	0	0	<=	0		
35	3)	0	0	<=	0		
36	4)	0	0	<=	0		
37	--						
38							

At this point, you are in READY mode and can use ordinary spreadsheet methods, using the cursor keys to move the cursor from cell to cell to enter the data. In the LP Obj Fn row, enter the profit contribution of each variable. In the next four rows, enter the constraint coefficients, the type of constraint (the default is ≤), and the right-hand side (RHS). To enter the type of constraint, type = or '<= or >=. (In 1-2-3, the < key acts the same as the / key, so you must type ' (single quote) first to show that it is a label. In addition, PROPS[+] assumes that < is ≤ and > is ≥.) Since you are in READY mode, typing errors can be corrected simply by moving the cursor to the cell and retyping the correct entry. The completed data entry area for our sample problem appears as follows:

	A	B	C	D	E	F	G
27							
28	INPUT DATA						
29		Variables:					
30	Row	X1	X2	Rel'n	RHS		
31	--						
32	Obj Fn:	400	300	(n/a)			
33	Rows: 1)	1	1	<=	8000		
34	2)	2	1	<=	10000		
35	3)	3	0	<=	12000		
36	4)	0	2	<=	14000		
37	--						

Pressing [Alt M] (i.e., pressing the [Alt] key and the M key simultaneously) shows the following menu at the top of the screen, and returns control to PROPS⁺.

```
A1:                                                                    MENU
Solve  Edit  Bound_defn  Integer_defn  Nonlinear_defn
Solve the problem
         A         B         C        D        E        F       G
```

Select **Solve** by pressing [Enter]. You will see the following menu:

```
A1:                                                                    MENU
LP  IP  NLP  Tableau_LP
Solve linear programming problem
         A         B         C        D        E        F
```

Select **LP**. The screen will flash as PROPS⁺ sets up the data and calls the Solver. When the Solver has completed its solution, it will beep, and at the top of your screen you will see a completion message similar to the following:

```
A50: [W10] 'SOLUTION                                                    EDIT
Results within tolerance; solution data follows  Press ENTER
Trial Solution: 3
         A         B         C        D        E        F       G
```

The program will pause. Press [Enter] to continue, and PROPS⁺ will generate the following table of output results:

```
         A         B         C        D        E        F        G
50  SOLUTION
51
52  Maximum Objective Function Value:      2600000
53
54                                     Sensitivity to Obj Fn Coeff Changes
55                         Reduced      Current ____Allowable____
56   Variable   Value      Cost         Coeff. Increase Decrease
57  -------------------------------     -------------------------
58       X1     2000         0             400     200      100
59       X2     6000         0             300     100      100
60
61                                     Sensitivity to Right Hand Side Changes
62              Slack      Dual         Current ____Allowable____
63   Constr.    Value      Price          RHS  Increase Decrease
64  -------------------------------     -------------------------
65  Rows:  1)      0        200           8000     500     2000
66         2)      0        100          10000    2000     1000
67         3)   6000          0          12000  1.0E+30    6000
68         4)   2000          0          14000  1.0E+30    2000
69
```

The optimal solution is to produce 2,000 trucks per month (X1) and 6,000 cars per month (X2), which results in a $2.6 million contribution to profits.

The output also shows that the capacity to assemble engines and bodies is fully utilized since the slack values are zero for the first two constraints. Constraints 3 and 4 show that there are 6,000 truck assembly worker-hours and 2,000 car assembly worker-hours that are unused each month.

The dual price associated with each constraint is the improvement in the objective function if the right-hand side is increased by one unit.

The reduced cost is
> **(a) the amount by which the objective coefficient would have to improve before the variable can have a positive value in the optimal solution, and**
> **(b) the deterioration in the objective function that occurs if the variable is forced to increase by one unit.**

The dual price (value) for constraint 1 (the number of bodies assembled per month) is $200/body, while the dual price for the engine assembly resource is $100/engine. This means that if we increase the number of bodies that can be assembled each month by 1, the profits will increase by $200. The dual prices for the last two constraints are 0, which implies there is no value in increasing the number of worker-hours per month available for truck or car assembly. This is reasonable since these capacities were not fully utilized.

The right-hand column of the output area contains the sensitivity range analysis. The first table shows the range over which the objective function coefficient can change without changing the optimal value of the variables. Thus, the contribution to profits from truck production can be in the range (400 − 100=) 300 to (400 + 200=) 600 without changing the optimal production schedule.

The Sensitivity to Right Hand Side Changes table shows the range over which the right-hand side (RHS) can change without changing the dual price of the resource and the current nonzero variables in the solution. For example, the number of engines per month that can be produced can vary over the range 9,000 to 12,000 without changing the dual price for engine production ($100 per engine/month) or the variables that are nonzero in the solution. (Of course, the optimal value for these variables will change as the RHS is changed.)

Solver Completion Message

When the Solver has completed its solution, it will beep and you will see a Solver completion message at the top of your screen. These messages were explained on page 10. Press [Enter] to continue; PROPS⁺ will generate a table of output results if a solution was found. If no solution was found, PROPS⁺ will display one of the following messages:

*** Max. time or iterations exceeded ***
*** Values did not converge (may be unbounded) ***
*** No feasible solution was found ***
*** Solution failed ***

It will also copy the last value for each variable used by the Solver. These values may be useful in diagnosing problems in the formulation.

LP Tableaux

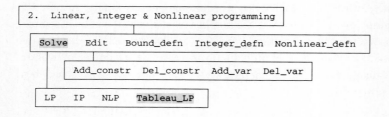

You may wish to follow the sequence of steps as they are performed in the Linear Programming simplex method. PROPS⁺ has a macro program that can either calculate the final tableau or step through each iteration of the simplex method, displaying the tableau at each stage. When the final tableau is reached, the optimal solution, dual prices, and sensitivity range analysis are displayed as before.

Press [Alt M] to get the menu, select **Solve**, and then select **Tableau_LP**. The following menu will be displayed:

```
A1:                                                                    MENU
Solve  First_tableau
Solve and display the LP solution
        A         B         C         D         E         F         G
```

If you select **Solve**, PROPS⁺ will calculate the optimal solution and display the optimal and previous tableaux. If you select **First_tableau** (or **Next_tableau** in subsequent menus) the program will stop after each iteration of the simplex method and display the current tableau. To continue, select **Next_tableau** and repeat the process until the optimal solution is found, or until you select **Solve**. For the car-truck problem, the final screen appears as follows:

	A	B	C	D	E	F	G
50	SOLUTION SUMMARY						
51							
52	Maximum Objective Function Value:				2600000		
53							
54			Reduced			Slack	Dual
55	Variable	Value	Cost		Constr.	Value	Price
56	---------------------------				---------------------------		
57	X1	2000	0		_s1	0	200
58	X2	6000	0		_s2	0	100
59					_s3	6000	0
60					_s4	2000	0

You will then see the following menu:

```
A50: [W10] 'SOLUTION SUMMARY                                              MENU
No  Yes
Do not perform sensitivity analysis calculations
```

	A	B	C	D	E	F	G
50	SOLUTION SUMMARY						

Select **No** by pressing [Enter] or just type in the letter **n**. The work area that contains the current and previous tableaux is located below the output in the worksheet. Use the [PgDn] key to locate the tableau. Change the column width to 7, using the **Worksheet Global Column-width** command (**/WGC**), so that you can see the entire tableau. Your screen should look like this:

	A	B	C	D	E	F	G	H	I	J
73										
74	Work area: (Iteration 4 of Phase II)									
75										
76				Current Tableau						
77										
78	Column	(basis)	_z	_s1	_s2	_s3	_s4	X1	X2	b
79		_z	1	200	100	1E-15	0	5E-14	0	3E+06
80	F	_s3	0	3	-3	1	0	-2E-16	0	6000
81	I	X2	0	2	-1	0	0	0	1	6000
82	H	X1	0	-1	1	0	0	1	0	2000
83	G	_s4	0	-4	2	0	1	0	0	2000
84										
85										
86				Previous Tableau						
87		_z	1	0	300	-66.66	0	6E-14	0	2E+06
88		_s1	0	1	-1	0.3333	0	-6E-17	0	2000
89		X2	0	0	1	-0.666	0	1E-16	1	2000
90		X1	0	0	0	0.3333	0	1	0	4000
91		_s4	0	0	-2	1.3333	1	-2E-16	0	10000

Note that when you change column width, the decimal numbers are truncated to fit within the specified column width. Numbers in the "E format" (scientific notation) are rounded. If the column width is too small to contain the number, you will see ****** in the cell. In the tableau, Column A specifies which variables are in the basis. In this example, X1, X2, _s3, and _s4 are basic variables. (The variable _s3 is the slack in the third constraint.) The values in Column J are the values of the basic variables. (Note that the value of _z, the objective function, appears to be 3E+06, which has been rounded from 2.6E+06 to fit within the specified column width.)

Editing

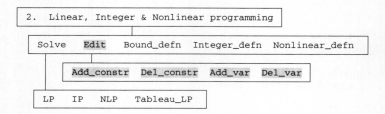

PROPS⁺ lets you edit a problem formulation by adding or deleting constraints or variables. For example, in the car-truck problem, suppose the opportunity to also produce snow vehicles arises. The profit contribution from a snow vehicle is $225, and each requires the equivalent of 1/2 a car body in the body assembly shop and the same time as a car engine in the engine production shop. Assembly requires 1.5 hours of car assembly worker-hours.

Before changing the problem, let us save this formulation for later use. Use the **File Save** command (**/FS**) and you will see the following menu:

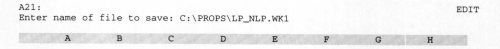

Type in a name for this file, for example, **car-tr**, and press [Enter]. (Note that if you did not change the name of the file, 1-2-3 would overwrite the original PROPS⁺ work-sheet.)

To edit the car-truck problem, move the cursor to the column in the input data table where you want the new variable(s) to appear. In this example, move the cursor to cell D30. Press [Alt M] and select **Edit** and **Add_Var**. Pressing [Enter] will add one new variable. If you want to add more than one variable, move the cursor one column to the right for each additional variable and then press [Enter]. In this example, we wish to add one variable, so we simply press [Enter]. The following screen will appear:

	A	B	C	D	E	F	G
28	INPUT DATA -- Press [Alt M] after entering coefficients						
29		Variables:					
30	Row	X1	X2	(new)	Rel'n	RHS	
31	---						
32	LP Obj Fn	400	300	0	(n/a)		
33	Rows: 1)	1	1	0	<=	8000	
34	2)	2	1	0	<=	10000	
35	3)	3	0	0	<=	12000	
36	4)	0	2	0	<=	14000	
37	---						
38							

You are now back in READY mode and you can use spreadsheet methods to move around the table and enter the new data. To make the problem easier to read, you can enter names for the variables and constraints as follows. Move the cursor over the variable name X1 in cell B30 and type **"truck**. Name the other variables in the same way. To name the rows, move the cursor over "Rows: 1)" in cell A33 and type **"body**. When the other constraints are named, the screen should look like this:

	A	B	C	D	E	F	G
28	INPUT DATA -- Press [Alt M] after entering coefficients						
29		Variables:					
30	Row	truck	car	snow	Rel'n	RHS	
31	---						
32	LP Obj Fn	400	300	225	(n/a)		
33	body	1	1	0.5	<=	8000	
34	engine	2	1	1	<=	10000	
35	t_m_hrs	3	0	0	<=	12000	
36	c_m_hrs	0	2	1.5	<=	14000	
37	---						
38							

To run the new model, press [Alt M], select **Solve** from the menu, and select **LP** from the next menu. The solution will look like this:

	A	B	C	D	E	F	G
50	SOLUTION						
51							
52	Maximum Objective Function Value:				2633333.		
53							
54					Sensitivity to Obj Fn Coeff Changes		
55			Reduced		Current	____Allowable____	
56	Variable	Value	Cost		Coeff.	Increase	Decrease
57			-------------------------			--------------------------	
58	truck	1333.333	0		400	50	400
59	car	6000	0		300	133.3333	66.66666
60	snow	1333.333	0		225	50	25

	A	**B**	**C**	**D**	**E**	**F**	**G**
61							
62					Sensitivity to Right Hand Side Changes		
63		Slack	Dual		Current	_____Allowable_____	
64	Constr.	Value	Price		RHS	Increase	Decrease
65	------------------------		----		--------------------------		
66	body	0	133.3333		8000	500	3000
67	engine	0	133.3333		10000	6000	1000
68	t_m_hr	8000	0		12000	1.0E+30	8000
69	c_m_hr	0	16.66666		14000	4000	2000

Car production stays at 6,000, truck production drops to 1,333.3, and snow vehicle production is 1,333.3, for an increase in profits of $33,333, to $2.633 million. We also note that the car assembly worker-hours are fully utilized, and has a dual price of $16.66 per worker-hour.

The edit feature can also be used to add new constraints or to delete variables or constraints, so that you can modify your problem without having to reenter your data.

Bounded Variables

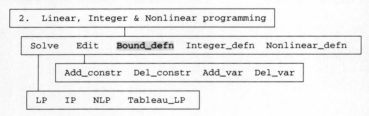

The Model:

$$\max \sum_{j=1}^{n} c_j x_j \quad \text{(or min)}$$

subject to

$$\sum_{j=1}^{n} a_{ij} x_j \ (\leq, \ =, \ \geq) \ b_i, \qquad\qquad i = 1, 2, \ldots, m$$

$$d_j \leq x_j \leq u_j, \qquad\qquad j = 1, 2, \ldots, n$$

Computation: PROPS⁺ uses the simplex method in the What-If Solver.
The specified bounds are added as constraints.

Limitations: The problem size is limited to 120 variables and 120 constraints, including the variable bounds. $d_j \geq 0$.

Often a problem calls for limits on the range of values that variables may assume. For example, in the vehicle problem, suppose we must produce at least 1500 trucks per month. In the last solution, truck production was 1,333.3 per month, so this requirement would be violated. We could add this restriction as a new constraint. However, it is usually easier, particularly if there are many bounds on the variables, to use the bounded-variable feature in PROPS+.

The first step is to define bounds on the variables. To do this, press [Alt M] and then select **Bound_defn**. The following screen will appear:

```
         A          B         C        D        E        F        G
30            Row     truck      car     snow    Rel'n      RHS
31       ---------------------------------------------------------------
32    LP Obj Fn       400       300      225     (n/a)
33    body             1         1       0.5      <=       8000
34    engine           2         1        1       <=      10000
35    tr. man-hr       3         0        0       <=      12000
36    car man-hr       0         2       1.5      <=      14000
37       ---------------------------------------------------------------
38
39    Bounds-Up infinity infinity infinity
40       Lower        0         0        0
41
```

The default values for the bounds are 0 and infinity (10^{30}). Change the lower bound on trucks to 1500 (cell B40), and run the model by selecting [Alt M], **Solve**, and **LP**. When the Solver has completed its solution, it will beep and at the top of your screen you will see a completion message similar to the following:

```
A50: [W10] 'SOLUTION                                                    EDIT
Results within tolerance; solution data follows   Press ENTER
Trial Solution: 4
          A          B         C        D        E        F        G
```

The program will pause. Press [Enter] to continue; PROPS+ will generate the following table of output results:

```
         A          B         C        D        E        F        G
50    SOLUTION
51
52    Maximum Objective Function Value:        2625000
53
54                                      Sensitivity to Obj Fn Coeff Changes
55                          Reduced       Current ____Allowable____
56    Variable    Value      Cost          Coeff. Increase Decrease
57    ---------------------------           ---------------------------
58     truck      1500        50             400      50    1.0E+30
59       car      6000         0             300     150      75
60      snow      1000         0             225      75      25
61
```

	A	B	C	D	E	F	G
62					Sensitivity to Right Hand Side Changes		
63		Slack	Dual		Current	___Allowable___	
64	Constr.	Value	Price		RHS	Increase	Decrease
65	-------------------------				-------------------------		
66	body	0	150		8000	500	3000
67	engine	0	150		10000	500	500
68	t_m_hrs	7500	0		12000	1.0E+30	7500
69	c_m_hrs	500	0		14000	1.0E+30	500
70							

The addition of the lower bound on the number of trucks reduced the profits from \$2.633 million to \$2.625 million. The lower constraint on truck production has a dual price of −\$50. That is, an additional truck would reduce profits by \$50, or conversely, reducing truck production to 1499 would increase profits by \$50.

Note that when bounds are defined, only those that have values other than **0** or **infinity** are included in the model. The simplex algorithm assumes a lower bound of 0 on all variables. To remove a bound, simply set its value to **0** or **infinity**.

Example: ALCOA

ALCOA has bauxite ore deposits in Guinea, Surinam, and Arkansas. Bauxite is converted to alumina (an intermediate high-grade material) in refineries in Surinam, Baltimore, and Arkansas. Finally, the alumina is converted to aluminum in smelting facilities in Baltimore and Kitimat.

Refining bauxite to alumina is relatively inexpensive. Smelting alumina into aluminum in electric furnaces (pot lines) is expensive. One ton of alumina yields 0.4 tons of finished aluminum ingot. The following data describe the process.

BAUXITE MINING

Mine Site	\$/ton	Annual Bauxite Capacity, tons	Alumina Yield
Guinea	8.40	36,000	6%
Surinam	7.20	52,000	8%
Arkansas	10.80	28,000	6.2%

BAUXITE TO ALUMINA REFINING

Refinery Site	\$/ton Alumina	Annual Bauxite Capacity, tons
Surinam	6.60	40,000
Baltimore	7.60	30,000
Arkansas	6.40	20,000

SMELTING ALUMINA TO ALUMINUM INGOT

Smelter Site	$/ton Alumina	Annual Alumina Capacity, tons
Baltimore	170	4,000
Kitimat	104	7,000

FINISHED PRODUCT DEMANDS

Plant Site	Annual Sales of Aluminum Ingot, tons
Baltimore	1,000
Kitimat	1,200

BAUXITE TRANSPORTATION COSTS, $/TON

From\To	Surinam	Baltimore	Arkansas
Guinea	8.00	10.20	40.20
Surinam	0.20	4.40	32.60
Arkansas	32.60	12.40	0.20

ALUMINA TRANSPORTATION COSTS, $/TON

From\To	Baltimore	Kitimat
Surinam	4.40	30.20
Baltimore	0.00	32.30
Arkansas	13.40	18.80

Finished ingots are not transported between Baltimore and Kitimat, or vice versa.

A model of the ALCOA operation must contain several capacity constraints; for example, total bauxite mined in Guinea must be equal to or less than 36,000 tons per year. Then, since there is no refinery in Guinea, bauxite mined in Guinea *and* shipped to Surinam, Baltimore, and Arkansas must be less than or equal to 36,000 tons per year. In total there are three mining, three refining, two smelting, and two demand equations, for a total of ten required constraints. To make the model easier to work with, we will add product balance equations (three into the refineries, three out of the refineries, and two for ingot demand) resulting in a total of 18 constraints.

We shall use the following notation to define the variables. Let XRS be the size of the shipment from mine R to refinery S, where R and S are the first letters in the names of the mine and refinery respectively (e.g., XGS is the shipment in tons from the mine at Guinea to the refinery at Surinam). Similarly, let YT be the production of alumina at refinery T, and YTU the shipment of alumina from refinery T to smelter U. Finally, let ZV be the production of ingot in tons at smelter V. The model can then be written as

min   16.4 XGS + 18.6 XGB + 48.6 XGA
    + 7.4 XSS + 11.6 XSB + 39.8 XSA
    + 43.3 XAS + 23.2 XAB + 11 XAA
    + 6.6 YS + 7.6 YB + 6.4 YA
    + 174.4 YSB + 170 YBB + 183.4 YAB
    + 134.2 YSK + 136.3 YBK + 122.8 YAK

subject to
   XGS + XGB + XGA ≤ 36000
   XSS + XSB + XSA ≤ 52000
   XAS + XAB + XAA ≤ 28000
   XGS + XSS + XAS ≤ 40000
   XGB + XSB + XAB ≤ 30000
   XGA + XSA + XAA ≤ 20000
   0.06 XGS + 0.08 XSS + 0.062 XAS − YS = 0
   0.06 XGB + 0.08 XSB + 0.062 XAB − YB = 0
   0.06 XGA + 0.08 XSA + 0.062 XAA − YA = 0
   YS − YSB − YSK = 0
   YB − YBB − YBK = 0
   YA − YAB − YAK = 0
   YSB + YBB + YAB ≤ 4000
   YSK + YBK + YAK ≤ 7000
   0.4 YSB + 0.4 YBB + 0.4 YAB − ZB = 0
   0.4 YSK + 0.4 YBK + 0.4 YAK − ZK = 0
   ZB ≥ 1000
   ZK ≥ 1200

To solve using PROPS⁺, select **2. LP, IP and NLP** from the ACCESS menu and define a problem with 20 variables, 18 constraints, and minimize.

	A	B	C	D	E	F	G
21		Analyst Name		Your_name			
22		Problem Name		ALCOA			
23							
24		Number of Variables			20		
25		Number of Constraints			18		
26		Problem type (max or min)		min			

When you have entered the data and changed the names of the variables and constraints, the worksheet should contain the following data:

	A	B	C	D	E	F	G	H	I	J	K
28	INPUT DATA -- Press [Alt-M] after entering coefficients										
29		Variables:									
30	Row	XGS	XGB	XGA	XSS	XSB	XSA	XAS	XAB	XAA	YS
31											
32	LP Obj Fn	16.4	18.6	48.6	7.4	11.6	39.8	43.4	23.2	11	6.6
33	G_mine	1	1	1	0	0	0	0	0	0	0
34	S_mine	0	0	0	1	1	1	0	0	0	0
35	A_mine	0	0	0	0	0	0	1	1	1	0
36	S_in_ref	1	0	0	1	0	0	1	0	0	0
37	B_in_ref	0	1	0	0	1	0	0	1	0	0
38	A_in_ref	0	0	1	0	0	1	0	0	1	0
39	S_alumina	0.06	0	0	0.08	0	0	0.062	0	0	-1
40	B_alumina	0	0.06	0	0	0.08	0	0	0.062	0	0
41	A_alumina	0	0	0.06	0	0	0.08	0	0	0.062	0
42	S_out_ref	0	0	0	0	0	0	0	0	0	1
43	B_out_ref	0	0	0	0	0	0	0	0	0	0
44	A_out_ref	0	0	0	0	0	0	0	0	0	0
45	B_smelt_in	0	0	0	0	0	0	0	0	0	0
46	K_smel_in	0	0	0	0	0	0	0	0	0	0
47	B_ingot	0	0	0	0	0	0	0	0	0	0
48	K_ingot	0	0	0	0	0	0	0	0	0	0
49	B_demand	0	0	0	0	0	0	0	0	0	0
50	K_demand	0	0	0	0	0	0	0	0	0	0
51											

	L	M	N	O	P	Q	R	S	T	U	V	W
28												
29												
30	YB	YA	YSB	YBB	YAB	YSK	YBK	YAK	ZB	ZK	Rel'n	RHS
31												
32	7.6	6.4	174.4	170	183.4	134.2	136.3	122.8	0	0	(n/a)	
33	0	0	0	0	0	0	0	0	0	0	<=	36000
34	0	0	0	0	0	0	0	0	0	0	<=	52000
35	0	0	0	0	0	0	0	0	0	0	<=	28000
36	0	0	0	0	0	0	0	0	0	0	<=	40000
37	0	0	0	0	0	0	0	0	0	0	<=	30000
38	0	0	0	0	0	0	0	0	0	0	<=	20000
39	0	0	0	0	0	0	0	0	0	0	=	0
40	-1	0	0	0	0	0	0	0	0	0	=	0
41	0	-1	0	0	0	0	0	0	0	0	=	0
42	0	0	-1	0	0	-1	0	0	0	0	=	0
43	1	0	0	-1	0	0	-1	0	0	0	=	0
44	0	1	0	0	-1	0	0	-1	0	0	=	0
45	0	0	1	1	1	0	0	0	0	0	<=	4000
46	0	0	0	0	0	1	1	1	0	0	<=	7000
47	0	0	0.4	0.4	0.4	0	0	0	-1	0	=	0
48	0	0	0	0	0	0.4	0.4	0.4	0	-1	=	0
49	0	0	0	0	0	0	0	0	1	0	>=	1000
50	0	0	0	0	0	0	0	0	0	1	>=	1200
51												

To scan the input data area easily, use the **Worksheet Global Column-width** command (**/WGC**) to set the width of the columns as narrow as possible, so that more columns can be seen on the screen. This allows you to see the structure of the model and to check the data. Press [Alt M] to call up the menu; select **Solve** and **LP** from the successive menus. After the model has been run, the output should look like this:

	A	B	C	D	E	F	G
64	SOLUTION						
65							
66	Minimum Objective Function Value:				1543112		
67							
68					Sensitivity to Obj Fn Coeff Changes		
69			Reduced		Current	____Allowable____	
70	Variable	Value	Cost		Coeff.	Increase	Decrease
71	---------	-----	------		------	--------	--------
72	XGS	0	1.932		16.4	1.0E+30	1.932
73	XGB	1666.666	0		18.6	1.932	8.446838
74	XGA	0	38.2364		48.6	1.0E+30	38.2364
75	XSS	40000	0		7.4	1.932	1.0E+30
76	XSB	12000	0		11.6	13.2	1.932
77	XSA	0	36.2724		39.8	1.0E+30	36.2724
78	XAS	0	28.3188		43.4	1.0E+30	28.3188
79	XAB	0	3.98		23.2	1.0E+30	3.98
80	XAA	20000	0		11	8.7284	1.0E+30
81	YS	3200	0		6.6	49.1	1.0E+30
82	YB	1060	0		7.6	2015.133	49.1
83	YA	1240	0		6.4	140.7806	2015.133
84	YSB	1440	0		174.4	20.4	6.5
85	YBB	1060	0		170	6.5	49.1
86	YAB	0	20.4		183.4	1.0E+30	20.4
87	YSK	1760	0		134.2	6.5	20.4
88	YBK	0	6.5		136.3	1.0E+30	6.5
89	YAK	1240	0		122.8	20.4	2015.133
90	ZB	1000	0		0	1.0E+30	1219
91	ZK	1200	0		0	1.0E+30	1118.5
92							
93					Sensitivity to Right Hand Side Changes		
94		Slack	Dual		Current	____Allowable____	
95	Constr.	Value	Price		RHS	Increase	Decrease
96	-------	-----	-----		-----	--------	--------
97	G_mine	34333.33	0		36000	1.0E+30	34333.33
98	S_mine	0	13.2		52000	1250	12000
99	A_mine	8000	0		28000	1.0E+30	8000
100	S_in_ref	0	3.928		40000	12000	16333.33
101	B_in_ref	16333.33	0		30000	1.0E+30	16333.33
102	A_in_ref	0	8.7284		20000	1612.903	15806.45
103	S_alumina	0	-306.6		0	980	100
104	B_alumina	0	-310		0	980	100
105	A_alumina	0	-318.2		0	980	100
106	S_out_ref	0	-313.2		0	980	100
107	B_out_ref	0	-317.6		0	980	100
108	A_out_ref	0	-324.6		0	980	100
109	B_smelt_in	1500	0		4000	1.0E+30	1500
110	K_smel_in	4000	0		7000	1.0E+30	4000
111	B_ingot	0	-1219		0	392	40
112	K_ingot	0	-1118.5		0	392	40
113	B_demand	0	-1219		1000	392	40
114	K_demand	0	-1118.5		1200	392	40
115							

The optimal solution ships 1666.7 tons of bauxite from Guinea to Baltimore. At Surinam, 40,000 tons of bauxite are refined and 12,000 tons are shipped to Baltimore. In Arkansas, 20,000 tons are mined and refined. The only mine at capacity is Surinam, which has a dual price of $13.2 per ton of bauxite mining capacity. Similarly, other activities and the value of capacity can be read from the SOLUTION table.

Integer Programming

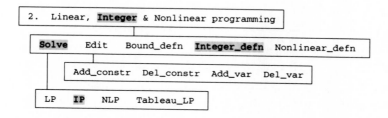

The Model:

$$\max \sum_{j=1}^{n} c_j x_j \quad \text{(or min)}$$

subject to

$$\sum_{j=1}^{n} a_{ij} x_j \ (\leq, \ =, \ \geq) \ b_i, \qquad i = 1, 2, \ldots, m$$

$$d_j \leq x_j \leq u_j, \qquad j = 1, 2, \ldots, n$$

$$x_j \text{ integer for } j \in I.$$

Computation: Branch and Bound is used, based on the simplex method in the What-If Solver. If bounds on variables are not at their default values, they are included as constraints.

Limitations: The problem size is limited to 120 variables in total, and at most 40 of these may be integers. A total of 120 constraints, including bounds on variables, are permitted. If bounds are not defined, the defaults are $d_j = 0$, $u_j = \infty$. $d_j \geq 0$.

Example: Karen Smith

Karen Smith has received an inheritance of $6,800 and is deciding on an investment strategy for this capital. She has identified some attractive investments, as described in the following table. Three of the securities are sold only in discrete units. Each has an associated measure of relative risk, in Karen's opinion. She wishes to maximize the return she earns on her portfolio, but wants to keep the weighted risk of her portfolio below 5.

Security Type	Unit of Investment	Rate of Interest	Risk Measure
Government Bond	$1,000	6%	1
Commercial Bond	$500	7%	4
Common Stock	any	8.5%	10
Deposit Certificate	$2,500	6.5%	2

Let g be the number of government bonds, b be the number of commercial bonds, d be the number of deposit certificates, and s be Karen's investment in stocks. Her problem can be formulated as follows:

$$\max\ 60g + 35b + 162.5d + .085s$$

subject to

$$1000g + 500b + 2500d + s \leq 6800$$
$$1000g + (4)500b + (2)2500d + 10s \leq 5\,(1000g + 500b + 2500d + s)$$
$$g,\ b,\ d\ \text{integer and} \geq 0,\ s \geq 0$$

(The second constraint can be rewritten as $-4000g - 500b - 7500d + 5s \leq 0$.)

To solve Karen's problem using PROPS[+], select **2. LP, IP and NLP** from the ACCESS menu and define a problem with four variables, two constraints, and maximization. You will see the following screen:

```
          A         B         C         D         E         F         G
22                  Problem Name        Karen Smith
23
24                  Number of Variables           4
25                  Number of Constraints         2
26                  Problem type (max or min)    max
27
28   INPUT DATA -- Press [Alt M] after entering coefficients
29              Variables:
30        Row       X1        X2        X3        X4      Rel'n      RHS
31   -----------------------------------------------------------------
32   LP Obj Fn        0         0         0         0     (n/a)
33     Rows: 1)       0         0         0         0       <=        0
34           2)       0         0         0         0       <=        0
35   -----------------------------------------------------------------
```

Enter the INPUT DATA and rename the variables and constraints so that your screen looks like this:

	A	B	C	D	E	F	G
28	INPUT DATA -- Press [Alt M] after entering coefficients						
29	Variables:						
30	Row	g	b	d	s	Rel'n	RHS
31	---						
32	LP Obj Fn	60	35	162.5	0.085	(n/a)	
33	budget	1000	500	2500	1	<=	6800
34	risk	-4000	-500	-7500	5	<=	0
35	---						
36							

To define which variables are integers, press [Alt M] to display the following menu:

```
A47: [W10]
Solve  Edit  Bound_defn  Integer_defn  Nonlinear_defn              MENU
Solve the problem
       A        B        C        D        E        F        G
```

and select **Integer_defn**. You will see this screen:

	A	B	C	D	E	F	G
28	INPUT DATA -- Press [Alt M] after entering coefficients						
29	Variables:						
30	Row	g	b	d	s	Rel'n	RHS
31	---						
32	LP Obj Fn	60	35	162.5	0.085	(n/a)	
33	budget	1000	500	2500	1	<=	6800
34	risk	-4000	-500	-7500	5	<=	0
35	---						
36	Integer:	no	no	no	no		
37							

Row 36, in this example, defines whether or not a variable can be fractional (no) or must be integer (yes). Change the definition for variables g, b, and d to **yes** and your screen should look like this:

	A	B	C	D	E	F	G
28	INPUT DATA -- Press [Alt M] after entering coefficients						
29	Variables:						
30	Row	g	b	d	s	Rel'n	RHS
31	---						
32	LP Obj Fn	60	35	162.5	0.085	(n/a)	
33	budget	1000	500	2500	1	<=	6800
34	risk	-4000	-500	-7500	5	<=	0
35	---						
36	Integer:	yes	yes	yes	no		
37							

You are now ready to solve Karen's problem. Press [Alt M] to display the following menu:

```
A1:                                                         MENU
Solve  Edit  Bound_defn  Integer_defn  Nonlinear_defn
Solve the problem
        A       B        C         D        E       F      G
```

Select **Solve** by pressing [Enter]. You will see the following menu:

```
A1:                                                         MENU
LP  IP  NLP  Tableau_LP
Solve linear programming problem
        A       B        C         D        E       F
```

Select **IP** by moving the cursor and pressing [Enter]. The screen will flash as PROPS⁺ sets up the data and calls the Solver. When the Solver has completed its solution, it will beep and at the top of your screen you will see a completion message similar to the following:

```
A48: [W10] 'SOLUTION SUMMARY                               EDIT
Results within tolerance; solution data follows  Press ENTER
Branch: 7B  Trial Solution: 6
        A       B        C         D        E       F      G
```

The program will pause. Press [Enter] to continue, and PROPS⁺ will generate the following table of output results:

```
        A         B         C        D       E        F      G
48   SOLUTION SUMMARY
49
50   Maximum Objective Function Value:          490.5
51                                                    Slack
52                                           Constr.  Value
53   Variable     Value
54   ------------------                       ------------------
55         g         0                        budget       0
56         b         5                        risk      1000
57         d         1
58         s      1800
59
```

Karen's optimal investment is to buy five commercial bonds (b) and one deposit certificate (d), and invest $1800 in stocks (s), for an annual return of $490.50. Note that the risk constraint is not binding.

Pure integer, mixed integer, and 0-1 integer programming models can be solved. To create a 0-1 variable, set the variable to integer, define bounds using the **Bound_defn** command in the PROPS⁺ menu, and set the upper bound to 1.

Example: Limestone Metalworks

David Smith has a small specialty metalworking shop, and has recently purchased a "plasma cutter" that cuts any desired pattern in a sheet of stainless steel. David has some free time on the cutter this week, and is considering four different standing contract jobs to fill up the unused time. The jobs are described in the following table:

Product Name	Contribution per unit	Set-up cost	Time required	Maximum required
End plate	$1.20	$36	5 min	100
Chassis	$.60	$12	2	40
Bracket	$.80	0*	3	unlimited
Drop plate	$.90	$5	1	50

* The cutter is currently set up for bracket production.

David wants to produce no more than three of these products. Which should he select, and how many of each should he make?

Define the variables E, C, B, and D as the number of each product to produce, respectively. Define XE to be equal to 1 if any E are produced, and to 0 if no E are produced. Define XC, XB, and XD in the same way. Then the problem becomes

$$\max\ 1.2E + 0.6C + 0.8B + 0.9D - 36XE - 12XC - 5XD$$

subject to

$$
\begin{aligned}
E - 100XE &\leq 0 \\
C - 40XC &\leq 0 \\
B - 1000XB &\leq 0 \\
D - 50XD &\leq 0 \\
5E + 2C + 3B + D &\leq 80 \\
XE + XC + XB + XD &\leq 3 \\
XE, XC, XB, XD &= 0 \text{ or } 1 \text{ integer} \\
E, C, B, D &\geq 0
\end{aligned}
$$

To solve this problem using PROPS⁺, select **2.LP, IP and NLP** from the ACCESS worksheet, define a problem with eight variables and six constraints, and enter the data as follows (note that the column width has been changed to 6 through the **Worksheet Global Column-width command (/WGC)**, to show the whole formulation on one screen):

	A	B	C	D	E	F	G	H	I	J	K
21		Analyst Name		Your_name							
22		Problem Name		Limestone	Metal						
23											
24		Number of	Variable		8						
25		Number of	Constrai		6						
26		Problem	type (max		max						
27											
28	INPUT DATA -- Press [Alt M] after entering coefficients										
29		Variables:									
30		Row	E	C	B	D	XE	XC	XB	XD Rel'n	RHS
31	--										
32	LP Obj Fn	1.2	0.6	0.8	0.9	-36	-12	0	-5 (n/a)	
33	Rows: 1)	1	0	0	0	-100	0	0	0 <=	0
34	2)	0	1	0	0	0	-40	0	0 <=	0
35	3)	0	0	1	0	0	0	-1000	0 <=	0
36	4)	0	0	0	1	0	0	0	-50 <=	0
37	5)	5	2	3	1	0	0	0	0 <=	80
38	6)	0	0	0	0	1	1	1	1 <=	3
39	--										
40											

Now press [Alt M] to call up the menu, and select **Integer_defn**. The bottom of the screen changes to

	A	B	C	D	E	F	G	H	I	J	K
38	6)	0	0	0	0	1	1	1	1	<=	3
39	--										
40	Integer:	no	no	no	no	no	no	no	no		
41											

Type **"yes** in the cells corresponding to the variables XE, XC, XB, and XD (that is, in cells F40, G40, H40, and I40). Now press [Alt M] again and select **Bound_defn** from the menu. You will see the bottom of your screen change to

	A	B	C	D	E	F	G	H	I	J	K
38	6)	0	0	0	0	1	1	1	1	<=	3
39	--										
40	Integer:	no	no	no	no	yes	yes	yes	yes		
41	Bounds-Up	infini	infini	infini	infini	infini	infini	infini	infinity		
42	Lower	0	0	0	0	0	0	0	0		
43											

Change the entries in cells F41, G41, H41, and I41 from **"infinity** to **1**. The result is

	A	B	C	D	E	F	G	H	I	J	K
38	6)	0	0	0	0	1	1	1	1	<=	3
39	--										
40	Integer:	no	no	no	no	yes	yes	yes	yes		
41	Bounds-Up	infini	infini	infini	infini	1	1	1	1		
42	Lower	0	0	0	0	0	0	0	0		
43											

You are now ready to solve the problem. Press [Alt M] and select **Solve** from the menu. Then select **IP** from the sub-menu. The screen will flash as PROPS⁺ sets up the data and calls the Solver. When the Solver has completed its solution, it will beep and at the top of your screen you will see a completion message similar to the following:

```
A52: [W10] 'SOLUTION SUMMARY                                          EDIT
Results within tolerance; solution data follows   Press ENTER
Branch: 1B   Trial Solution: 7
        A         B         C         D         E         F         G
52   SOLUTION SUMMARY
53
```

The program will pause. Press [Enter] to continue; PROPS⁺ will generate the following table of output results:

```
        A         B         C         D         E         F         G
52   SOLUTION SUMMARY
53
54   Maximum Objective Function Value:              48
55
56                                                      Slack
57   Variable    Value                   Constr.    Value
58   -------------------                  -------------------
59      E          0            Rows: 1)       0
60      C          0                  2)       0
61      B         10                  3)     990
62      D         50                  4)       0
63      XE         0                  5)       0
64      XC         0                  6)       1
65      XB         1
66      XD         1
67
```

David should make 10 brackets and 50 drop plates for a total contribution of $48.

Nonlinear Programming

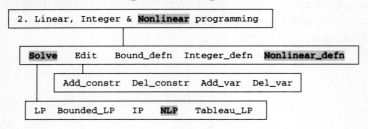

```
2. Linear, Integer & Nonlinear programming
```

```
Solve    Edit    Bound_defn   Integer_defn   Nonlinear_defn
```

```
        Add_constr   Del_constr   Add_var   Del_var
```

```
LP   Bounded_LP   IP   NLP   Tableau_LP
```

The Model:

$$\max f(x_1, x_2, \ldots, x_n) \quad \left(\text{or } \sum_{j=1}^{n} f_i(x_i)\right) \quad (\text{or min})$$

subject to

$$\sum_{j=1}^{n} a_{ij}x_j \ (\leq, \ =, \ \geq) \ b_i, \qquad i = 1, 2, \ldots, m$$

$$d_j \leq x_j \leq u_j, \qquad\qquad j = 1, 2, \ldots, n$$

Computation: The GRG2 algorithm in the What-If Solver is used.

Limitations: Problems are limited to 40 variables and 20 constraints. If bounds are not defined, the defaults are $d_j = -\infty$, $u_j = \infty$. Integer definitions are ignored.

Each programming method so far has assumed that the objective function is linear. This makes the solution methods easier and faster, and is often a good model. If the objective function has nonlinear terms, however, the nonlinear programming model is appropriate. Consider the following example.

Example: Sweet Creams

The Sweet Creams Bake Shop makes two types of pastry for the local Saturday market, tarts and popovers. Unsold pastry is donated to a local charity. For either product, uncertainty in the demand means that the expected marginal revenue declines as the quantity is increased. In addition, tarts and popovers are partial substitutes, so the expected marginal revenue of either also declines as the quantity of the other is increased. If Sweet Creams makes t tarts and p popovers, the expected revenue can be written as

$$R(t,p) = .5t - .001t^2 + .4p - .0007p^2 - .0002pt$$

Oven capacity limits Sweet Creams to a total of 500 tarts and popovers in any combination. Tarts need three minutes of labor each and popovers two minutes each. There are 12 hours of labor available for producing both pastries. Sweet Creams' costs are fixed in the short term, so its revenue maximization problem is

$$\max \quad .5t - .001t^2 + .4p - .0007p^2 - .0002pt$$

subject to
$$t + p \le 500$$
$$3\,t + 2\,p \le 720$$
$$t,p \ge 0$$

To solve Sweet Creams' problem using PROPS⁺, select **2. LP, IP and NLP** from the ACCESS menu and define a problem with two variables, two constraints, and maximization. You will see the following screen:

	A	B	C	D	E	F	G
21		Analyst Name		Your_name			
22		Problem Name		Sweet Cream			
23							
24		Number of Variables			2		
25		Number of Constraints			2		
26		Problem type (max or min)			max		
27							
28	INPUT DATA -- Press [Alt M] after entering coefficients						
29		Variables:					
30		Row	X1	X2	Rel'n	RHS	
31	--						
32	LP Obj Fn		0	0	(n/a)		
33	Rows: 1)		0	0	<=	0	
34	2)		0	0	<=	0	
35	--						

Enter the INPUT DATA and rename the variables and constraints so that your screen looks like this:

	A	B	C	D	E	F	G
28	INPUT DATA -- Press [Alt M] after entering coefficients						
29		Variables:					
30		Row	t	p	Rel'n	RHS	
31	--						
32	LP Obj Fn	0.5	0.4	(n/a)			
33	oven	1	1	<=	500		
34	labor	3	2	<=	720		
35	--						

In the preceding table we entered the linear coefficients in the objective. We now need to define the nonlinear objective function before we can solve the problem. To do this, press [Alt M] and select **Nonlinear_defn**. You will now see the following input data area:

```
          A          B          C          D          E          F          G
28  INPUT DATA -- Press [Alt M] after entering coefficients
29          Variables:
30      Row        t          p        Rel'n      RHS
31  ------------------------------------------------------
32  LP Obj Fn    0.5        0.4       (n/a)
33  oven          1          1         <=        500
34  labor         3          2         <=        720
35  ------------------------------------------------------
36
37
38
39  ------------------------------------------------------
40  NLP Obj Fn                                    0  =NLP_obj
41  Var Values
42  Optional |
43  NLP data |
44  area     |
45           |
46  ------------------------------------------------------
47
```

Nonlinear objective functions can have many different forms. The number of terms in the expression may vary, and the same variable may appear in more than one term. For this reason, the description of the objective function for nonlinear problems takes a somewhat different form. PROPS⁺ creates a working area in which you can define the various terms and coefficients in your objective function using spreadsheet functions. In this case, the value for each variable is stored in the row marked "Var Values" (in row 41 in this example). That is, cell B41 contains the value for the variable t and C41 contains the value for the variable p. The objective function is created in the "NLP Obj Fn" row (in cell E40 in this example) using the variable values in "Var Values." (When creating your objective function, it is a good idea to set each variable value to 1, so you can easily check that the objective function formulas you enter are correct.) Components of the objective function can be built up in the other cells in row 40, and rows 42 through 45 may be used for additional data.

For this example, the objective function contains both linear and nonlinear components. The linear coefficients are already in place in the worksheet, in cells B32 and C32. To incorporate the nonlinear components, enter their coefficients in cells in the working area. For instance, enter 0.001 in B42, 0.0007 in C42, and 0.0002 in C43. Move the cursor to cell E40 and enter the following formula for the objective function:

+B32*B41-B42*B41^2+C32*C41-C42*C41^2-C43*B41*C41

Your screen should appear as follows:

```
E40: U +B32*B41-B42*B41^2+C32*C41-C42*C41^2-C43*B41*C41                    READY
```

	A	B	C	D	E	F	G
29		Variables:					
30	Row	t	p	Rel'n	RHS		
31	--						
32	LP Obj Fn	0.5	0.4	(n/a)			
33	oven	1	1	<=	500		
34	labor	3	2	<=	720		
35	--						
36							
37							
38							
39	--						
40	NLP Obj Fn				**0.8981**	=NLP_obj	
41	Var Values	1	1				
42	Optional |	0.001	0.0007				
43	NLP data |		0.0002				
44	area |						
45	|						
46	--						
47							

To run the model, press [Alt M] and select **Solve** and **NLP**. When the Solver has completed its solution, it will beep and at the top of your screen you will see a completion message similar to the following:

```
A48: [W10] 'SOLUTION SUMMARY                                               EDIT
Results within tolerance; solution data follows  Press ENTER
Trial Solution: 1
```
A	B	C	D	E	F	G

Press [Enter] to continue; PROPS+ will generate the following output screen:

	A	B	C	D	E	F	G
48	SOLUTION SUMMARY						
49							
50	Maximum Objective Function Value:				90.75868		
51							
52			Reduced			Slack	Dual
53	Variable	Value	Cost		Constr.	Value	Price
54	--------------------------				--------------------------		
55	t	128.3516	0		oven	204.1758	0
56	p	167.4725	-0.00000		labor	0.000000	0.069934
57							
58							

Sweet Creams' optimal solution is to make about 128 tarts and 167 popovers, for a revenue of $90.76.

Example: The Car-Truck Problem Revisited

In the car-truck problem, we assumed that the contributions to profits were $400 for each truck and $300 for each car. This means that the marginal profitability is constant, independent of how many cars or trucks are produced.

Suppose that the profitability decreases as the number of units produced increases. For example, suppose if we make X_1 trucks, the marginal profitability is $400 - 0.1X_1$; if X_2 cars are made, the marginal profitability is $300 - 0.05X_2$. The contribution to profits for each activity is the integral from 0 to X of the marginal profitability. Thus for each activity, the profit as a function of production is

$$f_1(X_1) = 400X_1 - .1X_1^2/2$$

and

$$f_2(X_2) = 300X_2 - .05X_2^2/2$$

(Note that the "1/2" term in each function is the result of integrating the marginal cost function.) Total profit is the sum of these contributions. We now have a nonlinear objective function.

To solve this problem using PROPS$^+$, begin by retrieving the data for the original car-truck example, which we saved on page 38 as the file CAR-TR.WK1. Use the menu **Nonlinear_defn** to define the data area for the nonlinear objective function. Your screen should look like this:

```
           A          B          C          D          E          F          G
29                 Variables:
30         Row         X1         X2       Rel'n        RHS
31    -------------------------------------------------------
32  LP Obj Fn        400        300       (n/a)
33    Rows:  1)         1          1         <=        8000
34           2)         2          1         <=       10000
35           3)         3          0         <=       12000
36           4)         0          2         <=       14000
37    -------------------------------------------------------
38
39
40
41    -------------------------------------------------
42  NLP Obj Fn                                           0 =NLP_obj
43  Var Values
44  Optional |
45  NLP data |
46  area     |
47           |
48    -------------------------------------------------
49
50
```

The objective function is created in the "NLP Obj Fn" row (row 42 in this example) using the variable values in "Var Values" (row 43 here). Rows 44 through 47 may be used for additional data. The 400 and 300 coefficients are already available, so we need only enter the 0.1 and 0.05 coefficients in cells B44 and C44, for example. Then move the cursor to cell B42 and define the profit function ($f_1(X_1)$) for the truck activity using the cell pointing method. The formula should be

$$+B32*B43-(B44*B43^2)/2$$

This formula is then copied to cell C42, to calculate $f_2(X_2)$. The formula for the total objective function is entered in the cell to the left of "=NLP_Obj (cell E42 in this example). The default formula

$$@sum(C42 .. B42)$$

is already in the cell, which creates an objective function equal to the sums of the indicated cells (the contribution from each variable).

Note that the structure of the data area is particularly convenient when the objective function is separable by variables. However, any nonlinear objective function can be defined. If it is complicated, you may have to use other areas in the spreadsheet to store data and define the function. The final formula for $f(x_1\ x_2\ ...\ x_n)$ must be in the "NLP Obj Fn" row and the "RHS" column (cell E42 in this example).

Your screen should look like this:

```
          A         B         C         D         E          F          G
41   -------------------------------------------------
42   NLP Obj Fn  399.95    299.975             699.925  =NLP_obj
43   Var Values       1         1
44   Optional |     0.1      0.05
45   NLP data |
46   area     |
47            |
48   ---------------------------------------------------
49
```

To run the model, press [Alt M] and select **Solve** and **NLP**. When the Solver has completed its solution, it will beep, and at the top of your screen you will see a completion message similar to the following:

```
A50: [W10] 'SOLUTION SUMMARY                                              EDIT
Results within tolerance; solution data follows  Press ENTER
Trial Solution: 1
          A         B         C         D         E          F          G
```

Press [Enter] to continue; PROPS⁺ will generate the following output screen:

```
         A          B          C        D        E          F          G
50   SOLUTION SUMMARY
51
52   Maximum Objective Function Value:        1566666.
53
54                        Reduced                          Slack      Dual
55   Variable    Value      Cost            Constr.        Value      Price
56   -------------------------------        -------------------------------
57       X1 2666.666          0          Rows: 1) 666.6666              0
58       X2 4666.666 0.000000                2) 0.000053 66.66666
59                                             3) 3999.999              0
60                                             4) 4666.666              0
61
```

The optimal profits have dropped to $1.567 million, due to the decreasing profitability with increasing production. The optional production schedule is to produce 2,666.7 trucks and 4,666.7 cars each month. Only the engine assembly is fully utilized, with slack in the other constraints. The dual price on engine assembly is $66.67 per unit of engine per month capacity.

Beyond PROPS⁺

PROPS⁺ provides standardized data input formats for the common mathematical programming formulations. PROPS⁺ creates a spreadsheet model for the problem by setting up specific cells to contain the value of the decision variables and by defining formulas in other cells to calculate the objective function and each constraint based on these variables. PROPS⁺ then calls the Solver to find the optimal solution. The definition of the objective, constraints, and solution procedures are all handled automatically by PROPS⁺.

As you become familiar with spreadsheet modeling, you may create your own spreadsheet models for specific problems. Often you will wish to carry out "what-if" analysis by changing the value of certain cells to determine their effect on the value in a particular cell of interest. This type of analysis can be formalized as the following optimization problem: Find the value of certain cells (decisions) to maximize or minimize the value in another cell (objective), subject to constraints on either the range of values in the decision cells (bounds) or on other cells (constraints). Although such a problem can be rewritten as a standard mathematical programming model, it is often more convenient to work directly with the spreadsheet model that you have created. The What-If Solver optimization package will find optimal solutions for such spreadsheet models. (The student version of What-If Solver is available from Addison-Wesley and the professional version from Frontline Systems, Inc.) With this approach, you work with the existing spreadsheet model, and you can use nonlinear constraints. Working directly with the spreadsheet model usually requires fewer constraints and decision variables than a standard optimization formulation.

Features

1. **Transportation Problem**

   - calculates the minimum cost transportation plan.

   - allows the supply to exceed the demand.

   - provides a problem editing menu.

2. **Assignment Problem**

   - computes the minimum cost or maximum profit assignments.

   - allows either single or multiple assignments.

Chapter 3. Transportation and Assignment Models

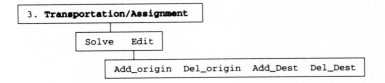

The Model:

$$\max \sum_{i=1}^{m} \sum_{j=1}^{n} c_{ij} x_{ij} \quad \text{(or min)}$$

subject to

$$\sum_{j=1}^{n} x_{ij} \leq s_i, \qquad i = 1, 2, \ldots, m \qquad \text{(supply)}$$

$$\sum_{i=1}^{m} x_{ij} = d_j, \qquad j = 1, 2, \ldots, n \qquad \text{(demand)}$$

$$x_{ij} \geq 0, \qquad \text{for all } i, j$$

Computation: Solved using the simplex method in the What-If Solver.

Limitations: The number of variables $n \times m \leq 120$.

Transportation, assignment, and transshipment problems (described later in Chapter 4) belong to a special class of linear programming problems called network flow problems. These problems have a wide variety of applications. Special algorithms are available to solve very large problems with thousands of variables, but the Solver simplex algorithm is adequate for the problems of moderate size. While these problems could be solved with the LP spreadsheet, we will create separate spreadsheet models to take advantage of the special problem structure to automatically define the constraints. In addition, the data input is tailored to each type of problem.

The Transportation Model

The transportation problem consists of finding the cheapest way to ship from several sources to several destinations, where the capacity of each source is specified and the demand at destination is known.

63

Example: The Newsprint Problem

International paper has newsprint mills in Trois Rivieres, North Bay, and Kenora, from which it supplies its major markets in New York, Toronto, Chicago, and Los Angeles. The following table summarizes the mills' capacities, demands, and the production and transportation costs from each mill to each market.

Mill	Markets				
	New York	Toronto	Chicago	Los Angeles	Mill Capacity
Trois Rivieres	15	16	30	70	700
North Bay	15	9	24	56	500
Kenora	36	24	15	45	400
Market Demand	500	100	400	300	

The entry for each mill and market pair is the cost in dollars per ton to ship the newsprint from the mill to that market. For example, it costs $24 per ton to ship from North Bay to Chicago. Mill capacity is the annual production in thousands of tons from each mill; for example, the Kenora mill can produce 400 thousand tons per year. The bottom row in the table is the annual demand, in thousands of tons, in each market.

To solve this problem using PROPS+, retrieve the ACCESS worksheet as described in Chapter 1. You will see the following screen:

```
                         A                              B
1                                             Copyright (C)
2             PROPS+    v1.00               E.R.Petersen & A.J.Taylor
3        Probabilistic and Optimization     Queen's University at Kingston
4               Spreadsheets                 programmed by G.D.Thompson
5        ==============================      ==============================
6
7       move cursor to the desired menu item and press [Enter]
8
9        1. Quit                            11. Simulation
10       2. LP, IP and NLP                  12. Probability Distributions
11       3. Transportation/Assignment       13. Decision Analysis
12       4. Transshipment                   14. Markov Chains
13       5. Networks                        15. Dynamic Programming (DP)
14       6. Project Management              16. Stochastic DP
15       7. Forecasting
16       8. Inventory
17       9. Production planning
18      10. Queueing
19
20
```

Move the cursor down two rows to **3. Transportation/Assignment** and press [Enter]. You will see the following screen:

	A	B	C	D	E	F	G	H
1	================================							
2		PROPS+			TRANSPORTATION/ASSIGNMENT			
3					-supply may be exceed demand			
4		Copyright (C)			-single or multiple assignments			
5		PROPS SYSTEMS			-simplex method solution			
6								
7		01/11/92 05:08 PM						
8		==============================						
9								
10	Instructions:							
11		STEP 1: Enter number of variables, number of constraints						
12			and problem type (max or min) when prompted. An					
13			appropriate data-input area will be constructed.					
14		STEP 2: Enter coefficients for the objective function and						
15			constraints. Rename the "X" variables [optional].					
16		STEP 3: Press [Alt M] for the command menu.						
17								
18		PROMPT mode when CMD is on. Type response, press [ENTER].						
19								
20					Press [Enter] to begin...			

On pressing [Enter], you will be in PROMPT mode (note that CMD appears at the bottom of the screen), and will be asked in sequence for the problem name, the number of Origin nodes (supply points), the number of Destination nodes (demand points), and the type of objective function: min (the default) or max. Respond to each by typing your response followed by [Enter]. Remember, if you make a typing error, press [Esc] and retype or backspace and correct the error before you press the [Enter] key. If you notice an error after pressing [Enter], you should abort the program with the key combination [Ctrl Break], followed by [Esc]. Then press **/FR** to retrieve the ACCESS worksheet and begin again.

For the newsprint problem, after you enter the relevant information, the screen should appear as follows:

	A	B	C	D	E	F	G
21		Analyst Name		Your_name			
22		Problem Name		newsprint			
23							
24		Number of Origins			3		
25		Number of Destinations			4		
26		Problem type (max or min)			min		
27							
28	INPUT DATA -- Press [Alt M] after entering coefficients						
29							
30		Destination:					
31	Origin		D1	D2	D3	D4	Supply
32	---						
33		O1	0	0	0	0	0
34		O2	0	0	0	0	0
35		O3	0	0	0	0	0
36	---						
37	Demand		0	0	0	0	
38							

At this point, use ordinary spreadsheet methods to enter the data, using the cursor keys to move the cursor from cell to cell. If you want to make the problem more readable, you can change the names of the origins and destinations by typing their names in the cells that contain the origin names O1, O2, and O3 and the destination names D1, D2, and D3. Your screen should then look like this:

	A	B	C	D	E	F	G
28	INPUT DATA -- Press [Alt M] after entering coefficients						
29							
30		Destination:					
31	Origin	NY	Toronto	Chicago	LA	Supply	
32	--						
33	Trois_R	15	16	30	70	700	
34	North Bay	15	9	24	56	500	
35	Kenora	36	24	15	45	400	
36	--						
37	Demand	500	100	400	300		

Press [Alt M] to get the following menu:

```
A1:                                                              MENU
Solve  Edit
Solve the problem
           A         B         C         D         E
```

Select **Solve** by pressing [Enter]. PROPS[+] will set up the data and call the Solver. When the Solver is finished, it will beep, and at the top of your screen you will see a completion message similar to the following:

```
A40:                                                             EDIT
Results within tolerance; solution data follows  Press ENTER
Trial Solution: 9
           A       B       C       D       E       F       G       H
```

Press [Enter] and PROPS[+] will generate the following tables of output results:

	A	B	C	D	E	F	G	H
40	SOLUTION SUMMARY							
41								
42		OPTIMAL ROUTE/ASSIGNMENT						
43								
44		origin	dest.	quantity	cost			
45		-------------------------------------						
46		Trois_R	NY	400	6000			
47		North Bay	NY	100	1500			
48			Toronto	100	900			
49			Chicago	300	7200			
50		Kenora	Chicago	100	1500			
51			LA	300	13500			
52					---------			
53					30600			
54								

```
         A        B        C        D        E        F        G        H
55
56           DUAL PRICES and REDUCED COSTS
57
58                   Reduced Cost Table                    Origin
59                   Destination                            Dual
60           Origin        NY  Toronto  Chicago      LA    price
61           ---------------------------------------------------------
62           Trois_R        0       7        6       16      0
63           North Bay      0       0        0        2      0
64            Kenora       30      24        0        0      9
65           ---------------------------------------------------------
66           Destin.      -15      -9      -24      -54
67           Dual price
68
```

Use the [PgUp] and [PgDn] keys and the cursor controls to look over the solution. The optimal solution has a cost of $30.6 million (supply and demand in thousands of tons per year).

The Assignment Model

The assignment problem occurs in a variety of decision-making situations; for example, the assignment of jobs to machines, workers to tasks or projects, sales personnel to sales territories, and contracts to suppliers. The single assignment problem assigns one job or worker to one and only one machine or project. Usually we want to find the assignment that minimizes cost or time or maximizes profits. This problem is a special form of the transportation problem, with supply being assigned to demand. If all demands are set equal to 1, then only one supply point will be assigned to each demand node.

Example: Assigning Consultants to Projects

Suppose you manage a consulting firm and want to assign consultants to projects in such a way as to minimize the completion time of the projects. The following table summarizes the expected time in days each consultant would take to complete each project.

Consultant	Project		
	Proj 1	Proj 2	Proj 3
Joe	11	15	8
Bob	9	18	5
Cathy	6	14	4

To solve this problem using PROPS⁺, load the transportation/assignment worksheet by selecting **3. Transportation/Assignment** from the ACCESS menu. Press [Enter] to start, and specify three origin nodes, three destination nodes, and the problem type as min. Enter the data, name the variables, and set all the supply and demand values to 1. Your worksheet should look like this:

	A	B	C	D	E	F	G
21		Analyst Name	Your_name				
22		Problem Name	consultant				
23							
24		Number of Origins			3		
25		Number of Destinations			3		
26		Problem type (max or min)			min		
27							
28	INPUT DATA -- Press [Alt M] after entering coefficients						
29							
30		Destination:					
31	Origin	Proj1	Proj2	Proj3	Supply		
32	--						
33	Joe	11	15	8	1		
34	Bob	9	18	5	1		
35	Cathy	6	14	4	1		
36	--						
37	Demand	1	1	1			

Press [Alt M] and select **Solve** from the menu. The Solver completion message will be displayed. Press [Enter] to continue, and the following output screen will appear:

	A	B	C	D	E	F	G
40	SOLUTION SUMMARY						
41							
42		OPTIMAL ROUTE/ASSIGNMENT					
43							
44		origin	dest.	quantity	cost		
45		-----------------------------------					
46		Joe	Proj2	1	15		
47		Bob	Proj3	1	5		
48		Cathy	Proj1	1	6		
49					---------		
50					26		
51							
52							
53		DUAL PRICES and REDUCED COSTS					
54							
55			Reduced Cost Table			Origin	
56			Destination			Dual	
57		Origin	Proj1	Proj2	Proj3	price	
58		---					
59		Joe	0	0	1	0	
60		Bob	0	5	0	2	
61		Cathy	0	4	2	5	
62		---					
63		Destin.	-11	-15	-7		
64		Dual price					

Joe is assigned to Proj2, Bob to Proj3, and Cathy to Proj1, for a total completion time of 26 days.

Editing

Suppose consultant Gerry becomes available. His completion times for each project are estimated to be 6, 16, and 6 days for Proj 1, Proj 2, and Proj 3, respectively. To modify the problem, press [Alt M], select **Edit** and **Add_Origin**. Then press [Esc] and move the cursor to the point in the table where you want the new origin to appear. In this case, move the cursor to A36 and press [Enter]. The revised input table will look like this:

	A	B	C	D	E	F	G
28	INPUT DATA -- Press [Alt M] after entering coefficients						
29							
30		Destination:					
31	Origin	Proj1	Proj2	Proj3	Supply		
32	--						
33	Joe	11	15	8	1		
34	Bob	9	18	5	1		
35	Cathy	6	14	4	1		
36	(new)	0	0	0	0		
37	--						
38	Demand	1	1	1			
39							

Enter the new data and your worksheet will look like this:

	A	B	C.	D	E	F	G
30		Destination:					
31	Origin	Proj1	Proj2	Proj3	Supply		
32	--						
33	Joe	11	15	8	1		
34	Bob	9	18	5	1		
35	Cathy	6	14	4	1		
36	Gerry	6	16	6	1		
37	--						
38	Demand	1	1	1			
39							

Rerun the model by pressing [Alt M] and selecting **Solve**. The completion code will appear at the top of the screen. Press [Enter] and the solution appears as follows:

	A	B	C	D	E	F	G
41	SOLUTION SUMMARY						
42							
43		OPTIMAL ROUTE/ASSIGNMENT					
44							
45		origin	dest.	quantity	cost		
46		--------------------------------					
47		Joe	Proj2	1	15		
48		Cathy	Proj3	1	4		
49		Gerry	Proj1	1	6		
50					---------		
51					25		
52							

	A	B	C	D	E	F	G
54		DUAL PRICES and REDUCED COSTS					
55							
56			Reduced Cost Table			Origin	
57			Destination			Dual	
58		Origin	Proj1	Proj2	Proj3	price	
59		--					
60		Joe	4	0	3	0	
61		Bob	2	3	0	0	
62		Cathy	0	0	0	1	
63		Gerry	0	2	2	1	
64		--					
65		Destin.	-7	-15	-5		
66		Dual price					
67							

Note that Bob is not assigned to any projects, Cathy is switched to Proj3, and Gerry is assigned to Proj1. The completion time has been reduced from 26 to 25 days.

Multiple assignments are possible. For example, it may be possible to assign each consultant up to two projects. This is modeled by increasing the supply for each consultant (origin) to 2, as shown in the following table:

	A	B	C	D	E	F
30		Destination:				
31	Origin	Proj1	Proj2	Proj3	Supply	
32	---					
33	Joe	11	15	8	2	
34	Bob	9	18	5	2	
35	Cathy	6	14	4	2	
36	Gerry	6	16	6	2	
37	---					
38	Demand	1	1	1		

When the problem is solved, you will see the following assignment:

	A	B	C	D	E	F
41	SOLUTION SUMMARY					
42						
43		OPTIMAL ROUTE/ASSIGNMENT				
44						
45		origin	dest.	quantity	cost	
46		---				
47		Cathy	Proj2	1	14	
48			Proj3	1	4	
49		Gerry	Proj1	1	6	
50					---------	
51					24	
52						

Note that Gerry is still used on Proj1, but Cathy is assigned to both Proj2 and Proj3.

More than one consultant may be assigned to one project. For instance, suppose Proj2 requires 2 consultants. To find the optimal assignment, enter the number 2 in the Demand for Project 2 (cell C38) as shown below.

	A	B	C	D	E	F
30		Destination:				
31	Origin	Proj1	Proj2	Proj3	Supply	
32	-------	-------	-------	-------	-------	
33	Joe	11	15	8	2	
34	Bob	9	18	5	2	
35	Cathy	6	14	4	2	
36	Gerry	6	16	6	2	
37	-------	-------	-------	-------	-------	
38	Demand	1	2	1		
39						

Now press [Alt M] and select **Solve** to find the following assignment.

	A	B	C	D	E	F
43		OPTIMAL ROUTE/ASSIGNMENT				
44						
45		origin	dest.	quantity	cost	
46		-------	-------	-------	-------	
47		Joe	Proj2	1	15	
48		Cathy	Proj2	1	14	
49			Proj3	1	4	
50		Gerry	Proj1	1	6	
51					---------	
52					39	
53						

Cathy and Gerry have the same assignments as before, but now Joe is also assigned to Proj2.

Features

Transshipment Problem

- uses a directed arc network.

- minimizes sum of supply plus transportation cost.

- allows for capacitated arcs.

- can have nonlinear costs.

Chapter 4. Transshipment Models

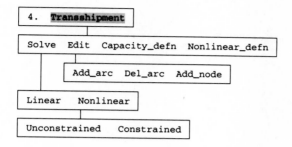

The Model:

$$\max \sum_{\text{all arcs } a} f_a(x_a) \quad \text{(or min)}$$

subject to

$$\sum_{i(a)=i} x_a - \sum_{j(a)=i} x_a \leq s_i, \quad \text{(supply)}$$

$$\sum_{j(a)=i} x_a - \sum_{i(a)=i} x_a = 0, \quad \text{(transshipment)}$$

$$\sum_{j(a)=i} x_a - \sum_{i(a)=i} x_a = d_i, \quad \text{(demand)}$$

$$0 \leq x_a \leq u_a, \text{ for all } a,$$

where arc a is directed from node $i(a)$ to node $j(a)$,
and u_a is the capacity of arc a.

Computation: Solved using the What-If Solver simplex method for linear
objectives and GRG2 for nonlinear objective functions.

Limitations: Limits on problem size:
  linear: number of arcs plus number of nodes $\leq$ 120.
  nonlinear: if uncapacitated, number of arcs $\leq$ 40;
        if capacitated, number of arcs $\leq$ 20.

The Transshipment Problem

Consider the directed arc network shown in the following diagram. Suppose that nodes 1 and 2 are supply nodes, with supply capacities of 40 and 20 respectively. Let nodes 7 and 8 be demand nodes, with demands 30 and 20 respectively. The cost of shipping over each arc is given in the following table.

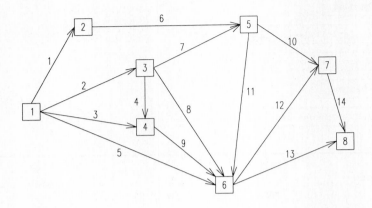

Arc	Start Node	End Node	Cost
1	1	2	6
2	1	3	6
3	1	4	8
4	3	4	3
5	1	6	9
6	2	5	3
7	3	5	6
8	3	6	7
9	4	6	8
10	5	7	3
11	5	6	4
12	6	7	6
13	6	8	7
14	7	8	5

We note that total supply is greater than total demand, and that shipments can move over the arcs only in the directions shown. We want to determine how shipments can be routed through the network to satisfy demand at minimum total transportation costs.

To solve this problem using PROPS⁺, retrieve the ACCESS menu and select **4. Transshipment**. The screen should look like this:

```
            A       B        C        D        E        F       G        H
 1   =================================
 2              PROPS+                    TRANSSHIPMENT SPREADSHEET
 3                                          - directed arcs
 4          Copyright (C)                   - linear costs
 5          PROPS SYSTEMS                   - capacitated arcs
 6                                          - nonlinear costs
 7          01/11/92 05:35 PM
 8   =================================
 9
10
11
12
13            Note: -nodes must be numbered consecutively from
14                    1 to the number of nodes
15                  -arcs may have any number or name
16
17            PROMPT mode when CMD is on. Type response, press [ENTER].
18
19                                      Press [Enter] to begin...
```

Press [Enter] and enter the problem name; the number of nodes, 8; the number of arcs, 14; and that it is a minimization problem. The following input data tables will be generated:

```
            A         B        C        D        E        F
21              Analyst Name    Your_name
22              Problem Name    transshipment
23
24              Number of Nodes                  8
25              Number of Arcs                  14
26              Problem type (max or min)       min
27
28   INPUT DATA
29                  start     end
30       arc        node      node     cost
31       ----       ----      ----     ----
32    arc_1
33    arc_2
34    arc_3
 :        :
47   SUPPLY and DEMAND DATA
48                            type              supply
49                  node      s,d,t   quantity   cost
50                  ----      ----     ----      ----
51                   1
52                   2
53                   3
54                   4
55                   5
56                   6
57                   7
58                   8
59
```

Enter the data into the tables, using spreadsheet methods. The first table contains the information on the network, while the second shows the information on the nodes. The type of node is s, d, or t, corresponding to supply, demand, or transshipment nodes. The quantity is the supply capacity for supply nodes or demand at demand nodes. The cells corresponding to transshipment nodes (i.e., nodes that do not have any supply or demand) are left blank. For supply nodes, a supply cost may be specified, and the model will then minimize the sum of supply plus transportation costs. When you have entered the data the screen will look like this:

	A	B	C	D	E
28	INPUT DATA				
29		start	end		
30	arc	node	node	cost	
31	----	----	----	----	
32	arc_1	1	2	6	
33	arc_2	1	3	6	
34	arc_3	1	4	8	
35	arc_4	3	4	3	
36	arc_5	1	6	9	
37	arc_6	2	5	3	
38	arc_7	3	5	6	
39	arc_8	3	6	7	
40	arc_9	4	6	8	
41	arc_10	5	7	3	
42	arc_11	5	6	4	
43	arc_12	6	7	6	
44	arc_13	6	8	7	
45	arc_14	7	8	5	
46					
47	SUPPLY and DEMAND DATA				
48			type		supply
49		node	s,d,t	quantity	cost
50		----	----	----	----
51		1	s	40	0
52		2	s	20	0
53		3	t		
54		4	t		
55		5	t		
56		6	t		
57		7	d	30	
58		8	d	20	
59					

Use the [PgUp], [PgDn], and cursor control keys to scan the input data for accuracy. (If the node type is not specified, it is assumed to be a transshipment node.)

To run the model, press [Alt M] and select **Solve**, **Linear**, and **Unconstrained** by pressing [Enter] each time. The Solver completion message will be displayed. Press [Enter], and the following output screen will appear:

	A	B	C	D	E	F	G
61	SOLUTION SUMMARY						
62							
63		OPTIMAL NETWORK FLOWS					
64							
65	arc	origin	dest.	flow	cost		
66	----	----	----	-,---	----		
67	arc_1	1	2	10	60		
68	arc_5	1	6	20	180		
69	arc_6	2	5	30	90		
70	arc_10	5	7	30	90		
71	arc_13	6	8	20	140		
72					---------		
73					560		
74							
75							
76	DUAL PRICES and REDUCED COSTS						
77							
78			Dual			reduced	
79	node	slack	price		arc	cost	
80	----	----	----		----	----	
81	1	10	0		arc_1	0	
82	2	0	6		arc_2	0	
83	3	0	-6		arc_3	0	
84	4	0	-8		arc_4	1	
85	5	0	-9		arc_5	0	
86	6	0	-9		arc_6	0	
87	7	0	-12		arc_7	3	
88	8	0	-16		arc_8	4	
89					arc_9	7	
90					arc_10	0	
91					arc_11	4	
92					arc_12	3	
93					arc_13	0	
94					arc_14	1	
95							

Nonlinear Arc Costs

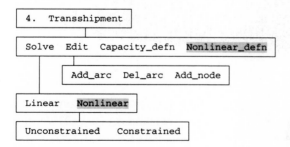

PROPS⁺ permits the cost of shipping over each arc to be nonlinear. For example, suppose the cost of shipping over arc a is given by the function

$$f_a(x_a) = c_a \, x_a + d_a \, x_a^2$$

As the traffic on each arc increases, the arc becomes more congested and the cost of shipping over it increases. To include nonlinear costs in the model, press [Alt M] and select **Nonlinear_defn**. The following data area will be created to the right of the arc input data table:

	A	B	C	D	E	F	G	H	I	J
28	INPUT DATA							0 =nonlinear obj fn		
29		start	end					nonlinear coef's		
30	arc	node	node	cost		flow	fa(x)			
31	----	----	----	----		----	----	----	----	
32	arc_1	1	2	6						
33	arc_2	1	3	6						
34	arc_3	1	4	8						
35	arc_4	3	4	3						
36	arc_5	1	6	9						
37	arc_6	2	5	3						
38	arc_7	3	5	6						
39	arc_8	3	6	7						
40	arc_9	4	6	8						
41	arc_10	5	7	3						
42	arc_11	5	6	4						
43	arc_12	6	7	6						
44	arc_13	6	8	7						
45	arc_14	7	8	5						
46										

The arc flows are calculated and stored in column F. In column G, the equation for the arc cost is entered. Columns H, I, and J can be used to store data for the cost functions. Column H will be used to store the coefficients d_a, which we will suppose are equal to 1 for each arc. Enter these coefficients in column H in the spreadsheet. The formula for the cost function for each arc is entered in column G as a formula. For example, go to G32 and enter the formula

+D32*F32+H32*F32^2

This is the cost function for arc_1. Use the **Copy** command (**/C**) to copy this formula into cell range [G33..G45]. The formula for the total objective function is in cell G28, which has the default formula @SUM(G32..G45) to sum the costs for each arc. To check your formula, enter a value for the arc flow in column F (a good value is 5). The model is now specified and the INPUT DATA table should look like this:

	A	B	C	D	E	F	G	H	I	J
28	INPUT DATA						755	=nonlinear obj fn		
29		start	end					nonlinear coef's		
30	arc	node	node	cost		flow	fa(x)			
31	----	----	----	----		----	----	----	----	
32	arc_1	1	2	6		5	55	1		
33	arc_2	1	3	6		5	55	1		
34	arc_3	1	4	8		5	65	1		
35	arc_4	3	4	3		5	40	1		
36	arc_5	1	6	9		5	70	1		
37	arc_6	2	5	3		5	40	1		
38	arc_7	3	5	6		5	55	1		
39	arc_8	3	6	7		5	60	1		
40	arc_9	4	6	8		5	65	1		
41	arc_10	5	7	3		5	40	1		
42	arc_11	5	6	4		5	45	1		
43	arc_12	6	7	6		5	55	1		
44	arc_13	6	8	7		5	60	1		
45	arc_14	7	8	5		5	50	1		
46										

The **/WGC** command was used to set the column width equal to 7, so that all the columns can be seen simultaneously. To run the model with nonlinear costs, press [Alt M] and select **Solve**, **Nonlinear**, and **Unconstrained** from the successive menus. When the Solver has completed its solution, it will beep, and at the top of your screen you will see a completion message similar to the following:

```
A61:                                                                    EDIT
Results within tolerance; solution data follows  Press ENTER
Trial Solution: 20
        A       B       C       D       E       F       G       H       I       J
```

Press [Enter] to continue; PROPS⁺ will generate the following output:

	A	B	C	D	E	F	G	H
61	SOLUTION SUMMARY							
62								
63		OPTIMAL NETWORK FLOWS						
64								
65	arc	origin	dest.	flow	cost			
66	----	----	----	----	----			
67	arc_2	1	3	9.160816	138.8854			
68	arc_3	1	4	6.839899	101.5034			
69	arc_5	1	6	17.20671	450.9315			
70	arc_6	2	5	16.79256	332.3680			
71	arc_7	3	5	3.134081	28.62695			
72	arc_8	3	6	6.026734	78.50867			
73	arc_9	4	6	6.839899	101.5034			
74	arc_10	5	7	18.53423	399.1204			
75	arc_11	5	6	1.392416	7.508492			
76	arc_12	6	7	13.64530	268.0661			
77	arc_13	6	8	17.82046	442.3121			
78	arc_14	7	8	2.179537	15.64807			
79					---------			
80					2364.982			
81								
82								

	A	B	C	D	E	F	G	H
83	DUAL PRICES and REDUCED COSTS							
84								
85			dual			reduced		
86	node	slack	price		arc	cost		
87	----	----	----		----	----		
88	1	6.792567	0		arc_1	6.000391		
89	2	3.207431	0		arc_2	0.005120		
90	3	-0.00000	-24.3165		arc_3	-0.01038		
91	4	-2.7E-15	-21.6901		arc_4	5.626298		
92	5	-0.00000	-36.5851		arc_5	0.043452		
93	6	-0.00000	-43.3699		ar _6	0		
94	7	-0.00000	-76.6518		arc_7	-0.00045		
95	8	-0.00000	-86.0109		arc_8	0		
96					arc_9	0		
97					arc_10	0.001775		
98					arc_11	0		
99					arc_12	0.008763		
100					arc_13	0		
101					arc_14	0		
102								

Note that with nonlinear costs, twelve of the arcs have nonzero flows compared to five nonzero arcs when the costs were linear. Since cost increases rapidly with flow when the cost function is nonlinear, the optimal flow over each arc is much lower. (**Note:** Since a nonlinear programming algorithm is used, you may find slight variations in the solution when run on different machines. The reduced cost on all arcs except arc_1 and arc_4 are essentially zero.)

Capacity Constraints on Arcs

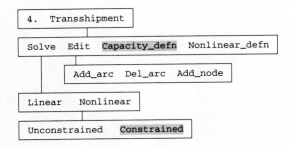

Capacity constraints can be imposed on any arc for both the linear and nonlinear model. To include capacity limits on each arc, press [Alt M] and select **Capacity_defn**. A new column will be added to the arc input data table, in which the capacity of each arc can be entered, as shown in the following screen:

	A	B	C	D	E	F	G	H	I
28	INPUT DATA						755	=nonlinear obj f	
29		start	end					nonlinear coef	
30	arc	node	node	cost	capacity	flow	fa(x)		
31	----	----	----	----	----	----	----	----	----
32	arc_1	1	2	6		5	55	1	
33	arc_2	1	3	6		5	55	1	
34	arc_3	1	4	8		5	65	1	
35	arc_4	3	4	3		5	40	1	
36	arc_5	1	6	9		5	70	1	
37	arc_6	2	5	3		5	40	1	
38	arc_7	3	5	6		5	55	1	
39	arc_8	3	6	7		5	60	1	
40	arc_9	4	6	8		5	65	1	
41	arc_10	5	7	3		5	40	1	
42	arc_11	5	6	4		5	45	1	
43	arc_12	6	7	6		5	55	1	
44	arc_13	6	8	7		5	60	1	
45	arc_14	7	8	5		5	50	1	
46									

If the value is left blank, the capacity is assumed to be infinite. Suppose there is a capacity constraint of 15 on arc_10. Enter 15 in cell E41 and press [Alt M] to run either the linear or nonlinear model, selecting the **Constrained** option. If the linear model is run, the following output is obtained:

	A	B	C	D	E	F	G
61	SOLUTION SUMMARY						
62							
63		OPTIMAL NETWORK FLOWS					
64							
65	arc	origin	dest.	flow	cost		
66	----	----	----	----	----		
67	arc_5	1	6	30	270		
68	arc_6	2	5	20	60		
69	arc_10	5	7	15	45		
70	arc_11	5	6	5	20		
71	arc_12	6	7	15	90		
72	arc_13	6	8	20	140		
73					---------		
74					625		
75							

Note that with the capacity constraint on arc_10, the cost has increased from 560 to 625, and quite different paths through the network are used.

Minimum Cost Flow Problem

The minimum cost flow problem has broad applications in transportation, assignment, transshipment, and network problems because each can be formulated as a minimum cost flow problem, and efficient algorithms are available to solve very large problems. The problem consists of finding the minimum cost flow circulation in a network with capacitated arcs. Consider the following network:

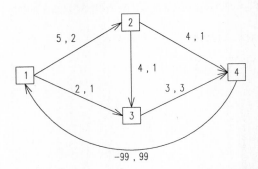

The first number on each arc is the cost of a unit flow on that arc, and the second is the arc capacity.

This problem can be solved using the transshipment model with capacity constraints on each arc. All node types are defined as transshipment (leave the type blank), with no supply or demand nodes. Using PROPS[+], the following is the input for the network:

	A	B	C	D	E	F	G	H
21		Analyst Name		Your_name				
22		Problem Name		min cost flow				
23								
24		Number of Nodes			4			
25		Number of Arcs			6			
26		Problem type (max or min)			min			
27								
28	INPUT DATA							
29		start	end					
30		arc	node	node	cost	capacity		
31		----	----	----	----	----		
32		arc_1	1	2	5	2		
33		arc_2	1	3	2	1		
34		arc_3	2	3	4	1		
35		arc_4	2	4	4	1		
36		arc_5	3	4	3	3		
37		arc_6	4	1	-99	99		
38								
39	SUPPLY and DEMAND DATA							
40			type			supply		
41		node	s,d,t	quantity		cost		
42		----	----	----		----		
43		1						
44		2						
45		3						
46		4						
47								

To solve, press [Alt M] and select **Solve, Linear,** and **Constrained** from the successive menus. Press [Enter] to clear the completion message, and the following output table is generated:

	A	B	C	D	E	F	G	H
49	SOLUTION SUMMARY							
50								
51		OPTIMAL NETWORK FLOWS						
52								
53	arc	origin	dest.	flow	cost			
54	----	----	----	----	----			
55	arc_1	1	2	2	10			
56	arc_2	1	3	1	2			
57	arc_3	2	3	1	4			
58	arc_4	2	4	1	4			
59	arc_5	3	4	2	6			
60	arc_6	4	1	3	-297			
61					---------			
62					-271			
63								
64								
65	DUAL PRICES and REDUCED COSTS							
66								
67			dual			reduced		
68	node	slack	price		arc	cost		
69	----	----	----		----	----		
70	1	0	99		arc_1	-87		
71	2	0	7		arc_2	-94		
72	3	0	3		arc_3	0		
73	4	0	0		arc_4	-3		
74					arc_5	0		
75					arc_6	0		
76								

The optimal solution is to send three units from node 1 through the network to node 4 and back to node 1. Arcs 1 to 4 are at capacity.

Features

Network Problem

- uses an undirected arc network.

- allows for capacitated arcs.

- calculates the shortest path between any two nodes, or between the origin and all other nodes.

- calculates the maximum flow between any two nodes.

- calculates the minimum spanning tree.

Chapter 5. Network Models

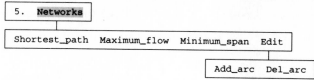

Network Definition

A number of important scheduling and routing problems can be expressed in the form of a network (also called a "graph"). For instance, the transshipment problem in the last chapter was a specialized form of network. Although linear programming can be used to solve some of these problems, general methods are based on network theory. This worksheet uses these network-theoretic techniques to solve for the shortest (or longest) path, the maximum flow through a capacitated network, and the minimum spanning tree (the minimum cost set of arcs that connect all nodes).

These models will be demonstrated using the network defined in the following table and diagram. Note that the arcs are *undirected*, so flow can be in either direction. The cost of shipping each unit of flow and the capacity, or maximum permitted flow, over each arc is contained in the table that follows.

Arc	Start Node	End Node	Cost	Capacity
1	1	2	6	4
2	1	3	6	3
3	1	4	8	5
4	3	4	3	7
5	1	6	9	5
6	2	5	3	3
7	3	5	6	7
8	3	6	7	5
9	4	6	8	4
10	5	7	3	6
11	5	6	4	5
12	6	7	6	4
13	6	8	7	7
14	7	8	5	6

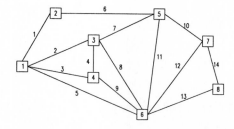

85

To analyze this network, select **5. Networks** from the ACCESS menu. You will see the following screen:

```
         A       B        C        D        E        F        G        H
1     ===============================
2                  PROPS+                    NETWORK ANALYSIS SPREADSHEET
3                                            - capacitated network
4              Copyright (C)                 - undirected arcs
5              PROPS SYSTEMS
6                                            - shortest or longest path
7              01/12/92 05:49 AM             - minimum spanning tree
8     ===============================        - maximum flow at minimum cost
9
10
11
12            Note: - nodes must be numbered consecutively from
13                      1 to the number of nodes
14                  - arcs may have any number or name
15
16
17            PROMPT mode when CMD is on. Type response, press [ENTER].
18
19                                           Press [Enter] to begin...
```

Press [Enter] and respond to the prompts by entering the problem name and the number of arcs in the network, pressing [Enter] after each entry. The following input table will be generated:

```
         A        B        C        D        E        F        G
21            Analyst Name    Your_name
22            Problem Name    network
23
24            Number of Arcs            14
25
26    INPUT DATA
27
28            Origination Node...........    1
29            Destination Node...........    2
30
31                        start     end
32                arc      node     node     cost capacity
33                ----     ----     ----     ----     ----
34            arc_1
35            arc_2
36            arc_3
37            arc_4
38            arc_5
39            arc_6
40            arc_7
41            arc_8
42            arc_9
43            arc_10
44            arc_11
45            arc_12
46            arc_13
47            arc_14
```

You are in READY mode and can use ordinary spreadsheet methods to enter the data. When the data is entered, your screen should look like this:

	A	B	C	D	E	F	G
31			start	end			
32		arc	node	node	cost	capacity	
33		----	----	----	----	----	
34		arc_1	1	2	6	4	
35		arc_2	1	3	6	3	
36		arc_3	1	4	8	5	
37		arc_4	3	4	3	7	
38		arc_5	1	6	9	5	
39		arc_6	2	5	3	3	
40		arc_7	3	5	6	7	
41		arc_8	3	6	7	5	
42		arc_9	4	6	8	4	
43		arc_10	5	7	3	6	
44		arc_11	5	6	4	5	
45		arc_12	6	7	6	4	
46		arc_13	6	8	7	7	
47		arc_14	7	8	5	6	

At any time, you can edit the network by adding or deleting one or more arcs. To do this, press [Alt M] and select **Edit**. Then pick the desired menu item and follow the menu instructions.

You are now ready to solve one of the following problems (shortest path, maximum flow, or minimum spanning tree) with this data.

Shortest Path

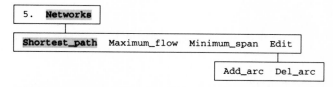

The Model:

$$f_i = \min \left[c_{ij} + f_i \right] \quad \text{(or max)}$$

where

$$f_j = \text{shortest distance from the origin to node j;}$$
$$f_{origin} = 0$$

Computation:

Step 0: assign label 0 to origin node, other nodes $+ \infty$.

Step 1: choose a labeled but unscanned node i.

Step 2: scan nodes j adjacent to i and calculate

$$f_j = \min (f_j, c_{ij} + f_i)$$

Node i is now scanned. Label node with smallest f_j.

Step 3: repeat steps 1 and 2 until all nodes are labeled.

Limitations: Assumes all arcs are undirected.

PROPS⁺ will find the shortest path between any two pairs of nodes in the network. Suppose you want the shortest path between node 7 and node 4. Move the cursor to E28 and enter 7 for the origin node; then move down one cell and enter 4, the destination node. To run the model, press [Alt M] and select **Shortest_path** by pressing [Enter]. The following output table will be created:

```
        A          B          C     .   D        E          F
51   SOLUTION  SUMMARY
52
53   SHORTEST  PATH is            12
54      from origin               7
55      to destination            4
56
57            Optimal Route is
58                  from        to
59                  node      node
60                  ----      ----
61                     7         5
62                     5         3
63                     3         4
64
65   SHORTEST  PATH
66      from origin              7
67      to all destinations  is
68                             min.  predecessor
69            to node         cost      node
70               ----         ----      ----
71                  1           12         2
72                  2            6         5
73                  3            9         5
74                  4           12         3
75                  5            3         7
76                  6            6         7
77                  7            0         7
78                  8            5         7
```

The shortest path is from 7 to 5 to 3 and then to 4, with a total distance or cost of 12. The output also shows the shortest distance from the origin node 7 to all other nodes. To find the longest path between two nodes, change the sign of the cost coefficient for each arc in the input data and re-solve.

Maximum Flow

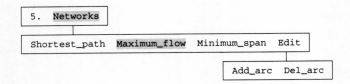

The Model:

$$\max \sum_{i(a)=source} x_a$$

subject to

$$x_a \leq u_a$$

where

x_a = flow on arc a from $i(a)$ to $j(a)$, and
u_a = capacity of arc a

Computation:

Step 0: label the origin $+ \infty$.

Step 1: choose a labeled but unscanned node i.

Step 2: scan all arcs j adjacent to i:
label $j(a)$ with [min $(f_i, u_a - x_a)$; $+a$], if a is a forward arc
label $i(a)$ with [min $(f_i, u_a + x_a)$; $-a$], if a is a reverse arc
This step scans node i.

Step 3: Repeat steps 1 and 2 until destination node labeled. Augment the flow along a path from origin to destination by the first part of the destination nodes label, using the second part to trace the path.

Step 4: Repeat steps 0 to 3 until no more nodes can be labeled. Stop.

Limitations: Assumes that arcs are undirected.

The problem is to determine the maximum possible flow between one pair of nodes when the arcs in the network have capacity constraints. For example, suppose the network represents a city's water system. Fire-fighters would want to know the maximum flow (using all possible paths) between two nodes. This is called the maximum flow network problem, and can be solved using PROPS[+]. Suppose you want to find the maximum flow that you can send from node 7 to node 4. On the initial network model set-up screen, set the origin node to **7** and the destination node to **4** (in cells E28 and E29 in this example). Press [Alt M] and select **Maximum_flow**. The following table of results will be created:

	A	B	C	D	E
51	SOLUTION SUMMARY				
52					
53	MAXIMUM FLOW is		16		
54	from origin		7		
55	to destination		4		
56					
57					
58		NETWORK FLOWS			
59		from	to	on	
60		node	node	arc	flow
61		----	----	----	----
62		1	4	arc_3	5
63		3	4	arc_4	7
64		6	1	arc_5	5
65		5	3	arc_7	6
66		6	3	arc_8	1
67		6	4	arc_9	4
68		7	5	arc_10	6
69		7	6	arc_12	4
70		8	6	arc_13	6
71		7	8	arc_14	6
72					

The maximum flow from origin 7 to destination 4 is 16. To check this, observe that the total flow out of node 7 and into node 4 is 16. Many different paths are used to get the flow from node 7 to node 4.

Minimum Spanning Tree

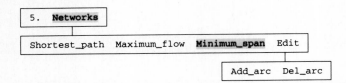

The Model:

        Find the minimum cost tree to reach all nodes.

        Let c_{ij} be the cost of the arc joining i to j.

Computation:

    Step 0:   Designate the root node by 1. Begin with set A = node 1.

    Step 1:   Calculate $\displaystyle\min_{i,\,j}\ (c_{ij})$ for all $i \in A, j \notin A$.

             Denote the minimizing j by s, and let $A = A \cup s$.

    Step 2:   Repeat Step 1 until $A = \{all\ nodes\}$.

Limitations: None.

If the network has n nodes, then a "spanning tree" is a set of n−1 arcs that connects all the nodes of the network and contains no loops. The "minimum spanning tree" is the spanning tree of minimum length or cost. The minimum spanning tree is useful if you wish to find the cheapest or shortest way to ensure that each node is connected to the network. An example of such a problem is that facing a utility wishing to connect all its customers with the shortest possible network.

To find the minimum spanning tree for the example network, press [Alt M] and select **Minimum_span**. PROPS⁺ will run the model and create the following output table:

```
        A           B          C         D         E
51  SOLUTION SUMMARY
52
53  MINIMUM SPANNING TREE
54
55              from        to
56              node        node      cost
57              ----        ----      ----
58                 1           2         6
59                 2           5         3
60                 5           7         3
61                 5           6         4
62                 7           8         5
63                 1           3         6
64                 3           4         3
65                                   ---------
66                        Total        30
67
```

The total cost of this tree is 30 and connects 1 to 2 and 3, 2 to 5, 3 to 4, 5 to 6 and 7, and 7 to 8. Note there are (8−1)=7 arcs in the tree and no loops.

Features

1. ## Problem Description

   - uses a single input format for CPM and PERT.

   - combines activity-on-arc and activity-on-node problem descriptions.

2. ## CPM Analysis

   - computes the time to complete the project and the critical activities.

   - schedules the start and finish times for each activity.

   - uses linear programming to find the minimum-cost method to reduce project time.

   - draws a GANTT chart.

3. ## PERT Analysis

   - computes the mean and variance of the time to complete the project.

   - estimates the probability that the project duration is greater than any specified time.

   - simulates activities to estimate the actual distribution of project completion time.

Chapter 6. Project Management

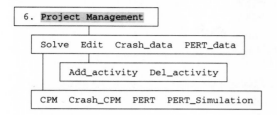

```
6. Project Management

   Solve   Edit   Crash_data   PERT_data

        Add_activity   Del_activity

   CPM   Crash_CPM   PERT   PERT_Simulation
```

Managers are often responsible for planning, scheduling, and controlling projects that consist of large numbers of tasks or activities, each carried out by separate departments, individuals, or subcontractors. Often these projects are so complex that no manager can keep track of the activities in his or her head, and a project management system is required. The system should answer the following types of questions:

1. What is the total time required to complete the project?
2. What are the earliest and latest start and finish times for each activity?
3. Which activities are critical and must be completed on schedule if the overall project is to be completed on schedule?
4. How long can noncritical activities be delayed without delaying the total project?
5. If extra effort, with resulting higher costs, is assigned to individual activities, what is the cheapest way to shorten the completion time for the total project?
6. If the time to complete each activity is random, what is the probability that the project will take longer than a given time?

The two most common project management techniques are described in the following paragraphs.

CPM (Critical Path Method) assumes that the time to complete each activity is known with certainty. CPM identifies the sequence(s) of events that cannot be delayed without delaying the whole project (the "critical path"), and the duration of this critical path. Results are displayed as a list of activities with schedule times, or in a graphical format called a GANTT chart. CPM also determines the "float" for each noncritical activity, the amount by which the activity can be delayed without affecting the overall project length.

If a shorter overall duration is desired, the model assumes that activities can be "crashed" (shortened) at an additional cost. In PROPS⁺, the **Crash_CPM** routine uses linear programming to determine the least-cost combination of activity shortenings to achieve the desired goal (if it is feasible).

PERT (Project Evaluation and Review Technique) assumes that the time to complete each activity is random. The usual assumption is that activity times follow a Beta distribution. For this distribution, if a most optimistic time a, most pessimistic time b, and most likely time m are specified, then the expected duration E is

$$E = (a + 4m + b)/6$$

and the variance V is

$$V = (b - a)^2 /36.$$

The method identifies the critical path based on the mean completion time for each activity. Activity durations are assumed to be independent of each other, and the resulting overall project duration is typically assumed to be approximately normal with a mean and variance corresponding to the sums of the means and variances of the activities on a critical path. (In our implementation, if there is more than one critical path, PROPS⁺ finds the mean and variance of the critical path that has the maximum variance.) This distribution is used to estimate the probability that the project will exceed any specified time horizon.

PERT techniques have been criticized because, in any particular realization of activity times, the actual critical path may not be the path that was originally identified based on the mean times. That is, in a particular case, some activity that was not designated as critical may take longer than expected and become critical. This means that the normal approximation described in the preceding paragraph may give an incorrect result. PROPS⁺ provides an option called **PERT_Simulation** that simulates the actual distribution of total project completion time, assuming the time for each activity follows a Beta distribution. Although the simulation can be quite time-consuming for a large problem, it gives a useful check on the normality assumption of standard PERT analysis.

Example: A Circuit Design Problem

The following table describes the sequence of activities that go into the design of a new electrical process control unit.

Job #	Description	Activity Time	Preceding Activities
1	block design	4 days	-
2	spec circuit design	8	1
3	test std circuits	6	1
4	test spec circuits	5	2,3
5	rack design	8	2
6	pre-test	5	4
7	make rack drawing	7	5,6
8	make circ drawing	5	6
9	deliver	1	7,8

Traditional CPM and PERT models allow for two forms of problem description, called activity-on-arc and activity-on-node. The problem can be shown as an activity-on-arc diagram, as follows:

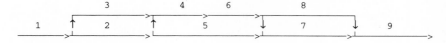

As an activity-on-node diagram, the problem appears as follows:

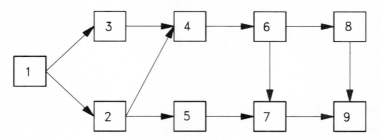

PROPS⁺ does not make this distinction. The input format simply requests information about which activities immediately precede each activity in the project.

The Project Management Spreadsheet

Begin by retrieving the ACCESS worksheet. The following menu appears on the screen:

```
                           A                                        B
 1                                                Copyright (C)
 2              PROPS+    v1.00                    E.R.Petersen & A.J.Taylor
 3        Probabilistic and Optimization          Queen's University at Kingston
 4              Spreadsheets                       programmed by G.D.Thompson
 5        ==============================          ==============================
 6
 7          Move cursor to the desired menu item and press [Enter]
 8
 9      1. Quit                             11. Simulation
10      2. LP, IP and NLP                   12. Probability Distributions
11      3. Transportation/Assignment        13. Decision Analysis
12      4. Transshipment                    14. Markov Chains
13      5. Networks                         15. Dynamic Programming (DP)
14      6. Project Management               16. Stochastic DP
15      7. Forecasting
16      8. Inventory
17      9. Production planning
18     10. Queueing
19
```

Select **6. Project Management** from this menu by moving the cursor down to item 6 and pressing [Enter], and you will see the following screen:

```
        A       B       C       D       E       F       G       H
 1     ==============================
 2                  PROPS+              PROJECT MANAGEMENT SPREADSHEET
 3                                      - CPM Analysis
 4              Copyright (C)             - normal
 5              PROPS SYSTEMS             - optimal crash (LP)
 6                                      - PERT Analysis
 7            03/10/92 01:54 PM           - normal dist for horizon exceeded
 8     ==============================     - simulates exact probability
 9                                          any horizon is exceeded
10     Instructions:
11              STEP 1: Enter number of activities when prompted. Input
12                      tables of the appropriate size will be constructed.
13              STEP 2: Enter the information associated with each
14                      activity. Rename the activities, if desired.
15              STEP 3: Press [Alt M] for the command menu. If you wish to do
16                      analysis, select PERT and define the extra times required.
17
18              PROMPT mode when CMD is on. Type response, press [ENTER].
19
20                                      Press [Enter] to begin...
```

Pressing [Enter] will display the following questions, one by one. Respond to each by typing your answer and pressing the [Enter] key.

	A	B	C	D	E	F	G
21			Analyst Name			Your_name	
22			Problem Name			circuit design	
23			Number of Activities			9	

At this point, PROPS⁺ will present the following table for you to complete. This table defines the interrelationships between activities:

	A	B	C	D	E	F	G	H
24								
25	INPUT DATA							
26								
27				Predecessor Activity Numbers [max. 5 each]:				
28	Activity Name_____		Number	_____	_____	_____	_____	_____
29	a_1		1					
30	a_2		2					
31	a_3		3					
32	a_4		4					
33	a_5		5					
34	a_6		6					
35	a_7		7					
36	a_8		8					
37	a_9		9					
38								
39								
40			Do Not					
41			Start	Activity				
42	Activity Name		Before	Time				
43	---------------------------------							
44	a_1		0	0				
45	a_2		0	0				
46	a_3		0	0				
47	a_4		0	0				
48	a_5		0	0				
49	a_6		0	0				
50	a_7		0	0				
51	a_8		0	0				
52	a_9		0	0				
53								

For the circuit design problem, this table should be completed as follows. Note that the default activity names (a_1, a_2, etc.) can be overwritten with names of up to eighteen characters of your choice. To the right of each activity, enter the activity numbers of those activities that *immediately precede* that activity. (There is a limit of five preceding activities. If more than five activities precede a particular activity, you can insert a dummy activity with 0 duration to include the overflow.) When all the predecessor activities have been specified, move down the worksheet and enter the time required for each activity. For the circuit design problem, the screen should look like this:

	A	B	C	D	E	F	G	H
21			Analyst Name			Your_name		
22			Problem Name			circuit design		
23			Number of Activities			9		
24								
25	INPUT DATA							
26								
27				Predecessor Activity Numbers [max. 5 each]:				
28	Activity Name_____		Number	_____	_____	_____	_____	_____
29	block design		1					
30	spec circuits		2	1				
31	test std circuits		3	1				
32	test spec circuits		4	2	3			
33	rack design		5	2				
34	pre-test		6	3	4			
35	make rack drawing		7	5	6			
36	make circuit drawi		8	6				
37	deliver		9	7	8			
38								
39								
40			Do Not					
41			Start	Activity				
42	Activity Name		Before	Time				
43	------------------------------------							
44	block design		0	4				
45	spec circuits		0	8				
46	test std circuits		0	6				
47	test spec circuits		0	5				
48	rack design		0	8				
49	pre-test		0	5				
50	make rack drawing		0	7				
51	make circuit drawi		0	5				
52	deliver		0	1				
53								

If there are constraints on the earliest starting time for any of the activities, these should also be entered in column C. Otherwise the default value of zero is assumed, as shown above. You are now ready to analyse the circuit design project.

The Critical Path Method

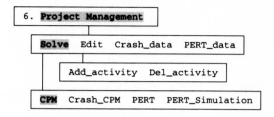

The Model:

$$ES_k = \max\left(B_k, \; \max_{i \in P_k} \left[EF_i\right]\right) \qquad \text{(earliest start)}$$

$$EF_k = ES_k + t_k \qquad \text{(earliest finish)}$$

$$CP = \max_i \left[EF_i\right] \qquad \text{(critical path)}$$

$$LF_k = \min\left[CP, \; t_k + \min_{i \in S_k} \left[LS_i\right]\right] \qquad \text{(latest finish)}$$

$$LS_k = LF_k - t_k \qquad \text{(latest start)}$$

$$Float_k = LF_k - EF_k, \; k = 1, 2, \ldots, N$$

where:

t_k = time to complete activity k
B_k = imposed earliest start time for activity k
P_k = the set of predecessor activities to activity k
S_k = the set of successor activities to activity k
$Float_k$ = the possible delay to k causing no increase in CP.

Computation: PROPS[+] recursively computes times for each activity.

Limitations: Problem size limited only by spreadsheet size.

The CPM method calculates the earliest start time for every activity, and the latest time that each can finish, in order that the overall project is not delayed. The difference between these two values is called the "float" for that activity, which is the maximum amount by which that activity can be delayed without causing delay in the project. The critical path is defined as the set of activities that have zero float.

To illustrate the use of PROPS⁺, press [Alt M] to call up a command menu that looks like this:

```
A52: PR                                                              MENU
Solve  Edit  Crash_data  PERT_data
Solve the current problem
          A         B         C         D         E         F         G         H
```

Select **Solve** by pressing [Enter]. You will then see the following menu:

```
A52: PR                                                              MENU
CPM  Crash_CPM  PERT  PERT_Simulation
Critical Path Analysis
          A         B         C         D         E         F         G         H
```

Select **CPM** by pressing [Enter]. PROPS⁺ will identify the critical path and present the following output:

```
          A         B         C         D         E         F         G
55
56   CPM OUTPUT
57                      Earliest  Latest Earliest  Latest
58   Name                 Start   Start   Finish   Finish      Float
59   ------------------------------------------------------------------
60   block design           0       0        4        4   *critical
61   spec circuits          4       4       12       12   *critical
62   test std circuits      4       6       10       12        2
63   test spec circuits    12      12       17       17   *critical
64   rack design           12      14       20       22        2
65   pre-test              17      17       22       22   *critical
66   make rack drawing     22      22       29       29   *critical
67   make circ drawing     22      24       27       29        2
68   deliver               29      29       30       30   *critical
69
70            Length of critical path:      30
```

As this output shows, the project will take 30 days to complete. Activities 1,2,4,6,7 and 9 are critical in the sense that any delay in these activities will cause the project to be delayed. The other (noncritical) activities have a float of 2, which means that, considered separately, they could each take an extra two days without delaying the project. The critical path is highlighted in the following activity diagram:

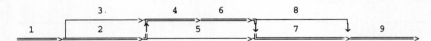

GANTT Chart

A useful tool for visualizing the critical path and float for each activity is called a GANTT chart. PROPS⁺ uses the spreadsheet Graph feature to draw the GANTT chart. Once the table just shown has been generated, you can call up the chart by pressing the [F10] key. The chart for the preceding example appears as follows:

GANTT CHART

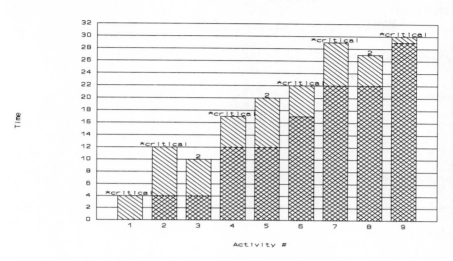

In this graph, the critical activities are labeled as critical, and the float is shown for noncritical activities.

Sensitivity Analysis

A major advantage of the PROPS[+] project management model is that sensitivity analysis is easy, since the critical path and the project times are automatically recalculated when activity time data is changed.

For example, consider what happens if the time required to test std circuits (activity 3) increases from six to nine days. To examine this, move the cursor to cell D46 and enter 9. The CPM OUTPUT table automatically changes:

	A	B	C	D	E	F	G	H
55								
56	CPM OUTPUT							
57			Earliest	Latest	Earliest	Latest		
58	Name		Start	Start	Finish	Finish	Float	
59	-------		------	------	------	------	------	
60	block design		0	0	4	4	*critical	
61	spec circuits		4	5	12	13	1	
62	test std circuits		4	4	13	13	*critical	
63	test spec circuits		13	13	18	18	*critical	
64	rack design		12	15	20	23	3	
65	pre-test		18	18	23	23	*critical	
66	make rack drawing		23	23	30	30	*critical	
67	make circ drawing		23	25	28	30	2	
68	deliver		30	30	31	31	*critical	
69								
70	Length of critical path:				31			

Note that the length of the critical path is now 31 and the activity "spec circuits" is now not critical, but the activity "test std circuits" has become critical. The new start and finish times for each activity are also automatically updated to reflect this new data.

CPM Crash Analysis

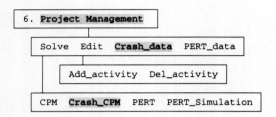

The Model:

In the CPM model, replace t_k by $(t_k - c_k)$, and solve

$$\min \sum_{k \in N} a_k c_k$$

subject to

$$CP \leq H$$
$$c_k \leq b_k$$

where

c_k = reduction in time through crashing activity k

a_k = cost of crashing activity k per unit time

b_k = maximum reduction in time for activity k

H = desired maximum project duration

Computation: The What-If Solver is used to find the minimum-cost solution.

Limitations: The desired maximum duration may not be feasible.

In many situations, it is possible to assign extra resources to an activity in order to shorten its duration. In project management, this is called "crashing" the activity. Of course, crashing results in higher costs, and the problem is to determine by how much each activity should be shortened to achieve a specified overall project duration at minimum cost.

We assume that the cost of crashing an activity is linear in the amount of time saved, and any fractional amount of crashing is possible. For example, suppose an activity normally requires six days, but it could be shortened by two days at a cost of $400. The crashing cost per unit time for this activity is $200 per day, with a maximum reduction in time of two days. Crashing by 0.5 days to give a duration of 5.5 days would cost an extra $100.

Suppose the activities in the circuit design problem can be crashed according to the following table:

Job #	Description	Normal Time	Crash Cost per unit Time	Max Reduction in Time
1	block design	4 days	$200	1 day
2	spec circuit design	8	100	2
3	test std circuits	6	200	1
4	test spec circuits	5	--	--
5	rack design	8	50	2
6	pre-test	5	250	2
7	make rack drawing	7	250	2
8	make circ drawing	5	300	1
9	deliver	1	--	--

Note that activities 4 and 9 cannot be shortened. To interpret this table, note that activity 1 can be shortened by as much as one day (from 4 days to 3) at an additional cost of $200.

Recall that the original critical path for this project was 30 days. Which activities should be crashed to achieve, say, a 29-day deadline? Let us use PROPS+ to find out. To return to the original problem, change the 9 in cell D46 back to 6. To define the crash data, call up the menu with [Alt M]:

```
A68:                                                                        MENU
Solve  Edit  Crash_data  PERT_data
Solve the current problem
        A        B        C        D        E        F        G        H
```

Select **Crash_data** and you will see the following screen:

	A	B	C	D	E	F	G	H
39						___CRASH DATA___		
40			Do Not		Crash	Max.		
41			Start	Activity	Cost per	Reduction		
42	Activity Name		Before	Time	unit time	in Time		
43	--
44	block design		0	4				
45	spec circuits		0	8				
46	test std circuits		0	6				
47	test spec circuits		0	5				
48	rack design		0	8				
49	pre-test		0	5				
50	make rack drawing		0	7				
51	make circ drawing		0	5				
52	deliver		0	1				
53								
54					Desired Project Duration =	1.0E+30		
55								

Note that the original problem data is retained (along with the logical relationship among the activities). At this point, you are in READY mode and can use ordinary spreadsheet methods to enter the crash data. The result for this project appears as follows:

	A	B	C	D	E	F	G	H
39						___CRASH DATA___		
40			Do Not		Crash	Max.		
41			Start	Activity	Cost per	Reduction		
42	Activity Name		Before	Time	unit time	in Time		
43	--
44	block design		0	4	200	1		
45	spec circuits		0	8	100	2		
46	test std circuits		0	6	200	1		
47	test spec circuits		0	5				
48	rack design		0	8	50	2		
49	pre-test		0	5	250	2		
50	make rack drawing		0	7	250	2		
51	make circ drawing		0	5	300	1		
52	deliver		0	1				
53								
54					Desired Project Duration =		29	
55								

Note that for activities "test spec circuits" and "deliver", which cannot be crashed, the crash cost and reduction in time are left blank. Now press [Alt M] and the menu reappears:

```
G52: U 29                                                              MENU
Solve  Edit  Crash_data  PERT_data
Solve the current problem
          A         B         C         D         E         F         G         H
```

Select **Solve** by pressing [Enter], and you will see the following menu:

```
G52: U 29                                                          MENU
CPM  Crash_CPM  PERT  PERT_Simulation
Critical Path Analysis
         A        B        C        D        E        F        G        H
```

Select **Crash_CPM**. The screen will flash as PROPS⁺ sets up the data and calls the Solver. When the Solver has completed its solution, it will beep, and at the top of your screen you will see a completion message similar to the following:

```
D56:                                                              EDIT
Results within tolerance; solution data follows  Press ENTER
Trial Solution: 34
         A        B        C        D        E        F        G        H
```

The program will pause. Press [Enter] to continue; PROPS⁺ will generate the following table of output results:

```
         A        B        C        D        E        F        G        H        I
54                      Desired Project Duration     29
55
56  CPM "CRASH" OUTPUT
57                 Earliest Latest  Earliest Latest                Crash    Extra
58  Name            Start    Start  Finish   Finish   Float        Time     Cost
59  --------------------------------------------------------------------------------
60  block design        0    1E-11       4        4 *critica         0        0
61  spec circuits       4       4       11       11 *crash..         1  100.000
62  test std circuit    4       5       10       11      1           0        0
63  test spec circui   11      11       16       16 *critica         0        0
64  rack design        11      13       19       21      2           0        0
65  pre-test           16      16       21       21 *critica         0        0
66  make rack drawin   21      21       28       28 *critica         0        0
67  make circ drawin   21      23       26       28      2           0        0
68  deliver            28      28       29       29 *critica         0        0
69                                                               ----------------
70        Length of critical path:    29                            1  100.000
71
72        -- (press [Alt-R] to re-solve after changes to data) --
73
```

To see the full table, change the column width to 8 with the **Worksheet Global Column-width** command (**/WGC**). As you can see from this output, the second activity, "spec circuits," was crashed by one day to meet the imposed 29-day horizon, at a cost of $100. Note that any activity that is crashed will also be critical. Also note that the float for the third activity, "test std circuit", has been reduced from two days in the original solution to one day as a result of crashing the second activity.

If a desired project duration that cannot be met without exceeding the crash limits is imposed, the linear program will be infeasible. In this case, the following message will appear at the top of the screen:

```
A52:                                                                              EDIT
Feasible point not found; solution data follows   Press ENTER
Trial Solution: 19
         A          B          C          D          E          F          G          H          I
```

Press [Enter] to continue and you will see the following message in the worksheet:

```
         A          B          C          D          E          F          G          H
56   CPM "CRASH" OUTPUT                 *** No feasible solution was found ***
```

PERT Analysis

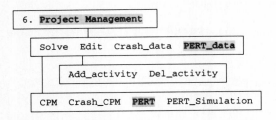

The Model:

Approximates the project duration with a normal distribution with

$$\text{mean } E = \sum_c E_k \text{ and variance } V = \sum_c V_k$$

where

C = the set of activities on the maximum variance critical path

$$E_k = \left(\frac{a_k + 4m_k + b_k}{6}\right) \text{ and } V_k = \left(\frac{(b_k - a_k)^2}{36}\right)$$

a_k = the most optimistic time for activity k
b_k = the most pessimistic time for activity k
m_k = the most likely time for activity k

Computation: The same computations as for CPM.

Limitations: Assumes that the critical path that is based on mean activity times always applies.

The CPM method assumed that activity times were deterministic and known. PERT is designed to deal with randomness in the length of time required for each activity. The typical assumption is that the probability distribution of time for each activity is a Beta distribution. The following graph illustrates a typical Beta distribution. Note the right tail of this distribution.

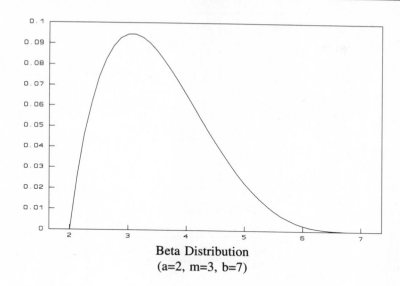

Beta Distribution
(a=2, m=3, b=7)

This distribution is characterized by three parameters: the most optimistic time a (= 2 in the example), the most likely time m (= 3 above), and the most pessimistic time b (=7 above). The mean and variance of the activity time are calculated directly from these parameters. If there are a reasonable number of activities on the critical path and the activity durations are independent, the resulting sum of the component random times will be approximately normally distributed (by the central limit theorem), with a mean and variance equal to the sum of the critical activities' means and variances.

If there is more than one critical path in a problem, there will be more than one normal distribution. PROPS⁺ chooses the critical path with the maximum variance for the best approximation to the overall project duration. We can now estimate the probability that the project will require more than any arbitrary length of time.

Returning to the circuit design problem, suppose the most optimistic, most likely, and most pessimistic time for each activity have been estimated as shown in the following table:

Job #	Description	Most Optimistic Duration	Most Likely Duration	Most Pessimistic Duration
1	block design	3 days	4 days	5 days
2	spec circuit design	6	8	11
3	test std circuits	5	6	8
4	test spec circuits	5	5	9
5	rack design	5	8	12
6	pretest	4	5	8
7	make rack drawing	5	7	8
8	make circ drawing	4	5	6
9	deliver	1	1	1

To enter this data for a PERT analysis, press [Alt M] to call up the following menu:

```
C53:                                                                    MENU
Solve  Edit   Crash_data   PERT_data
Solve the current problem
         A        B        C        D       E       F       G       H
```

Select **PERT_data** from this menu, and the data input table is presented for you to complete:

```
         A        B        C        D       E       F       G        H       I
38
39                                  ___CRASH DATA__    _____PERT DATA_____
40                         Do Not     Crash    Max.    Most    Most     Most
41                         Start  ActivityCost perReductio Optim. Likely Pessim.
42   Activity Name         Before  Time unit timin Time   Time    Time    Time
43   ---------------------------------------------------------------------------
44   block design            0       4     200       1
45   spec circuits           0       8     100       2
46   test std circuit        0       6     200       1
47   test spec circui        0       5
48   rack design             0       8      50       2
49   pre-test                0       5     250       2
50   make rack drawin        0       7     250       2
51   make circ drawin        0       5     300       1
52   deliver                 0       1
53
```

Note that if you have already run a CPM analysis, column D will contain the mean time for the activity and columns E and F will show the CPM crash data. This data is ignored in the PERT analysis, since PERT relies solely on estimates for the most optimistic, most likely, and most pessimistic estimates for each activity's duration. When this data is entered, the following screen should appear (columns D through F are not relevant for this analysis, and have been hidden):

	A	B	C		G	H	I	J
38								
39					___PERT DATA___		
40			Do Not		Most	Most	Most	
41			Start		Optim.	Likely	Pessim.	
42	Activity Name		Before		Time	Time	Time	
43	---
44	block design		0		3	4	5	
45	spec circuits		0		6	8	11	
46	test std circuits		0		5	6	8	
47	test spec circuits		0		5	5	9	
48	rack design		0		5	8	12	
49	pre-test		0		4	5	8	
50	make rack drawing		0		5	7	8	
51	make circ drawing		0		4	5	6	
52	deliver		0		1	1	1	
53								

The input table extends across the spreadsheet to the right. To make it easier to see the data, move the cursor to column D and use the **Worksheet Title Vertical** command (**/WTV**). Now as you move the cursor to the right, the columns will scroll and you see only the columns of interest. (Columns A, B, and C will always be seen, but columns D-F will be hidden, as shown in the figure.) When you are finished entering data, use the **Worksheet Title Clear** command (**/WTC**) to remove the title columns. Alternatively, you can change the column width using the **Worksheet Global Column-width** command (**/WGC**).

Note that the most likely observation corresponds to the peak of the Beta distribution. Since the Beta is not symmetric because of its right tail, the mean value will in general be larger than the most likely value. The mean value is calculated from the three parameters, and thus may not be precisely the same as that used in the CPM analysis. To run a PERT analysis, press [Alt M] to bring up the following menu:

```
C50: U 1                                                                    MENU
Solve  Edit  Crash_data  PERT_data
Solve the current problem
       C        D        E        F        G        H        I        J
```

Select **Solve** to call up the following menu:

```
C50: U 1                                                                    MENU
CPM  Crash_CPM  PERT  PERT_Simulation
Critical Path Analysis
       C        D        E        F        G        H        I        J
```

Select **PERT** and the following output will be generated:

```
         A          B         C         D         E         F         G         H
55
56  PERT OUTPUT       ----------EXPECTED VALUES ----------
57                    Earliest  Latest Earliest  Latest
58  Name              Start     Start  Finish    Finish         Float
59  --------------------------------------------------------------------
60  block design            0         0        4         4 *critical
61  spec circuits           4         4 12.16666 12.16666 *critical
62  test std circuits       4         6 10.16666 12.16666         2
63  test spec circuits12.16666 12.16666 17.83333 17.83333 *critical
64  rack design      12.16666       15 20.33333 23.16666 2.833333
65  pre-test         17.83333 17.83333 23.16666 23.16666 *critical
66  make rack drawing 23.16666 23.16666       30       30 *critical
67  make circ drawing 23.16666       25 28.16666       30 1.833333
68  deliver                30        30       31       31 *critical
69
70               Expected Project Duration:        31
71               Standard Deviation: 1.394433
72
73           The likelihood total time
74           for the project will exceed          31
75                                  is   0.500000
76
```

The expected duration time for the project is estimated to be 31 days, with a standard deviation of 1.4 days. You can now estimate the probability that the project will take longer than any specified time. For example, suppose you want to estimate the probability that the project will take longer than 33 days. To do this, enter 33 (in this example in cell E74). You will see the following screen:

```
         A          B         C         D         E         F         G         H
69
70               Expected Project Duration:        31
71               Standard Deviation: 1.394433
72
73           The likelihood total time
74           for the project will exceed          33
75                                  is   0.075739
76
```

Thus there is about a 7.6% chance that the project will take longer than 33 days.

Note that the usual parametric analysis can be performed, since PROPS⁺ is designed to automatically recalculate the model. In addition, you can alternate between the various project management techniques as you carry out the analysis of the project.

PERT Simulation

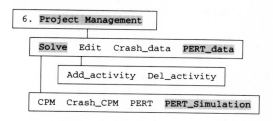

In PERT analysis it is assumed that the critical path calculated using mean activity times will in fact be the critical path when the random values for the activity times are realized. PROPS+ includes a procedure that simulates random draws from each activity's Beta probability distribution, and thereby simulates the overall project duration. The results form a check on the validity of PERT's normality assumption.

To simulate the overall project duration in the sample problem, press [Alt M] to call up the menu. Select **Solve** and the following menu appears:

```
E77:
CPM   Crash_CPM   PERT   PERT_Simulation                              MENU
Critical Path Analysis
        A           B          C         D         E       F        G        H
```

Move the cursor to **PERT_Simulation** and press [Enter]. PROPS+ will perform some calculations; you will then see the following screen:

```
        A           B          C         D         E       F
71
72   PERT Simulation Output
73
74   Total number of simulated points?        100
75
```

If you select the default value by pressing [Enter], PROPS+ will simulate 100 different occurrences of the project. (The maximum number of points that can be simulated is 8000.) On completion, you will see the following screen:

	A	B	C	D	E	F	G	H	I	J
73					Project Duration					
74	Project				Frequency Distribution					
75	--------------------			-------	-------------------------------------					
76	average 31.91271			Duration	25	26	27	28	29	30
77	std dev 2.241229			freq	0	0	0	0	0.05	0.19
78				cum.freq	0	0	0	0	0.05	0.24
79										
80		The likelihood total time								
81		for the project will exceed			31.91					
82				is	0.58					
83										

The frequency distribution for project completion time continues to the right on the spreadsheet beyond column H. This table contains the number of times (from the 100 trial simulations of the project) that the project required each duration. To see a graph of this distribution, press [F10].

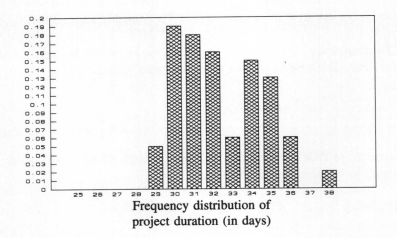

Frequency distribution of
project duration (in days)

Press any key to exit from the graph.

The simulation output can also be used to estimate the probability that the project will exceed any specified duration. In the above screen, the model reports that the probability that the actual duration will exceed the average of 31.91 days is 58% (indicating that the distribution is skewed toward the higher values).

As in the preceding PERT analysis, you can specify any project length in cell E81 and PROPS⁺ will calculate the proportion of simulation runs that exceed this length. For example, the following screen shows the result of inserting the number 33 in cell E81.

	A	B	C	D	E	F	G	H	I	J
72	PERT Simulation Output									
73					Project Duration					
74	Project				Frequency Distribution					
75	------------------				-------------------------------------					
76	average 31.91271			Duration	25	26	27	28	29	30
77	std dev 2.241229			freq	0	0	0	0	0.05	0.19
78				cum.freq	0	0	0	0	0.05	0.24
79										
80		The likelihood total time								
81		for the project will exceed			33					
82				is	0.48					
83										

Your output may have different numeric values. The above distribution is based on a simulation and your simulated values will likely be different, giving different statistics.

Features

1. ## Time Series Models

   - models are explicitly defined.

   - goodness of fit criteria and forecast are automatically recalculated when model definition or forecasting method is changed.

2. ## Regression Models

   - no growth.

   - linear growth.

   - percentage, or exponential, growth.

   - Gompertz nonlinear (S-curve) growth.

3. ## Exponential Smoothing Models

   - simple first order.

   - Holt model with trend correction.

   - Winters model with seasonality updating.

   - optimal selection of exponential smoothing coefficients.

4. ## Forecasting Models

   - regression.

   - regression with exponentially smoothed residual.

   - simple exponential smoothing.

   - simple moving average.

   - exponential smoothing with trend correction (Holt model).

   - exponential smoothing with trend correction and seasonal factor update (Winters model).

Chapter 7. Forecasting

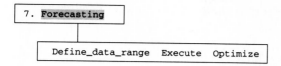

Many decision problems involve making estimates about the future value of some variable based on observed values of the variable in the past called a time series. Examples include weekly sales levels for a retail product, monthly housing starts in a city, number of business failures in each quarter in a state, national annual gross domestic product, and so on. A typical time series is shown in the following graph.

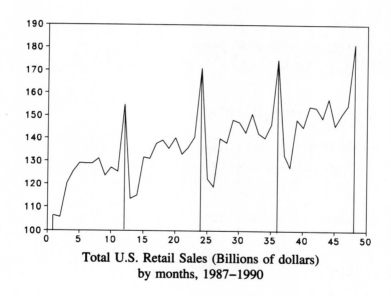

Total U.S. Retail Sales (Billions of dollars)
by months, 1987–1990

In this series, you can see that each December has a relatively high level of sales, and January and February are relatively low. Also, June and August appear to have slightly higher sales than average, and July is a little under average. This example shows that time series patterns can be quite complex. One useful way to think about the pattern is to imagine that the series is made up of four components, superimposed on one another: a long-term trend, a seasonal pattern, a cyclical variation, and a random "noise" component. Each of these is described in the next section. Using these components, different models can be created for any given set of data. A later section of this chapter will discuss how to choose the most appropriate model. As is true of other operations research methods, the value of an analysis will depend on how well the chosen model reflects reality.

Forecasting involves two activities: creating a model to describe the observed time series, and using this model to predict future observations. To create the model, the first step is to identify the seasonal component, if any, and isolate it from the data. This is called "deseasonalizing." Next, the trend component is identified and isolated from the data; this is called "detrending." Finally, the cyclical variation can be identified from the remaining deseasonalized, detrended data.

In principle, prediction reverses the order of these steps. First the cyclical pattern is projected, then the trend term applied, and finally the seasonal adjustment incorporated. In some model implementations, these steps are not carried out separately, but are still done implicitly.

Components of a Time Series Model

Trend This refers to the long-term average value of the time series. In the Total U.S. Retail Sales graph on page 115, there is a general upward movement, with an apparent approximately linear increase over time. PROPS$^+$ allows for four general trend types, illustrated in the following graphs.

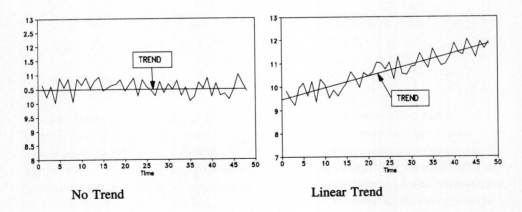

No Trend   Linear Trend

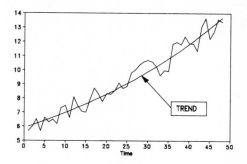

Exponential or Percentage Trend

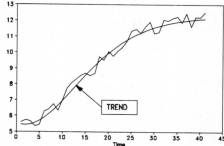

Gompertz or S-curve Trend

Seasonality   This component corresponds to a repetitive general pattern in the series over time. For example, the graph of U.S. retail sales on page 115 showed a series with a strong seasonal pattern: a high in December (Christmas sales), a low in January and February (the post-Christmas slump), and smaller peaks in June and August with a dip in July. The seasonal variation may be one of two forms—additive or multiplicative—as illustrated in the following figures (which assume a linear trend in each case).

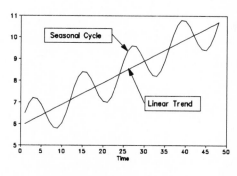

Additive Seasonality

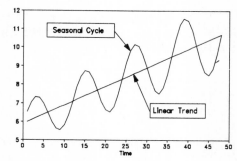

Multiplicative Seasonality

Additive seasonality assumes that each time period has a seasonal component added to the trend. Multiplicative seasonality assumes that the size of the seasonal component depends on the trend value at that point; that is, the size of the seasonal swing increases as the trend increases.

Cyclic Variation   This refers to variations in the series that don't show a repetitive pattern. Based on the concept of the business cycle, the cyclical component describes the departure of the series from the trend for a number of consecutive periods. The following figure illustrates a linear trend with a cyclic variation component.

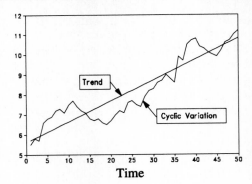

Time

Because of its irregularity and nonperiodic nature, identifying the cyclic pattern is more difficult than recognizing either the trend or seasonal components in a time series. Thus we do not directly model the cyclical component, but rather use techniques such as exponential smoothing to describe the correlation of this component from period to period.

Random error, or noise   Some of the variation in a time series is due to factors that affect the variable's values, but are unpredictable. Variation in a series from these factors taken together is called random fluctuation, or noise. Noise is equivalent to the residual in a regression model.

These components can be combined in a variety of ways, depending on the nature of the data. A typical example in many texts is a strictly additive model, which can be represented as

$$x_t = s_t + r_t + c_t + e_t$$

where

s_t = seasonal factor applying to period t
r_t = the long-term trend at t
c_t = the cyclical component at t
e_t = the random error associated with period t

Another model that often arises in empirical time series has a multiplicative seasonal component and an additive cyclical component (this is the default model in PROPS[+]) can be represented as:

$$x_t = s_t (r_t + c_t) + e_t$$

Deseasonalizing a Time Series

If the time series x_t has a seasonal pattern, PROPS[+] begins by estimating the seasonal factors. Seasonal adjustment factors can be either additive or multiplicative. For the additive case, for each season PROPS$^+$ averages the deviations between the observed value and the centered moving average, based on the length of the seasonal pattern. For the multiplicative case, PROPS$^+$ finds the average ratio of the observation to the centered moving average. Each time period t will thus have an associated seasonal factor, with a repeating pattern from cycle to cycle. For notational convenience, we denote the estimated seasonal factor for period t as S_t. Note that with this definition, if the cycle length is m, then $S_t = S_{t-m} = S_{t-2m}$ and so on. (We will use capital letters to denote estimates or smoothed values.)

To deseasonalize the time series x_t, we assume that the seasonal factors remain constant over time. The deseasonalized time series is

$$y_t \quad = x_t / S_t \qquad \text{multiplicative seasonality}$$
$$= x_t - S_t \qquad \text{additive seasonality}$$

If there is reason to suspect that the seasonal adjustment factors are not constant over time, then the Winters model is appropriate. This model uses exponential smoothing to estimate and forecast the seasonal adjustment factors.

Forecasting Models

Forecasting methods develop estimates of the future value of a time series by projecting the model components into the future. The two main types of forecasting models in current use are regression models and exponential smoothing models.

Regression models are particularly useful in modeling the long-term trend component of a time series, and are most appropriate when the time interval to be forecasted is long.

Exponential smoothing is a forecasting technique that uses a weighted average of the past value of the components of a time series to forecast the value in the next period. The technique can be used to forecast each component of the time series, and is most often used for short-term forecasts. Exponential smoothing can also be combined with regression methods to forecast the cyclical component of a time series.

Another popular technique (used in deseasonalizing the time series) is moving averages. PROPS$^+$ includes a simple moving average forecasting model for comparative purposes.

Regression Models

Regression models forecast the deseasonalized series y_t, obtained from the original observations x_t. The regression models used in PROPS$^+$ are described in the following paragraphs. In the descriptions, we refer to the point on the regression line in time period t as R_t and use the letters a, b, and q to describe model coefficients that are to be estimated.

1. no growth

$$R_t = a = \bar{y} \quad \text{(the average value of the deseasonalized series)}$$

2. linear growth

$$R_t = a + bt$$

3. percentage growth

$$R_t = e^{(a + bt)}$$

4. Gompertz

$$R_t = Ka^{b^t}$$

In each model, the coefficients are chosen to minimize the sum of the squared errors; that is, $\Sigma(y_t - R_t)^2$, where the summation is over the number of observations.

With n observations, the forecast for the deseasonalized value that will occur j periods in the future, using the regression model, is

$$\hat{y}_{n+j} = R_{n+j}$$

The seasonal adjustment is then applied to this forecast to estimate the actual observation that is anticipated j periods hence.

Exponential Smoothing Models

Simple exponential smoothing is used to forecast a time series that has no trend, such as for a deseasonalized time series without trend, or for the residual in a regression-based forecasting model. Let d_t represent the series to be forecast, so

$$\begin{aligned} d_t &= y_t & \text{for a deseasonalized time series} \\ &= y_t - R_t & \text{the residual in a regression-based model} \end{aligned}$$

The simple exponential smoothing model finds a smoothed estimate F_t for each observed d_t through the relation:

$$F_t = \alpha\, d_t + (1 - \alpha)\, F_{t-1}$$

where α is the smoothing coefficient ($0 \leq \alpha \leq 1$). That is, the smoothed value F_t is the weighted average of the current observation, d_t, and the previous smoothed value, F_{t-1}. If α is large, the most recent data is weighted more heavily, whereas a small α places more weight on past data. This procedure smooths out the random component. (Note that exponential smoothing is similar to a moving average model.) To initialize the model, in PROPS$^+$ we let $F_1 = d_1$, which assumes we had a perfect forecast for the first period. The forecast after n observations for period n+h is then

$$\hat{y}_{n+h} = F_n \qquad \text{for a deseasonalized series forecast}$$

$$= R_{n+h} + F_n \qquad \text{for a regression-based forecast}$$

If there is a trend in the deseasonalized time series y_t, the smoothed series F_t will tend to lag behind the actual time series. In this case, we introduce a term to incorporate the changing trend, as follows. Let B_t be a smoothed estimate for the current slope of the trend in the time series; the exponential smoothing formulas are then

$$F_t = \alpha \, y_t + (1 - \alpha) \, (F_{t-1} + B_{t-1})$$

$$B_t = \beta \, (F_t - F_{t-1}) + (1 - \beta) \, B_{t-1}$$

Here β ($0 \leq \beta \leq 1$) is the trend smoothing coefficient, and is used to smooth and update the estimate of the current trend. The equations are initialized by setting

$$F_1 = d_1$$

$$B_1 = (y_n - y_1)/(n - 1)$$

The deseasonalized time series forecast after n observations for time period n+j is then

$$\hat{y}_{n+j} = F_n + j*B_n$$

This is called the Holt model.

Suppose the series contains both a trend and a seasonal component. If the seasonality is constant, the series can be deseasonalized as just described and the Holt model applied to the result. If the seasonal characteristics are slowly changing over time, then exponential smoothing can be applied to the seasonal adjustment factor through the relation:

$$S_t = \gamma \, x_t/F_t + (1 - \gamma) \, S_{t-m} \qquad \text{for multiplicative seasonality}$$

$$= \gamma(x_t - F_t) + (1 - \gamma) \, S_{t-m} \qquad \text{for additive seasonality}$$

Here γ is the seasonal smoothing coefficient and m is the period of the seasonality. To initialize, the first m values for S_t are calculated as described in the earlier section on deseasonalizing a time series. When this smoothed seasonal adjustment is combined with the preceding Holt model, so that y_t is calculated using the value S_{t-m}, it is referred to as the Winters model.

In all models, the seasonal adjustment is applied to the deseasonalized forecast to estimate the actual observation that is anticipated j periods hence. The forecast of future values after n observations is

$$\hat{x}_{n+j} = S_{n+j-m} * \hat{y}_{n+j} \qquad \text{for multiplicative seasonality}$$
$$= S_{n+j-m} + \hat{y}_{n+j} \qquad \text{for additive seasonality}$$

where S_{n+j-m} is the latest estimate for the seasonality factor.

To summarize, PROPS$^+$ provides the following forecasting models:
1. regression
2. regression with exponentially smoothed cyclical component
3. simple exponential smoothing
4. simple moving average
5. exponential smoothing with trend correction (Holt model)
6. exponential smoothing with trend correction and seasonal factor update (Winters model)

Example: U.S. Retail Sales
We will illustrate using the U.S. retail sales data discussed earlier. The data is listed below.

U.S. Retail Sales (Billions of U.S. dollars)

	1987	1988	1989	1990
JAN	106.4	113.6	122.5	132.6
FEB	105.8	115.1	118.9	127.3
MAR	120.4	131.6	139.8	148.3
APR	125.4	131.0	137.9	145.0
MAY	129.1	137.6	148.2	154.1
JUN	129.0	139.1	147.1	153.5
JUL	129.0	135.4	142.6	148.9
AUG	131.0	140.2	150.9	157.4
SEP	123.8	133.0	142.1	145.6
OCT	127.2	135.9	140.2	150.7
NOV	125.4	140.3	146.3	154.6
DEC	154.8	170.8	174.8	181.4

Source: U.S. Dept. of Commerce, Bureau of the Census, BR-87-12,BR-88-12,BR-89-12,BR-90-12

This data is graphed on page 115, at the beginning of this chapter. From the graph, you can see that there is an annual seasonal cycle (12 periods). The seasonality is multiplicative, since by inspection, December sales appear to be a certain percentage above the average yearly sales and July sales appear to be a certain percentage below. We will use PROPS$^+$ to forecast retail sales for the next 12 months.

The Forecasting Spreadsheet

Begin by retrieving the ACCESS worksheet. The following menu appears on the screen:

```
                    A                              B
1                                         Copyright (C)
2          PROPS+      v1.00          E.R.Petersen & A.J.Taylor
3    Probabilistic and Optimization    Queen's University at Kingston
4            Spreadsheets              programmed by G.D.Thompson
5    ==============================    ==============================
6
7         Move cursor to the desired menu item and press [Enter]
8
9     1. Quit                          11. Simulation
10    2. LP, IP and NLP                12. Probability Distributions
11    3. Transportation/Assignment     13. Decision Analysis
12    4. Transshipment                 14. Markov Chains
13    5. Networks                      15. Dynamic Programming (DP)
14    6. Project Management            16. Stochastic DP
15    7. Forecasting
16    8. Inventory
17    9. Production planning
18   10. Queueing
```

Select **7. Forecasting** from this menu by moving the cursor to item 7 on row 15 and pressing [Enter]. You will see the following screen:

```
      A       B       C       D       E       F       G       H
1    ==============================    FORECASTING SPREADSHEET
2              PROPS+                  - models: no growth, linear,
3                                        exponential, or nonlinear growth
4           Copyright (C)             - nonseasonal, additive,
5           PROPS SYSTEMS                or multiplicative seasonality
6                                     - forecast uses
7          10/13/92 04:30 PM             regression,
8    ==============================       exponential smoothing, or
9                                         moving average.
10   INSTRUCTIONS:
11    1.   Import or create the time series (multiple) in the data area.
12    2.   Use the menu to define the range of the current time series.
13    3.   Define the type of model underlying the time series.
14    4.   Specify the type of forecasting procedure to be used.
15    5.   Press [Alt M] to run the forecast model.
16    6.   Press [F10] to graph the forecast results.
17
18               Analyst Name:     Your_name
19               Problem Name:
```

When you have typed a problem name and pressed [Enter], you will see the following screen:

```
      C       D       E       F       G       H       I       J
41   -------------------------------------------------------------------
42        forecast          |   DATA AREA: *** Enter/import time series data
43   series    error        |              below this line ***
44   -------------------------------------------------------------------
45                          |
```

The area in the worksheet down and to the right from F45 is a work area for entering time series data. This is free format, but the observed values for the time series you wish to forecast must all appear in one column. More than one time series may be entered, but each series must be in its own single column. When the retail sales data is entered, the worksheet will look like this:

```
        C       D       E       F       G       H       I       J
41 ----------------------------------------------------------------------------
42      forecast           |   DATA AREA: *** Enter/import time series data
43  series    error        |                 below this line ***
44 ----------------------------------------------------------------------------
45                         |    1987     JAN    106.4
46                         |             FEB    105.8
47                         |             MAR    120.4
48                         |             APR    125.4
49                         |             MAY    129.1
50                         |             JUN    129.0
51                         |             JUL    129.0
52                         |             AUG    131.0
53                         |             SEP    123.8
54                         |             OCT    127.2
55                         |             NOV    125.4
56                         |             DEC    154.8
57                         |    1988     JAN    113.6
58                         |             FEB    115.1
59                         |             MAR    131.6
60                         |             APR    131.0
61                         |             MAY    137.6
62                         |             JUN    139.1
63                         |             JUL    135.4
64                         .             AUG    140.2
65                         .             SEP    133.0
66                         .             OCT    135.9
67                                       NOV    140.3
68                                       DEC    170.8
69                              1989     JAN    122.5
70                                       FEB    118.9
71                                       MAR    139.8
72                                       APR    137.9
73                                       MAY    148.2
74                                       JUN    147.1
75                                       JUL    142.6
76                                       AUG    150.9
77                                       SEP    142.1
78                                       OCT    140.2
79                                       NOV    146.3
80                                       DEC    174.8
81                              1990     JAN    132.6
82                                       FEB    127.3
83                                       MAR    148.3
84                                       APR    145.0
85                                       MAY    154.1
86                                       JUN    153.5
87                                       JUL    148.9
88                                       AUG    157.4
89                                       SEP    145.6
90                                       OCT    150.7
91                                       NOV    154.6
92                                       DEC    181.4
```

If the data is in another worksheet, use the **File Combine Copy** command (**/FCC**) to import either a Range or the Entire-File; see page 21. If the data is in an ASCII file, use the **File Import Numbers** command (**/FIN**). To define the input data range, move the cursor to the top of the time series (cell H45 in this example) and press [Alt M] to get the following menu:

```
F45: 1987                                                                        MENU
Define_data_range   Execute   Optimize
Define the range containing the observed data
         A         B         C         D         E         F         G         H
```

Select **Define_data_range** by pressing [Enter]. You will be asked to enter the range of the _DATA_COLUMN, which is [H45..H92] in this example. You can indicate a different time series, or a different length for a time series, by selecting the **Define_data_range** command again. You will see the following screen:

```
          A         B         C         D         E   |    F         G         H
21  MODEL SPECIFICATION                                | SUMMARY STATISTICS
22   Seasonal        length of cycle           1 | ==================
23               multiplicative or additive    m | # of obs n              48
24   Trend    no growth             n           1 | series mean
25            linear growth         l             | std deviation
26            percentage            p             | MSE(mean sq err)
27            Gompertz (S-curve)    g             | R-squared
28  FORECAST METHOD                            1 | MAD(mean abs dv)
29   1. regression                               | MAPE(mean % err)
30   2. regression with exp. smoothed residual   | Durbin-Watson
31   3. simple exponential smoothing             | Standard BIC
32   4. simple moving average                    *** NOTE: Press [Alt M] ***
33   5. exp. smoothing with trend corr. (Holt)   *** to re-run model.  ***
34   6. exp. sm, tc, seasonal update (Winters)   | curr growth rate
35  Smoothing factors (if used)                  | REGRESSION MODEL
36    Exponential    cyclical (alpha)      0.20       a         b         k
37    smoothing         trend (beta)       0.15
38                   seasonal (gamma)      0.10   EXP. SMOOTHING MODEL
39    moving average period               5         Fn       Bn
40  Forecast horizon (periods forward)    4
```

If you press [F10], you can view the time series just defined. Press any key to return to the worksheet. The preceding screen is used to define the model and the forecasting method. The following cells contain the information defining the model:

cell E22: enter the seasonality cycle length. For this example, the data is monthly with a seasonal cycle of 12 months. Enter this value in cell E22. If the value is 1, then no seasonality is assumed.

cell E23: enter **m** if multiplicative seasonality and **a** if additive seasonality. In this example, leave the cell at the default, m.

cell E24: enter **n**o, **l**inear, **p**ercentage, or **g**ompertz to specify the trend *if a regression model* is used (forecast methods 1 and 2). In this example, use the default, l (lower case L).

cell E28: enter the number for the forecasting method desired. For now, leave its value at 1.

cell E40: enter the forecast horizon. Enter 12 in this example.

cells E36–E39: these cells contain the smoothing coefficients.

Press [Alt M] to get the menu, and select **Execute** to run the model. PROPS⁺ sets up the calculations for each method, and presents the following screen:

```
         A        B         C         D         E   |   F         G         H
21  MODEL SPECIFICATION                             | SUMMARY STATISTICS
22    Seasonal          length of cycle        12   | ===================
23                 multiplicative or additive   m   | # of obs n            48
24    Trend    no growth              n          1  | series mean      138.37
25             linear growth          l             | std deviation     15.80
26             percentage             p             | MSE(mean sq err) 3.3434
27             Gompertz (S-curve)     g             | R-squared       0.985658
28  FORECAST METHOD                            1    | MAD(mean abs dv) 1.4177
29    1. regression                                 | MAPE(mean % err)  1.01%
30    2. regression with exp. smoothed residual     | Durbin-Watson  1.929646
31    3. simple exponential smoothing               | Standard BIC   4.196521
32    4. simple moving average                      |
33    5. exp. smoothing with trend corr. (Holt)     |
34    6. exp. sm, tc, seasonal update (Winters)     | curr growth rate   0.44%
35  Smoothing factors (if used)                     | REGRESSION MODEL
36      Exponential     cyclical (alpha)    0.20    |     a         b         k
37      smoothing          trend (beta)     0.15    | 121.7424 0.672346
38                      seasonal (gamma)     0.10    | EXP. SMOOTHING MODEL
39      moving average period               5       |    Fn        Bn
40  Forecast horizon (periods forward)      12
```

The default forecast based on a linear growth regression model is used. To see a graph of the actual and forecast values, press [F10] and you will see the following graph:

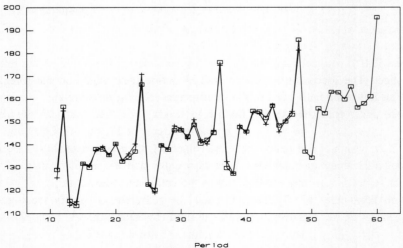

Period
□ Forecast   + Actuals

Press any key to return to the spreadsheet. Because the length of the seasonal cycle is greater than 1, the original time series, x_t, is deseasonalized and the regression model is fitted to the deseasonalized data. The seasonality factors are applied to the forecast deseasonalized values to produce the forecast. If the seasonal cycle is 1, the models are fitted to the original time series.

Summary statistics showing the "goodness of fit" measures for the forecasting model are displayed on the main screen. For this model the mean square error (MSE) is 3.3434, the R-squared value between forecasted and actual data is 0.985658, the mean absolute deviation (MAD) is 1.4177, and the mean absolute percentage error (MAPE) is 1.01%. The Durbin-Watson statistic is 1.9296. The Durbin-Watson statistic is not an accuracy measure per se, but rather indicates whether there is first-order autocorrelation in the errors after the forecasting method has been applied. If the errors are essentially random, the Durbin-Watson statistic will be approximately 2. Positive correlation between successive errors will give a value of less than 2, and negative correlation a value greater than 2. (A rule of thumb is that Durbin-Watson values in the range 1.5-2.5 indicate little autocorrelation in the error terms, so this model output supports the conclusion that the errors are random.)

The objective of forecasting is to find the model that will produce the best forecast, not the best fit to the historical data. The model that explains the historical data best may not be the best predictive model for two reasons. The first is that the model may involve too many parameters. For example, if the model has the same number of parameters as data points, the fit could be perfect but the forecasting capability very poor. The second reason is that the time series may be nonrecurrent. A common measure used to compare models is the standardized BIC (Bayes Information Criterion) measure. The lower the value, the better the predictive capability. This measure is useful for comparison of different models for the same historical data set.

The model parameters are summarized in the range [F36..H40]. If a regression model is used, the estimated coefficients are displayed. Similarly, if exponential smoothing is used, the smoothed estimates for the last observation (time period n) are displayed.

You can change the model specifications on the main screen to see the impact on the model fit of a change in assumption or forecasting method. For example, you can select a different forecasting method simply by changing the number in cell E28. Try different values and observe the resulting "goodness of fit" measures. You can press [F10] to see a plot of the series and the fitted model in each case.

PROPS+ also provides a special feature that allows you to determine optimal values for the exponential smoothing coefficients, to minimize the mean squared error of the fitted model. For instance, for the above data, suppose you select forecast method 5 (the Holt model). The resulting MSE is 3.6460, based on the default smoothing coefficients of $\alpha = .20$ and $\beta = .15$. This indicates that the Holt model with these coefficients does not fit quite as well as the linear regression model. To find the optimal values of the smoothing coefficients for the minimum MSE, press [Alt M], select **Optimize**, and press [Enter]. When the Solver has completed its solution, it will beep and you will see a completion message similar to the following:

```
E28: U[W6]5                                                                    EDIT
Results within tolerance; solution data follows   Press ENTER
Trial Solution: 11
          A         B         C         D         E         F         G         H
```

Press [Enter] and PROPS+ will return the optimal values $\alpha = .03$ and $\beta = 1.00$, which yield the minimum MSE for a Holt model, 3.4566. Note that even the best Holt model does not fit this data as well as the linear regression model.

You can scan columns C and D to examine the fitted deseasonalized series and errors. Use the [PgDn] key to see the forecast values in column C for time periods n to n+h.

```
                A         B          C         D       E      F       G         H
41   -----------------------------------------------------|-------------------------------
42   time      seasonal      forecast              |  DATA AREA: *** Enter/import
43   period     factor    series    error          |                      below thi
44   -----------------------------------------------------|-------------------------------
45   1         0.884834                             |  1987 JAN            106.4
46   2         0.864008 104.4478  1.352112          |       FEB            105.8
47   3         0.998415 121.4299 -1.02997           |       MAR            120.4
48   4         0.980515 119.8645  5.535431          |       APR            125.4
49   5         1.036411 127.7359  1.364060          |       MAY            129.1
                   :                                |
                   :                                |
89   45        0.975885 147.3597 -1.75978           |       SEP            145.6
90   46        0.982683 148.7390  1.960942          |       OCT            150.7
91   47        0.998153 151.6163  2.983637          |       NOV            154.6
92   48        1.207019 184.1378 -2.73785           |       DEC            181.4
93   49 est.   0.884834 135.3655
94   50 est.   0.864008 132.6094
95   51 est.   0.998415 153.7353
96   52 est.   0.980515 151.4670
97   53 est.   1.036411 160.6175
98   54 est.   1.030478 160.2109
99   55 est.   1.006519 156.9869
100  56 est.   1.037843 162.3891
101  57 est.   0.975885 153.1804
102  58 est.   0.982683 154.7364
103  59 est.   0.998153 157.6691
104  60 est.   1.207019 191.2625
```

The seasonality factors for each period are shown in column B.

Example: Purr-fect Cat Food

The Purr-fect Cat Food company has recorded the following quarterly gross sales (measured in thousands of dollars) for a certain line of dry cat kibble and is interested in forecasting future kibble sales.

period	sales	period	sales	period	sales
1	4.21	15	46.31	29	54.37
2	13.12	16	38.33	30	59.32
3	16.13	17	41.23	31	59.49
4	15.93	18	36.69	32	58.77
5	10.61	19	28.47	33	46.36
6	8.64	20	32.39	34	51.90
7	10.78	21	36.50	35	61.02
8	13.57	22	33.01	36	59.99
9	15.99	23	46.66	37	57.76
10	14.39	24	49.74	38	63.18
11	27.68	25	47.97	39	53.76
12	33.12	26	55.09	40	48.49
13	30.80	27	54.61	41	50.96
14	37.17	28	61.60		

To forecast the future kibble sales using PROPS⁺, access the forecasting spreadsheet from the main menu and enter the data into a single column. Define the data range and press [F10] to plot the time series. The following graph appears:

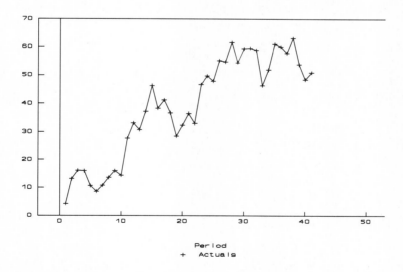

No seasonal pattern is apparent from the graph, and so the seasonality cycle is left at 1. Since the sales appear to be increasing at a reasonably linear rate, you might choose to fit a linear regression model to this data. This is the PROPS⁺ default, so you can simply press [Alt M] and select **Execute**, which gives the following screen:

```
          A         B          C         D        E    |    F          G          H
21  MODEL SPECIFICATION                               |  SUMMARY STATISTICS
22  Seasonal          length of cycle           1  |  ==================
23                    multiplicative or additive m  |  # of obs n              41
24  Trend   no growth              n            1  |  series mean          38.69
25          linear growth          1               |  std deviation        17.80
26          percentage             p               |  MSE(mean sq err) 57.3865
27          Gompertz (S-curve)     g               |  R-squared         0.805537
28  FORECAST METHOD                              1  |  MAD(mean abs dv)   6.4718
29   1. regression                                  |  MAPE(mean % err)   22.15%
30   2. regression with exp. smoothed residual      |  Durbin-Watson     0.598441
31   3. simple exponential smoothing                |  Standard BIC     74.36011
32   4. simple moving average                       |
33   5. exp. smoothing with trend corr. (Holt)      |
34   6. exp. sm, tc, seasonal update (Winters)      |  curr growth rate     2.07%
35  Smoothing factors (if used)                    |  REGRESSION MODEL
36    Exponential    cyclical (alpha)     0.20     |        a          b          k
37    smoothing         trend (beta)      0.15  10.08785 1.361797
38                   seasonal (gamma)     0.10     EXP. SMOOTHING MODEL
39      moving average period              5          Fn        Bn
40  Forecast horizon (periods forward)     4
```

Press [F10] to see the following plot:

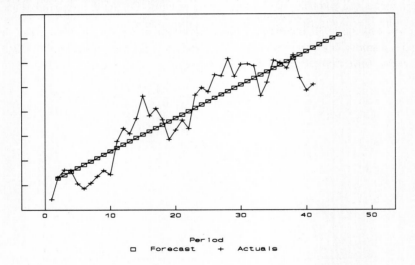

The regression line in this graph appears to overstate the sales in the later periods. That is, it looks like sales are starting to "tail off" in the later periods. To select a different model, change the trend specification in cell E24 to **g** for the Gompertz S-shaped curve, and press [F10] to generate the following graph. (**Note:** you do not need to execute the model again—changing cell E24 automatically brings up the new model.)

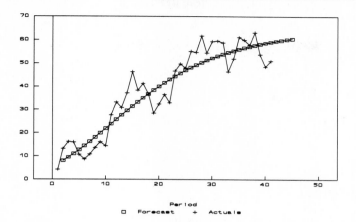

Note that the MSE has dropped from 57.3865 to 41.1657, and the nonlinear regression line fits the data much better. The Durbin-Watson statistic is 0.82, which suggests that the successive residuals are correlated. If forecast method 2 is used, these residuals are smoothed, and the MSE increases slightly. However, if we use the **optimize** command, the optimal smoothing coefficient is $\alpha=0.79$ and the MSE decreases to 33.95. The actual and forecast series appear in the following graph:

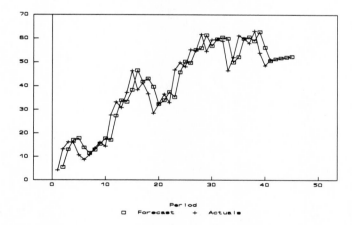

The optimize command uses the Solver to search for the values of the smoothing coefficients that will minimize the MSE. Starting from the initial coefficient settings, this procedure will find locally optimal values for the coefficients. Usually these will also be globally optimal values, but this cannot be guaranteed in all instances. To ensure that global values for the smoothing coefficients have been found, you can start with different initial settings and repeat the optimization procedure.

Features

1. **<u>Deterministic EOQ Model</u>**

   ■ allows price breaks.

   ■ permits comparison of optimal and actual policy costs.

2. **<u>Probabilistic EOQ Model</u>**

   ■ uses a continuous review model.

   ■ allows normally distributed demand during lead time.

   ■ permits use of an arbitrary distribution of demand during lead time.

Chapter 8. Inventory

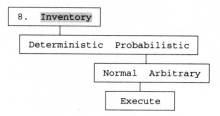

The two principal questions in inventory control are how much of a good or material should be ordered or produced, and how often should this be done, to provide a reasonable level of service at the lowest cost. Higher levels of inventory mean higher storage costs and higher interest costs on the capital investment in the inventory. On the other hand, lower levels of inventory mean higher costs from not having the material when needed ("stockout"), and higher costs from less efficient production or ordering (smaller orders or shorter runs). Inventory control models seek an optimal balance between these sources of cost.

This chapter describes Economic Order Quantity ("EOQ") inventory models, in both deterministic and probabilistic forms. The deterministic EOQ model is useful when the demand for an item is steady and the purchaser wishes to determine the size of order to place to take fixed ordering costs and price breaks into account. The probabilistic EOQ model is used to establish order quantities and safety stock when the demand for the item fluctuates over time.

We begin with an overview of the single-item inventory control problem to establish a common vocabulary and point of view. We then examine each of the models in turn, illustrating in particular the power of PROPS⁺ in examining the sensitivity of model results to assumptions.

The Inventory Control Problem: Definitions and Notation

Suppose we are stocking a single item that has an uncertain demand over time. One possible rule for maintaining inventory is "when the inventory level drops below s (the reorder point), order Q units, which will bring the inventory level up to S (the order-up-to point)." If there is a "lead time," or delay, between submitting an order and receiving the units, we may run out of inventory and suffer a shortage. When inventory is received, the units in shortage ("backorders") are made up first and the remainder of the shipment of Q units is available for use during the next time period. The level of inventory over time with this control system is shown in the following figure. (If backorders are not allowed, the inventory level would remain at zero until the shipment arrives. At that point the inventory level would jump to Q and the process would repeat.)

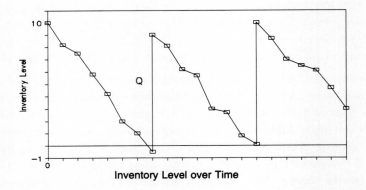

Inventory Level over Time

In order to find the optimal inventory control policy, we must make some assumptions about the costs involved in the problem. Typical parameters, which may or may not apply to given situations, are discussed in the following paragraphs.

Ordering or Setup Cost K: A fixed cost incurred each time the level of inventory is increased that does not depend on the size of the increase. This cost may reflect the cost of preparing an order or of setting up and shutting down a machine for a production run of this item.

Unit Purchase Cost c: The variable cost incurred by purchasing or producing one unit. If quantity discounts are available, c depends on quantity ordered.

Holding or Carrying Cost h: The annual cost of carrying one unit in inventory. This cost includes the lost interest from having capital tied up in inventory, plus any storage charges, warehouse handling costs, and spoilage.

Stockout Cost p: the cost (whether real or intangible) incurred when shortages occur. In the deterministic EOQ model, shortage cost is per item short per unit time. In the probabilistic EOQ model, shortage cost is assumed to be proportional to the shortage quantity, and does not take "shortage time" into account. This cost includes the loss of goodwill from not being able to supply the customer. If shortages are not backlogged, p should also include the lost contribution to profits. A convenient way to model an inventory problem in which stockout is not permitted is to make p a very large number, so that a cost-minimizing solution will not allow shortages.

Annual Demand Rate *a:* This is the expected annual demand for the item and is assumed to occur uniformly over the year.

In the model descriptions that follow, we discuss assumptions and computational formulas but suggest you consult standard textbooks for mathematical derivations (see the Preface, page iv). For each model, a short description will be followed by an example and further analysis, concluding with some observations on the application of the model where appropriate.

Deterministic EOQ Model

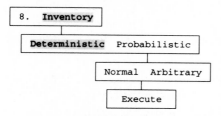

The Model:

$$Q = \sqrt{\frac{2aK}{h} \frac{p+h}{p}} \qquad s = \sqrt{\frac{2aK}{p} \frac{h}{p+h}} \ ; \quad S = Q + s$$

Computations: PROPS[+] directly calculates the policy variables and cost components from these formulas.

Limitations: The model assumes demand is deterministic and that orders arrive at a uniform rate.

The inventory level over time with this model appears as follows:

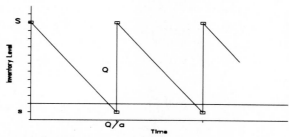

Deterministic Inventory Level over Time

The most fundamental of inventory models, this model assumes that demand is uniform and known with certainty and that resupply is instantaneous. The optimal policy is to order Q units every (Q/a) of a year, and as shown in the figure, the inventory level fluctuates between s and S. We will use the following example (with modifications) to illustrate each of the PROPS⁺ models.

Example: The Widget Problem

Suppose you are maintaining an inventory of widgets for sale. It costs $40 to submit an order for more widgets, which have a purchase price of $100 each. Your cost of capital is 12%, so that holding one widget in inventory for one year costs $12 in foregone interest income. The cost of warehousing one widget for a year is $2 (widgets don't spoil or become obsolete), making the total cost of holding one widget for a year $14. There is a constant demand for widgets of 520 per year, spread evenly across the year. If shortages are allowed, we will impose a shortage cost of $10 per widget short each time there is a shortage.

To analyze this model using PROPS⁺, begin by retrieving the ACCESS worksheet, and select **8. Inventory**. The following menu appears:

```
A16:                                                                  MENU
Deterministic  Probabilistic
EOQ Calculation under deterministic conditions
         A         B         C         D         E         F         G         H
```

Select **Deterministic** from this menu; the following screen will appear:

```
         A         B         C         D         E         F         G         H
1    ==============================
2              PROPS+                      DETERMINISTIC EOQ SPREADSHEET
3                                          (Economic Order Quantity)
4         Copyright (C)          - quantity discounts
5         PROPS SYSTEMS
6
7         03/11/92 08:15 PM
8    ==============================
9
10   Instructions:
11           Enter values into the INPUT DATA area. The decision variables
12           (Q and s) and the other derived figures will be automatically
13           re-calculated and entered into the "Optimal" column. You can
14           then change the "Actual" column to see the cost effects of
15           deviations from the optimal policy.
16
17           PROMPT mode when CMD is on. Type response, press [ENTER].
18
```

When you press [Enter], you are prompted for a problem name. Type a name and press [Enter]. You are then presented with the following worksheet. (The worksheet assumes default values for the variables, as shown, which you can later modify.)

	A	B	C	D	E	F	G	H
21		Analyst Name		Your_name				
22		Problem Name		widget				
23								
24	INPUT DATA:							
25		Fixed Transaction (Ordering) cost per order ("K")						50
26		Purchase (Production) Quantity Discounts						
27		unit cost "c"		if buy at least				
28			0	0				
29			0	0				
30			0	0				
31			0	0				
32			0	0				
33		Inventory Holding cost						
34			warehousing cost per unit per year					1
35			annual cost of capital in percent				%	0
36		Annual Demand ("a")						100
37								
38		Shortage cost per unit per year ("p")						1.0E+30
39		(very large ==> shortages not allowed)						

You can now enter the problem data directly into the worksheet. In this example, the fixed transaction cost is $40, the purchase cost is $100 per widget, the warehousing cost is $2 per year, the cost of capital is 12%, and the annual demand is 520. The optimal values are recalculated automatically as data is entered. After you enter the data the worksheet appears as follows:

	A	B	C	D	E	F	G	H
24	INPUT DATA:							
25		Fixed Transaction (Ordering) cost per order ("K")						40
26		Purchase (Production) Quantity Discounts						
27		unit cost "c"		if buy at least				
28			100	0				
29			0	0				
30			0	0				
31			0	0				
32			0	0				
33		Inventory Holding cost						
34			warehousing cost per unit per year					2
35			annual cost of capital in percent				%	12
36		Annual Demand ("a")						520
37								
38		Shortage cost per unit per year ("p")						1.0E+30
39		(very large ==> shortages not allowed)						
40								
41	DECISION VARIABLES:					Optimal	Actual	
42		Order Quantity ("Q")				54.51	54.51	
43		Re-Order Point ("s")				0.00	0.00	
44								
45	==>	Order-Up-To Point ("S")				54.51	54.51	
46		Number of Orders per year				9.54	9.54	
47		Purchase (Production) cost per unit				100	100	
48		Total holding cost per year ("h")				14	14	
49								
50	COST BREAKDOWN:					Optimal	Actual	
51		Annual Fixed Ordering cost				381.58	381.58	
52		Annual Unit Ordering cost				52000.00	52000.00	
53		Annual Inventory Holding cost				381.58	381.58	
54		Annual Shortage cost				0.00	0.00	
55						------------------		
56		Total Annual Cost				52763.15	52763.15	
57						==================		

In this worksheet, the "Optimal" column contains the optimal values for the decision variables, assuming that all the variables are continuous. The "Actual" column permits you to determine the total cost if values other than the optimal ones for Q and s are chosen (for instance, if you choose integer values or standard order quantities for these variables, or values corresponding to current practice). For example, you could move the cursor to cell G42 and enter 60 to see the effect of ordering 60 units every time the inventory level reaches zero. This is illustrated in the following figure:

	A	B	C	D	E	F	G	H
41	DECISION VARIABLES:					Optimal	Actual	
42		Order Quantity ("Q")				54.51	60.00	
43		Re-Order Point ("s")				0.00	0.00	
44								
45	==> Order-Up-To Point ("S")					54.51	60.00	
46		Number of Orders per year				9.54	8.67	
47		Purchase (Production) cost per unit				100	100	
48		Total holding cost per year ("h")				14	14	
49								
50	COST BREAKDOWN:					Optimal	Actual	
51		Annual Fixed Ordering cost				381.58	346.67	
52		Annual Unit Ordering cost				52000.00	52000.00	
53		Annual Inventory Holding cost				381.58	420.00	
54		Annual Shortage cost				0.00	0.00	
55						------------------		
56		Total Annual Cost				52763.15	52766.67	
57						==================		
58								

Note that the cost per year has risen by $3.52 as a result of selecting nonoptimal values. A natural question is: How sensitive is the total cost to variations across a range of Q values? The clearest way to show this is by a graph, and you can use the capabilities of the spreadsheet to construct such a graph, as described on page 23. The **Data Fill** command can be used to create a set of Q values in the range [A61..A68]. Move the cursor to B60 and enter the formula **+G56**. Now, using the **Data Table 1** command (**/DT1**), define the table range as **[A60..B68]** and the input cell as **G42**. A table of costs corresponding to these Q values is generated. Titles have been added in [A58..B59] to describe the column contents, as shown in the following table:

	A	B	C	D	E	F
58	order					
59	Q	Cost				
60		52766.67				
61	30	52903.33				
62	40	52800.00				
63	50	52766.00				
64	60	52766.67				
65	70	52787.14				
66	80	52820.00				
67	90	52861.11				
68	100	52908.00				
69						

A convenient way to visualize the results is via the **Graph** command (**/G**) using the graph type **XY**, and adding titles with the **Graph Options Titles** command (**/GOT**). This sequence produces the following graph:

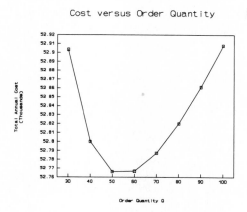

A similar procedure can be used to examine the sensitivity of the model results to any of the assumptions in the model (the **Data Table 2** command (**/DT2**) permits sensitivity analysis on two parameters). Sensitivity to multiple value changes can be determined by selecting an appropriate grid of parameter values and copying model output directly to a tabular representation of the grid.

In the preceding example, the unit ordering cost is constant because 520 widgets must be ordered each year at a cost of $100 each, for a total cost of $52,000. The annual capital carrying cost for a widget is 12% of $100, or $12 per widget per year. Note that the same solution would have been obtained if the unit ordering cost had been set to 0 and the warehousing cost had been increased from $2 to $14 per item per year. In this case, the unit ordering cost could have been disregarded in determining the optimal decision, as is done in many texts.

Quantity Discounts

Suppose volume discounts are available when ordering widgets. For example, suppose the following price schedule is available from the supplier:

price per unit	quantity ordered
$100	0 to <100
95	100 to <500
90	500 or more

In this case the cost of ordering becomes very important and must always be included, since the objective is to minimize the sum of the annual ordering and inventory costs. To include the quantity discounts, you can enter the purchasing price breaks as follows. The basic cost is $100 (cell C28). The cost drops to $95 (cell C29) if you order at least 100 (cell D29), and if you order at least 500 (cell D30) the cost is $90 (cell C30). With these values entered, the spreadsheet will look like this:

```
          A        B         C        D        E        F        G        H
21                Analyst Name       Your_name
22                Problem Name       Widgets with price breaks
23
24   INPUT DATA:
25                Fixed Transaction (Ordering) cost per order ("K")         40
26                Purchase (Production) Quantity Discounts
27                     unit cost "c"   if buy at least
28                          100          0
29                           95        100
30                           90        500
31                            0          0
32                            0          0
33                Inventory Holding cost
34                          warehousing cost per unit per year             2
35                          annual cost of capital in percent       %     12
36                Annual Demand ("a")                                     520
37
38                Shortage cost per unit per year ("p")          1.0E+30
39                (very large ==> shortages not allowed)
40
41   DECISION VARIABLES:                          Optimal   Actual
42                Order Quantity ("Q")             500.00   500.00
43                Re-Order Point ("s")               0.00     0.00
44
45       ==> Order-Up-To Point ("S")               500.00   500.00
46                Number of Orders per year           1.04     1.04
47                Purchase (Production) cost per unit     90       90
48                Total holding cost per year ("h")     12.8     12.8
49
50   COST BREAKDOWN:                              Optimal   Actual
51                Annual Fixed Ordering cost        41.60    41.60
52                Annual Unit Ordering cost      46800.00 46800.00
53                Annual Inventory Holding cost   3200.00  3200.00
54                Annual Shortage cost               0.00     0.00
55                                               ------------------
56                Total Annual Cost              50041.60 50041.60
57                                               ==================
58
```

Note that with quantity discounts, the orders are much larger (500 versus 54), yielding an annual saving of $52763 − 50041 = $2722 over the case without quantity discounts. Again, we can perform a sensitivity analysis to see how costs change with the quantity ordered. Use the **Data Fill** command (**/DF**) to create a range of order quantities from 25 to 700 in steps of 25, and then the **Data Table 1** command (**/DT1**) to create the following table:

	A	B	C	D
58		Quantity	Total	
59		ordered	cost	
60			50041.6	
61		25	53007	
62		50	52766	
63		75	52802.33	
64		100	50278	
65		125	50403.9	
66		150	50543.66	
67		175	50691.35	
68		200	50844	
69		225	50999.94	
70		250	51158.2	
71		275	51318.13	
72		300	51479.33	
73		325	51641.5	
74		350	51804.42	
75		375	51967.96	
76		400	52132	
77		425	52296.44	
78		450	52461.22	
79		475	52626.28	
80		500	50041.6	
81		525	50199.61	
82		550	50357.81	
83		575	50516.17	
84		600	50674.66	
85		625	50833.28	
86		650	50992	
87		675	51150.81	
88		700	51309.71	

The effect of price breaks is shown in the following graph:

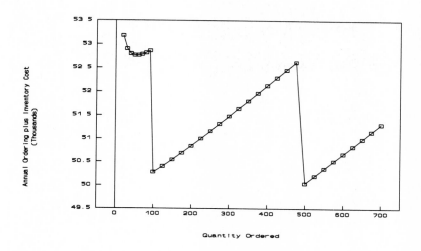

Note that buying "right" is more important in this example than the cost of carrying extra inventory.

Shortages

You can use this model to explore what happens if shortages are allowed. To illustrate, we shall assume that the ordering cost is $100, and no quantity discounts are available. Assume a cost of $10 per widget each time there is a stockout. Recall that the optimal inventory policy with large stockout cost suggested ordering widgets about 10 times per year. Since you will have a stockout each period with a deterministic model, this suggests an annual stockout charge of about (10 x $10 =) $100 per widget short. However, the average duration of a stockout will be at most 10% of the total time, corresponding to a shortage cost of $1,000 per widget for a full year. As you see, this "appropriate" shortage cost is approximate at best, and the model results should be checked for sensitivity. Changing the stockout cost to $1,000 (cell H38) yields the following solution:

	A	B	C	D	E	F	G	H
24	INPUT DATA:							
25		Fixed Transaction (Ordering) cost per order ("K")						40
26		Purchase (Production) Quantity Discounts						
27			cost "c"	if buy more than				
28			100	0				
29			0	0				
30			0	0				
31			0	0				
32			0	0				
33		Inventory Holding cost						
34				warehousing cost per unit per year				2
35				annual cost of capital in percent		%	12
36		Annual Demand ("a")						520
37								
38		Shortage cost per unit per year ("p")						1000
39		(very large ==> shortages not allowed)						
40								
41	DECISION VARIABLES:					Optimal	Actual	
42		Order Quantity ("Q")				54.89	54.89	
43		Re-Order Point ("s")				-0.76	-0.76	
44								
45	==> Order-Up-To Point ("S")					54.13	54.13	
46		Number of Orders per year				9.47	9.47	
47		Purchase (Production) cost per unit				100	100	
48		Total holding cost per year ("h")				14	14	
49								
50	COST BREAKDOWN:					Optimal	Actual	
51		Annual Fixed Ordering cost				378.93	378.93	
52		Annual Unit Ordering cost				52000.00	52000.00	
53		Annual Inventory Holding cost				373.70	373.70	
54		Annual Shortage cost				5.23	5.23	
55						------------------		
56		Total Annual Cost				52757.86	52757.86	
57						==================		
58								

In a deterministic inventory problem with stockouts allowed, it is optimal to allow some shortages. However, these shortages will be small (here, about one unit each inventory cycle).

Probabilistic EOQ Model

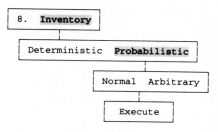

The Model:

$$Y = \int_{x=s}^{\infty} (x - s)p(x)dx \qquad Q = \sqrt{\frac{2a(K + pY)}{h}} \qquad \int_{x=s}^{\infty} p(x)dx = \frac{hQ}{pa}$$

where

$p(x)$ = the probability distribution of demand
Y = the expected shortage
Q = the reorder quantity
s = the reorder point
a = the expected annual demand

Computation: PROPS⁺ uses an iterative procedure to calculate Q and s. This procedure converges if

$$\frac{pa}{h} \geq \sqrt{\frac{2a(K + pE[x])}{h}}$$

where $E[x]$ is the expected demand during the lead time.

Limitations: i) Holding costs are based on average inventory, including shortages.

ii) Shortage cost is assumed to be proportional to the shortage, quantity without taking shortage time into account.

This problem is similar to the deterministic EOQ problem in that the expected annual demand is known, along with the fixed cost of ordering, holding cost, and penalty cost. However, this model allows for a random demand during the lead time between the time an order is placed and the time that the material ordered is available for distribution. Thus it is particularly useful in determining the safety stock level.

PROPS⁺ provides two versions of this model. The first assumes that the demand during lead time is normally distributed, and the second solves the problem for any arbitrary discrete distribution of demand during lead time.

Normal Demand during Lead Time

Return to the widget problem, but now suppose that replenishment of widgets is not instantaneous, and that it takes two weeks for an order to be filled. The mean demand during lead time is 20, and suppose the standard deviation is 5.

To find the optimal inventory policy, access PROPS+ and select **8. Inventory,** **Probabilistic**, and **Normal** from the successive menus. You will see the following screen:

```
         A        B        C        D        E        F        G        H
1    ==============================     PROBABILISTIC EOQ SPREADSHEET
2              PROPS+                       (Economic Order Quantity)
3                                         - continuous review model
4            Copyright (C)                - normal demand distribution during
5            PROPS SYSTEMS                    lead time
6                                         - ref: Hamdy Taha, Optns R. 5th Ed.
7            09/24/92 05:32 PM                  MacMillan, pp. 515-517
8    ==============================     - an iterative procedure is used to
9                                           calculate the reorder point and
10                                          the order quantity
11   Instructions:
12
13           PROMPT mode when CMD is on.  Type response, press [Enter].
14
15           [Alt M] -- Presents user with MENU of possible actions.
16
17
18           Analyst Name?      Your_name
19           Problem Name?
20
```

Type in the problem name and press [Enter]. You will see the following screen:

```
         A        B        C        D        E        F        G
21   INPUT DATA:
22
23       Demand during lead time probability distribution: NORMAL
24           Mean            2
25           Std Dev         1
26
27           Fixed Transaction cost per order ("K")              0
28           Purchase cost per unit [optional] ("c")             0
29           Expected Annual Demand ("a")                        0
30           Holding cost per unit per year ("h")                0
31           Shortage cost per unit ("p")                        0
32
33           Max. No. of Iterations            10
34
35                   (Enter data, then hit [Alt M] for the commands menu)
36
```

You are now in READY mode and can enter the problem data, as follows:

	A	B	C	D	E	F	G	H
21	INPUT DATA:							
22								
23	Demand during lead time probability distribution: NORMAL							
24		Mean	20					
25		Std Dev	5					
26								
27		Fixed Transaction cost per order ("K")					40	
28		Purchase cost per unit [optional] ("c")					0	
29		Expected Annual Demand ("a")					520	
30		Holding cost per unit per year ("h")					14	
31		Shortage cost per unit ("p")					10	
32								
33		Max. No. of Iterations	10					

In this model, you enter the holding cost per unit per year, which is the sum of the warehousing cost plus the capital carrying cost. Press [Alt M] to call up the execution menu and select **Execute**. The solution appears in the worksheet as follows:

	A	B	C	D	E	F	G	H
36								
37	DECISION VARIABLES:					Optimal	Actual	
38		Order Quantity ("Q")				57.18	57.18	
39		Re-Order Point ("s")				25.10	25.10	
40								
41	==>	Order-Up-To Point ("S")				82.28	82.28	
42		Number of Orders per year				9.09	9.09	
43		Probability of Shortage				0.15	0.15	
44		Expected Shortage ("Y")				0.40	0.40	
45								
46	COST BREAKDOWN:					Optimal	Actual	
47		Annual Ordering (Setup) cost				363.78	363.78	
48		Annual Purchase (Production) cost				0.00	0.00	
49		Annual Inventory Holding cost				471.63	471.63	
50		Annual Shortage Penalty cost				36.46	36.46	
51						------------------		
52		Total Annual Cost				871.88	871.88	
53						==================		

Note that the order size is similar to the deterministic EOQ model, but because of the uncertain demand during lead time, we must order sooner, and on the average carry more inventory. Inventory holding costs have increased by about $90.

You can use the "Actual" column (G) to test the sensitivity of the inventory costs as the order quantity and reorder point are changed. For example, suppose the order quantity is 60 and the reorder point is 25. Inserting these values into the "Actual" column yields the following worksheet entries:

```
         A          B          C          D          E          F          G          H
36
37  DECISION VARIABLES:                                             Optimal    Actual
38            Order Quantity ("Q")                                   57.18     60.00
39            Re-Order Point ("s")                                   25.10     25.00
40
41    ==>     Order-Up-To Point ("S")                                82.28     85.00
42            Number of Orders per year                               9.09      8.67
43            Probability of Shortage                                 0.15      0.16
44            Expected Shortage ("Y")                                 0.40      0.42
45
46  COST BREAKDOWN:                                                 Optimal    Actual
47            Annual Ordering (Setup) cost                          363.78    346.67
48            Annual Purchase (Production) cost                       0.00      0.00
49            Annual Inventory Holding cost                         471.63    490.00
50            Annual Shortage Penalty cost                           36.46     36.10
51                                                                --------------------
52            Total Annual Cost                                     871.88    872.76
53                                                                ====================
```

The deviation from an optimal policy results in increased expected costs of about $0.88 per year.

Arbitrary Demand during Lead Time

Now suppose that in the widget problem you have the following distribution for demand during the lead time:

Demand x	5	10	15	20	25	30	35
Probability P(x)	.05	.1	.2	.3	.2	.1	.05

This arbitrary distribution has the same mean as the previous normal distribution, but a larger variance. To find the optimal policy, select **8. Inventory** from the ACCESS worksheet. Then select **Probabilistic** and **Arbitrary** from the successive menus. Enter a problem name and press the [Enter] key. PROPS⁺ then requests information about the random demand during the lead time. The following screen appears:

```
         A          B          C          D          E          F          G          H
21  INPUT DATA:
22
23      Demand during lead time probability distribution:
24
25            Demand ranges from
```

Type a number for the lowest value of demand during lead time and press [Enter]. Then type the highest value and again press [Enter]. Finally, when the prompt calls for an increment size (the default is 1), type the increment you wish to use in the distribution.

In the example, the demand varies from 5 to 35 in steps of 5. Once the increment is entered, the following screen appears:

	A	B	C	D	E	F	G	H
24								
25		Demand ranges from		5	to	35		
26		in increments of		5				
27								
28		*** Warning: Probabilities do not sum to one ***						
29	Demand	5	10	15	20	25	30	35
30	Prob.	0	0	0	0	0	0	0
31								
32		==> Expected Demand during lead time =					0	
33								
34								
35		Fixed Transaction cost per order ("K")					0	
36		Purchase cost per unit [optional] ("c")					0	
37		Expected Annual Demand ("a")					0	
38		Holding cost per unit per year ("h")					0	
39		Shortage cost per unit ("p")					0	
40								
41		Max. No. of Iterations		10				

(If the distribution does not have uniform increments, begin with a uniform increment scale to create the correct number of sample points. Later, you can alter the demand values as well as the probabilities to create a nonuniform scale.) You can now move the cursor to enter the probability distribution for the demand over the range of values you have indicated. (As soon as the probability distribution is completed and sums to 1, the warning message above the distribution disappears.) In addition, you can enter the cost data that corresponds exactly to the previous case. When you enter the widget data with the above distribution for demand during the lead time, the following worksheet appears:

	A	B	C	D	E	F	G	H
28								
29	Demand	5	10	15	20	25	30	35
30	Prob.	0.05	0.1	0.2	0.3	0.2	0.1	0.05
31								
32		==> Expected Demand during lead time =					20	
33								
34								
35		Fixed Transaction cost per order ("K")					40	
36		Purchase cost per unit [optional] ("c")					0	
37		Expected Annual Demand ("a")					520	
38		Holding cost per unit per year ("h")					14	
39		Shortage cost per unit ("p")					10	
40								
41		Max. No. of Iterations		10				
42								
43		(Enter data, then hit [Alt M] for the commands menu)						
44								

With this probabilistic data, PROPS⁺ uses an iterative technique to find the optimal solution. You can control how many iterations PROPS⁺ will go through by altering the cell corresponding to "Max. No. of Iterations", although for most reasonable problems 10 iterations is sufficient.

To find the optimal solution, press [Alt M] and a menu appears at the top of the screen with only one choice—**Execute**. Pressing [Enter] to select **Execute** yields the following worksheet:

	A	B	C	D	E	F	G	H
44								
45	DECISION VARIABLES:					Optimal	Actual	
46		Order Quantity ("Q")				60.94	60.94	
47		Re-Order Point ("s")				25.00	25.00	
48								
49	==>	Order-Up-To Point ("S")				85.94	85.94	
50		Number of Orders per year				8.53	8.53	
51		Probability of Shortage				0.15	0.15	
52		Expected Shortage ("Y")				1.00	1.00	
53								
54	COST BREAKDOWN:					Optimal	Actual	
55		Annual Ordering (Setup) cost				341.29	341.29	
56		Annual Purchase (Production) cost				0.00	0.00	
57		Annual Inventory Holding cost				496.61	496.61	
58		Annual Shortage Penalty cost				85.32	85.32	
59						------------------		
60		Total Annual Cost				923.23	923.23	
61						==================		

As before, you can determine the effect on costs of choosing nonoptimal decision variable values by altering numbers in the "Actual" column. Observe that changing these values cause an instantaneous change in the cost figures shown, since no reoptimization is necessary. For example, if the order quantity is 60, then entering this value in cell G46 results in the following output:

	A	B	C	D	E	F	G	H
44								
45	DECISION VARIABLES:					Optimal	Actual	
46		Order Quantity ("Q")				60.94	60.00	
47		Re-Order Point ("s")				25.00	25.00	
48								
49	==>	Order-Up-To Point ("S")				85.94	85.00	
50		Number of Orders per year				8.53	8.67	
51		Probability of Shortage				0.15	0.15	
52		Expected Shortage ("Y")				1.00	1.00	
53								
54	COST BREAKDOWN:					Optimal	Actual	
55		Annual Ordering (Setup) cost				341.29	346.67	
56		Annual Purchase (Production) cost				0.00	0.00	
57		Annual Inventory Holding cost				496.61	490.00	
58		Annual Shortage Penalty cost				85.32	86.67	
59						------------------		
60		Total Annual Cost				923.23	923.33	
61						==================		

You can perform the same sorts of sensitivity analysis on the impacts of changes in decision variable values as in the deterministic case, complete with tables and graphs. Changes in costs or in the demand distribution will require reoptimization through the [Alt M], **Execute** command sequence, however, so that tables for sensitivity analysis must be constructed on an element-by-element basis rather than with a **Data Table** command. That is, you must successively run the model with different values and, after each run, copy the values of the results you're interested in to a blank area of the worksheet (using the **Range Value** command) for later analysis.

The EOQ models are continuous review models, which assume "steady state" models and minimize expected costs per unit time. Two other inventory models are available in PROPS[+]. The next chapter describes the Production Planning model, which solves for the optimal production (and hence inventory) schedule for a multi-period problem with different deterministic demands each period. The optimal multi-period inventory model with probabilistic demand each period is solved in the Stochastic DP module, using the Optimal_(s,S) model (see Chapter 16).

Features

1. **<u>Optimal Deterministic Inventory Model</u>**

   ■ calculates the optimal production plan with fixed setup costs.

   ■ considers a finite planning horizon with periodic review.

   ■ uses dynamic programming to calculate the solution.

Chapter 9. Production Planning

The Model:

$$C_i = \min_{j=i,\ i+1,\ \ldots,\ n} \left(C_{j+1} + K + c\sum_{k=i}^{j} r_k + h\sum_{k=i+1}^{j}(k-i)r_k \right)$$

where

C_i = total cost of optimal policy from the start of period i, with no stock available, to the end of the horizon

$C_{n+1} = 0$

r_i = the requirement (demand) in period i

Computations: PROPS⁺ uses the Wagner-Whitin theorem and dynamic programming to calculate the optimal policy.

Limitations: The model assumes a fixed setup cost and linear unit ordering (production) and holding costs. Holding costs are charged on inventory carried from one period to the next.

The Production Planning model, often called the periodic review deterministic inventory model, determines when and in what quantities a single item should be ordered or produced. Production or ordering is assumed to involve both a fixed and a variable cost, and the known demand must be satisfied. Production during any period can be stored for demand in future periods, and an inventory carrying cost is charged on inventory carried over from one period to the next. No shortages are allowed. The special form of the cost functions permits the use of an efficient solution algorithm. If the inventory problem has more general costs, the deterministic dynamic programming model in Chapter 15 is the appropriate solution method.

Example: Widgets Revisited

Suppose you are producing widgets (see page 136 for a description of the problem) and plan production (ordering) on a weekly basis. Also, suppose that you know the demand for the next eight weeks, as shown in the following table.

Week	1	2	3	4	5	6	7	8
Demand	8	14	6	12	5	15	8	12

The weekly cost of holding inventory, from the widget data on page 136, is $14/52 per widget. How large should we make each production run (or order size) to minimize costs?

From the PROPS+ ACCESS worksheet, select **9. Production Planning**. You will see the following screen:

```
        A       B       C       D       E       F       G       H
1   ============================== DETERMINISTIC PRODUCTION or
2                PROPS+              INVENTORY SPREADSHEET
3                                  - demand each period known
4            Copyright (C)         - no shortages
5            PROPS SYSTEMS         - uses dynamic programming and the
6                                    Wagner-Whitin theorem to calculate
7            03/08/92 01:15 PM       the optimal production plan
8   ============================== - will only produce (order) when
9                                    inventory is zero
10  Instructions:
11
12        PROMPT mode when CMD is on. Type response, press [ENTER].
13
14        [Alt M] -- Presents user with MENU of possible actions.
15
16                              Press [ENTER] to begin...
17
18
```

Press [Enter] and you are prompted for the problem name and the number of periods in the planning horizon. Press [Enter] after typing each response. PROPS+ then constructs the work area based on the specified number of periods, as follows (note that the "Period" and "Quantity" rows continue off the screen into columns I and J in this example):

```
        A       B       C       D       E       F       G       H
21          Analyst Name?   Your_name
22          Problem Name?   widget IV
23
24          Number of periods?              8
25
26  INPUT DATA:
27
28  Demands:  Period      1       2       3       4       5       6
29            Quantity    0       0       0       0       0       0
30
31  Costs:    Fixed Setup (or Ordering) cost per "run" (or order)      0
32            Production (or Purchase) cost per unit [optional]        0
33            Inventory Holding cost per unit per period               0
34
```

Insert the data for your example problem, being sure to move the cursor far enough to the right to enter data in cells I29 and J29. To see all the columns, you can use the **Worksheet Global Column-width command (/WGC)** to set the column width to 7. After the data has been entered, the worksheet should look like this:

	A	B	C	D	E	F	G	H	I	J
21		Analyst Name? Your_name								
22		Problem Name? widget IV								
23										
24		Number of periods?			8					
25										
26	INPUT DATA:									
27										
28	DemandsPeriod		1	2	3	4	5	6	7	8
29		Quantit	8	14	6	12	5	15	8	12
30										
31	Costs: Fixed Setup (or Ordering) cost per "run" (						40			
32		Production (or Purchase) cost per unit [op						0			
33		Inventory Holding cost per unit per period0.2692									
34										

(The holding cost per period is 14/52.) Pressing [Alt M] displays the execute menu at the top of the screen; in this case the menu has only one option, **Execute** (recall that the [Esc] key will abort the menu call if you wish). Pressing [Enter] to execute yields the following worksheet:

	A	B	C	D	E	F	G	H	I
36	STAGE-BY-STAGE ANALYSIS:								
37									
38		Stage 1: Period 8							
39									
40	Action	12							
41	Cost	40							
42									
43		=> Minimum Cost		40					
44									
45									
46		Stage 2: Period 7							
47									
48	Action	8	20						
49	Cost	80	43.2307						
50									
51		=> Minimum Cost 43.2307							
52									
53									
54		Stage 3: Period 6							
55									
56	Action	15	23	35					
57	Cost 83.2307	82.1538	48.6153						
58									
59		=> Minimum Cost 48.6153							
60									
61									
62		Stage 4: Period 5							
63									
64	Action	5	20	28	40				
65	Cost 88.6153	87.2692	88.3461	58.0384					
66									
67		=> Minimum Cost 58.0384							
68									

	A	B	C	D	E	F	G	H	I
69									
70		Stage 5: Period 4							
71									
72	Action	12	17	32	40	52			
73	Cost	98.0384	89.9615	92.6538	95.8846	68.8076			
74									
75		=> Minimum Cost	68.8076						
76									
77									
78		Stage 6: Period 3							
79									
80	Action	6	18	23	38	46	58		
81	Cost	108.807	101.269	94.5384	101.269	106.653	82.8076		
82									
83		=> Minimum Cost	82.8076						
84									
85									
86		Stage 7: Period 2							
87									
88	Action	14	20	32	37	52	60	72	
89	Cost	122.807	110.423	106.115	100.730	111.5	119.038	98.4230	
90									
91		=> Minimum Cost	98.4230						
92									
93									
94		Stage 8: Period 1							
95									
96	Action	8	22	28	40	45	60	68	80
97	Cost	138.423	126.576	115.807	114.730	110.692	125.5	135.192	117.807
98									
99		=> Minimum Cost	110.692						
100									
101									
102	OPTIMAL PRODUCTION PLAN: (Note: Other optimal plans may exist)								
103									
104		Cost of Optimal Plan =		110.692					
105									
106		Period	Amount						
107		---------------							
108		1	45						
109		2	0						
110		3	0						
111		4	0						
112		5	0						
113		6	35						
114		7	0						
115		8	0						

The worksheet shows the steps in the solution of this problem, and then summarizes the optimal ordering policy. The optimal production policy is to order 45 widgets now, and at the beginning of period 6 order an additional 35, resulting in a minimal cost of $110.69 for the eight weeks. In this model, instantaneous replenishment is assumed. The intermediate tables show the cost of alternative actions. For example, in period 1 (Stage 8), if the action is to order 8, which is enough for period 1, then the total cost would be $138.42 if you ordered optimally thereafter. If you ordered 22, enough for periods 1 and 2, and then ordered optimally thereafter, the cost would be $126.58.

Note that the average demand in this example is 10 widgets per week, which is comparable to the first deterministic EOQ problem in the previous chapter. Other costs are similar. The EOQ model called for producing 54.5 units every 5.45 weeks, for an annual cost of $763.15. The annual cost for this model is $719.48 (110.69 x 52/8). The difference arises from a) the assumption in this case that we only charge for the inventory carried over from one period to the next, and b) the order sizes of 45 and 35 in this case are smaller than the other model, which had order sizes in the 50- to 60-widget range. In this case, the finite horizon limits the order size. From the dynamic programming table for stage 8 (period 1), if all 80 widgets were ordered at the beginning, the cost would increase to $117.81.

Features

1. ## Poisson Queues

   - multiserver queues.

   - finite queue length.

   - finite calling population.

   - state-dependent parameters.

2. ## Non-Poisson Queues

   - general service time.

   - constant service time.

   - Erlang service time.

   - general arrival and service time approximation.

3. ## Priority Queues

   - multiserver case.

   - general service time, class-dependent parameters.

Chapter 10. Queueing

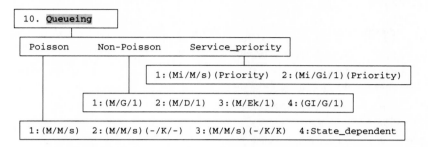

```
┌──────────────────────┐
│ 10. Queueing         │
└──────────────────────┘
  ┌────────────────────────────────────────────────┐
  │  Poisson     Non-Poisson     Service_priority   │
  └────────────────────────────────────────────────┘
              ┌───────────────────────────────────────────────────────┐
              │ 1:(Mi/M/s)(Priority)   2:(Mi/Gi/1)(Priority)           │
              └───────────────────────────────────────────────────────┘
         ┌──────────────────────────────────────────────────────┐
         │ 1:(M/G/1)   2:(M/D/1)   3:(M/Ek/1)   4:(GI/G/1)       │
         └──────────────────────────────────────────────────────┘
 ┌────────────────────────────────────────────────────────────────────┐
 │ 1:(M/M/s)   2:(M/M/s)(-/K/-)   3:(M/M/s)(-/K/K)   4:State_dependent  │
 └────────────────────────────────────────────────────────────────────┘
```

Queues, or line-ups of people or things awaiting a service, are everywhere in modern life. A relevant managerial question is, "Should more or less resources be devoted to the service facilities, and what will be the effect on the time spent in line?" The answer to this question involves describing the way the people or things ("calling units") that need service arrive, and the way in which that service is provided. As with other problems in operations research, we construct a model of the waiting line that is sufficiently detailed to capture the essence of these two system characteristics while being simple enough to be analytically solved.

Models of waiting lines describe the probability distribution of the arrival process, the number of serving units, any priority or queue discipline, and the distribution of service times. Other system characteristics are also included, such as whether the population of calling units is finite, or whether there is a maximum permissible length of queue (with any extra calling units being turned away when this is reached).

This chapter begins with a discussion of ways to describe these system characteristics. We then outline the options available in PROPS[+] for analyzing a variety of queueing problems. Finally, we present several examples of the use of PROPS[+]. For a discussion of the theory of queueing problems, we refer you to any of the texts mentioned in the Preface.

As you will see, PROPS[+] allows a great deal of flexibility in the choice of assumptions made about the queueing system. This permits ready testing of the model conclusions under different assumptions, which allows you to determine how sensitive the results are to the approximations in the model. In addition, the user has the full power of the spreadsheet system for post-solution analysis of problems. The examples in this chapter, particularly the first one dealing with an (M/M/s) model, show some of the capabilities of the spreadsheet approach to problem analysis.

Queueing Models

Queueing systems are usually described with Kendall-Lee notation, which takes the general form (a/b/s) or (a/b/s)(d/e/f), in which a stands for the arrival distribution, b for the service time distribution, and s for the number of parallel servers. In the longer form, d is the service discipline (assumed to be FCFS, or first come, first served, unless specified otherwise), e is the maximum number of calling units in the system (those in line plus those being served), and f is the size of the calling unit population. Standard notation is used to describe commonly used assumptions for a and b. These are

M : Markovian arrival or service times, or, equivalently, exponential
          interarrival or service time distributions
D : constant or deterministic interarrival or service time
E_k : Erlang, or gamma, distribution with parameter k
GI : general independent distribution of interarrival time
G : general distribution for service time

To illustrate, imagine a factory in which there are two repairmen and 20 machines, with each operating machine breaking down according to a Markovian process. Machines are serviced in the order in which they break down, and time between breakdowns follows an exponential distribution. This system is described as (M/M/2)(FCFS/20/20). Of course, solution of the system requires specification of the parameters of the Markov arrival and service time distributions.

In analyzing waiting lines, typically one is interested in how long calling units must wait for service and how much of the time the service facilities remain idle. In either case, one may be interested in either short-run transient characteristics given some starting condition, or in long-run average values ("steady state characteristics"). PROPS$^+$ focuses on steady state statistics as being generally of the most interest. In particular, we typically calculate the following quantities for queues:

W : the expected total delay (time in line plus service time) per unit
W_q : the expected time spent in the queue
L : the expected number of calling units in the system (including those
          being served)
L_q : the expected length of the waiting line
p_n : the probability of n calling units in the system at steady state
P(W>t) : the probability that the wait in the system is greater than t

The values of these queueing characteristics will depend on the interarrival and service time probability distributions. Following the usual convention, we use λ to represent the average arrival rate of calling units, and we denote the mean of the inter-arrival time as a (= $1/\lambda$). We use μ for the service rate, and b (=$1/\mu$) for the mean of the service time distribution. The number of parallel servers is s. For models that permit an infinite queue length, if $\lambda > s\mu$, so that on average more calling units arrive in a given time than can be served, the queue length will increase without limit and there will be no steady state average values.

The comparison of arrival and service rates is usually done through computing the traffic intensity $\rho = \lambda/\mu s$. If $\rho \geq 1$, the steady state is not usually attainable (except for problems with finite calling populations or maximum queue lengths). In addition, it is often particularly interesting in queueing problems to examine the change in waiting time as ρ changes. We will see how PROPS$^+$ facilitates this analysis.

Most problems have, at their root, some economic consequences that follow from any particular resolution of the queueing problem. For instance, increasing the service rate can generally be done at some cost, and the question is whether the reduced expected waiting time warrants the increased cost. Often an imputed cost of waiting is used to facilitate this comparison, and we will see how to use PROPS$^+$ to examine trade-offs between these two types of cost. Our focus is problem *analysis*, and we will not review the mathematics of queueing models; rather, we will accept the models as given and explore how one can use them to deepen understanding about the problem itself.

PROPS$^+$ has three categories of queueing problems: Poisson queues, with exponentially distributed interarrival and service times; non-Poisson queues, with some other distribution for interarrival and/or service times; and priority queues, with precedence given to some classes of calling units over others. Within each category, we have a variety of models.

Poisson Queues

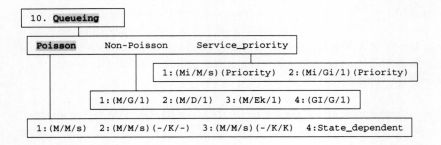

We will begin with the simplest of these models, the (M/M/s) model, and use an example to illustrate the extensive problem analysis that can be done using PROPS⁺. For the remaining models, we will show how to input data and interpret results. The same in-depth analysis is possible with any of the queueing models.

(M/M/s) Markov Arrival, Markov Service, s Server Queue

The Model:

$$P_O = \left[\sum_{n=0}^{s-1} \frac{(\lambda/\mu)^n}{n!} + \frac{(\lambda/\mu)^s}{s!} \frac{1}{1-(\lambda/s\mu)} \right]^{-1}$$

$$P_n = \begin{cases} \dfrac{(\lambda/\mu)^n}{n!} P_O & \text{if } O \leq n \leq s \\[2mm] \dfrac{(\lambda/\mu)^n}{s!s^{n-s}} P_O & \text{if } n \geq s \end{cases}$$

$$L_q = \frac{P_O(\lambda/\mu)^s \rho}{s!(1-\rho)^2}$$

$$W_q = \frac{L_q}{\lambda}$$

$$W = W_q + \frac{1}{\mu}$$

$$L = \lambda\left(W_q + \frac{1}{\mu}\right) = L_q + \frac{\lambda}{\mu}$$

$$P\{W > t\} = e^{-\mu t}\left[1 + \frac{P_O(\lambda/\mu)^s}{s!(1-\rho)}\left(\frac{1 - e^{-\mu t(s-1-\lambda/\mu)}}{s-1-\lambda/\mu}\right)\right]$$

$$P\{W_q > t\} = \left[1 - P\{W_q = O\}\right]e^{-s\mu(1-\rho)t}$$

$$P\{W_q = O\} = \sum_{n=0}^{s-1}P_n$$

Computation: PROPS+ defines the finite summations and directly calculates the expressions above. As parameters are altered, you may have to type [Alt R] to recalculate.

Limitations: $\rho < 1$; $s \leq 69$.

Example: A Bank Problem

A local branch of a bank has three tellers on duty at the peak hour of the day. During this time, sample observations have shown that the time it takes to service a customer is approximately exponentially distributed, with a rate of .25 customers per minute (i.e., the mean service time per customer is four minutes). Customers arrive independently, and the time between arrivals is approximately exponentially distributed. The mean time between customers is two minutes, for a rate of .5 customers per minute. Customers wait in a single queue for the first available teller, and the service rule is first come, first served.

The bank manager has observed that the line is sometimes quite long, and is considering having a fourth teller on duty during this peak period. Since additional hiring is involved, the cost of doing so is quite high, and the manager estimates that direct and indirect costs will be $12 per hour for this extra service. Is it worth it to have an extra teller?

To analyze this problem using PROPS⁺, invoke the ACCESS menu and select **10. Queueing** from the menu. You will then see the following menu at the top of the page:

```
A18:                                                                    MENU
Poisson  Non-Poisson  Service_Priority
Queueing problems with Poisson arrival and service-time distributions
         A        B        C        D        E        F     G        H
```

Selecting **Poisson** from this menu generates the following menu at the top of the screen:

```
A18:                                                                    MENU
1:(M/M/s)  2:(M/M/s)(-/K/-)  3:(M/M/s)(-/K/K)  4:State-dependent
Single or Multi-server, infinite queue length
         A        B        C        D        E        F     G        H
```

Select **1:(M/M/s)** and the following screen appears:

```
         A        B        C        D        E        F     G        H
1        ===============================
2                      PROPS+                POISSON QUEUEING SPREADSHEET
3                                                 M/M/s (-/-/-)
4                 Copyright (C)            - infinite queue length
5                 PROPS SYSTEMS            - single or multi-server
6
7            03/08/92 01:43 PM
8        ===============================
9
10  Instructions:
11
12          PROMPT mode when CMD is on. Type response, press [ENTER].
13
14          [Alt M] -- Presents user with MENU of possible actions.
15
16                                        Press [ENTER] to begin...
```

Press [Enter] and respond to the prompts to set up the following problem description:

```
         A        B        C        D        E        F     G        H
21            Analyst Name:     Your_name
22            Problem Name:     bank-1
23
24  INPUT DATA:
25            Mean Arrival Rate      0.5 ("lambda")
26            Mean Service Rate     0.25 ("mu")
27            Number of Servers        3 ("s")
28
```

When the number of servers is entered, PROPS⁺ immediately calculates the standard steady state queue characteristics as follows:

```
        A          B          C          D          E          F          G          H
29  MOMENTS:
30          Traffic Intensity 0.666666 ("rho")
31                                                        Queue   System
32          Expected Number of Customers            0.888888 2.888888
33          Expected Waiting Time per Customer      1.777777 5.777777
34
35  WAITING TIME PROBABILITIES:                     t =        0
36
37                                  FIFO
38          P{W >t} (system)          1
39          P{Wq>t} (queue)       0.444444
40
41  PROBABILITY DISTRIBUTION:  (random arrival finds exactly n in system)
42
43                  n      Pn        Cn
44              --------------------------
45              0 0.111111 0.111111
46              1 0.222222 0.333333
47              2 0.222222 0.555555
48              3 0.148148 0.703703
49              4 0.098765 0.802469
50              5 0.065843 0.868312
51              6 0.043895 0.912208
52              7 0.029263 0.941472
53              8 0.019509 0.960981
54              9 0.013006 0.973987
55             10 0.008670 0.982658
56             11 0.005780 0.988438
```

From this output, you see that the expected queue length is 0.89, and each customer can expect to wait for 1.778 minutes in the queue before being served. There is a 44.4% chance that a customer will have to wait in the queue before being served (or a 55.6% chance that a customer will be served immediately). The probability distribution, P_n, is the probability that there are n customers in the system. C_n is the cumulative probability that the number in the system is less than or equal to n. For example, the entry for n=8 shows that there is a 4% chance that there will be 8 or more in the system (i.e., 5 or more in the queue).

In examining the customer waiting time, you might want to know the probability that a customer must wait more than five minutes. To answer this, move the cursor to cell F35, which contains the value for the waiting time probability parameter, and change it to 5. You will see the following worksheet:

```
        A          B          C          D          E          F          G          H
29  MOMENTS:
30          Traffic Intensity 0.666666 ("rho")
31                                                        Queue   System
32          Expected Number of Customers            0.888888 2.888888
33          Expected Waiting Time per Customer      1.777777 5.777777
34
35  WAITING TIME PROBABILITIES:                     t =        5
36
37                                  FIFO
38          P{W >t} (system)      0.286504
39          P{Wq>t} (queue)       0.127335
```

The probability that the customer must wait more than 5 minutes in the system (waiting in line and being served) is thus 0.287, and that the customer's wait in the queue will be more than 5 minutes is 0.127.

To address the bank's economic problem, you can now examine the situation if the number of tellers was increased to 4. Move the cursor to the INPUT DATA section and replace the number of servers with four, reset the time in cell F35 to 0, and press [Alt R] to recalculate the output data for four servers:

```
          A         B         C         D        E        F        G        H
29   MOMENTS:
30             Traffic Intensity        0.5  ("rho")
31                                                          Queue    System
32             Expected Number of Customers          0.173913 2.173913
33             Expected Waiting Time per Customer    0.347826 4.347826
34
35   WAITING TIME PROBABILITIES:                   t =         0
36
37                                       FIFO
38             P{W >t} (system)            1
39             P{Wq>t} (queue)       0.173913
40
41   PROBABILITY DISTRIBUTION:   (random arrival finds exactly n in system)
42
43                     n      Pn       Cn
44                    -------------------------
45                    0  0.130434 0.130434
46                    1  0.260869 0.391304
47                    2  0.260869 0.652173
48                    3  0.173913 0.826086
49                    4  0.086956 0.913043
50                    5  0.043478 0.956521
51                    6  0.021739 0.978260
52                    7  0.010869 0.989130
53                    8  0.005434 0.994565
```

Observe that the expected number of customers in the system has dropped from 2.8889 with three tellers to 2.1739 with four. Thus there are 0.715 fewer customers waiting. Since the cost of an additional teller is $12/hr, if customer waiting time is valued at any more than (12/.715) = $16.80 per hour, the extra teller is worth the cost. Note also that the probability of a customer having any delay in the queue at all has dropped from 44.4% to 17.4%, so that fewer customers are inconvenienced by having to wait.

You can explore the relationship between additional service, customer arrivals, and total costs further by considering the way in which total costs change with the customer arrival rate. That is, with assumed values for teller cost and cost of customer waiting in the queue, you can use PROPS[+] to see how these costs change with an increasing customer arrival rate. To do so, we will describe how you can construct tables of total cost for different arrival rates, and use the spreadsheet Graph utility to create plots of the functional relationships.

Change the number of servers back to 3 and press [Alt R] to recalculate the model. Find a blank area to use as a work area. (For all worksheets, the range [I1..P20] is clear for use.) Set up a cell, say J1, that will contain the cost per hour of teller time ($12), and another (J2) for the cost per hour of customer waiting time (say, $30). It is tidy to put labels for these in I1 and I2. We will want to construct a table that will contain values of lambda in the first column and total cost in the second. Begin by selecting a range of values for the arrival rate. Now, with three servers, an arrival rate of 0.75 will force ρ to 1, so this is the maximum arrival rate to consider. For example, you might choose 11 values for lambda, between .25 and .75 customers per minute. Using the **D**ata **F**ill command (**/DF**) over the range [I6..I16], with START .25, STEP .05, and STOP .80, produces the following worksheet:

	I	J	K	L	M	N	O	P
1	Teller $=	12						
2	Cust $=	30						
3								
4								
5								
6	0.25							
7	0.3							
8	0.35							
9	0.4							
10	0.45							
11	0.5							
12	0.55							
13	0.6							
14	0.65							
15	0.7							
16	0.75							
17								

Now you can set up the cost function for any parameter setting. The total cost given s tellers and Lq customers waiting in the queue can be written

(Teller cost)*s + (Customer cost)*Lq

Put the total cost formula in, say, cell J5 as

+J1*D27+J2*F32

You can now complete the table of costs as follows. Type the **D**ata **T**able **1** command (**/DT1**), give the table range as [I5..J16] and the input cell as the cell containing lambda in the problem input area (in this case, D25). The spreadsheet system then completes the cost table. Put labels in cells I4 and J4 to identify the variables, and you should see the following:

	I	J	K	L	M	N	O	P
1	Teller $=	12						
2	Cust $=	30						
3								
4	rate	cost/hr	(3 tellers)					
5		62.66666						
6	0.25	37.36363						
7	0.3	38.82352						
8	0.35	41.31194						
9	0.4	45.38731						
10	0.45	51.96350						
11	0.5	62.66666						
12	0.55	80.72810						
13	0.6	113.6629						
14	0.65	183.9844						
15	0.7	404.2044						
16	0.75	ERR						
17								

Observe that the spreadsheet shows "ERR" for the cost for an arrival rate of .75. At this point, the traffic intensity ρ is 1, and the queue will increase without limit.

Now you can repeat this exercise for s=4. Begin by setting up the same sort of table for lambda and cost in columns M and N of the scratch area. Now return to the input area and change the number of servers to 4. Either pressing [Alt R] or recalculating through the menu obtained with [Alt M] will determine the queue characteristics for this number of servers. Repeating the data table construction using the range [M5..N16] yields the following worksheet:

	I	J	K	L	M	N	O	P
1	Teller $=	12						
2	Cust $=	30						
3								
4	rate	cost/hr	(3 tellers)		rate	cost/hr	(4 tellers)	
5		53.21739				53.21739		
6	0.25	37.36363			0.25	48.20408		
7	0.3	38.82352			0.3	48.47635		
8	0.35	41.31194			0.35	48.97414		
9	0.4	45.38731			0.4	49.81399		
10	0.45	51.96350			0.45	51.15491		
11	0.5	62.66666			0.5	53.21739		
12	0.55	80.72810			0.55	56.31595		
13	0.6	113.6629			0.6	60.91694		
14	0.65	183.9844			0.65	67.74630		
15	0.7	404.2044			0.7	78.00580		
16	0.75	ERR			0.75	93.84905		
17								

The most effective presentation of this analysis is through the spreadsheet Graph function. The following graph was produced using this table and the XY graph type with the rate column I as the X value and the cost columns in columns J and N as graph ranges A and B respectively, and then adding suitable titles and legends. Observe that, whereas costs of three or four tellers are very similar when the arrival rate is 0.5, once the rate increases, staying with three tellers is very expensive, reflecting the great increase in customer waiting time in the queue.

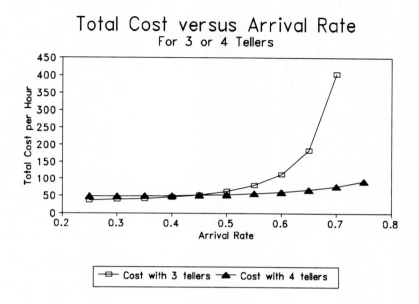

You could continue the analysis with alternative assumptions about the cost of additional servers, or different imputed costs for customer delay. This sensitivity analysis is simple within this spreadsheet construction. To revalue the tables on a change of costs, you need only repeat the **Data Table 1** command (**/DT1**), modifying the cost formula in cells J5 and N5 as appropriate.

(M/M/s)(-/K/-) Finite Poisson Queue

The Model:

$$P_O = \left[1 + \sum_{n=1}^{s} \frac{(\lambda/\mu)^n}{n!} + \frac{(\lambda/\mu)^s}{s!} \sum_{n=s+1}^{K} \left(\frac{\lambda}{s\mu} \right)^{n-s} \right]^{-1}$$

$$P_n = \begin{cases} \dfrac{(\lambda/\mu)^n}{n!} P_O, & \text{for } n = 1, 2, \ldots, s \\[2ex] \dfrac{(\lambda/\mu)^n}{s!s^{n-s}} P_O, & \text{for } n = s, s+1, \ldots, K \\[2ex] 0, & \text{for } n > K \end{cases}$$

$$L_q = \frac{P_O(\lambda/\mu)^s \rho}{s!(1-\rho)^2} \left[1 - \rho^{K-s} - (K-s)\rho^{K-s}(1-\rho) \right]$$

$$W = \frac{L}{\overline{\lambda}}, \quad W_q = \frac{L_q}{\overline{\lambda}}$$

$$\overline{\lambda} = \lambda(1 - P_K)$$

Computation: For a given model specification, PROPS+ calculates the finite summations and then the derived expressions. As parameters are changed [Alt R] recalculates queue characteristics.

Limitations: $K \leq 69$ and $s \leq 69$.

This model is the same as the preceding M/M/s model except that the maximum number of units both in the queue and being served is K. Units needing service that arrive when the system has K members do not join the queue but must go elsewhere for service. This is a useful model for service facilities that have a limited ability to store up calling units, such as a barbershop with a limited number of waiting chairs.

The problem input is identical to that of the preceding M/M/s model, except that the maximum permissible number in the system, K, is requested. The output format is the same as for the M/M/s model.

Example: Bank 2

Imagine a bank with three tellers; customers arrive at rate $\lambda = 0.5$ and are served at rate $\mu = 0.25$. Also suppose that when the queue length becomes 5 (meaning that there are $K = 8$ in the system), subsequent customers refuse to wait for service and do not join the queue (they "balk"). It may be interesting to know how often a balk occurs in such a system.

Calling up the **2:(M/M/s)(-/K/-)** spreadsheet within PROPS+ displays this screen:

```
          A       B       C       D       E       F       G       H
 1    ==============================
 2                 PROPS+                POISSON QUEUEING SPREADSHEET
 3                                         M/M/s (-/K/-)
 4             Copyright (C)             - finite queue length
 5             PROPS SYSTEMS              (K = max. no. in system)
 6                                       - single or multi-server
 7             03/08/92 02:32 PM
 8    ==============================
 9
10    Instructions:
11
12             PROMPT mode when CMD is on. Type response, press [ENTER].
13
14             [Alt M] -- Presents user with MENU of possible actions.
15
16                                         Press [ENTER] to begin...
```

When you press the [Enter] key, you will be presented with a series of questions. For each, type your response followed by the [Enter] key.

```
          A       B       C       D       E       F       G       H
21             Analyst Name:    Your_name
22             Problem Name:    bank-2
23
24    INPUT DATA:
25
26             Mean Arrival Rate    0.5  ("lambda")
27             Mean Service Rate    0.25 ("mu")
28             Number of Servers      3  ("s")
29             Max. System Size       8  ("K")
30
```

Once the system size is entered, PROPS+ immediately computes the following characteristics of the queueing system:

	A	B	C	D	E	F	G	H
31	MOMENTS:							
32		Expected Arrival Rate			0.489849	("lambda_bar")		
33								
34		Expected Traffic Intensity		0.653132		("rho_bar")		
35								
36						Queue	System	
37		Expected Number of Customers			0.600158	2.559555		
38		Expected Waiting Time per Customer			1.225190	5.225190		
39								
40	PROBABILITY DISTRIBUTION: (random arrival finds exactly n in system)							
41								
42			n	Pn	Cn			
43			----------------------------					
44			0	0.115622	0.115622			
45			1	0.231245	0.346867			
46			2	0.231245	0.578112			
47			3	0.154163	0.732275			
48			4	0.102775	0.835051			
49			5	0.068517	0.903568			
50			6	0.045678	0.949246			
51			7	0.030452	0.979698			
52			8	0.020301	1			
53			9	0	1			

With a finite queue length of 5 (8 in the system), there is a 2% probability that the queue will be full, and during this period arriving customers will balk. Contrast this with the infinite queue length model on page 163 where the probability was 4% that there would be 5 or more customers in the queue.

(M/M/s)(-/K/K) Finite Population Poisson Queue

The Model:

$$P_O = \left[\sum_{n=O}^{s-1} \frac{K!}{(K-n)!n!} \left(\frac{\lambda}{\mu}\right)^n + \sum_{n=s}^{K} \frac{K!}{(K-n)!s!s^{n-s}} \left(\frac{\lambda}{\mu}\right)^n \right]^{-1}$$

$$P_n = \begin{cases} P_O \dfrac{K!}{(K-n)!n!} \left(\dfrac{\lambda}{\mu}\right)^n & \text{if } O \leq n \leq s \\[2ex] P_O \dfrac{K!}{(K-n)!s!s^{n-s}} \left(\dfrac{\lambda}{\mu}\right)^n & \text{if } s \leq n \leq k \\[2ex] O & \text{if } n > k \end{cases}$$

$$L_q = \sum_{n=s}^{K} (n-s)P_n$$

$$L = \sum_{n=0}^{s-1} nP_n + L_q + s\left(1 - \sum_{n=0}^{s-1} P_n\right)$$

$$W = \frac{L}{\overline{\lambda}}, \qquad W_q = \frac{L_q}{\overline{\lambda}}$$

$$\overline{\lambda} = \lambda(K - L)$$

Computation: For a given model specification, PROPS+ calculates the finite summations and then the derived expressions. As parameters are changed, [Alt R] recalculates the queue characteristics.

Limitations: $K \leq 69$, $s \leq 69$, $s \leq K$.

This model is similar to the preceding one, except that here there is a finite calling population of size K. Each member of the calling population, when not in the queueing system, generates a demand for service at rate λ, according to a Markovian process. Thus, if the queue is empty, customers arrive at rate $K\lambda$. If all K members of the calling population are in the system, then the arrival rate is zero. Thus, there can never be more than a total of K in the queue and being served at any time. The input and output follow the same format as in the M/M/s case; the only differences are the need to specify K in the input, and that the arrival rate λ is expressed as "per unit of population not in the system".

Example: A Machine Repair Problem

Suppose we have a factory with 20 machines and two repair persons. A machine that is currently operating breaks down on the average once every 15 days and requires an average of one day to repair. Assuming Poisson processes for breakdown and repair, what is the expected number of machines under repair at any time?   Select the **3:(M/M/s)(-/K/K)** model; the following screen is generated:

```
        A         B         C         D         E         F         G         H
 1    ==============================
 2                 PROPS+                     POISSON QUEUEING SPREADSHEET
 3                                                  M/M/s (-/K/K)
 4             Copyright (C)                  - finite calling population
 5             PROPS SYSTEMS                  - single or multi-server
 6
 7           03/08/92 02:38 PM
 8    ==============================
 9
10    Instructions:
11
12            PROMPT mode when CMD is on. Type response, press [ENTER].
13
```

Press [Enter] and respond to each question, ending each response by pressing [Enter]. The completed data entry appears as follows:

```
         A        B         C         D         E         F        G        H
21               Analyst Name:      Your_name
22               Problem Name:      machine repair
23
24    INPUT DATA:
25               Mean Demand Rate                        0.066666 ("lambda")
26                 (for each member of calling population)
27               Mean Service Rate                              1 ("mu")
28               Number of Servers                              2 ("s")
29               Maximum System (Population) Size              20 ("K")
```

When the last entry is complete, PROPS⁺ computes the queueing system characteristics:

```
         A        B         C         D         E         F        G        H
31    MOMENTS:
32               Expected Arrival Rate        1.217891 ("lambda_bar")
33
34               Expected Traffic Intensity 0.608945 ("rho_bar")
35
36                                                          Queue    System
37               Expected Number of Customers          0.513738 1.731629
38               Expected Waiting Time per Customer     0.421825 1.421825
39
40    PROBABILITY DISTRIBUTION:   (random arrivals)
41
42                        n      Pn        Cn
43                      --------------------------
44                       0 0.234632 0.234632
45                       1 0.312843 0.547476
46                       2 0.198134 0.745610
47                       3 0.118880 0.864490
48                       4 0.067365 0.931856
49                       5 0.035928 0.967784
50                       6 0.017964 0.985748
51                       7 0.008383 0.994132
52                       8 0.003632 0.997764
53                       9 0.001453 0.999218
54                      10 0.000532 0.999750
55                      11 0.000177 0.999928
56                      12 0.000053 0.999981
57                      13 0.000014 0.999995
58                      14 0.000003 0.999999
59                      15 0.000000 0.999999
60                      16 0.000000 0.999999
61                      17 0.000000 0.999999
62                      18 0.000000 0.999999
63                      19  9.8E-11        1
64                      20  3.3E-12        1
65                      21        0        1
```

On average, 1.73 machines are broken down and are awaiting repair or are being repaired (the mean number of customers in the system). Both repair persons are idle 23% of the time (P_0) and both are busy 45% of the time ($1-P_0-P_1$). On average, there are 1.22 breakdowns per day ("lambda-bar").

State Dependent Finite Queue

The Model:

$$P_O = \frac{1}{1 + \sum_{n=1}^{N} C_n}$$

$$C_n = \frac{\lambda_{n-1}\lambda_{n-2}\cdots\lambda_O}{\mu_n\mu_{n-1}\cdots\mu_1} \qquad \text{for } n = 1, 2, \ldots, N$$

$$L = \sum_{n=O}^{N} nP_n$$

$$W = \frac{L}{\overline{\lambda}} \qquad\qquad \overline{\lambda} = \sum_{n=O}^{N} \lambda_n P_n$$

where λ_i = arrival rate with i in the system
μ_i = service rate with i in the system

Computation: For a given population size, PROPS+ defines the required calculations and evaluates the expressions. As parameters are changed, queue characteristics are automatically recalculated. If the population size is changed, [Alt R] must be used to recalculate.

Limitations: None.

This model solves the general Poisson finite queueing problem. The input is again similar to the M/M/s model, except that you must specify the arrival and service rates for each state. PROPS+ eases the amount of input by assuming that each arrival and service rate is a multiple of the "base" rate.

Example: Bank 3

Consider the same finite queue banking problem as in Bank Example 2, except that as the queue length gets longer, the tellers work faster. In particular, suppose that the service rate increases by 5% for each customer in the queue (over three in the system). Thus $\lambda = 0.5$, s = 3, K = 8, and $\mu = 0.25$ (base rate). The state-dependent service rate is

$$\begin{aligned}
\mu_i &= i\mu & i &= 1, 2, 3 \\
&= 3\mu(1 + .05(i - 3)) & 4 &\leq i \leq 8
\end{aligned}$$

Calling up the PROPS+ **4:State_dependent** worksheet, pressing [Enter], and completing the data entry produces the following worksheet:

	A	B	C	D	E	F	G	H	I	J	K	L
21		Analyst Name		Your_name								
22		Problem Name		bank-3								
23												
24	INPUT DATA:											
25			Base Arrival		0.5	("lambda")						
26			Base Service		0.25	("mu")						
27												
28			Max. Number i		8	("N")						
29												
30	RATE MULTIPLIERS:											
31			System	0	1	2	3	4	5	6	7	8
32			Arrival	1	1	1	1	1	1	1	1	0
33			Service	0	1	1	1	1	1	1	1	1

The arrival and service rate multipliers default to a value of 1, as shown above. At this point, you can alter the values in the service rate multiplier cells to the appropriate ones for this question by manually inserting the new values or using a function defined elsewhere in the worksheet. With these changes, the input data appears as follows:

	A	B	C	D	E	F	G	H	I	J	K	L
30	RATE MULTIPLIERS:											
31			System	0	1	2	3	4	5	6	7	8
32			Arrival	1	1	1	1	1	1	1	1	0
33			Service	0	1	2	3	3.15	3.3	3.45	3.6	3.75

PROPS[+] automatically recalculates the queue statistics, giving the following moments and distribution for the system:

	A	B	C	D	E	F	G	H
35	MOMENTS:							
36								
37		Expected customer demand rate				0.494654	("lambda_bar")	
38								
39						System		
40		Expected Number of Customers				2.377296		
41		Expected Waiting Time per Customer				4.805968		
42								
43	PROBABILITY DISTRIBUTION:		(random arrival finds exactly n in system)					
44								
45			n	Pn	Cn			
46			---------------------------					
47			0	0.121303	0.121303			
48			1	0.242607	0.363911			
49			2	0.242607	0.606519			
50			3	0.161738	0.768258			
51			4	0.102691	0.870949			
52			5	0.062237	0.933186			
53			6	0.036079	0.969265			
54			7	0.020044	0.989309			
55			8	0.010690	1			

Comparison with the previous example shows that the increase in service rates with longer queue lengths reduces the expected waiting time in the system from 5.2 minutes to 4.8 minutes.

Non-Poisson Queues

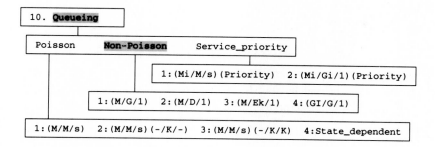

(M/G/1) Markov Arrival, General Service Time, Single Server Queue

---

The Model:

Pollaczek-Khintchine Formula:

$$P_O = 1 - \rho$$

$$L_q = \frac{\lambda^2 \sigma^2 + \rho^2}{2(1 - \rho)}$$

$$L = \rho + L_q$$

$$W_q = \frac{L_q}{\lambda}$$

$$W = W_q + b$$

Computation: PROPS[+] computes the queue characteristics directly from the equations, with $\rho = \lambda b$.

Limitations: $\rho < 1$, $0 \leq \sigma < \infty$.

This model assumes that interarrival times are exponentially distributed with mean $(1/\lambda)$, and that service times follow a distribution with a known mean b and standard deviation σ. You may observe that if the service distribution is exponential, these equations reduce to the M/M/1 model discussed earlier.

As a demonstration of this model, let us examine the relationship between the waiting time in the queue and the standard deviation of the service time for different arrival rates. For comparison, we will assume that the mean service time stays constant at 1 and will vary the arrival rate.

Selecting **Non-Poisson** and **1:(M/G/1)** from the successive menus through PROPS[+] and pressing [Enter] when prompted by the title screen displays a sequence of parameters with their default values as shown in the following screen. PROPS[+] immediately computes the moments of the queue parameters based on these default values:

	A	B	C	D	E	F	G	H
21		Analyst Name:		Your_name				
22		Problem Name:		general service time				
23								
24	INPUT DATA:							
25								
26		Mean Arrival Rate			0.8	("lambda")		
27		Service Time: Mean			1	("b")		
28			Std Dev		1	("sigma_b")		
29								
30								
31	MOMENTS:							
32								
33		Traffic Intensity		0.8	("rho")			
34	===>	Idle time =		0.2	("P_0")			
35								
36							Queue	System
37		Expected Number of Customers					3.2	4
38		Expected Waiting Time per Customer					4	5
39								

In order to examine the impact of changes in the arrival rate λ and service time standard deviation σ on the waiting time in the queue, we will use the spreadsheet **Data Table 2** command (**/DT2**). To set up the spreadsheet, find a currently unused portion of the worksheet. The range [I1..P20] is always available for your use. Using the **Data Fill** command (**/DF**) in the ranges [K4..O4] and [J5..J13] and inserting descriptive titles in L3 and [I6..I7] yields the following table in the worksheet:

	I	J	K	L	M	N	O	P
1								
2								
3				standard deviation of service time				
4			0	0.5	1	1.5	2	
5		0.1						
6	arrival	0.2						
7	rate	0.3						
8		0.4						
9		0.5						
10		0.6						
11		0.7						
12		0.8						
13		0.9						
14								

Now move the cursor to cell J4 and enter the formula **+F38**, the expected waiting time for the current values of standard deviation and arrival rate. Finally, enter the **Data Table 2** command (**/DT2**). In this example, the range will be [J4..O13]; input cell 1 is E26 and input cell 2 is E28. Finally, using the **Range Format Fixed 2** command (**/RFF2**) over the range [J4..O13] to put the table in a clearer format, you produce the following worksheet:

	I	J	K	L	M	N	O	P
1								
2								
3				standard	deviation of	service	time	
4		4.00	0.00	0.50	1.00	1.50	2.00	
5		0.10	0.06	0.07	0.11	0.18	0.28	
6	arrival	0.20	0.13	0.16	0.25	0.41	0.63	
7	rate	0.30	0.21	0.27	0.43	0.70	1.07	
8		0.40	0.33	0.42	0.67	1.08	1.67	
9		0.50	0.50	0.63	1.00	1.63	2.50	
10		0.60	0.75	0.94	1.50	2.44	3.75	
11		0.70	1.17	1.46	2.33	3.79	5.83	
12		0.80	2.00	2.50	4.00	6.50	10.00	
13		0.90	4.50	5.63	9.00	14.63	22.50	

The response of the waiting time to variations in the arrival rate and service time standard deviation is even more clearly shown using the spreadsheet **Graph** commands (**/G**). Use an XY graph and name each column in the table as one of the inputs A through E in the graph menu. After adding appropriate titles, the graph showing the sensitivity analysis of waiting time to variations in arrival rate and service time standard deviation appears as follows:

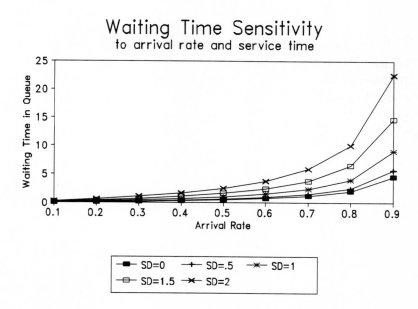

(M/D/1) Markov Arrival, Constant Service Time, Single Server Queue

The Model:

$$P_O = 1 - \rho$$

$$L_q = \frac{\rho^2}{2(1 - \rho)}$$

$$L = \rho + L_q$$

$$W_q = \frac{L_q}{\lambda}$$

$$W = W_q + b$$

Computation: PROPS$^+$ computes $\rho = \lambda b$ and the preceding queue characteristics directly from ρ.

Limitations: $\rho < 1$.

This model assumes that customers arrive according to a Markov process at rate λ and that service time is a fixed constant b. Note that this model is just a special case of the previous model (M/G/1) with the standard deviation of the service time set at zero. Use of the model is similar to that of the queueing models discussed earlier.

(M/Ek/1) Markov Arrival, Erlang Service, Single Server Queue

The Model:

$$L_q = \frac{\lambda^2 / k\mu^2 + \rho^2}{2(1 - \rho)} = \frac{1 + k}{2k} \frac{\lambda^2}{\mu(\mu - \lambda)}$$

$$W_q = \frac{1 + k}{2k} \frac{\lambda}{\mu(\mu - \lambda)}$$

$$W = W_q + b$$

$$L = \lambda W$$

Computation: PROPS$^+$ computes $\rho = \lambda b$, $\mu = \dfrac{1}{b}$ and the preceding queue characteristics directly from ρ.

Limitations: $\rho < 1$.

This model requests the calling unit arrival rate, the mean service time, and the Erlang shape parameter k as input, and computes the standard queue character-istics directly. The Erlang distribution is a two-parameter generalization of the single-parameter exponential distribution, and has often been found to match observed distributions very well. Varying the shape parameter k but holding the mean constant yields distributions with different variances and degrees of skewness, permitting good approximations to a wide variety of empirical distributions, as follows. Given an empirical distribution with mean E[t] and variance σ^2, you can approximate it with the Erlang of rate $\mu = 1/E[t]$ and shape parameter k equal to the integer value that makes $(1/k\mu^2)$ closest to σ^2.

It can be shown that an Erlang order k distribution with mean $(1/\mu)$ has the same distribution as the sum of k independent identically distributed exponential random variables with mean $(1/k\mu)$. Hence, it is often convenient to think of this distribution as being equivalent to a system having k identical memoryless components to the service.

Use of this model is similar to that of the queueing models discussed earlier.

(GI/G/1) General Independent Arrival, General Service, Single Server Queue

The Model:

Approximation Form:

$$W_q \simeq \frac{1 + \left(\dfrac{\sigma_b}{b}\right)^2}{\dfrac{1}{\rho^2} + \left(\dfrac{\sigma_b}{b}\right)^2} \left[\frac{\sigma_a^2 + \sigma_b^2}{2a(1 - \rho)}\right]$$

$$W = W_q + b$$

$$L = \frac{W}{a}$$

$$L_q = \frac{W_q}{a}$$

Computation: PROPS$^+$ computes $\rho = \lambda/\mu$ and the preceding queue characteristics directly from ρ.

Limitations: $\rho < 1$.

As input, this model requests the mean interarrival time $a = 1/\lambda$ and its standard deviation σ_a, and the service time mean $b = 1/\mu$ and standard deviation σ_b, from which the standard queue characteristics are computed. This approximation is exact for the M/G/1 and D/D/1 queues and for all queues as $\rho \to 1$.

Priority Queues

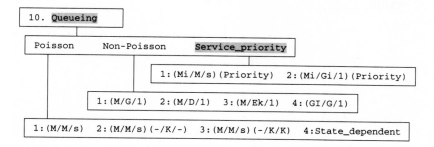

The models we have discussed to this point generally follow the rule first come, first served, or FCFS. In many situations, however, some types of calling unit may have priority on service. Examples include job shops with normal and rush categories for work, hospital emergency rooms, in which some classes of trauma must be dealt with immediately and others can be delayed, and so on. Priority can be of two forms. Preemptive priority permits a higher priority request to interrupt current service to a lower priority unit. Non-preemptive priority places a higher priority request at the head of the line but the current service is completed without interruption. PROPS[+] deals with both forms. In the following discussion, priority classes are numbered i=1,2,...,N from the highest (i=1) to the lowest (i=N) priority.

(Mi/M/s) (priority) Poisson Queue with s Servers

The Model:

Non-preemptive Priorities:

$$W_k = \frac{1}{AB_{k-1}B_k} + \frac{1}{\mu} \quad \text{for } k = 1, 2, \ldots, N$$

$$A = s! \left(\frac{s\mu - \lambda}{\rho^2} \right) \sum_{j=0}^{s-1} \frac{\rho^j}{j!} + s\mu$$

$$B_O = 1, \quad B_k = 1 - \frac{\sum_{i=1}^{k} \lambda_i}{s\mu} \quad \text{for } k = 1, 2, \ldots, N$$

where
    s = the number of servers
    μ = mean service rate per busy server
    λ_i = mean arrival rate for priority class i, for $i = 1, 2, \ldots, N$

$$\lambda = \sum_{i=1}^{N} \lambda_i, \quad \rho = \frac{\lambda}{\mu}$$

Preemptive Priorities:

$$W_k = \frac{1/\mu}{B_{k-1}B_k} \quad \text{for } k = 1, 2, \ldots, N$$

$$L_k = \lambda_k W_k \quad \text{for } k = 1, 2, \ldots, N$$

Computation: PROPS$^+$ sets up a worksheet based on the given number of
priority classes and servers. Queue characteristics are then found directly.

Limitations: $\rho < 1$, $s \le 69$. Preemption with $s > 1$ is not solved.

As with the previous classes of queueing models, PROPS$^+$ requests data on the mean service rate μ per server, the arrival rates λ_i for each of the N classes, and the number of servers s. PROPS$^+$ then immediately calculates the standard queue characteristics. Changing μ or any λ_i causes instant recalculation of the waiting and queue length statistics. However, if s or N is changed, you must use [Alt R] to recalculate the complete queue characteristics.

Priority Queues. Queueing models with priorities apply whenever some calling units are served with a preferential service order and jump the waiting lower priority units in their order of service. Examples include emergency services in hospitals in which victims of major trauma are treated first, secretarial pools in which some jobs are treated as "rush" and preempt whatever else a worker may be doing, and airport check-in counters in which business class passengers are served as soon as the next economy class passenger is served (nonpreemptive service). PROPS+ solves both preemptive and nonpreemptive queueing models.

Example: Computer Scheduling

Suppose a mainframe computer schedules jobs according to each user's priority. In some installations, for example, priority class 1 users pay using real dollars, while class 2 customers pay with allocated computer "funny money." Suppose that the time to process a job is exponentially distributed with a mean of five seconds, so the average rate $\mu = 0.2$ jobs/second, and the computer is 90% utilized. How does the service for each job class vary as the proportion of high priority jobs changes?

To answer this with PROPS+, select **10. Queueing** from the ACCESS menu; then **Service_priority** and **1:(Mi/M/s)(Priority)**, and you will see the following screen:

```
         A        B        C        D        E        F        G        H
 1   ==============================
 2              PROPS+                PRIORITY QUEUEING SPREADSHEET
 3                                       Mi/M/s
 4           Copyright (C)            - infinite queue length
 5           PROPS SYSTEMS            - preemptive or non-preemptive
 6                                    - single or multi-server
 7           09/25/92 06:49 AM
 8   ==============================
 9
10   Instructions:
11
12           PROMPT mode when CMD is on.  Type response, press [Enter].
13
14           [Alt M] -- Presents user with MENU of possible actions.
15
16                                           Press [Enter] to begin...
17
```

Press [Enter] and respond to each prompt, pressing [Enter] after each entry. Set the number of servers s = 1, the service rate mu = 0.2, the number of classes N = 2, and leave the Preemptive Priorities? response at its default value n (simply press [Enter]). You will see the following screen:

	A	B	C	D	E	F	G
21		Analyst Name:		Your_name			
22		Problem Name:		computer load			
23							
24	INPUT DATA:						
25		Number of Servers			1	("s")	
26		Mean Service Rate			0.2	("mu")	
27							
28		Number of Priority Classes			2	("N")	
29		Preemptive Priorities? y/n			n		
30							
31		Mean Arrival Rates:					
32	class	1	2				
33	rate	0.5	0				
34							
35		====> "lambda" =		0.5			
36							
37	MOMENTS:						
38							
39		Traffic Intensity = ≥ 1 [ERR] ("rho")					
40							
41		class	Wq	W	Lq	L	
42		---					
43		1	-8.33333	-3.33333	-4.16666	-1.66666	
44		2	5.555555	10.55555	0	0	
45							

In this table, the default values for the arrival rates of the two classes are 0.5 and 0 respectively. (With these default values, the traffic intensity $\rho > 1$, so the queue would increase without limit. This is indicated by the ERR message in the worksheet.)

Since we are assuming that the computer is 90% utilized, the times between the arrivals of jobs has a mean of (5/.9) = 5.55 seconds, corresponding to 0.18 jobs per second. To vary the split of this job stream between the two classes, set up a variable alpha at some convenient place on the worksheet to record the fraction of jobs of class 1 (in cell G33, for example). Choose an initial value of, say, 0.5. (It is good practice to put a descriptive tag in cell F33, as shown.) Now, since the mean service rate μ is contained in cell E26, you can set up a function for the arrival rates of each class: in cell B33, enter **+G33*0.9*E26**, and in C33, enter **+(1-G33)*0.9*E26**. The result of these operations is

	A	B	C	D	E	F	G	H
31		Mean Arrival Rates:						
32	class	1	2					
33	rate	0.09	0.09			alpha=	0.5	
34								
35		====> "lambda" =		0.18				
36								

PROPS[+] immediately computes queueing characteristics for each class in the system, including

> Wq: the average time spent in the queue awaiting service
>
> W : the average time spent in the queue and being serviced
>
> Lq: the average length of the queue for each class
>
> L : the average number of members of each class in the system

These are displayed in the worksheet immediately below the input area above. If you make changes in the input data, these statistics are automatically updated to reflect the changes.

	A	B	C	D	E	F	G
39			Traffic Intensity =		0.9	("rho")	
40							
41		class	Wq	W	Lq	L	
42		-----	-----	-----	-----	-----	--
43		1	8.181818	13.18181	0.736363	1.186363	
44		2	81.81818	86.81818	7.363636	7.813636	
45							

Now we can examine how the wait in the queue for each class varies as the proportion of class 1 jobs (alpha) changes. To do so, we can construct two tables recording the values of Wq for each class for a range of alpha values by using the **Data Fill** and **Data Table** commands.

	I	J	K	L	M	N
1	class 1			class 2		
2	alpha	Wq		alpha	Wq	
3		8.18			81.82	
4	0.00	4.50		0.00	45.00	
5	0.10	4.95		0.10	49.45	
6	0.20	5.49		0.20	54.88	
7	0.30	6.16		0.30	61.64	
8	0.40	7.03		0.40	70.31	
9	0.50	8.18		0.50	81.82	
10	0.60	9.78		0.60	97.83	
11	0.70	12.16		0.70	121.62	
12	0.80	16.07		0.80	160.71	
13	0.90	23.68		0.90	236.84	
14	1.00	45.00		1.00	450.00	

Note that the table reports a queue wait of 4.5 seconds for job class 1 when alpha = 0 (there aren't any class 1 jobs). This is an asymptotic result, as is the Wq for class 2 when alpha = 1. A graph of these values dramatically illustrates the impact of an increasing fraction of class 1 jobs. If alpha = 0.1, that is 10% of the jobs have priority class 1, then the waiting time for priority class 2 jobs is 10 times that for jobs in class 1.

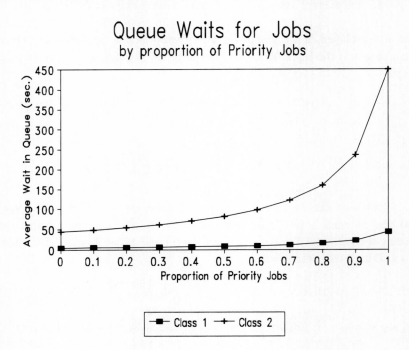

(Mi/Gi/1) (priority) Markov Arrival, General Service Queue

The Model:

$$W_q^{(k)} = \frac{\sum\limits_{i=1}^{N} \lambda_i (E_i^2\{t\} + var_i\{t\})}{2(1 - S_{k-1})(1 - S_k)}$$

$$L_q^{(k)} = \lambda_k W_q^{(k)}$$

$$W^{(k)} = W_q^{(k)} + E_k\{t\}$$

$$L^{(k)} = L_q^{(k)} + \rho_k$$

$$\rho_k = \lambda_k E_k\{t\}$$

$$S_k = \sum_{i=1}^{k} \rho_i < 1, \qquad k = 1, 2, \ldots, N$$

$$S_O = O$$

$$W_q = \sum_{k=1}^{N} \frac{\lambda_k}{\lambda} W_q^{(k)}, \qquad \lambda = \sum_{k=1}^{N} \lambda_k$$

where

$E_i\{t\}$ is the mean service time for class i and
$var_i\{t\}$ is the variance of service times for class i

Computation: PROPS$^+$ sets up a worksheet based on the given number of priority classes and servers. Queue characteristics are then found directly.

Limitations: $\rho_N < 1$, $s \leq 69$.

As in the preceding model, PROPS$^+$ prompts for the arrival and service time characteristics of each class and computes queue characteristics directly. With the same number of classes, any alteration of the arrival or service rate data is instantly reflected in these characteristics. If the number of classes is altered, you must use [Alt R] to recalculate the values. This model is particularly useful when the priority classes are selected on the basis of service times. This model is used in the same way as the preceding priority queueing model.

Features

1. **Simulation**

   - simulates any spreadsheet model.

   - discrete time simulation model.

   - risk analysis.

   - financial analysis.

Chapter 11. Simulation

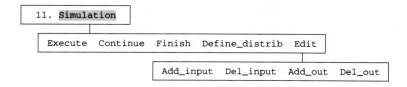

Spreadsheets are powerful tools in modeling complex relationships between variables. An especially useful feature of spreadsheets is the ability to perform "what if" analysis. That is, you can change the value of any variable and see what happens to the output variables. PROPS⁺ extends this capability by permitting you to identify any variables in the model as random variables and then to use Monte Carlo simulation techniques to analyze the impact of this randomness on any other set of variables.

For example, spreadsheets are often used to model financial problems, which typically involve a number of cash flows that contribute to some overall objective. PROPS⁺ permits you to specify probability distributions for any set of the component variables, and through simulation generate the mean and standard deviation of the output variables. If desired, the frequency distributions for these variables can also be calculated. Consider the following example.

Example: Financial Analysis Model
Suppose you invest $20,000 in a new machine and expect to realize a cash flow of $5,000 in each of the next six years. Suppose an interest rate of 10% per annum. What is the net present value (NPV) and internal rate of return (IRR) generated by the machine? What happens if the cash flow is not $5,000 in each year, but is a random variable?

To analyze this problem, let us create a spreadsheet model of this investment. Use the Worksheet Erase command (**/WE**) to clear the worksheet. Enter the interest rate in cell D4 and the cash flows for each year in [D6..D12]. Period 0 represents the initial investment of 20 (1000) and is negative since it is an outlay of cash. Periods 1-6 represent the cash inflow in each year. To compute the net present value and internal rate of return, you can use the spreadsheet functions **@NPV** and **@IRR**. Put the formulas **@NPV(.01*D4,D6..D12)** in cell D13 and **@IRR(.01*D4,D6..D12)*100** in cell D14. Entering the year number and titles in appropriate cells, you generate the following worksheet:

```
           A        B        C        D        E        F        G
1
2     FINANCIAL ANALYSIS MODEL
3
4              interest rate %              10
5                      period    cash flow
6                            0         -20
7                            1           5
8                            2           5
9                            3           5
10                           4           5
11                           5           5
12                           6           5
13              net present value  1.614821
14       internal rate of return  12.97800
15
16
```

You can now see what happens if the cash flows change. For example, suppose the cash flow in period 1 is only 3. If you change cell D7 to 3, the net present value becomes slightly negative. A more general risk analysis would assume that the cash flows each period are random. For example, suppose that the cash flow in each period is normally distributed with a mean of 5 (thousand) and a standard deviation of 1 (thousand), and that observations are independent from period to period. We shall use PROPS+ to perform this analysis. First, change the value in cell D7 back to 5 and then save this worksheet for later inclusion in the simulation model using the **File Save** command (**/FS**), calling the file **FINANCE**.

The Simulation Worksheet

From the PROPS+ ACCESS worksheet, select the **11. Simulation** model. You will see the following screen:

```
           A        B        C        D        E        F        G        H
1     ==============================   SIMULATION SPREADSHEET
2                PROPS+               - simulates any spreadsheet,
3                                     - assigns cells as random vbls.
4             Copyright (C)           - built in distributions:
5             PROPS SYSTEMS               Normal
6                                         Exponential
7          04/06/92 07:38 AM              Uniform
8     ==============================       Triangular
9                                          Bernoulli
10                                    - Arbitrary continuous or discrete
11                                            distribution
12                                    - Risk analysis
13    Instructions:
14       1. Use the File Combine Copy command to import Spreadsheet
15             model, or create model below.
16       2. Move cursor below spreadsheet model, and press [Alt M] for
17             simulation menus.
18
19                                          Press [ENTER] to begin...
20
```

Press [Enter] and you will see the screen:

```
         A        B        C        D        E        F        G        H
21  ----------------------------------------------------------------------
22   Area for  spreadsheet model: import or create below, then press [Alt M]
23
24
25
26
27
28
29
```

You are now prompted to import or create the spreadsheet model you wish to simulate. Since you have already created and saved the model, use the **File Combine Copy Entire-file** command (**/FCCE**) and select the file FINANCE.WK1 to import. Your screen should look like this:

```
         A        B        C        D        E        F        G        H
21  ----------------------------------------------------------------------
22    Area for spreadsheet model: import or create below, then press [Alt M]
23  FINANCIAL ANALYSIS MODEL
24
25          interest rate %          10
26                   period   cash flow
27                        0       -20
28                        1         5
29                        2         5
30                        3         5
31                        4         5
32                        5         5
33                        6         5
34          net present value 1.614821
35          IRR              12.97800
36
37
```

You are now ready to attach the simulation model. Move the cursor to an area just below the spreadsheet model, say row 36. Press [Alt M] and you will see the following menu:

```
A37:                                                              MENU
No  Yes
CONFIRM: Is it okay to ERASE everything below the current row?  NO
         A        B        C        D        E        F        G        H
```

Select **Yes.** You will be prompted for the problem name, "cashflow," and the number of input and output variables. The cash flows in each year (1-6) are random variables and are called the input (independent) variables. There are two dependent or output variables of interest, NPV and IRR. After you input this information, PROPS[+] generates the following SIMULATION SETUP DATA tables:

```
         A        B        C        D        E        F        G        H
38  SIMULATION SETUP DATA                    Distribution: parameter list
39                                           ---------------------------
40  Analyst Name       Your_name             Normal:      mean, std_dev
41  Simulation Name    cashflow              Exponential: mean
42                                           Uniform:     lower, upper
43                                           Triangular:  lower, median, upper
44                                           Bernoulli:   p
45     Input    Input   Type of             Arbitrary:   d or c, name, n_pts
46   Variable    Cell    Prob.
47    Number  Location Distr'tn <-distribution parameters->
48   -------- -------- -------- -------- -------- --------
49        1
50        2
51        3
52        4
53        5
54        6
55
56   Output    Name    Output
57  Variable    of      Cell   ----- frequency distribution -----
58   Number   Output Location  record?    start    stop interval
59   -------- -------- -------- -------- -------- -------- --------
60        1                        n         0        0        1
61        2                        n         0        0        1
62
63            Total number of simulated points?          100
64
65  ----------------------------------------------------------------------
66  >>> Fill in the above tables, then hit [Alt M] for the menu. <<<
67
68  ----------------------------------------------------------------------
```

This first table is used to specify the location of the input cells and to identify the probability distribution for each variable. Move the cursor to cell B49 and type in the cell location of the first input variable, D28. Enter the type of distribution (give the full name, normal, or the first letter, n) in cell C49 and the parameters of the selected distribution (5 and 1 in this example) in cells [D49..E49]. The screen should look like this:

```
         A        B        C        D        E        F        G        H
38  SIMULATION SETUP DATA                    Distribution: parameter list
39                                           ---------------------------
40  Analyst Name       Your_name             Normal:      mean, std_dev
41  Simulation Name    cashflow              Exponential: mean
42                                           Uniform:     lower, upper
43                                           Triangular:  lower, median, upper
44                                           Bernoulli:   p
45     Input    Input   Type of             Arbitrary:   d or c, name, n_pts
46   Variable    Cell    Prob.
47    Number  Location Distr'tn <-distribution parameters->
48   -------- -------- -------- -------- -------- --------
49        1  d28      normal       5        1
50        2
51        3
52        4
```

Enter the cell locations for the other input variables, and use the Copy command (/C) to define their distributions to be normal with mean 5 and standard deviation 1 also. (Note that each variable could have different parameters or distributions.) The input variable definition will look like this:

	A	B	C	D	E	F
45	Input	Input	Type of		Arbitrary:	d or
46	Variable	Cell	Prob.			
47	Number	Location	Distr'tn	<-distribution parameters->		
48	--------	--------	--------	--------	--------	--------
49	1	d28	normal	5	1	
50	2	d29	normal	5	1	
51	3	d30	normal	5	1	
52	4	d31	normal	5	1	
53	5	d32	normal	5	1	
54	6	d33	normal	5	1	
55						

Now define the output cells. Move the cursor to the table of output variable definitions, cell B60 in this example, and enter the name and cell location of each output variable. Call the first output variable NPV and the second IRR. The completed table should look like this:

	A	B	C	D	E	F	G	H
56	Output	Name	Output					
57	Variable	of	Cell	-----	frequency	distribution	-----	
58	Number	Output	Location	record?	start	stop	interval	
59	--------	--------	--------	--------	--------	--------	--------	
60	1	NPV	d34	n	0	0	1	
61	2	IRR	d35	n	0	0	1	
62								
63		Total number of simulated points?				100		
64	Fill in the above tables, then press [Alt M] for the menu.							
65	--							

For now we shall not record the frequency distribution of the output variables. The simulation has now been defined and you are ready to run it. Press [Alt M] to see the following menu:

```
F63: U 100                                                          MENU
Execute   Continue   Finish   Define_distrib   Edit
Begin simulating
        A         B         C         D         E       F       G       H
```

Select **Execute** by pressing [Enter]; PROPS⁺ will set up the simulation and run 100 independent simulations of the spreadsheet. The output in the worksheet appears as follows:

	A	B	C	D	E	F	G	H
69	Simulation Sample:							
70	No.	in_1	in_2	in_3	in_4	in_5	in_6	out_1
71	100	5.559563	4.181490	5.327287	4.639019	2.896754	3.902111	-0.28890
72	--							
73	OUTPUT AREA							
74	Output #1: NPV							
75								
76	mean	1.505504						
77	std dev	1.887494						
78								
79								
80	Output #2: IRR							
81								
82	mean	12.77170						
83	std dev	3.499184						

(Because of the random nature of the model, the output from one run to the next will be different. Thus the numbers in your output table may be slightly different.)

The Simulation Sample table is included in the output. This table displays the number of the current simulation run and the current input and resulting output values for each repetition. You can observe how these values change as the simulation proceeds. If you press [F9], the recalculation key, a new set of random input variables will be generated with the resulting output variables. This table is particularly useful in ensuring that the simulation is working correctly, because each time you press [F9], new random selections for each input will be shown with the corresponding output variable values. Note that at the end of a simulation, the values shown in this table have been recalculated for the next sample point.

Also notice that when the simulation is running, the mean and standard deviation for each output variable change as the sample size increases. This is useful for deciding how many points you need to simulate. This initial run consisted of 100 sample points. If you wish to simulate more points, say 200, move the cursor to F63, type **200** [Enter], press [Alt M] to get the menu, and select **Continue** from the menu. PROPS⁺ will then continue the simulation for 100 more independent simulations of the spreadsheet model. (If you selected **Execute**, the simulation would have been redefined and would run for 200 new iterations.) The output now appears as follows:

	A	B	C	D	E
74	Output #1: NPV				
75					
76	mean	1.880976			
77	std dev	1.690707			
78					
79					
80	Output #2: IRR				
81					
82	mean	13.42677			
83	std dev	3.099803			

There is no limit on the number of observations that can be simulated (except for the time required). If you wish to interrupt the simulation when it is executing, press [Ctrl Break] followed by [Esc]. You could then, for example, save the worksheet and carry on with some other tasks. When you wish to continue with the simulation, you can retrieve the worksheet and restart the simulation from the break point by pressing [Alt M] and selecting **Continue**.

You may wish to repeat the simulation and create a frequency distribution for each of the output variables. To do so, change the default value in the "record?" column from n to y for the output variables and define the range for each. From the initial run, we can estimate the range of each output variable. Let NPV run from −3 to 6 with an interval size of 1, and IRR from 7 to 18 in steps of 1. Your screen should appear as follows:

	A	B	C	D	E	F	G	H
58	Number	Output	Location	record?	start		stop	interval
59	--------	--------	--------	--------	--------		--------	--------
60	1	NPV	d34	y	−3		6	1
61	2	IRR	d35	y	7		18	1
62								
63		Total number of simulated points?					200	

To repeat the simulation, press [Alt M] and select **Execute**. The simulation will be initialized and then run, giving the following output. (The "Sum(***" cells are created by PROPS+ to compute the mean and variance of the output variables.)

	A	B	C	D	E	F	G	H	I	J	K	L	M	N	O
73	OUTPUT AREA														
74	Output #1: NPV								Sum(314			Sum(****			
75					frequency distribution										
76	mean	1.571163	x	−3	−2	−1	0	1	2	3	4	5	6		
77	std dev	1.634735	freq	2	4	14	34	45	39	36	18	7	1		
78															
79															
80	Output #2: IRR								Sum(****			Sum(****			
81					frequency distribution										
82	mean	12.85206	x	7	8	9	10	11	12	13	14	15	16	17	18
83	std dev	2.994900	freq	9	4	15	13	23	34	20	19	24	15	14	10
84															

To see the full table, the column width in columns C-O was changed to 4 using the **Worksheet Column Column-Range Set-width** command (**/WCCS**). The reported frequency distribution is the number of occurrences for the output variable (x) in the range [x−(interval/2), x+(interval/2)]. Occurrences outside this range are assigned to the lowest or highest range, as appropriate. The mean and standard deviation are computed from the actual occurrence data, not the frequency distribution. The 1-2-3 Graph command can be used to show the frequency distributions, as follows:

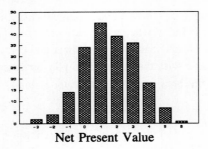
Net Present Value

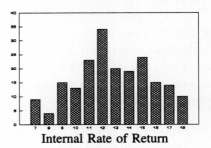
Internal Rate of Return

We will now discuss the probability distributions you can use to describe the input variables. First save this worksheet for later use using the **File Save** command (**/FS**), under the filename **F_SIMM**.

Probability Distributions

PROPS[+] is designed so that the distribution of input variables can be defined easily. The following probability distributions can be used:

Distribution	Parameter list	Variable range
Normal:	mean, std_dev	$-\infty < X < +\infty$
Exponential:	mean	$X > 0$
Uniform:	lower, upper	lower $< X <$ upper
Triangular:	lower, median, upper	lower $< X <$ upper
Bernoulli:	p	$X = 0$ or 1
Arbitrary:	d or c, name, n_pts	

The first four distributions listed describe continuous random variables. These distributions are illustrated in the following diagrams.

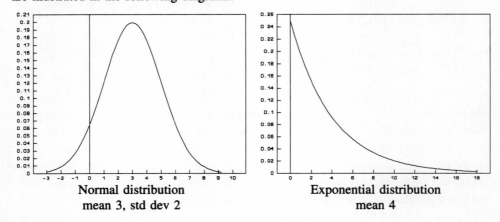

Normal distribution
mean 3, std dev 2

Exponential distribution
mean 4

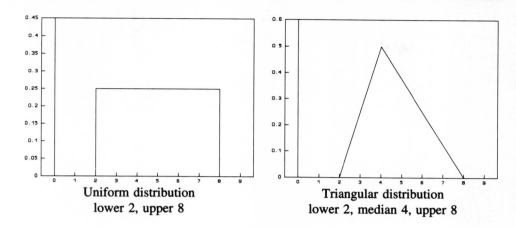

Uniform distribution
lower 2, upper 8

Triangular distribution
lower 2, median 4, upper 8

The Bernoulli distribution describes a discrete random variable that takes on the values X=1 with probability p, and X=0 with probability 1–p. Arbitrary distributions are discussed in the next section.

Arbitrary probability distributions   Arbitrary (any) distribution for continuous or discrete random variables can also be defined. In the Input Variable definition table, if the distribution is defined as "arbitrary," then the first item in the parameter list is d or c, indicating whether the distribution is discrete or continuous. The second item is a unique name followed by the number of points used to specify the distribution. For example, suppose you want one of the input random variables to be described by the following discrete distribution:

Cumulative distribution	F(x)	.1	.4	.7	.9	1
Probability distribution	f(x)	.1	.3	.3	.2	.1
Random variable	x	1	3	7	8	12

That is, the variable x will only take on the values 1, 3, 7, 8, or 12 with the above probabilities. Use the PROPS⁺ ACCESS worksheet and select **11. Simulation** to load a new simulation worksheet. The following screen illustrates how to define this distribution for an input variable called x in cell D28. Move the cursor down to row 24, press [Alt M] and select the default values for each prompt. The definition in the Input Variable table would look like

	A	B	C	D	E	F	G	H
33	Input	Input	Type of		Arbitrary:	d or c,	name,	n_pts
34	Variable	Cell	Prob.					
35	Number	Location	Distr'tn	<-distribution parameters->				
36	--------	--------	--------	--------	--------	--------	--------	
37	1	D28	arb	d	x	5		

(Note that in defining the type of distribution, you need only type the first letter.) To create this distribution, press [Alt M] and select **Define_distrib** from the menu. You will see the following screen:

```
        A         B         C     '   D         E         F         G         H
47  -------------------------------------------------------------------------
48  Area for arbitrary probability distributions
49
50  Note: F(x) = Probability X <= x.
51
52                                   <---- 5 points ---->
53     Name: X              F(x)        0         0         0         0         0
54     Type: discrete         x         0         0         0         0         0
55                          index       0         1         2         3         4
56
57  -------------------------------------------------------------------------
```

Enter the values for x that the variable can assume and the probability that the random variable is less than or equal to x; that is, the cumulative distribution function (cdf), or F(x). The worksheet should look like this:

```
        A         B         C         D         E         F         G         H
47  -------------------------------------------------------------------------
48  Area for arbitrary probability distributions
49
50  Note: F(x) = Probability X <= x.
51
52                                   <---- 5 points ---->
53     Name: X              F(x)       0.1       0.4       0.7       0.9        1
54     Type: discrete         x         1         3         7         8        12
55                          index       0         1         2         3         4
56
57  -------------------------------------------------------------------------
```

The cdf for this random variable is graphed as follows:

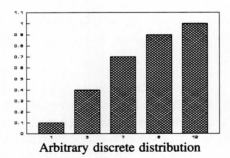

Arbitrary discrete distribution

Suppose you now want to use a continuous random variable that has the following cumulative probability distribution:

Cumulative distribution F(x)	0	.1	.4	.7	.9	1
Random variable x	0	1	3	7	8	12

Note that the probability distribution must be specified in terms of F(x), the cdf. Also note that the smallest x must have F(x)=0, and the largest F(x)=1. The random variable can take on any value in the range from 0 to 12. The following screen illustrates its definition in the Input Variable table:

	A	B	C	D	E	F	G	H
33	Input	Input	Type of		Arbitrary:	d or c,	name,	n_pts
34	Variable	Cell	Prob.					
35	Number	Location	Distr'tn	<-distribution parameters->				
36	--------	--------	--------	--------	--------	--------		
37	1	C23	arb		c	X	6	

To create this distribution, press [Alt M] and select **Define_distrib** from the menu. When you have entered the data, you will see the following screen:

	A	B	C	D	E	F	G	H
47	---							
48	Area for arbitrary probability distributions							
49								
50	Note: F(x) = Probability X <= x.							
51								
52				<---	6 points	----->		
53	Name: X		F(x)	0	0.1	0.4	0.7	0.9	1
54	Type: contin.		x	0	1	3	7	8	12
55			index	0	1	2	3	4	5
56				<----	6 points	---->		

Note that F(x) is 0 for the lowest value of x and 1 for the highest value of x.

Editing

PROPS+ also allows you to add or delete both input and output variables to or from the model you have constructed. Suppose you wish to modify the financial simulation discussed earlier. Begin by retrieving the previously saved simulation file **F_SIMM.WK1** using the File Retrieve command (**/FR**). Suppose, for example, that you wish to have a record of the cash flow in period 1. To do so, add a new output variable 3 to the Output Variable table, name it "cash1", and give its cell location, D28. To edit the model, move the cursor to the row in the SIMULATION SETUP DATA table where you want to add or delete a variable. In this case, move the cursor to A62. Press [Alt M] and select **Edit** from the menu. You will see the following new menu:

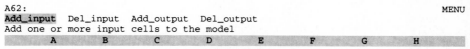

```
A62:                                                          MENU
Add_input  Del_input  Add_output  Del_output
Add one or more input cells to the model
         A       B       C       D       E       F       G       H
```

Select **Add_output** and you will see the following screen:

```
A62:                                                                        POINT
Enter name: _ROWS_TO_ADD_                        Enter range: A62..A62
```

	A	B	C	D	E	F	G	H
56	Output	Name	Output					
57	Variable	of	Cell	-----	frequency	distribution	-----	
58	Number	Output	Location	record?	start	stop	interval	
59	--------	--------	--------	--------	--------	--------	--------	
60	1 NPV		d34	n	0	0	1	
61	2 IRR		d35	n	0	0	1	
62								

Since you wish to add only one variable, press [Enter]. Space for the new variable is created, and after you have added its description you should see the following screen:

	A	B	C	D	E	F	G	H
58	Number	Output	Location	record?	start	stop	interval	
59	--------	--------	--------	--------	--------	--------	--------	
60	1 NPV		d34	n	0	0	1	
61	2 IRR		d35	n	0	0	1	
62	3 cash1		d28	n	0	0	1	

You can now rerun the simulation by pressing [Alt M] and selecting **Execute**. The output statistics for the new variable will now be recorded. You can also add or delete input variables to or from the simulation model in the same fashion.

When finished with a simulation, press [Alt M] and select **Finish**. This deletes all internal references to the spreadsheet model being simulated and to the input distributions and deletes any range name definitions created during the simulation.

The range of possible simulation models that can be created is almost limitless. To illustrate, the following examples demonstrate simulation models of an inventory system, a queueing system and of the gambling game called blackjack.

Example: Inventory System

Suppose a periodic review inventory system, in which the order quantity is Q and the safety-stock is s. Suppose the inventory level is reviewed at the beginning of each week and if the inventory level is s or lower, an order is placed for Q items. Replenishment is instantaneous. Assume the demand each week is approximately normally distributed with mean 10 and standard deviation 3, and our initial policy has Q=50 and s=5. (We will set up the simulation so that different values of Q and s can be chosen.) Finally, suppose the cost each time an order is placed is K=$40, the annual cost of holding an item in inventory is $14 (14/52 per week) and the cost per item short is $10.

To simulate this system we first create a spreadsheet model. The following model describes the inventory system for a single period:

```
          A         B         C       D       E         F         G         H
 1   Inventory Simulation Model
 2                                            Cost coefficients
 3   safety-stock, s        5             order (optional),c          0
 4   order quantity, Q     50             setup, K                   40
 5                                        holding, h           0.269230
 6   initial inventory     10             shortage, p                10
 7            order         0
 8   r.v.      3.093910
 9   rounded demand         3
10   ending inventory       7
11   cost this period  1.884615
12
```

The initial or starting inventory level is in cell C6. The formulas for the model are:

    C7: @IF(C6<=C3,C4,0).
    B8: 20*@RAND
    C9: @ROUND(B8,0)
    C10: +C6+C7-C9
    C11: @IF(C7>0,G4+G3*C7,0)+@IF(C10>=0,G5*C10,-G6*C10)

For testing purposes, the random demand is assumed to be uniformly distributed between 0 and 20, generated by the 1-2-3 formula **@rand**. Since demand is integer, the generated demand is rounded to the nearest integer in cell C9. The inventory at the end of the period is calculated in cell C10, with the costs for the period calculated in cell C11. To test the model, press the recalculation key [F9] to generate a new random demand. Change the initial inventory level, the order quantity, Q, and the safety-stock, s, to ensure that the calculations are performed correctly.

To make the model into a multi-period one, enter the formula **+C10** in cell C6. You will now see the **CIRC** indicator at the bottom of your screen. This indicates that there is a circular reference in the spreadsheet model. The initial inventory is made equal to the ending inventory (for the previous period), and the ending inventory depends on the initial inventory. Each time you press the recalculation key [F9] the model recalculates the spreadsheet and shows the results for the next period. Try it! When you are satisfied that the model is correct, use the **File Save** command (**/FS**) to save this model under the name **INV_SIMM**.

From the PROPS+ ACCESS worksheet, select **11. Simulation**. Use the **File Combine Copy Entire-File** command (**/FCCE**) and give the file name **INV_SIMM**. This operation will import the inventory model into the simulation spreadsheet. Your screen should look like:

```
         A         B         C         D        E        F        G         H
21   ---------------------------------------------------------------------------
22    Area for spreadsheet model: import or create below, then press [Alt M]
23                    Inventory Simulation Model
24                                          Cost coefficients
25    safety-stock, s        5             order (optional),c           0
26    order quantity, Q     50             setup, K                    40
27                                         holding, h        0.269230
28    initial inventory      9             shortage, p                 10
29           order           0
30    r.v.      2.026956
31    rounded demand         2
32    ending inventory       7
33    cost this period  1.884615
34
```

Move the cursor down the spreadsheet to row 35. Press [Alt M], and in response to the prompts enter the problem name and specify 1 input and 1 output variable. Define the input variable to be cell B30, with a normal distribution with mean 10 and standard deviation 3. The output is cell C33. When you have finished defining the simulation setup, your screen should look like:

```
         A         B         C         D        E        F        G         H
37   SIMULATION SETUP DATA                   Distribution: parameter list
38                                           --------------------------
39   Analyst Name         Your_name          Normal:      mean, std_dev
40   Simulation Name      simulate inventory Exponential: mean
41                                           Uniform:     lower, upper
42                                           Triangular:  lower, median, upper
43                                           Bernoulli:   p
44    Input     Input   Type of              Arbitrary:   d or c, name, n_pts
45   Variable   Cell     Prob.
46   Number   Location  Distr'tn  <-distribution parameters->
47   --------  --------  --------  --------  --------  --------
48      1        b30        n         10        3
49
50   Output     Name    Output
51   Variable     of     Cell    ----- frequency distribution -----
52   Number    Output  Location  record?    start     stop  interval
53   --------  --------  --------  --------  --------  --------  --------
54      1        cost      c33        n         0         0        1
55
56              Total number of simulated points?         100
```

To run the simulation, press [Alt M] and select **Execute**. PROPS[+] will run 100 independent simulations of the spreadsheet. The output in the worksheet appears:

```
         A         B         C         D        E        F        G
62   Simulation Sample:
63      No.     in_1     out_1
64      100  14.00464  49.96153
65   --------------------------
66   OUTPUT AREA
67   Output #1: cost
68
69      mean 17.17807
70   std dev 19.88402
71
```

That is, for a simulation of 100 weeks, the mean cost is $17.18. Note that, since simulation is a random process, the cost you calculate will probably be different since you will have a different random sample.

A simulation run of 100 observations is very small. To get a longer sample, change the number of simulated points to 1000 (cell F56), press [Alt M] and select **Continue**. The simulation will continue and you will see the following screen:

```
        A          B          C        D        E        F        G
62  Simulation Sample:
63       No.       in_1     out_1
64      1000  16.92574  5.115384
65  --------------------------
66  OUTPUT AREA
67  Output #1: cost
68
69       mean 16.69111
70   std dev 20.20818
```

The cost estimate is now $16.69 per week. If the simulation is run for 10,000 weeks, the estimate is

```
        A          B          C        D        E        F        G
62  Simulation Sample:
63       No.       in_1     out_1
64     10000  9.603761        30
65  --------------------------
66  OUTPUT AREA
67  Output #1: cost
68
69       mean 16.50428
70   std dev 20.13794
```

Simulations generally require very long runs (many observations) to accurately estimate the mean or the distribution of the output variables. An estimate for the standard deviation of the estimated (sample) mean is (std dev)/$\sqrt{n}$, where n is the number of independent observations. Since our observations are not independent, we would expect the standard deviation of our estimate for the cost each week is *at least* 0.2 (= $20.1/\sqrt{10000}$).

Suppose you were interested in the cost implications of varying the safety-stock level. Changing the value in cell C25 to 13, and running the simulation for another 10,000 points resulted in a cost estimate of $15.75 per week, which is clearly an improvement over the cost with a safety stock of 10. You could use this simulation model in this trial-and-error fashion, to search for the optimal value for the order quantity and safety-stock. You will find, however, that very long simulation runs are required, particularly as you get near the optimal values and the changes in cost are small.

Example: Queueing

Our next example is a simulation of a single server queueing system. Initially, we shall assume an M/M/1 queue (see Chapter 10), but arbitrary distributions for the interarrival and service times could also be simulated.

The first step is to create a spreadsheet model of the customer's arrival and departure time to and from the system. Several approaches are possible; however, the simplest is to use a renewal model with the recursive recalculation capability of the spreadsheet. The following spreadsheet demonstrates such a model for a single server queue.

	A	B	C	D	E	F	G	H
1	Single Server Queue Simulation							
2							0-1 rv	sample
3	arrival rate		0.8		int-arrival time		0.432345	0.707803
4	service rate		1		service time		0.468223	0.631531
5								
6	last arrival time			21.33787				
7	inter-arrival time			0.707803				
8	last service comp. time			31.92553				
9								
10	time of next arrival			22.04567				
11	service time			0.631531				
12	next service comp. time			32.55706				
13								
14	time waiting in system			10.51139				
15	idle time per service			0				
16								

The following formulas are in the specified cells:

    D6:   +D10
    D7:   +H3
    D8:   +D12
    D10: @IF(D6+D7>D8,0,D6+D7)
    D11: +H4
    D12: @IF(D10=0,D11,D8+D11)
    D14: +D12-D10
    D15: @IF(D10=0,D6+D7-D8,0)
    G3:   @RAND
    H3:   -@LN(1-G3)/C3
    G4:   @RAND
    H4:   -@LN(1-G4)/C4

The time of the last arrival is in cell D6, and the completion time for the last service is in D8. Cell D10 calculates the time of the next arrival. If the time of the next arrival (D6+D7) is greater than the time of the last service completion (D8), the queue is empty, and the time of the next arrival is re-set to zero (a new cycle). Cell D12 calculates the time when the customer will complete service. The customer's time in the system and the idle time per service are calculated in cells D14 and D15.

To generate exponentially distributed random variables for the interarrival and service times, uniformly distributed random variables are generated in cell G3 and G4 using the 1-2-3 function **@rand**. The inverse cumulative distributions for the exponential distributions are entered in cells H3 and H4, which transform the uniformly distributed random variables into the appropriate exponentially distributed variables.

The order of recalculation in the spreadsheet must be from top to bottom. To control this, use the **W**orksheet **G**lobal **R**ecalculation **R**owwise command (**/WGRR**). Note that the **CIRC** indicator at the bottom of the screen will turn off. To test the spreadsheet model, press the recalculation key [F9] repeatedly. When you are satisfied that the spreadsheet model is correct, use the **F**ile **S**ave command (**/FS**) to save this model under the name **Q_SIMM**.

From the PROPS⁺ ACCESS worksheet, select **11. Simulation**. Use the **F**ile **C**ombine **C**opy **E**ntire-File command (**/FCCE**) and select the file **Q_SIMM** to import the model into the simulation spreadsheet. After you have imported the model, you will have to again use the **W**orksheet **G**lobal **R**ecalculation **R**owwise command (**/WGRR**) to set the order of recalculation as the function setting is not transferred with the saved worksheet. Move the cursor to row 39, press [Alt M], and in response to the prompts enter the problem name, and define 0 input and 2 output variables. (Note that the PROPS⁺ simulation routine can use random variables defined in the spreadsheet model, and new values for these variables will be selected each time the simulation recalculates. If no input variables are defined, PROPS⁺ will collect the output statistics.) Define the output variables to be "wait" in cell D36 and "idle" in cell D37. Your screen should look like this:

```
        A         B         C         D      ·  E         F         G          H
41   SIMULATION SETUP DATA                    Distribution: parameter list
42                                            ----------------------------
43   Analyst Name        Your_name           Normal:       mean, std_dev
44   Simulation Name     simulate queue      Exponential: mean
45                                            Uniform:      lower, upper
46                                            Triangular:   lower, median, upper
47                                            Bernoulli:    p
48     Input     Input   Type of             Arbitrary:    d or c, name, n_pts
49   Variable     Cell    Prob.
50    Number   Location Distr'tn <-distribution parameters->
51   --------  -------- --------  --------  --------  --------
52
53    Output     Name    Output
54   Variable     of      Cell    ----- frequency distribution -----
55    Number   Output  Location record?    start     stop  interval
56   --------  -------- --------  --------  --------  --------  --------
57      1        wait     d36       n         0         0        1
58      2        idle     d37       n         0         0        1
59
60             Total number of simulated points?        100
61
```

To run the simulation, press [Alt M] and select **Execute.** PROPS[+] will run 100 customers through the queue. The output in the worksheet appears:

```
        A         B         C         D         E         F         G
66   Simulation Sample:
67      No.      out_1     out_2
68      100   1.754678  0.640331
69   --------------------------
70   OUTPUT AREA
71   Output #1: wait
72
73       mean 2.852115
74    std dev 1.942427
75
76
77   Output #2: idle
78
79       mean 0.212445
80    std dev 0.667503
81
```

The estimate for the waiting time in the system is 2.85 (the expected wait from queueing theory is 5.0, but for this number of observations an estimate between 2 and 10 is likely). If you run the simulation for longer periods, you will see how the mean waiting time estimate changes. After 1000 customers the following output appears:

```
        A         B         C         D         E         F         G
66   Simulation Sample:
67      No.      out_1     out_2
68     1000   15.51057        0
69   --------------------------
70   OUTPUT AREA
71   Output #1: wait
72
73       mean 3.857791
74    std dev 3.401365
75
```

After 10,000 customers the estimate was 4.43, while after 100,000 customers we obtained the following output:

```
        A         B          C       D       E       F       G
66   Simulation Sample:
67        No.     out_1    out_2
68    100000 17.13230           0
69   --------------------------
70   OUTPUT AREA
71   Output #1: wait
72
73        mean 4.976333
74    std dev 4.866147
75
76
77   Output #2: idle
78
79        mean 0.250588
80    std dev 0.761583
81
```

The estimated waiting time in the system is 4.98. This example highlights the need for long simulation runs for an accurate estimation of system characteristics. (Theoretically, the standard deviation of the estimate after 100,000 customers is 0.04, which is consistent with the above results.)

If you wish to use different interarrival or service time distributions, use the PROPS[+] edit command to add these input variables and to define the appropriate distributions.

Example: Blackjack

In Chapter 16 on page 339 we describe the game of blackjack and use stochastic dynamic programming to solve for the optimal strategy that the player should follow. In that problem we need to know the probabilities of each outcome should the dealer play (i.e., if the player doesn't break). This example shows how to use simulation to estimate these probabilities.

The casino rules require that the dealer must always take a card if she has 16 or less and does not take a card (she "stands") on 17 or more. Aces count as either 1 or 11. If the dealer exceeds 21, she "breaks" and the player wins. Start with a clean spreadsheet. The following spreadsheet models the dealer's hand.

	A	B	C	D	E	F	G	H
1								
2								
3	BLACKJACK	SPREADSHEET						
4						corr	corr	
5				total	sum	1st	2nd	
6	card no.	card	ace	aces	0	ace	ace	over
7	1	0	0	0	0	0	0	99999
8	2	0	0	0	0	0	0	99999
9	3	0	0	0	0	0	0	99999
10	4	0	0	0	0	0	0	99999
11	5	0	0	0	0	0	0	99999
12	6	0	0	0	0	0	0	99999
13	7	0	0	0	0	0	0	99999
14								
15						number of cards		7
16						final hand "Z"=		0

Column A contains the sequence number of the card (we assume the dealer will never take more than seven cards). Column B shows a possible sequence of card values that the dealer could obtain in seven draws. The formulas for columns C through H are

> **C7: @IF(B7=11,1,0)**
> **D7: +D6+C7**
> **E7: +E6+B7**
> **F7: @IF(E7>21#and#D7>0,E7-10,E7)**
> **G7: @IF(F7>21#and#D7>1,F7-10,F7)**
> **H7: @IF(G7>16,A7,99999)**

These formulas are copied into rows 8 through 13. Finally, in H15 and H16 we place the formulas:

> **H15: @IF(@MIN(H7..H13)>7,7,@MIN(H7..H13))**
> **H16: @INDEX(G7..G13,0,H15-1)**

Having constructed this model in the worksheet, check that the logic is correct by typing in different sequences of cards in column B (cards have values of 2-11). When you are satisfied that the model is correct, use the File Save command (**/FS**) to save the file under the name **BJ_MDL**.

From the PROPS[+] ACCESS worksheet, select **11. Simulation**. Leaving the cursor on cell A22, use the File Combine Copy Entire-file command (**/FCCE**), and select the file **BJ_MDL.WK1** to import the model into the simulation spreadsheet. Move the cursor down the spreadsheet to below the model, say row 39. Press [Alt M], enter the problem name, and define seven input and two output variables. Your screen should look like this:

	A	B	C	D	E	F	G	H
41	SIMULATION SETUP DATA				Distribution: parameter list			
42					---------------------------			
43	Analyst Name		Your_name		Normal:	mean, std_dev		
44	Simulation Name		blackjack		Exponential:	mean		
45					Uniform:	lower, upper		
46					Triangular:	lower, median, upper		
47					Bernoulli:	p		
48	Input	Input	Type of		Arbitrary:	d or c, name, n_pts		
49	Variable	Cell	Prob.					
50	Number	Location	Distr'tn	<-distribution parameters->				
51	--------	--------	--------	--------	--------	--------		
52		1						
53		2						
54		3						
55		4						
56		5						
57		6						
58		7						
59								
60	Output	Name	Output					
61	Variable	of	Cell	----- frequency distribution -----				
62	Number	Output	Location	record?	start	stop	interval	
63	--------	--------	--------	--------	--------	--------	--------	
64	1			n	0	0	1	
65	2			n	0	0	1	
66								
67	Total number of simulated points?					100		
68								
69	---							
70	>>> Fill in the above tables, then hit [Alt M] for the menu. <<<							

Complete the SIMULATION SETUP DATA table for this problem as follows:

	A	B	C	D	E	F	G	H
41	SIMULATION SETUP DATA				Distribution: parameter list			
42					---------------------------			
43	Analyst Name		Your_name		Normal:	mean, std_dev		
44	Simulation Name		blackjack		Exponential:	mean		
45					Uniform:	lower, upper		
46					Triangular:	lower, median, upper		
47					Bernoulli:	p		
48	Input	Input	Type of		Arbitrary:	d or c, name, n_pts		
49	Variable	Cell	Prob.					
50	Number	Location	Distr'tn	<-distribution parameters->				
51	--------	--------	--------	--------	--------	--------		
52	1	b28	arb	d	card	10		
53	2	b29	arb	d	card	10		
54	3	b30	arb	d	card	10		
55	4	b31	arb	d	card	10		
56	5	b32	arb	d	card	10		
57	6	b33	arb	d	card	10		
58	7	b34	arb	d	card	10		
59								
60	Output	Name	Output					
61	Variable	of	Cell	----- frequency distribution -----				
62	Number	Output	Location	record?	start	stop	interval	
63	--------	--------	--------	--------	--------	--------	--------	
64	1	no_cards	h36	y	2	7	1	
65	2	hand	h37	y	17	22	1	
66								
67	Total number of simulated points?					1000		
68								

Before running the simulation, you must create the distribution for the possible draws that the dealer would observe, using the **Define_distrib** command in the menu. In this example, we will approximate the distribution by assuming that each draw is independent of the others, so that the probability of drawing each value from 2 through 9 is 1/13, a 10 (or face card counting as 10) is 4/13, and an ace is 1/13. Remember to enter the cumulative probabilities. Changing the column widths to show more of the worksheet, the distribution appears as follows:

```
        A       B       C     D     E     F     G     H     I     J     K     L     M
69   -----------------------------------------------
70   Area for arbitrary probability distributions
71
72   Note: F(x) = Probability X <= x.
73
74                              <- 10 points ----->
75   Name: CARD       F(x) 0.07 0.15 0.23 0.30 0.38 0.46 0.53 0.61 0.92   1
76   Type: discrete    x     2     3     4     5     6     7     8     9    10    11
77                    index  0     1     2     3     4     5     6     7     8     9
78
```

We have requested 1,000 points in the simulation. To run, press [Alt M] and select **Execute** by pressing [Enter]. The following output is generated:

```
        A       B       C     D     E     F     G     H     I     J     K
84   OUTPUT AREA
85   Output #1: no_cards                                    Sum(x) 2909
86                              frequency distribution
87      mean    2.909    x     2     3     4     5     6     7
88   std dev 0.846592 freq.   348   446   163    36     6     1
89
90
91   Output #2: hand                                        Sum(x)20485
92                              frequency distribution
93      mean   20.485    x    17    18    19    20    21    22
94   std dev 2.666041 freq.   119   149   143   169   123   297
95
```

Thus, in the 1,000 hands simulated, the dealer broke 29.7% of the time. On average the dealer took about three cards, and only once took seven cards. Remember, your results may be slightly different due to the randomness within the model. (For this problem, you also could use the Markov model in Chapter 14 to calculate the exact probabilities.)

You can now modify this model to include other features of blackjack. In the casino version of this game, the player sees the dealer's first card before he decides whether to take a card. Suppose the dealer's first card is a 2. In the above model, we could enter 2 in cell B28 for the dealer's first card. Move the cursor to the first variable in the input description (cell A52). Use the commands **Edit** and **Del_input** to delete the first input variable. (You now have only six input variables, with the same output definitions.) Simulating this model for 1,000 hands yields this output:

	A	B	C	D	E	F	G	H	I	J
83	OUTPUT AREA									
84	Output #1: no_cards								Sum(x)	3694
85				frequency distribution						
86	mean	3.694	x	2	3	4	5	6	7	
87	std dev	0.756547	freq.	0	463	402	114	20	1	
88										
89										
90	Output #2: hand								Sum(x)	20541
91				frequency distribution						
92	mean	20.541	x	17	18	19	20	21	22	
93	std dev	2.750330	freq.	126	148	139	112	134	341	
94										

Thus, if the dealer shows a 2 as her first card, she has approximately a 34% chance of breaking and takes on the average 3.7 cards. We could repeat this exercise for each possible initial card held by the dealer.

Features

1. **<u>Discrete Probability Distributions</u>**

   - geometric.

   - binomial.

   - Poisson.

   - arbitrary.

2. **<u>Continuous Probability Distributions</u>**

   - normal.

   - exponential.

   - Erlang.

   - lognormal.

3. **<u>Conditional Distributions</u>**

   - Bayesian revision.

4. **<u>Functions of Random Variables</u>**

   - distribution for any function of random variables.

   - demand during lead time distributions.

Chapter 12. Probability Distributions

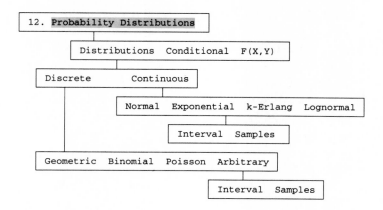

```
12. Probability Distributions
        │
        Distributions  Conditional  F(X,Y)
        │
  Discrete        Continuous
                        │
                Normal  Exponential  k-Erlang  Lognormal
                        │
                    Interval   Samples
        │
  Geometric  Binomial  Poisson  Arbitrary
                                    │
                            Interval   Samples
```

This worksheet provides a utility for manipulating probability distributions to support the other worksheets in PROPS⁺. Both discrete and continuous probability distributions can be generated. In PROPS⁺, probabilistic manipulations use either discrete random variables or discrete approximations of continuous random variables. In forming the discrete approximations, you specify the range of the random variable (from "start value" to "stop value") and either the **Interval** size or the number of **Sample** points. That is, the degree of accuracy of the approximation is up to you.

To use this module, retrieve the PROPS⁺ ACCESS worksheet and select **12. Probability Distributions** from the menu. You will see the following screen:

```
         A        B        C        D        E        F        G        H
 1   =============================   PROBABILITY DISTRIBUTION SPREADSHEET
 2              PROPS+               - discrete probability distributions
 3                                     (geometric, binomial, Poisson,
 4            Copyright (C)            general)
 5            PROPS SYSTEMS         - continuous probability distrib's
 6                                     (normal, exponential, Erlang,
 7          09/26/92 05:42 AM         lognormal)
 8   =============================   - Bayesian revision
 9                                   - calculates the probability
10      Your_name                      distribution for any function
11                                     of two random variables
12   Instructions:
13
14   Probability distribution tables will extend DOWN and RIGHT from the
15   location of the cursor when the macro is invoked.  Make sure you have
16   clear worksheet BELOW and RIGHT of the highlighted cell before execut'n
17
18         [Alt M] - Presents user with MENU of possible actions
19
20                                      Press [PgDn] for data area...
```

Defining Probability Distributions

PROPS[+] allows you to generate common discrete and continuous probability distributions, and in addition permits you to describe any arbitrary distribution in a discrete form. This section describes how to define each distribution. To set up a distribution using PROPS[+], press [Alt M] to reveal the following menu at the top of the screen:

```
A21:                                                                          MENU
Distributions  Conditional  F(X,Y)
Create probability distributions
```

Select **Distributions** and the menu changes to the following one:

```
A21:                                                                          MENU
Discrete  Continuous  (Return)
Create a discrete probability distribution
          A        B        C        D        E        F        G        H
```

You are now ready to define a probability distribution in the worksheet.

Discrete Distributions

Press [Enter] to select **Discrete** from the preceding menu. The menu then changes to the following:

```
A21:                                                                          MENU
Geometric  Binomial  Poisson  Arbitrary  (Return)
Geometric Distribution
          A        B        C        D        E        F        G        H
```

We will describe how to define distributions for each of these in turn.

Geometric Distribution

The geometric distribution describes the probability distribution of the number of observations (X) required to obtain the first "success" in a series of independent trials, each of which has a probability p of being a success. The equation for this distribution is

$$\text{Probability } [X = j] = p(1 - p)^{j-1} \quad j = 0, 1, 2, \ldots$$

$$\text{mean} = \frac{1}{p} \quad \text{standard deviation} = \sqrt{\frac{(1 - p)}{p}}$$

Note that this is a single-parameter distribution: setting a value for p completely defines the distribution.

Select **Geometric** from the menu. PROPS⁺ then asks you for a name for the distribution, in this case leaving the cursor in the worksheet above the question. Simply type in a name of your choice (from 1 to 14 characters long), which will be used to refer to this distribution from now on. PROPS⁺ then requests a value for p. Enter this value as a decimal, and PROPS⁺ constructs the complete distribution. As an example, suppose we want the geometric distribution for p=0.68. Naming it GEO-1 and entering .68 when requested generates the following entries in the worksheet:

	A	B	C	D	E	F	G	H	I	J
21		Geometric	distribution:	GEO-1						
22										
23	prob *p	0.68 |	cdf:	0.68	0.8976	0.9672	0.9895	0.9966	0.9989	0.9996
24	mean	1.4705 |	pdf:	0.68	0.2176	0.0696	0.0222	0.0071	0.0022	0.0007
25	std dev	0.8318 |	x:	1	2	3	4	5	6	7
26										

Note that PROPS⁺ provides the probability distribution function (pdf), the cumulative distribution function (cdf), and the mean and standard deviation of the distribution. (The distribution description in PROPS⁺ is truncated when the cdf reaches 0.999.)

Binomial Distribution

The binomial distribution describes the probability of observing j successes in n independent observations, when the probability of a success for any observation is p. Its equation is

$$\text{Probability } [X = j] = \left(\frac{n!}{j!(n - j)!} \right) p^j (1 - p)^{n-j} \quad j = 0, 1, 2, \ldots$$

$$\text{mean} = np \quad \text{standard deviation} = \sqrt{np(1 - p)}$$

This is a two-parameter distribution that requires values for the number of observations n and the success probability on a single observation p.

To construct a binomial distribution in PROPS+, select **Binomial** from the menu; you will be prompted for a distribution name. Type in a name (1-14 characters) and you will be prompted for values for n and p. On receiving these values, PROPS+ builds the corresponding binomial distribution. PROPS+ requires that n be < 55. Of course, for large n the normal approximation to the binomial can be used. Below are the worksheet entries for creating a binomial distribution named BIN-1 with n=6, p=0.5.

	A	B	C	D	E	F	G	H	I	J
21		Binomial	distribution:	BIN-1						
22										
23	size "N	6	cdf:0.0156	0.1093	0.3437	0.6562	0.8906	0.9843		1
24	prob "p	0.5	pdf:0.0156	0.0937	0.2343	0.3125	0.2343	0.0937	0.0156	
25	mean	3	x: 0	1	2	3	4	5	6	
26	std dev	1.2247								
27										

Poisson Distribution

The Poisson distribution describes the probability distribution for a process (X) that counts the number of occurrences of some event in space or time, when the likelihood of an occurrence at any instant is identical and independent for all instants. Letting λ (lambda) be the average rate of occurrence per unit of space or time, in an interval of length t we would expect λt occurrences. The probability of exactly j occurrences in an interval t is

$$\text{Probability }[X = j] = \frac{(\lambda t)^j e^{-\lambda t}}{j!} \qquad j = 0, 1, 2, \ldots$$

$$\text{mean} = \lambda t \qquad \text{standard deviation} = \sqrt{\lambda t}$$

In PROPS+, a Poisson distribution is created by selecting **Poisson** from the menu. You will be asked for a name (1–14 characters) and the value for λt (the default value for λt is 1). PROPS+ then constructs the distribution, extending the sample space (j) to the right in the worksheet until the cdf reaches 0.999 or a maximum of 69 points is created. Entering the name (here POISSON-1), followed by the value 2.4 for the parameter λt, constructs the following distribution in the worksheet:

	A	B	C	D	E	F	G	H	I	J	K	L
21		Poisson	distribution:	POISSON-1								
22												
23	Lambda	2.4	cdf0.090	0.308	0.569	0.778	0.904	0.964	0.988	0.996	0.999	
24	mean	2.4	pdf0.090	0.217	0.261	0.209	0.125	0.060	0.024	0.008	0.002	
25	std de	1.549	x 0	1	2	3	4	5	6	7	8	
26												

Arbitrary Distributions

You can enter any discrete probability distribution. PROPS[+] labels the sample points with a numeric value, and assumes a constant increment in this value from sample point to sample point. Thus, if you wish to describe a discrete variable with values that are not separated with a constant increment, you must first create a distribution with a constant step size that has the same number of points as your distribution, and with probabilities corresponding to your distribution. After creating this distribution, you can overwrite the constant increment random variable values with the ones you wish.

Suppose we wish to enter the following discrete distribution for a random variable X (note that there are seven sample points):

x	0	4	5	8	15	18	22
Prob(X=x)	.05	.1	.18	.22	.12	.3	.03

Selecting **Arbitrary** from the menu causes PROPS[+] to ask for a distribution name (1-14 characters in length). Choosing the name **GEN-1** yields the following screen:

```
       A         B         C         D         E         F         G         H
21               Probability distribution: GEN-1
22
23
24
25                                     0
26                           Start x at?
27
```

The prompt "Start x at?" requests a value for the sample point with the lowest value, which can be any decimal number (default value 0). In this example we want seven sample points, so we can start at 0 and end at 6. Using the default value of 0 produces the screen:

```
       A         B         C         D         E         F         G
21               Probability distribution: GEN-1
22
23
24
25                                    10
26                           Stop x at?
27
```

The second prompt, "Stop x at?" asks for the largest value (default 10). On entering 6 in the highlighted cell, you are asked to select from a menu at the top of the screen:

```
D25:
Interval  Samples
You specify the interval ("step"), I calculate the number of sample points
        A       B       C       D       E       F       G
21                  Probability distribution: GEN-1
```

This menu allows you to choose one of two options for specifying the interval between sample points:

Interval - Choosing this option generates the prompt "How big?", which is a request for the interval size (1 in this example).

Samples - This option generates the prompt "How many?", which requests the number of sample points you wish in your distribution. PROPS[+] determines the interval length between the maximum and minimum values of the range to yield this many points. In the example, you would respond with 7.

Choosing the first option and responding to "How big?" with the default value of 1, pressing [Enter] results in the following screen:

```
        A       B       C       D       E       F       G       H       I       J
21                  Probability distribution: GEN-1
22
23   mean      0 |  cdf:    0       0       0       0       0       0       0
24   std dev   0 |  pdf:    0       0       0       0       0       0       0
25             |    x:      0       1       2       3       4       5       6
26             |   Px:      0       0       0       0       0       0       0
27             | Px^2:      0       0       0       0       0       0       0
28
29
```

You can now enter the probability distribution in the worksheet row designated "pdf" (row 24 in this example) by moving the cursor to each cell and typing in the probability for each successive sample point. The cdf is computed automatically. This yields the following worksheet:

```
        A       B       C       D       E       F       G       H       I       J
21                  Probability distribution: GEN-1
22
23   mean   3.28 |  cdf:  0.05    0.15    0.33    0.55    0.67    0.97      1
24   std dev1.5942|  pdf:  0.05     0.1    0.18    0.22    0.12     0.3    0.03
25             |    x:      0       1       2       3       4       5       6
26             |   Px:      0      0.1    0.36    0.66    0.48     1.5    0.18
27             | Px^2:      0      0.1    0.72    1.98    1.92     7.5    1.08
28
29
```

Finally, you can overwrite the random variable values with the actual values you want (in row 25 in this example):

	A	B	C	D	E	F	G	H	I	J
21		Probability distribution: GEN-1								
22										
23	mean	10.92	cdf:	0.05	0.15	0.33	0.55	0.67	0.97	1
24	std dev	6.2971	pdf:	0.05	0.1	0.18	0.22	0.12	0.3	0.03
25			x:	0	4	5	8	15	18	22
26			Px:	0	0.4	0.9	1.76	1.8	5.4	0.66
27			Px^2:	0	1.6	4.5	14.08	27	97.2	14.52
28										

Note that summary statistics (mean, standard deviation) are automatically updated as you enter the new values. Also, note that in the worksheet for the general distribution, values labeled "Px:" and "Px^2:" appear below the constructed distribution (in rows 26 and 27 in the example). These rows are used in computing the mean and standard deviation of the distribution.

Continuous Distributions

PROPS$^+$ allows definition of four common continuous models: normal, exponential, Erlang, and lognormal. In each case, PROPS$^+$ asks you for parameters defining the distribution, and uses these parameters to construct a discrete analogue of the continuous distribution. (Should a distribution other than these four be desired, you can enter the discrete form directly, using the **Arbitrary** option under the **Discrete** menu option.) In all cases, you have control over the degree of fineness of the approximation as follows. First, you have control over the low and high values in the approximation (though PROPS$^+$ will suggest default values). Second, you will be requested via a menu to specify either how many sample points are desired in the approximation or what the interval size should be. A narrow interval with many sample points implies a better approximation, but this larger sample space means that manipulations and computations will be carried out more slowly. You control this trade-off.

Interval - Choosing this option generates the prompt "How big?", which is a request for the interval size. If the previously specified range is not an integral multiple of the interval, the first interval starts at the low value and the last interval will contain the high value.

Samples - This option asks for the number of sample points desired ("How many?"). PROPS$^+$ chooses the specified low and high values as two of these points and evenly spaces the remaining points between these values.

To enter a continuous random variable in PROPS$^+$, press [Alt M] to display the following menu:

```
A21:                                                                       MENU
Distributions  Conditional  F(X,Y)
Create probability distributions
         A         B         C         D         E         F         G         H
```

Choosing **Distributions** and then **Continuous** changes the menu at the top of the screen as follows:

```
A21:                                                                       MENU
Normal  Exponential  K-Erlang  Lognormal  (Return)
Normal Distribution
         A         B         C         D         E         F         G         H
```

Normal Distribution

The equation describing the probability distribution for a normally distributed random variable X is

$$f(x) = \frac{1}{\sqrt{2\pi}\sigma}\, e^{-\frac{1}{2}\left(\frac{x-\mu}{\sigma}\right)^2} \qquad -\infty < x < \infty$$

$$\text{mean} = \mu \qquad \text{standard deviation} = \sigma$$

This is a distribution with two parameters, the mean μ and standard deviation σ. To define a normal distribution in PROPS⁺ with, say, a mean of 6.2 and standard deviation of 1.3, select **Normal** from the menu. You are then prompted for a name for the distribution (say, NORMAL-1), its mean, and its standard deviation. The following screen appears:

```
         A         B         C         D         E         F         G         H
21             Normal distribution: NORMAL-1
22
23     mean    6.2
24  std dev    1.3
25                                    2.3
26                            Start x at?
```

Following this, you are prompted for values at which to start and stop the distribution. (PROPS⁺ has default values of $(\mu-3\sigma)$ and $(\mu+3\sigma)$, or 2.3 and 10.1 in this example.) Finally, you are prompted for the number of sample points to use; you must specify either the interval size or the number of sample points, as described earlier. Here, using the default Start and Stop values, choosing **Samples,** and in response to the request "How many?" selecting 8 sample points in the distribution yields the following result:

	A	B	C	D	E	F	G	H	I	J	K	L
21		Normal distribution: NORMAL-1										
22												
23	mean	6.2	cdf	0.001	0.016	0.099	0.334	0.665	0.900	0.983	0.998	
24	std de	1.3	pdf	0.003	0.030	0.134	0.279	0.279	0.134	0.030	0.003	
25			x	2.3	3.414	4.528	5.642	6.757	7.871	8.985	10.1	
26			z	-3	-2.14	-1.28	-0.42	0.428	1.285	2.142	3	
27		Note: "pdf" is the value of f(x) at x										
28												

Observe that PROPS⁺ provides the value of the probability density function (pdf) at each value of x, the cumulative probability function (cdf), and the standardized normal z-score for each discrete value of the variable.

Note that the given pdf value at each point x is the *value* of the density function at that point. It is *not* a probability, so the set of given values does not sum to one. An approximation for the probability that the random variable X will take on the discrete value x can be found by multiplying the given value by the length of the interval between successive x values. Alternatively, you may assume the given pdf values are the relative values of observing a random variable value in each interval. A measure of the probability can be obtained by dividing the given pdf value by the sum of the pdf values across the range of the x values.

The value given for the cdf (the probability that the random variable value is less than or equal to x) is exact for the given x values. Thus the exact probability that X is between successive x values in the table is the difference between successive cdf values.

Exponential Distribution
The equation for the distribution for an exponential random variable is

$$f(x) = \lambda e^{-\lambda x} \qquad x \geq 0$$

$$\text{mean} = 1/\lambda \qquad \text{standard deviation} = 1/\lambda$$

Often used to model the time between occurrences of independent events, the exponential distribution is a single-parameter distribution that has both mean and standard deviation equal to 1/λ. Suppose we want an exponential distribution with parameter 0.3. Selecting **Exponential** from the menu causes PROPS⁺ to prompt for a distribution name (say, EXP-1) and a value for the parameter λ (here 0.3). You are then asked for a value at which to start the discrete distribution (default value 0). The screen looks like this:

A	B	C	D	E	F	G	H
21		Exponential distribution: EXP-1					
22							
23	Lambda	0.3					
24	mean	3.333333					
25	std dev	3.333333	0				
26			Start x at?				

PROPS⁺ then requests a value at which to stop the discrete form of the distribution, and suggests a default value of INT[−ln(.001/λ)]+1, where INT[.] stands for the integer part of the expression. Finally, PROPS⁺ requests the number of sample points through the prompt sequence: **Interval Samples.** If you use the defaults for the Start and Stop values and choose the **Interval** option, PROPS⁺ then requests the interval size with the following screen:

A	B	C	D	E	F	G	H
21		Exponential distribution: EXP-1					
22							
23	Lambda	0.3					
24	mean	3.333333					
25	std dev	3.333333	1				
26			How big?				
27							

PROPS⁺ always defaults to an interval size of 1. We can override the default value by typing in a new one, say 5, which yields the following distribution:

A	B	C	D	E	F	G	H	I
21		Exponential distribution: EXP-1						
22								
23	Lambda	0.3	cdf:	0	0.77686	0.95021	0.98889	0.99752	0.99944
24	mean	3.33333	pdf:	0.3	0.06693	0.01493	0.00333	0.00074	0.00016
25	std dev	3.33333	x:	0	5	10	15	20	25
26		Note: "pdf" is the value of f(x) at x							

As before, the cdf is the exact probability that the random variable is less than or equal to each x value, and the pdf is the value of the probability density function for each x.

Erlang Distribution

The equation for an Erlang distribution of order k is

$$f(x) = \frac{\mu k(\mu k t)^{k-1} e^{-\mu k t}}{(k - 1)!} \qquad \text{for } x \geq 0$$

$$\text{mean} = 1/\mu \qquad \text{standard deviation} = \sqrt{1/k\mu^2}$$

This two-parameter distribution (μ and k) corresponds to the sum of k independent and identically distributed exponential random variables, each with parameter kμ. The mean of this distribution is (1/μ) and its variance is (1/kμ²). In the most general form of this distribution, k is required merely to be nonnegative, in which case this is known as a Gamma distribution. In PROPS⁺, k is restricted to the positive integers less than 69.

This family of distributions is often used to describe the service time in queueing models. An Erlang with k=1 is the exponential distribution, and as k increases, the variance of the distribution decreases. In the limit, as k grows to infinity, the distribution represents a constant service time.

To use PROPS⁺ to construct an Erlang distribution with mean 2.0 and parameter k=3, select **K-Erlang** from the menu. After requesting a name for the distribution (say, ERL-1), PROPS⁺ requests the mean of the distribution (2), and the order k (3). It then requests a Start value (default 0) and a Stop value (default equal to the mean plus six standard deviations rounded off, which is 9 in this example), after which it again requests the number of points through **Interval** or **Samples** in the manner previously described. Selecting **Interval** with a step size of 1 yields the following screen:

```
        A    B    C    D    E    F    G    H    I    J    K    L    M    N
21          Erlang distribution: ERL-1
22
23   mean    2 |  cd   0 0.19 0.57 0.82 0.93 0.97 0.99 0.99 0.99 0.99
24      k    3 |  pd   0 0.37 0.33 0.16 0.06 0.02 0.00 0.00 0.00 0.00
25   std d1.15 |       0    1    2    3    4    5    6    7    8    9
26       Note: "pdf" is the value of f(x) at x
```

Lognormal Distribution

If Y is a normal random variable with mean μ and standard deviation σ and X $= e^Y$, then X has a lognormal distribution. Its density function is

$$f(x) = \frac{1}{\sqrt{2\pi}\sigma x} e^{-\frac{1}{2}\left[\frac{\ln(x) - \ln(\mu)}{\sigma}\right]^2}$$

$$\text{mean} = e^{\mu + \sigma^2/2} \qquad \text{standard deviation} = \sqrt{e^{(2\mu + 2\sigma^2)} - e^{(2\mu + \sigma^2)}}$$

This two-parameter distribution (μ and σ) has a minimum value of 0 (when the underlying normal distribution has a value of $-\infty$). You can change the minimum value by specifying a "shift" amount a, which merely translates the whole distribution by the constant a. To enter such a distribution in PROPS⁺, select **Lognormal** from the menu and provide a distribution name. You are prompted for "normal mu" and "normal sigma" (the parameters of the underlying normal process Y), and for the "shift a". Following this, PROPS⁺ asks for the Start value (default value $a+e^{(\mu-3\sigma)}$) and the Stop value (default value $a+e^{(\mu+3\sigma)}$). Finally, the number of points in the distribution is selected as before, using the **Interval** or **Samples** option.

The lognormal distribution can be highly skewed, with a long right-hand tail. The median value is $(a+e^{\mu})$, and the mean is a + the unshifted mean. Thus, as σ increases, the mean departs significantly from the median.

As an example, suppose you wish to enter a lognormal distribution named LOGN-1 with an underlying normal distribution with mean $\mu = 1$ and $\sigma = 0.5$, so that the resulting lognormal distribution will have a minimum value of 3. Following the preceding steps using the default Start and Stop values (3.60653 and 15.18249) and the **Samples** option to describe the sample space with, say, seven points, yields the following distribution:

	A	B	C	D	E	F	G	H	I	J
21		Lognormal	distribution:	LOGN-1						
22										
23	normal	1	cdf:0.0013	0.4447	0.8395	0.9564	0.9873	0.9960	0.9986	
24	& sig	0.5	pdf:0.0088	0.7902	0.4875	0.1846	0.0651	0.0234	0.0088	
25	shift "	3	x:3.6065	5.5358	7.4651	9.3945	11.323	13.253	15.182	
26	mean 6.0802		z:	-3	-0.138	0.9926	1.7108	2.2382	2.6551	3
27	std dev1.6415									
28	Note: "pdf" is the value of f(x) at x									

Conditional Distributions

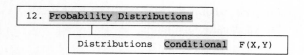

This spreadsheet allows you to work with discrete conditional probability distributions. Suppose you know the distribution of X, say f(x), and the conditional distribution of another variable Y given X, or f(y|x). PROPS[+] will construct the joint distribution f(x,y), the marginal distribution f(y), and the posterior distribution f(x|y).

To demonstrate, suppose X can assume values of 0, 1, or 2 with probabilities 0.5, 0.3, and 0.2, respectively. Suppose Y has a value of either 0 or 1, but the probability distribution for Y depends on which X value holds, as shown in this table:

	Y = 0	Y = 1
X = 0	0.5	0.5
X = 1	0.3	0.7
X = 2	0.1	0.9

Conditional Distribution f(y|x)

First, access the **12. Probability Distribution** spreadsheet from the PROPS[+] ACCESS menu. Enter the distribution for X by pressing [Alt M] and selecting **Distributions, Discrete,** and **Arbitrary** from the successive menus. Naming this distribution as X with values from 0 to 2 with an interval of 1, and entering the above probabilities, results in the following worksheet:

	A	B	C	D	E	F	G
21		Probability distribution: X					
22							
23	mean	0.7	| cdf:	0.5	0.8	1	
24	std dev	0.781024	| pdf:	0.5	0.3	0.2	
25			| x:	0	1	2	
26			| Px:	0	0.3	0.4	
27			| Px^2:	0	0.3	0.8	
28							

To enter the conditional distribution of Y given X, press [Alt M] and select **Conditional** from the menu. PROPS[+] asks for the name of the distribution to be created (say, Y) and the name of the existing (prior) distribution (enter X for the distribution just created), and the range of the Y distribution (0 to 1 with an interval of 1). PROPS[+] creates the following worksheet:

	A	B	C	D	E	F	G	H
30		Conditional distribution: Y						
31		(Y {P(y)} conditional on X {P(x)})						
32								
33			ENTER CONDITIONAL PROBABILITIES {P(y|x)} BELOW:					
34				y				
35				0	1	Check		
36		x	0	0	0	ERR		
37			1	0	0	ERR		
38			2	0	0	ERR		
39								
40			Joint probability distribution {P(x,y)}:					
41				y				
42				0	1			
43		x	0	0	0			
44			1	0	0			
45			2	0	0			
46								
47								
48			Marginal Probability Distribution {P(y)}: Y					
49								
50	mean	0	| cdf:	0	0			
51	std dev	0	| pdf:	0	0			
52			| y:	0	1			
53			| Py:	0	0			
54			| Py^2:	0	0			
55								
56			Posterior probability distribution {P(x|y)}:					
57				y				
58				0	1			
59		x	0	ERR	ERR			
60			1	ERR	ERR			
61			2	ERR	ERR			
62								

You can now enter the values of the conditional probability distribution in the appropriate cells (rows 36 to 38, columns D and E in this example). Note the "Check" column, which tests to see if the entries sum to 1 for each value of X. The joint, marginal, and posterior distribution are automatically calculated, yielding the following worksheet:

	A	B	C	D	E	F	G	H
30		Conditional distribution: Y						
31		(Y {P(y)} conditional on X {P(x)})						
32								
33			ENTER CONDITIONAL		PROBABILITIES {P(y|x)} BELOW:			
34				y				
35				0	1	Check		
36		x	0	0.5	0.5	ok		
37			1	0.3	0.7	ok		
38			2	0.1	0.9	ok		
39								
40			Joint probability distribution {P(x,y)}:					
41				y				
42				0	1			
43		x	0	0.25	0.25			
44			1	0.09	0.21			
45			2	0.02	0.18			
46								
47								
48			Marginal Probability Distribution {P(y)}: Y					
49								
50	mean	0.64	| cdf:	0.36	1			
51	std dev	0.48	| pdf:	0.36	0.64			
52			| y:	0	1			
53			| Py:	0	0.64			
54			| Py^2:	0	0.64			
55								
56			Posterior probability distribution {P(x|y)}:					
57				y				
58				0	1			
59		x	0	0.694444	0.390625			
60			1	0.25	0.328125			
61			2	0.055555	0.28125			
62								

From this worksheet, the unconditional probability of observing Y = 0 is 0.36, and of Y = 1 is 0.64. Further, given a Y value, the conditional distribution for X is given directly.

One common use for conditional distributions is in Bayesian revision of beliefs in decision analysis. This is discussed in detail in Chapter 13. Another use is in calculating the demand distribution during the lead time in inventory control models. The next section describes this use.

Function of Random Variables

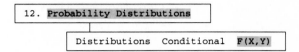

PROPS⁺ determines the probability distribution of any function of two random variables, and, by iteration, of any function of any number of independent random variables. The logic is as follows. Suppose you have already defined distributions in a worksheet for two random variables, X and Y, using the methods of the previous section. Recall that PROPS⁺ represents these distributions in a discrete form with a finite number of possible values for each X and Y. Suppose we have n values for X and m for Y. In constructing a function of X and Y, PROPS⁺ begins by determining the joint probability of each possible ordered pair of X,Y values, which would be (nm) values. (Because the underlying distributions may be either discrete or a discrete approximation to a continuous distribution, PROPS⁺ uses the normalized value of the pdf as the probability of each event.) PROPS⁺ then attaches a function value to each of these joint sample points, and finally summarizes the resulting distribution in a form specified by the user.

As an example, suppose you have defined two distributions in the worksheet; the first, called BIN, is a binomial with n=4 and p=.3, and the second, called GEN, is an arbitrary distribution with values 1, 3, 4, and 7 and probabilities P(1)=.2, P(3)=.5, P(4)=.1, and P(7)=.2. Suppose you wish to find the distribution for the random variable JNT = $BIN^2 - 2*GEN$.

Using the methods of the last section to enter the two distributions successively, the worksheet appears as follows:

	A	B	C	D	E	F	G	H
20		Binomial distribution: BIN						
21								
22	size "N"	4	| cdf:	0.2401	0.6517	0.9163	0.9919	1
23	prob "p"	0.3	| pdf:	0.2401	0.4116	0.2646	0.0756	0.0081
24	mean	1.2	| x:	0	1	2	3	4
25	std dev	0.916515						
26								
27								
28		Probability distribution: GEN						
29								
30	mean	3.5	| cdf:	0.2	0.7	0.8	1	
31	std dev	1.962141	| pdf:	0.2	0.5	0.1	0.2	
32			| x:	1	3	4	7	
33			| Px:	0.2	1.5	0.4	1.4	
34			| Px^2:	0.2	4.5	1.6	9.8	
35								

Press [Alt M] to display the following menu at the top of the screen:

```
A38:
Distributions  Conditional  F(X,Y)
Create probability distributions
        A         B         C         D         E         F         G         H
```

Selecting **F(X,Y)** from this menu causes PROPS⁺ to prompt you for a name for the new distribution (say JNT), and then for names for the two component distributions (BIN and GEN). PROPS⁺ then determines the number of ordered sample points and generates the following table in the worksheet and on the screen:

```
C47:                                                                    VALUE
+
        A         B         C         D         E         F
45
46      BIN       GEN       JNT       Prob.
47      0         1                   0.04802
48      0         3                   0.12005
49      0         4                   0.02401
50      0         7                   0.04802
51
```

PROPS⁺ then requests that you use POINT mode to construct the desired function. As an example, to specify the function (BIN^2 − 2*GEN), observe that the cursor is currently on the first row in the desired JNT distribution (cell C47 in this example). Move the cursor to the first row of the column labeled "BIN", cell A47. Then press the exponent symbol ^, followed by 2. Note that the cursor returns to the first row of column "JNT". Now enter a "−" sign and move the cursor to the first row of the column labeled "GEN" (cell B47). Finally, press * followed by 2 to multiply GEN by 2. The cell contents at the top of the screen appear as follows:

```
C47:                                                                    VALUE
+A47^2-B47*2
        A         B         C         D         E         F         G
45
46      BIN       GEN       JNT       Prob.
47      0         1                   0.04802
48      0         3                   0.12005
49      0         4                   0.02401
50      0         7                   0.04802
51
```

Pressing [Enter] causes PROPS⁺ to calculate the function value for each (BIN,GEN) sample point and store the result in "JNT". At the conclusion of this step, the top of the table in the worksheet appears as follows:

```
           A         B         C         D         E         F         G
42
43                                          -14
44                                    Start x at?
45
46       BIN       GEN       JNT      Prob.
47         0         1       -14    0.04802
48         0         3       -13    0.08232
```

Finally, PROPS⁺ requests information about how you would like to represent this distribution. You can select any level of summarization by specifying the starting and ending discrete values and either the interval width or the desired number of sample points. PROPS⁺ will request the smallest value by prompting "Start x at ?" (with a default value equal to the lowest observed value, here –14), and the largest value with "Stop x at ?" (the default value is the largest function value, here +14). Once you have specified the minimum and maximum desired values for the resulting JNT distribution, PROPS⁺ presents a menu for you to describe the intermediate values between these extremes. You can do this by specifying the interval size or the total number of points you want in the resulting distribution, by selecting from the following menu:

```
D43:                                                                              MENU
Interval  Samples
You specify the interval ("step"), I calculate the number of sample points
     A         B         C         D         E         F         G         H
```

Suppose we used the default values for the first and last point of –14 and +14, and selected **Interval** from this menu. PROPS⁺ requests the interval width with the prompt "How big?" (default 1, which we might override with a value of, say, 4). PROPS⁺ immediately constructs the desired probability distribution JNT in the worksheet, as follows:

```
      A    B    C    D    E    F    G    H    I    J    K    L
38         Probability distribution: JNT
39         (Function of BIN and GEN)
40
41   mean -4.72 |  cdf0.048 0.183 0.368 0.796 0.940 0.978 0.998     1
42   std de4.800 |  pdf0.130 0.052 0.406 0.289 0.099 0.015 0.004 0.001
43              |   x  -14   -10    -6    -2     2     6    10    14
44
```

Note: The values given for the cdf of JNT are the probabilities that the variable JNT will be less than or equal to each x, and are exact. Letting the interval between the x values be I, the value given for pdf is the relative frequency that JNT lies in the range $x - I/2$ $\leq$ JNT $< x + I/2$. Thus, in this aggregation process, all the points in each half-open interval $[x - (I/2), x + (I/2))$ are approximated by x. Any probability mass directly on the midpoint is assigned to the higher value. The extreme low and high end points of the new distribution are assigned the probabilities below the first midpoint and above the last, respectively.

Example: Distribution of Demand during Lead Time

In inventory control, the time between placing an order for more stock and the arrival of the stock, called the "lead time," is often random. The replenishment policy must take the demand during this time into account in determining how much to order the next time. You can use this spreadsheet to calculate a distribution for the demand during the lead time.

Suppose the demand each day, X, is random but independent from day to day and follows this distribution:

x	0	1	2	3
P(x)	.4	.3	.2	.1

The lead time, T, is 1, 2, or 3 days with the following probability distribution:

t	1	2	3
P(t)	.25	.5	.25

To find the distribution for the demand during the lead time, access the probability worksheet and enter the discrete distribution X (using the **Distributions, Discrete, Arbitrary** sequence of menu selections). Call up the menu with [Alt M]. From the menu, select **F(X,Y)** to create a random variable X2 that will be found by X2 = X + X, and will correspond to the demand given a lead time of two days. (In this construction, the first distribution name is X and the second is also X. Use the given default values for range and interval to summarize the X2 distribution.) Repeat the **F(X,Y)** procedure to construct X3 = X2 + X, the demand given a lead time of three days, again using default values to summarize. Finally, enter the distribution for the lead time T using the **Distributions, Discrete, Arbitrary** menu choices. The spreadsheet should then contain the following data:

```
       A     B     C     D     E     F     G     H     I     J     K     L     M     N
20           Probability distribution: X
21
22    mean    1  |  cd 0.4   0.7   0.9    1
23    std d   1  |  pd 0.4   0.3   0.2   0.1
24               |     0     1     2     3
25               |  P  0    0.3   0.4   0.3
26               |  Px^ 0   0.3   0.8   0.9
27
28
29
30           Probability distribution: X2
31           (Function of X and X)
32
33    mean    2  |  cd0.16  0.4  0.65  0.85  0.95  0.99    1
34    std d1.41  |  pd0.16 0.24  0.25   0.2   0.1  0.04  0.01
35               |     0     1     2     3     4     5     6
36       Note: "pdf" is the relative frequency of x in [x-int/2,x+int/2]
37
38
39           Probability distribution: X3
40           (Function of X and X2)
41
42    mean    3  |  cd0.06  0.20  0.41  0.63  0.80  0.91  0.97  0.99  0.99    1
43          1.73 |  pd0.06  0.14  0.20  0.21  0.17  0.11  0.05  0.02  0.00  0.00
44               |     0     1     2     3     4     5     6     7     8     9
45
46
47
48           Probability distribution: T
49
50    mean    2  |  cd0.25  0.75    1
51    std d0.70  |  pd0.25   0.5  0.25
52               |     1     2     3
53               |  P0.25    1  0.75
54               |  Px^0.25    2  2.25
```

Now X is the conditional demand during the lead time if T=1; X2 is the conditional demand if T=2; and X3 corresponds to T=3. You can use the **Conditional** spreadsheet to find the unconditional demand, D, during the lead time. First, D has a possible range from 0 to 9. To construct the distribution for D, press [Alt M] and select **Conditional**. Name the new distribution D, with the prior distribution T, and use the values Start 0, Stop 9, and Interval 1. PROPS⁺ generates this table:

	B	C	D	E	F	G	H	I	J	K	L	M	N	O
58	Conditional distribution: D													
59	(D {P(y)} conditional on T {P(x)})													
60														
61			ENTER CONDITIONAL PROBABILITIES {P(y|x)} BELOW:											
62			y											
63			0	1	2	3	4	5	6	7	8	9	Check	
64	x	1	0	0	0	0	0	0	0	0	0	0	ERR	
65		2	0	0	0	0	0	0	0	0	0	0	ERR	
66		3	0	0	0	0	0	0	0	0	0	0	ERR	
67														

To complete the table, use the spreadsheet Copy command (/C) to put the pdf values for X (row 23) into the first row (row 64 in the spreadsheet), the pdf for X2 (row 34) in the second row (row 65), and the pdf for X3 (row 43) in the third row (row 66). The resulting spreadsheet appears as follows:

	B	C	D	E	F	G	H	I	J	K	L	M	N	O
58	Conditional distribution: D													
59	(D {P(y)} conditional on T {P(x)})													
60														
61			ENTER CONDITIONAL PROBABILITIES {P(y|x)} BELOW:											
62			y											
63			0	1	2	3	4	5	6	7	8	9	Check	
64	x	1	0.4	0.3	0.2	0.1	0	0	0	0	0	0	ok	
65		2	0.16	0.24	0.25	0.2	0.1	0.04	0.01	0	0	0	ok	
66		3	0.06	0.14	0.20	0.21	0.17	0.11	0.05	0.02	0.00	0.00	ok	
67														
68			Joint probability distribution {P(x,y)}:											
69			y											
70			0	1	2	3	4	5	6	7	8	9		
71	x	1	0.1	0.07	0.05	0.02	0	0	0	0	0	0		
72		2	0.08	0.12	0.12	0.1	0.05	0.02	0.00	0	0	0		
73		3	0.01	0.03	0.05	0.05	0.04	0.02	0.01	0.00	0.00	0.00		
74														
75														
76	Marginal Probability Distribution {P(y)}: D													
77														
78	2	| cdf	0.19	0.42	0.65	0.83	0.92	0.97	0.99	0.99	0.99		1	
79	1.58	| pdf	0.19	0.23	0.22	0.17	0.09	0.04	0.01	0.00	0.00	0.00		
80		|	y	0	1	2	3	4	5	6	7	8	9	
81		|	Py	0	0.23	0.45	0.53	0.37	0.23	0.11	0.03	0.01	0.00	
82		|Py^y	0	0.23	0.90	1.61	1.49	1.19	0.68	0.25	0.09	0.02		
83														
84	Posterior probability distribution {P(x|y)}:													
85			y											
86			0	1	2	3	4	5	6	7	8	9		
87	x	1	0.51	0.32	0.22	0.13	0	0	0	0	0	0		
88		2	0.40	0.51	0.55	0.55	0.53	0.41	0.26	0	0	0		
89		3	0.08	0.15	0.22	0.30	0.46	0.58	0.73	1	1	1		
90														

The Marginal Probability Distribution P(y) in this worksheet, labeled D, is the distribution of demand during the lead time. The values for demand are located in row 80 in this example, and the probabilities are in row 79. (The rows labeled Py and Py^y are used to compute the mean and standard deviation of the random variable.)

Features

1. <u>Decision Analysis</u>

- draws the decision tree in the worksheet.

- allows a user-specified utility function or table.

- computes optimal expected values and utilities.

- identifies optimal decisions under both criteria.

2. <u>Sensitivity Analysis</u>

- instant updating allows rapid sensitivity analysis to changes in problem parameters.

3. <u>Value of Information</u>

- facilitates Bayesian updating of probabilities.

- data entry system allows easy computation of value of sample information.

- sensitivity to prior probabilities is easily computed.

4. <u>Special Features</u>

- calculates the certainty equivalent of the optimal expected utility.

- permits indirect references to subtrees.

- facilitates problem editing.

Chapter 13. Decision Analysis

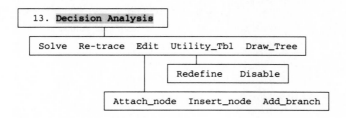

The Model:

At decision nodes: $f_i = \max_{k \in B_i} [f_k]$ (or min)

At chance nodes: $f_i = E_{k \in B_i} [f_k]$

where

f_i = the value of the objective at each node i

B_i = the set of successors to node i

E = the expected value operator

Computation: The terminal monetary value of each end node is calculated from the branch costs and rewards. The value f_i (monetary or utility value) is calculated for each end node. The value of the remaining nodes is then recursively calculated.

Limitations: The utility function must be monotonically increasing over the range of values in the problem.

Decision analysis is a method of analyzing problems that contain one or more choices with uncertain outcomes. Typically, such a problem is represented using a **decision tree**, which provides a graphical representation of the decision-making process. The tree shows the progression of events over time. The junction points in the tree are called **nodes**, and the arcs or connectors between the nodes are called **branches**. There are two types of nodes: a **decision** node corresponding to choosing from a set of alternatives, and a **chance** node corresponding to an uncertain or random event. The branches from a decision node represent the alternative actions that the decision maker can take, while the branches from a chance node represent the possible random events that can occur. The tree describes the sequence in which decisions are made and chance outcomes revealed.

Generally, each branch, whether from a decision or chance node, has costs and/or rewards associated with it. The decision problem is to select the set of actions at every

235

decision node that will maximize (for rewards) or minimize (for costs) the expected outcome. The rewards and/or costs are assumed to have a common scale, dollars. However, it is well known that the monetary value of an outcome does not necessarily reflect an individual's preference for that outcome. Typically, one's preference for additional income diminishes as wealth increases, reflecting diminishing marginal utility for money. To include this behavior in decision making, a common approach is to assume that individuals have an implicit **utility function**, which transforms monetary outcomes to a preference scale. Then the decision problem is to identify the actions that maximize the expected utility. PROPS+ calculates both the optimal expected value and the optimal expected utility, and the optimal decisions.

Decision analysis depends on effective encoding of beliefs about the relative likelihood of the alternative possibilities. In decision analysis, beliefs are typically expressed through a probability distribution for an appropriate sample space. Many texts have good descriptions of how to assess these distributions. Here, we will assume that you have established probabilities for uncertain events, and we will deal only with discrete probability distributions (either the events are discrete, or we use a discrete approximation for an event with a continuous outcome space).

Example: The Kitchen Gadget Decision

Imagine you are an inventor, and have just come up with an idea for a new kitchen gadget. You are not sure if it will work, but it looks promising. After some reflection, you feel that the probability that the gadget will work is 80%. At the moment, you see three options:

1) You could sell the idea "as is" to a manufacturer of kitchen implements. The manufacturer will give you an immediate fee of $2,000 for your idea. Then, if the gadget is successful, you will receive another lump sum of $1,000 plus a royalty of $.05 for each unit sold.

2) You could develop a prototype of the gadget. You estimate that it will cost $3,000 to develop it, and the prototype will show whether or not the gadget will work (probability 80%). If it doesn't work, you will scrap the idea. Should the prototype work as expected, you have two options:

   a) Sell the prototype. You predict that a working model should fetch a fee of $5,000 with a royalty of $.10 per unit sold.
   b) Manufacture and market the gadget yourself. This requires a cash outlay of $5,000 but will provide a revenue of $.50 per unit.

3) You could give up the idea, for a net outcome of $0.

Your choice obviously depends on the potential market for the gadget. Suppose that the following demand distribution summarizes your beliefs about the gadget's market potential, given that the gadget works:

Demand	Probability
Low (10,000 units)	0.3
Medium (30,000 units)	0.5
High (50,000 units)	0.2

Also, suppose you believe that this demand does not depend on which option for manufacture and distribution you choose.

Assuming that you wish to maximize the expected profits from your gadget, what should you do?

Your problem is summarized in the following tree. Decision nodes in the tree are shown with an open square (□), chance nodes with an open circle (O), and probabilities for chance noted are shown in parentheses ( ). Cash flows directly associated with branches are shown in brackets [ ].

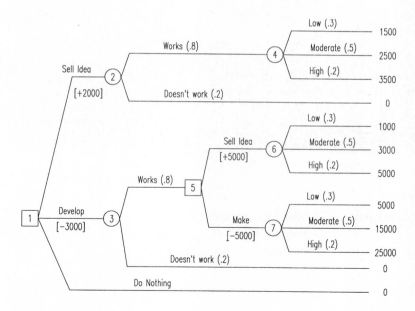

To solve this problem using PROPS⁺, first sketch the problem on paper, and assign a unique node number (numbered consecutively from 1) to every chance and decision node in the tree (in the figure, the node numbers are shown within the node symbol).

The Decision Analysis Worksheet

Now access PROPS⁺ and select **13. Decision Analysis** from the ACCESS menu. You will see the following screen:

```
              A        B        C        D        E        F        G        H
1      ===============================
2                    PROPS+                      DECISION ANALYSIS SPREADSHEET
3                                                - simplified problem definition
4                 Copyright (C)                  - sub-trees permitted
5                 PROPS SYSTEMS                  - draws the tree diagram
6                                                - utility function or table
7               05/09/92 07:57 AM               - identifies optimal actions for
8      ===============================                both expected value & utility
9                                                - automatic recalculation
10                                               - extensive editing
11     Instructions:
12
13             When prompted, enter problem name, whether maximization (max)
14             or minimization (min) problem, and number of nodes. Follow
15             each response by pressing [Enter].
16
17                                                          Press [Enter] to begin...
18
19
```

Pressing [Enter] will display the following questions, one by one. Respond to each by typing your answer and pressing the [Enter] key.

```
              A        B        C        D        E        F        G
21            Analyst Name:      Your_name
22            Problem Name:      gadget
23
24            Maximize or minimize?        max
25
26
```

At this point, PROPS⁺ asks you to enter the number of decision and chance nodes (seven in this problem). When you type **7** and press [Enter], PROPS⁺ will present the following table for you to complete, to describe the tree.

```
        A         B         C         D         E         F         G         H
26  PROBLEM definition:
27             Node type
28      Node (d, c or   No. of    List of successor decision
29    number    node) branches    or chance node numbers
30        1                       _____     _____     _____  ...
31        2
32        3
33        4
34        5
35        6
36        7
37
38            ...to continue press [Alt M]
```

Referring to the node numbers in the sketch, complete this table as shown for this problem. (For now, the node types will be either decision d or chance c. The use of subtrees will be explained later.) Note that you don't need to specify any node number for branches that end at the tips of the tree — PROPS+ inserts these automatically and labels them for future reference with "e#", where # is a number.

```
        A         B         C         D         E         F         G         H
26  PROBLEM definition:
27             Node type
28      Node (d, c or   No. of    List of successor decision
29    number    node) branches    or chance node numbers
30        1 d             3           2         3       _____  ...
31        2 c             2           4
32        3 c             2           5
33        4 c             3
34        5 d             2           6         7
35        6 c             3
36        7 c             3
37
38            ...to continue press [Alt M]
```

When the table is complete, press [Alt M]. PROPS+ will check that the problem as defined in the definition table is a tree (that is, it has a single root, is connected, and has no loops). If not, it will indicate an error. It then draws the decision tree and will create a table in the spreadsheet for you to complete to describe the values and probabilities for the problem. You will see the following table in your spreadsheet:

```
        A         B         C         D         E         F         G         H         I
38
39  D-1 _____ C-2 _____ C-4 _____ e1
40                                       _____ e2
41                                       _____ e3
42                      _____ e4
43      _____ C-3 _____ D-5 _____ C-6 _____ e5
44                                              _____ e6
45                                              _____ e7
46                                   _____ C-7 _____ e8
47                                              _____ e9
48                                              _____ e10
49              _____ e11
50      _____ e12
```

	A	B	C	D	E	F	G	H
51								
52								
53						Terminal value	$ value	
54	# of	_____	Branch	_____	Ending	----------------	end of	
55	node	Name	Reward	Prob.	node #	$	utils	branch
56	1	1-2	0		2			
57		1-3	0		3			
58		1-e12	0		e12			
59								
60	2	2-4	0	0	4			
61		2-e4	0	0	e4			
62				ERR				
63	3	3-5	0	0	5			
64		3-e11	0	0	e11			
65				ERR				
66	4	4-e1	0	0	e1			
67		4-e2	0	0	e2			
68		4-e3	0	0	e3			
69				ERR				
70	5	5-6	0		6			
71		5-7	0		7			
72								
73	6	6-e5	0	0	e5			
74		6-e6	0	0	e6			
75		6-e7	0	0	e7			
76				ERR				
77	7	7-e8	0	0	e8			
78		7-e9	0	0	e9			
79		7-e10	0	0	e10			
80				ERR				
81		UTILITY function						
82			x	u(x)				
83			1	1				
84								
85		...to continue press [Alt M]						
86								
87								

Use the [PgUp] and [PgDn] keys to examine the worksheet. (You may also use the
Worksheet Global Column-width command to change the width of the columns to display
the decision tree more clearly.) The decision tree is a useful check to ensure that the
problem you entered corresponds to the tree in your sketch.

At this point, you are in READY mode, and you can use normal data entry
methods to complete the table. Note that you can use the Copy command (/C) and also
formulas referring to values in other cells. Also note that you can enter names for the
various branches out of each node simply by typing the name you wish over the existing
name (1-2, 1-3, etc.) in column B. This will make later interpretation of the results easier.
For the kitchen gadget problem, the completed table appears as follows:

	A	B	C	D	E	F	G	H
52						----<for internal use>----		
53						Terminal value$ value		
54	# of	_____	Branch_____		Ending	----------------		end of
55	node	Name	Reward	Prob.	node #	$	utils	branch
56	1	sell	2000		2			
57		develop	-3000		3			
58		abandon	0		e12			
59								
60	2	works	0	0.8	4			
61		fails	0	0.2	e4			
62								
63	3	works	0	0.8	5			
64		fails	0	0.2	e11			
65								
66	4	high	3500	0.2	e1			
67		mod	2500	0.5	e2			
68		low	1500	0.3	e3			
69								
70	5	sell	5000		6			
71		make	-5000		7			
72								
73	6	high	5000	0.2	e5			
74		mod	3000	0.5	e6			
75		low	1000	0.3	e7			
76								
77	7	high	25000	0.2	e8			
78		mod	15000	0.5	e9			
79		low	5000	0.3	e10			
80								

To solve this decision problem using the expected monetary value criterion, press [Alt M], and the following menu will appear:

```
A80:
Solve  Re-trace  Edit  Utility_Tbl  Draw_Tree
Solve the decision tree
        A      B      C      D      E      F      G      H
```

Select **Solve** by pressing [Enter]. PROPS⁺ will create the formulas to perform the calculations and, when finished, will present the following screen:

	A	B	C	D	E	F	G	H
85								
86	·EXPECTED value		4200		EXPECTED utility		4200	
87					Certainty equiv.		4200	
88								
89		Dollar values				Utilities		
90		------------------				------------------		
91	node	value	action		node	value	action	
92	1	4200	develop		1	4200	develop	
93	2	3920			2	3920		
94	3	4200			3	4200		
95	4	4400			4	4400		
96	5	6000	make		5	6000	make	
97	6	4800			6	4800		
98	7	6000			7	6000		
99								

This table shows that the expected value of the gadget is $4,200, and that the optimal actions are to develop a prototype, and if it works, make and market the gadget yourself.

Utility Functions

The criterion used in the previous solutions was to maximize the expected monetary reward. Now suppose that your preferences for alternative monetary outcomes can be described through a utility function. PROPS⁺ allows you to either specify a mathematical function for this utility function or describe it by means of a table containing the utilities of specific monetary values. To illustrate the first case, suppose that your preferences for different outcomes can be summarized as a utility function of the mathematical form

$$u(x) = \frac{x}{1000} - (.01)\left(\frac{x}{1000}\right)^2$$

where x is the total monetary value, measured at the extreme tips of the tree. To enter the utility function, move the cursor to the cell under u(x), which is cell C83 in this example. You will see the following screen:

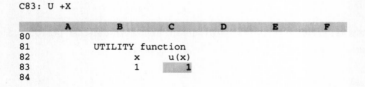

The default utility function contained in the cell immediately below u(x) is the linear function u(x) = x. To enter the desired function, with the cursor in the cell just below u(x) (cell C83 in this example), type

$$+(x/1000)-.01*(x/1000)^2$$

and press [Enter]. **Note:** There are no blanks allowed in this expression. PROPS⁺ has given cell B83 the name "x", so you can either use the letter x or point to cell B83 when you want to refer to the independent variable. The following screen appears:

C83: (X/1000)-(0.01)*(X/1000)^2

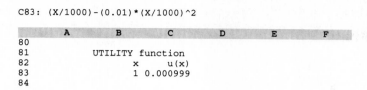

	A	B	C	D	E	F
80						
81		UTILITY function				
82			x	u(x)		
83			1	0.000999		
84						

Using this utility function, you can now resolve the gadget decision problem by pressing [Alt M] to bring up the menu and selecting **Solve**. You will see the following menu:

A85:   MENU
Stop Proceed
Save existing information

	A	B	C	D	E	F	G	H

This menu warns you that the existing solution information will be erased. Select **Proceed**, and the following new solution will appear:

	A	B	C	D	E	F	G	H
						----<for internal use>----		
52						Terminal values		$ value
53	# of		Branch		Ending	------------------		end of
54	node	Name	Reward	Prob.	node #	$	utils	branch
55								
56	1	sell	2000		2	3920	3.7532	2000
57		develop	-3000		3	4200	3.502	-3000
58		abandon	0		e12	0	0	0
59								
60	2	works	0	0.8	4	4400	4.2015	2000
61		fails	0	0.2	e4	2000	1.96	2000
62								
63	3	works	0	0.8	5	6000	5.15	-3000
64		fails	0	0.2	e11	-3000	-3.09	-3000
65								
66	4	high	3500	0.2	e1	5500	5.1975	5500
67		mod	2500	0.5	e2	4500	4.2975	4500
68		low	1500	0.3	e3	3500	3.3775	3500
69								
70	5	sell	5000		6	4800	4.55	2000
71		make	-5000		7	6000	5.15	-8000
72								
73	6	high	5000	0.2	e5	7000	6.51	7000
74		mod	3000	0.5	e6	5000	4.75	5000
75		low	1000	0.3	e7	3000	2.91	`3000
76								
77	7	high	25000	0.2	e8	17000	14.11	17000
78		mod	15000	0.5	e9	7000	6.51	7000
79		low	5000	0.3	e10	-3000	-3.09	-3000
80								
81		UTILITY function						
82			x	u(x)				
83			1	0.000999				
84								

	A	B	C	D	E	F	G	H
85								
86	EXPECTED value		4200		EXPECTED utility		3.7532	
87					Certainty equiv.		3905.748	
88								
89		Dollar values				Utilities		
90		------------------				------------------		
91	node	value	action		node	value	action	
92	1	4200	develop		1	3.7532	sell	
93	2	3920			2	3.7532		
94	3	4200			3	3.502		
95	4	4400			4	4.2015		
96	5	6000	make		5	5.15	make	
97	6	4800			6	4.55		
98	7	6000			7	5.15		
99								
100								

Observe that PROPS⁺ provides the optimal action and its expected value using both the maximum expected value and the maximum expected utility decision criteria. Further, the table summarizes these values at every decision node. Note that in this case the two criteria give different decisions. An expected-value decision maker would develop the gadget, while the utility maximizer would sell it. Before proceeding, save this worksheet for later use using the **File Save** command (**/FS**), calling the file GADGET.WK1.

Utility Table

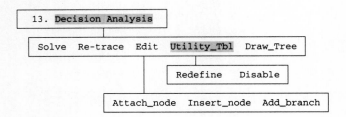

In many applications the utility function is estimated experimentally and is represented by a table of utility values corresponding to different monetary values. PROPS⁺ will use these values, with linear interpolation between the given points, to approximate the complete utility function. Suppose, for instance, that the kitchen gadget decision maker estimated the following points on his utility curve:

Monetary Value	Utility
- $5,000	0
0	.28
+ $5,000	.48
+ $15,000	.76
+ $20,000	.86
+ $30,000	1.00

Note: To permit interpolation, the range of this table *must* completely span the range of net possible outcomes in the tree.

To enter the table, press [Alt M] and select the **Utility_Tbl** option from the menu; you will be presented with the following screen:

```
        AA       AB      AC      AD      AE      AF      AG      AH
1
2   Empirical Utility Table      Enter monetary amounts in the "X" column
3                                and the corresponding utility value in the
4         X      U(X)           U(X) column.
5   ------------------
6
7
8                                       ...to continue press [Alt M]
9
10
```

Complete the screen as shown below:

```
        AA       AB      AC      AD      AE      AF      AG      AH
1
2   Empirical Utility Table      Enter monetary amounts in the "X" column
3                                and the corresponding utility value in the
4         X      U(X)           U(X) column.
5   ------------------
6     -5000        0
7         0     0.28                     ...to continue press [Alt M]
8      5000     0.48
9     15000     0.76
10    20000     0.86
11    30000        1
12
```

Press [Alt M] to complete the definition of the utility table and return to the main worksheet. To solve the gadget decision tree with this utility function, press [Alt M] and select the menu options **Solve** and then **Proceed**. For this problem, using the data table form of the utility description, the solution appears in the spreadsheet as follows:

	A	B	C	D	E	F	G	H
85								
86		EXPECTED value	4200		EXPECTED utility	0.43584		
87					Certainty equiv.		3896	
88								
89		Dollar values				Utilities		
90		------------------				------------------		
91	node	value action			node	value action		
92	1	4200 develop			1	0.43584 sell		
93	2	3920			2	0.43584		
94	3	4200			3	0.39616		
95	4	4400			4	0.4548		
96	5	6000 make			5	0.4672 sell		
97	6	4800			6	0.4672		
98	7	6000			7	0.4616		

If you wish to change the utility table, or use a utility function, press [Alt M] and select **Utility_Tbl** from the menu. You will see the new menu:

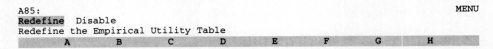

```
A85:                                                                         MENU
Redefine   Disable
Redefine the Empirical Utility Table
        A        B        C        D        E        F        G        H
```

Redefine lets you change the empirical utility table; **Disable** will terminate references to the utility table, and will use the linear utility function u(x)=x instead. (This could then be modified to some other function, as described in the last section.)

Subtrees

In many problems, portions of the decision tree are repeated. To make problem definition easier, PROPS⁺ permits the use of subtrees, which can be repeated (and nested) in different parts of the decision tree. For example, a decision problem may exactly repeat portions of the tree (to the tips) at various points in the diagram. Rather than requiring you to enter the same structure over and over, PROPS⁺ allows you to enter the structure once and then refer to this structure, using the subtree indication, at other points in the diagram.

In the PROBLEM definition table, you may specify a node as a decision node (node type d), a chance node (node type c), or a subtree by specifying the node number of the root of the subtree that should follow from this point. The gadget decision problem offers a simple example of the use of subtrees. The random market demand appears in three places in the decision tree (at nodes 4, 6, and 7). In defining the problem, nodes 6 and 7 could be specified as subtrees by indicating their node type as 4, meaning that node 4's structure will repeat from nodes 6 and 7. The steps in problem entry follow the same patterns as before, and the problem definition, using the subtree option, should appear as follows:

	A	B	C	D	E	F	G	H
21		Analyst Name:		Your_name				
22		Problem Name:		gadget				
23								
24		Maximize or minimize?			max			
25								
26	PROBLEM definition:							
27		Node type		List of successor decision				
28		Node (d, c or	No. of	or chance node numbers				
29	number	node)	branches	_____	_____	_____	...	
30	1	d	3	2	3			
31	2	c	2	4				
32	3	c	2	5				
33	4	c	3					
34	5	d	2	6	7			
35	6	4						
36	7	4						

Note the only difference now is that nodes 6 and 7 have type equal to the node number 4, the root of the subtree. Press [Alt M] and the following screen appears:

	A	B	C	D	E	F	G	H
38	Actual problem definition (with subtrees expanded)							
39								
40	Node	Type	Branches	Successors...				
41	1	d	3	2	3	e12		
42	2	c	2	4	e4			
43	3	c	2	5	e11			
44	4	c	3	e1	e2	e3		
45	5	d	2	6	7			
46	6	c	3	e5	e6	e7		
47	7	c	3	e8	e9	e10		
48								
49								
50	D-1	_____	C-2	_____	C-4	_____	e1	
51						_____	e2	
52						_____	e3	
53				_____	e4			
54		_____	C-3	_____	D-5	_____	C-6	_____ e5
55							_____	e6
56								e7
57					_____	C-7	_____	e8
58							_____	e9
59							_____	e10
60				_____	e11			
61		_____	e12					
62								
63						----<for internal use>----		
64						Terminal values		$ value
65	# of	_____	Branch	_____	Ending	-----------------		end of
66	node	Name	Reward	Prob.	node #	$	utils	branch
67	1	1-2	0		2			
68		1-3	0		3			
69		1-e12	0		e12			
70								
71	2	2-4	0	0	4			
72		2-e4	0	0	e4			
73				ERR				
74	3	3-5	0	0	5			
75		3-e11	0	0	e11			
76				ERR				

	A	B	C	D	E	F	G	H
77	4	4-e1	0	0	e1			
78		4-e2	0	0	e2			
79		4-e3	0	0	e3			
80				ERR				
81	5	5-6	0		6			
82		5-7	0		7			
83								
84	6 [4]	6-e5	0	0	e5			
85		6-e6	0	0	e6			
86		6-e7	0	0	e7			
87				ERR				
88	7 [4]	7-e8	0	0	e8			
89		7-e9	0	0	e9			
90		7-e10	0	0	e10			
91				ERR				
92								

The Actual problem definition table with subtrees expanded is created, followed by the tree diagram and the input data table. In the input data table, nodes 6 and 7 are followed by the notation [4], indicating that they are a repeat of node 4. When the data for node 4 is entered, the same values are repeated for nodes 6 and 7. These values for nodes 6 and 7 can be changed, which would be necessary for the branch values in this example. When the data is entered, [Alt M] will call up the menu and the solution can proceed as before.

The use of subtrees did not greatly simplify this problem, because the subtrees were at the end of the decision tree. In more complex decision problems, the simplification can be significant. An example will be presented later in this chapter.

Editing a Problem

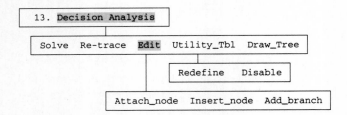

PROPS+ lets you edit the decision problem easily, through the following operations:

Attach_node changes a branch end to a node, prompts for the node type and number of branches, modifies the Actual problem definition table and creates space in the data table for the new data.

Insert_node inserts a node before a previously defined node and then prompts for node definition in a manner similar to **Attach_node**.

Add_branch adds a branch from a node and modifies the Actual problem definition and data input tables.

There are no specific commands to delete nodes or branches. In PROPS⁺ it is easier to simply modify the data so that undesired nodes or branches will not affect the solution. For example, a branch from a chance node can be effectively eliminated by setting its probability to zero. If the branch is from a decision node, a large penalty can be assigned to its branch value so that it will not be selected. In the same way, a node can be eliminated simply by eliminating the branch that leads to it.

Note: When subtrees have been used to define the decision tree, the Actual problem definition table is edited, and the original Problem definition table is left unchanged (and is no longer used). The following rules apply:

1) If a subtree is edited, then changes will appear in that part of the decision tree and in all parts of the tree that directly refer to that subtree.

2) If changes are made to a part of the decision tree that was defined using a subtree reference, then the change will be only in that part of the decision tree, and will not affect any other part of the tree.

As an example of these rules, suppose that in the gadget problem, a branch is added onto node 4 to represent a "very high" demand. That branch will also appear on nodes 6 and 7. However, if a branch is added onto node 6, only that branch will be added to the tree. This feature permits tremendous flexibility in editing the decision problem.

When the decision structure has been modified through this editing, a new decision tree can be drawn when **Draw_Tree** is selected from the main menu.

To explore these editing capabilities, we urge you to experiment with the gadget problem, noting what happens as you attach and insert nodes and add branches.

Sensitivity Analysis

A major advantage of the PROPS⁺ decision analysis system is that it makes sensitivity analysis easy: PROPS⁺ automatically calculates the optimal expected value and utility when any reward or probability value is altered in the data area. For example, suppose the selling price for the untested gadget were to increase from $2,000 to $4,000. Let's return to the original problem statement, as shown in the table on page 243, to see how expected value and utility are affected. Move the cursor to the appropriate cell in the worksheet (cell C56 contains the selling price) and change the value to 4000. The solution at the bottom of the worksheet instantly changes to

	A	B	C	D	E	F	G	H
85								
86	EXPECTED value		5920		EXPECTED utility		5.5564	
87					Certainty equiv. 5905.102			
88								
89		Dollar values				Utilities		
90		------------------				------------------		
91	node	value action			node	value action		
92	1	5920 *			1	5.5564 *		
93	2	5920			2	5.5564		
94	3	4200			3	3.502		
95	4	6400			4	5.9855		
96	5	6000 *			5	5.15 *		
97	6	4800			6	4.55		
98	7	6000			7	5.15		
99								
100		* = Must re-trace optimal decisions - use [Alt R]						
101								

The expected value and utilities have changed to reflect the new value. Note, however, that the old optimal decision may no longer be appropriate with the change in data. PROPS⁺ shows this by displaying a * in the "action" column with a warning message. Pressing [Alt R] will retrace the problem to produce the new optimal actions with the revised data. In the above example, this yields the following result:

	A	B	C	D	E	F	G	H
85								
86	EXPECTED value		5920		EXPECTED utility		5.5564	
87					Certainty equiv. 5905.102			
88								
89		Dollar values				Utilities		
90		------------------				------------------		
91	node	value action			node	value action		
92	1	5920 sell			1	5.5564 sell		
93	2	5920			2	5.5564		
94	3	4200			3	3.502		
95	4	6400			4	5.9855		
96	5	6000 make			5	5.15 make		
97	6	4800			6	4.55		
98	7	6000			7	5.15		
99								

You can also vary the probability distributions for any chance nodes (singly or in combination). As you change the probabilities, you will note that the warning message "ERR" appears to indicate when the probabilities don't sum to 1. As you enter new values for the probabilities, the expected values and utilities again change automatically to reflect this new information. (You must press [Alt R] to retrace if you want to know the corresponding optimal decisions.)

We can generalize this procedure. Suppose you are interested in how the expected value changes over a range of possible selling prices (currently set at $2,000). You can use the power of the spreadsheet system and PROPS+ to see what happens.

First, you need a portion of the worksheet that is currently empty as a working area — the space immediately to the right of the title page (that is, the cell range [I1..P30]) is always available for this purpose, though any clear range of cells will do. Let us build a table of alternative selling prices and determine the corresponding expected values for the decision problem. To do so, move the cursor to an initial data cell, say I4. Now enter the spreadsheet **Data Fill** command (**/DF**), indicate the range [I4..I12], and indicate the values as, say, Start = 1960, Step = 80, and Stop = 2600. This fills column I with the values of the selling price we are interested in. Now put the cell reference for the cell containing the expected value of the decision problem (+C86) into cell J3. Finally, enter the spreadsheet **Data Table 1** command (**/DT1**) with the range [I3..J12] and the input cell C56 (containing the selling price) to build the following table. (Titles have been entered in ranges [I1..I3] and [J1..J3] to complete the table.)

	I	J	K	L
1	selling	expected		
2	price	value		
3		5920		
4	1960	4200		
5	2040	4200		
6	2120	4200		
7	2200	4200		
8	2280	4200		
9	2360	4280		
10	2440	4360		
11	2520	4440		
12	2600	4520		
13				

The table shows that for selling prices less than or equal to $2,280, the expected value is unchanged. This is because the optimal decision in these cases is "Develop", so the selling price doesn't matter. On the other hand, if the selling price rises above $2,280, the best decision is "Sell Idea", and the expected value will increase with the selling price. The data in the table can be graphed using the spreadsheet **Graph** commands (**/G**) to show this more clearly.

PROPS⁺ can also deal with more complicated forms of sensitivity analysis, as shown in the following example. In the original kitchen gadget decision, we assumed three levels of demand for the product, with the following probability distribution:

Demand	Probability
Low (10,000 units)	0.3
Moderate (30,000 units)	0.5
High (50,000 units)	0.2

Suppose that you still believe that the probabilities for the demand levels are correct, but are less sure of the actual demand at each level. One way to model this is to suppose that the number of units sold if sales are low will be 10000r, where r can vary over some range of values. The moderate sales could be 30000r, and high sales 50000r. (That is, r can be thought of as a way to reflect more or less optimism about the potential market for the gadget.) How sensitive is the expected value of the decision to different values of r?

To answer this question, you can return to the worksheet, reset cell C56 to 2000, and redefine the rewards from the appropriate end tips of the tree as functions of r. To do this, find some currently unused part of the worksheet to store a value for r. In this example, we could use cells A52 and B52 for this purpose. It is handy to use the left-hand cell for a description of the adjacent cell. The worksheet entry appears as follows:

```
         A          B          C          D          E
51
52       r=        0.8
53
54     # of _____     Branch _____      Ending
55     node  Name        Reward     Prob.     node #
56        1  sell          2000                    2
57           develop      -3000                    3
58
59
```

Now alter the entries in the data table corresponding to branch rewards on the sales outcomes to reflect this value of r. For example, the entry in cell C66 changes from 3500 to 3500*B52. Repeat this change for cells C67, C68, C73, C74, C75, C77, C78 and C79. This operation results in the following data area for the problem with an r value of 0.8:

	A	B	C	D	E
52	r=	0.8			
53					
54	# of	_____	Branch	_____	Ending
55	node	Name	Reward	Prob.	node #
56	1	sell	2000		2
57		develop	-3000		3
58		abandon	0		e12
59					
60	2	works	0	0.8	4
61		fails	0	0.2	e4
62					
63	3	works	0	0.8	5
64		fails	0	0.2	e11
65					
66	4	high	2800	0.2	e1
67		mod	2000	0.5	e2
68		low	1200	0.3	e3
69					
70	5	sell	5000		6
71		make	-5000		7
72					
73	6	high	4000	0.2	e5
74		mod	2400	0.5	e6
75		low	800	0.3	e7
76					
77	7	high	20000	0.2	e8
78		mod	12000	0.5	e9
79		low	4000	0.3	e10
80					

You can now construct a table relating expected values of the decision problem to alternative values of r in the same way as in the previous example. That is, you can use the **Data Fill** command (**/DF**) to put r values of interest, say from .7 to 1.4, in the range [I4..I11], enter **+C86** in cell J3, and use the **Data Table 1** command (**/DT1**) on the range [I3..J11] with cell B52 as the input cell. This generates the following table:

	I	J	K	L
1	optimism	expected		
2	coeff r	value		
3		3536		
4	0.7	3344		
5	0.8	3536		
6	0.9	3728		
7	1	4200		
8	1.1	5320		
9	1.2	6440		
10	1.3	7560		
11	1.4	8680		
12				

Using the **Graph** commands (**/G**) on this data shows the relationship more clearly:

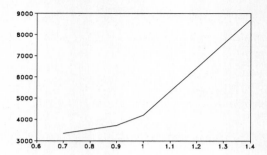

Sensitivity to other components of the problem can be tested in a similar fashion. The major advantage of PROPS⁺ is that changes in problem values that cause the optimal decisions to change are reflected immediately in the expected values, without user intervention. Sensitivity analysis is thus very easy to do. Note, however, that if the problem *structure* changes (that is, a change in the number of nodes or number of branches), the problem must be re-solved from the beginning.

Certainty Equivalent

The solution to the gadget problem under the maximum expected value criterion yielded an expected value of $4,200. The maximum expected utility rule, using the mathematical function, gave an expected utility of 3.7532. (These results were shown on page 244.) To relate these two values, note that PROPS⁺ calculates the *certainty equivalent* of the decision problem, or $3,905.75 in this case. This value is the certain amount of money that has the same utility as the expected utility of the decision problem. That is, for this problem, with the given utility function, you would be indifferent whether you "owned" the rights to the kitchen gadget or received a sure $3,905.75 in cash. The difference between the expected value and the certainty equivalent is called the *risk premium*, which is $294.25 in this case. It corresponds to an acceptable cost in foregone expected value that you would be willing to give up to avoid the risk in the decision problem. The risk premium is thus a measure of the degree of risk aversion shown by that utility function for the specific decision problem.

You can explore how the aversion to risk is reflected in the risk premium. One way to do this is to see how the premium changes as the probability that the gadget will work is altered. First, retrieve the previously saved worksheet file GADGET.WK1 using the **File Retrieve** command (**/FR**). Set up a cell, say B53, which will contain the probability that the gadget will work, and store an initial value in that cell (say 0.8). Now use the entry **+$B$53** in the problem data input, in place of the original 0.8 entries corresponding to the probability that the gadget will work, and insert **+1–$B$53** as the probability that the gadget won't work. Note that these probabilities occur in two separate places in the data array.

Now use a scratch area, [I1..P20] for instance, to construct a table with possible values for the probability that the gadget will work, say from 0.60 to 0.95. Then the spreadsheet **/D**ata Table 1 command (**/DT1**) (described in the previous section) can be used to create a table of the certainty equivalent (G87) for each of these probabilities.

Then you can repeat the table of probabilities and create a second table containing the expected value (C86) of the decision problem for each alternative probability that the gadget will work. Finally, subtracting the first value from the second will give the risk premium corresponding to each probability of the gadget working. The spreadsheet for the gadget problem created by these steps appears as follows:

	I	J	K	L	M	N	O	P
1	Prob			Prob				
2	Gadget	Certainty		Gadget	Expected		Risk	
3	Works	Equivalent		Works	Value		Premium	
4	------------------			------------------			---------	
5	0.6	3422.00		0.6	3440		18.00	
6	0.65	3542.47		0.65	3560		17.53	
7	0.7	3663.24		0.7	3680		16.76	
8	0.75	3784.34		0.75	3800		15.66	
9	0.8	3905.75		0.8	4200		294.25	
10	0.85	4080.51		0.85	4650		569.49	
11	0.9	4531.33		0.9	5100		568.67	
12	0.95	4986.67		0.95	5550		563.33	
13								

Note that the risk premium does not behave in a smooth, monotonic fashion as the probability changes. This is because the two criteria, maximizing expected value versus maximizing expected utility, may result in different decisions being chosen, with corresponding differences in impacts on the risk premium.

The Value of Information

Decision analysis can be used to determine how much you should pay to obtain additional information about the uncertain quantities in a problem. We will demonstrate by extending the kitchen gadget decision problem.

Suppose you have concluded your analysis of the problem as above, but just before you take action you meet an engineering consultant who will help you predict whether your design will eventually work, but will charge a fee for this help. Suppose that the consultant will come up with a rating for the gadget of either "Good" or "Poor". When you ask how to use this information, the consultant says that, in similar situations in the past, in cases in which the product turned out to be successful, he had said "Good" 70% of the time and "Poor" 30%. On the other hand, when the machine was eventually found not to work, he had said "Good" 40% of the time and "Poor" 60%. What is this consultant's advice worth to you?

You would like to incorporate the imperfect information that will be provided by the consultant into your earlier beliefs about the likelihood that the gadget will work. In decision analysis, the original probability distribution without the consultant's information, that is, P(works)=0.8, P(doesn't work)=0.2, is called the **Prior** distribution. PROPS⁺ requires a numeric value to represent possible values of a random variable, so we can associate the value 0 with the event "doesn't work" and 1 with the event "works". Thus your prior beliefs about whether the gadget will work can be represented by the probability distribution:

Prior Distribution		
X	0	1
P(X)	0.2	0.8

The consultant's advice is expressed as a **conditional** distribution, since the probabilities for each of his responses depend on whether the gadget will actually work or not. Let Y=0 correspond to the consultant saying "Poor," and Y=1 to his saying "Good." Then the consultant's accuracy in his statement can be described with the following probability distribution:

Conditional Distribution for Consultant's Response		
	P(Y=0|X)	P(Y=1|X)
X = 0	0.6	0.4
X = 1	0.3	0.7

What you need in the decision tree is not this conditional distribution, but rather the **marginal** probability for each response by the consultant, and the **posterior** distribution that the gadget will work, given each response. We can use PROPS⁺ to compute these quantities.

From the PROPS⁺ ACCESS menu, select **12. Probability Distributions** and you will see the following screen:

```
        A       B       C       D       E       F       G       H
1   ==============================      PROBABILITY DISTRIBUTION SPREADSHEET
2               PROPS+                   - discrete probability distributions
3                                           (geometric, binomial, Poisson,
4             Copyright (C)                  general)
5             PROPS SYSTEMS             - continuous probability distrib's
6                                           (normal, exponential, Erlang,
7             05/09/92 01:35 PM             lognormal)
8   ==============================      - Bayesian revision
9                                       - calculates the probability
10                                          distribution for any function
11                                          of two random variables
12  Instructions:
13
14  Probability distribution tables will extend DOWN and RIGHT from the
15  location of the cursor when the macro is invoked. Make sure you have
16  clear worksheet BELOW and RIGHT of the highlighted cell before execut'n
17
18          [Alt M] - Presents user with MENU of possible actions
19
```

PROPS⁺ allows you to generate common discrete and continuous probability distributions, and in addition permits you to describe any arbitrary distribution in a discrete form. This section describes how to define each distribution. Press [Alt M] to bring up the menu and select **Distributions, Discrete,** and **Arbitrary** from the successive menus. You then will be requested for a name for the prior distribution, say WORK/NOT. PROPS⁺ then asks a series of questions to establish the range of values in the prior distribution. Enter a "Start x at" value of 0, a "Stop x at" value of 1, and select **Interval** and choose its default value of 1. PROPS⁺ then sets up the following array to describe the prior distribution over the value [0,1] for x:

```
        A       B       C       D       E       F       G
20              Probability distribution: WORK/NOT
21
22      mean        0 |  cdf:        0       0
23    std dev       0 |  pdf:        0       0
24                    |   x:         0       1
25                    |  Px:         0       0
26                    |  Px^2:       0       0
```

In the row marked "pdf:" enter the probability **0.2** in cell D23 for the event X=0, and **0.8** in cell E23 for the event X=1. The worksheet changes as follows:

```
        A       B       C       D       E       F       G
20              Probability distribution: WORK/NOT
21
22      mean      0.8 |  cdf:       0.2      1
23    std dev     0.4 |  pdf:       0.2     0.8
24                    |   x:         0       1
25                    |  Px:         0      0.8
26                    |  Px^2:       0      0.8
```

You are now ready to compute the required marginal and posterior distributions. Move the cursor to cell A30 (so the worksheet to the right and below is empty) and call up the menu by pressing [Alt M]. Select **Conditional** and you will be asked for the name of the distribution to be created (say, POST), and then the name of the prior distribution (WORK/NOT). PROPS⁺ then prompts you for information about the values of the conditional variable corresponding to the consultant's responses. Letting Y=0 correspond to "Poor" and Y=1 to "Good", respond to the questions "Start y at?" with 0, "Stop y at?" with 1, choose **Interval** from the menu, and select the default value of 1 as before. PROPS⁺ then generates the following table so that you can enter the conditional probabilities:

	A	B	C	D	E	F	G	H
30		Conditional distribution: POST						
31		(POST {P(y)} conditional on WORK/NOT {P(x)})						
32								
33				ENTER CONDITIONAL PROBABILITIES {P(y|x)} BELOW:				
34				y				
35				0	1	Check		
36		x	0	0	0	ERR		
37			1	0	0	ERR		
38								
39			Joint probability distribution {P(x,y)}:					
40				y				
41				0	1			
42		x	0	0	0			
43			1	0	0			
44								
45								
46		Marginal Probability Distribution {P(y)}: POST						
47								
48	mean	0	| cdf:	0	0			
49	std dev	0	| pdf:	0	0			
50			| y:	0	1			
51			| Py:	0	0			
52			| Py^2:	0	0			
53								
54		Posterior probability distribution {P(x|y)}:						
55				y				
56				0	1			
57		x	0	ERR	ERR			
58			1	ERR	ERR			
59								
60								

(Note that the joint, marginal, and posterior distributions tables are set up below this area and will be updated automatically as you enter the conditional data.) The "Check" column ensures that the probability distribution conditional on each possible value of the prior random variable sums to 1. Filling the conditional probabilities for this problem yields the following worksheet:

	A	B	C	D	E	F	G	H
30			Conditional distribution: POST					
31			(POST {P(y)} conditional on WORK/NOT {P(x)})					
32								
33				ENTER CONDITIONAL	PROBABILITIES {P(y|x)} BELOW:			
34				y				
35				0	1	Check		
36			x	0	0.6	0.4	ok	
37				1	0.3	0.7	ok	
38								
39				Joint probability	distribution {P(x,y)}:			
40				y				
41				0	1			
42			x	0	0.12	0.08		
43				1	0.24	0.56		
44								
45								
46			Marginal Probability Distribution {P(y)}: POST					
47								
48		mean	0.64		cdf:	0.36	1	
49		std dev	0.48		pdf:	0.36	0.64	
50					y:	0	1	
51					Py:	0	0.64	
52					Py^2:	0	0.64	
53								
54			Posterior probability distribution {P(x|y)}:					
55				y				
56				0	1			
57			x	0	0.333333	0.125		
58				1	0.666666	0.875		
59								
60								

Observe that the required marginal and posterior distributions are computed. You can use the **File Xtract** (**/FX**) and **File Combine** (**/FC**) commands to copy the distributions to the decision analysis worksheet, or print the values for later entry in the decision worksheet.

Should you wish to do sensitivity analysis on the prior distributions at some later point in the analysis, you can return to this worksheet and carry out these steps for each alternative prior probability distribution you wish to consider.

Returning to the decision problem, the complete decision tree, including the consultant's advice (the "do nothing" option has been deleted, since we know it is not going to be chosen), is shown in the following figure with the marginal and posterior probabilities we computed.

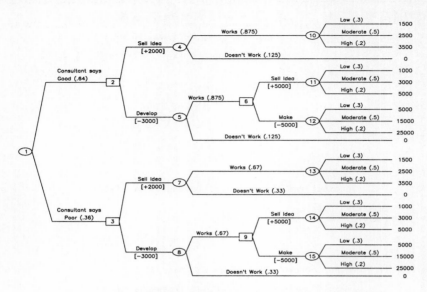

Decision Tree with Consultant's Advice

We will now show how subtrees can greatly simplify the description of this decision problem. In the decision tree, note that the tree from node 3 on is the same as that from node 2 on. Thus we can let node 3 be the subtree from 2. Also nodes 11 and 12 are subtrees equivalent to 10. Thus we need only nine nodes to define the problem, not 15. These nine nodes *must* be numbered consecutively from 1 to 9. To achieve this, renumber node 10 as 7, node 11 as 8, and node 12 as 9. We can now use PROPS[+] to solve this problem. From the ACCESS menu, select **13. Decision Analysis**, and set up the following PROBLEM definition:

	A	B	C	D	E	F	G	H
21		Analyst Name:		Your_name				
22		Problem Name:		gadget2				
23								
24		Maximize or minimize?			max			
25								
26	PROBLEM definition:							
27		Node type			List of successor decision			
28	Node	(d, c or	No. of	or chance node numbers				
29	number	node)	branches	___	___	___ ...		
30	1	c	2	2	3			
31	2	d	2	4	5			
32	3		2					
33	4	c	2	7				
34	5	c	2	6				
35	6	d	2	8	9			
36	7	c	3					
37	8		7					
38	9		7					

Pressing [Alt M] causes PROPS⁺ to create the Actual problem definition, draw the tree, and build the input data table. Your screen should look like this:

```
          A         B         C         D         E         F         G
40   Actual problem definition (with subtrees expanded)
41
42       Node      Type Branches    Successors...
43        1         c        2         2         3
44        2         d        2         4         5
45        3         d        2        10        12
46        4         c        2         7         e4
47        5         c        2         6        e11
48        6         d        2         8         9
49        7         c        3        e1        e2        e3
50        8         c        3        e5        e6        e7
51        9         c        3        e8        e9       e10
52       10         c        2        11       e15
53       11         c        3       e12       e13       e14
54       12         c        2        13       e22
55       13         d        2        14        15
56       14         c        3       e16       e17       e18
57       15         c        3       e19       e20       e21
58
59
60   C-1 _____ D-2 _____ C-4 _____ C-7 _____ e1
61                                      \_____ e2
62                                      \_____ e3
63                           \_____ e4
64            \_____ C-5 _____ D-6 _____ C-8 _____ e5
65                                              \_____ e6
66                                              \_____ e7
67                           \_____ C-9 _____ e8
68                                      \_____ e9
69                                      \_____ e10
70                 \_____ e11
71       \_____ D-3 _____ C-10 _____ C-11 _____ e12
72                                       \_____ e13
73                                       \_____ e14
74                 \_____ e15
75            \_____ C-12 _____ D-13 _____ C-14 _____ e16
76                                               \_____ e17
77                                               \_____ e18
78                            \_____ C-15 _____ e19
79                                        \_____ e20
80                                        \_____ e21
81            \_____ e22
82
83
```

To see the full decision tree, temporarily set the column width to 6 using the Worksheet Global Column-width command (**/WGC6**). Set up this problem in a fashion similar to the first version of the gadget problem. The complete data table and utility function appear as follows:

	A	B	C	D	E
84					
85	# of	_____ Branch	_____		Ending
86	node	Name	Reward	Prob.	node #
87	1	says good	0	0.64	2
88		says poor	0	0.36	3
89					
90	2	sell	2000		4
91		develop	-3000		5
92					
93	3 [2]	sell	2000		10
94		develop	-3000		12
95					
96	4	works	0	0.875	7
97		fails	0	0.125	e4
98					
99	5	works	0	0.875	6
100		fails	0	0.125	e11
101					
102	6	sell	5000		8
103		make	-5000		9
104					
105	7	low	1500	0.3	e1
106		mod	2500	0.5	e2
107		high	3500	0.2	e3
108					
109	8 [7]	low	1000	0.3	e5
110		mod	3000	0.5	e6
111		high	5000	0.2	e7
112					
113	9 [7]	low	5000	0.3	e8
114		mod	15000	0.5	e9
115		high	25000	0.2	e10
116					
117	10 [4]	works	0	0.666666	11
118		fails	0	0.333333	e15
119					
120	11 [7]	low	1500	0.3	e12
121		mod	2500	0.5	e13
122		high	3500	0.2	e14
123					
124	12 [5]	works	0	0.666666	13
125		fails	0	0.333333	e22
126					
127	13 [6]	sell	5000		14
128		make	-5000		15
129					
130	14 [8]	low	1000	0.3	e16
131		mod	3000	0.5	e17
132		high	5000	0.2	e18
133					
134	15 [9]	low	5000	0.3	e19
135		mod	15000	0.5	e20
136		high	25000	0.2	e21
137					
138		UTILITY function			
139		x	u(x)		
140		1	0.000999		
141					
142		...to continue press [Alt M]			
143					

To solve, press [Alt M] and select **Solve** from the menu. The following solution appears:

```
        A        B         C       D     E        F          G         H
142
143   EXPECTED value      4416          EXPECTED utility  3.88036
144                                     Certainty equiv. 4043.890
145
146          Dollar values                    Utilities
147        ------------------              ------------------
148   node    value action             node     value action
149     1     4416                        1   3.88036
150     2     4875 develop                2      4.12 develop
151     3     3600 sell                   3 3.454333 sell
152     4     4100                        4 3.921312
153     5     4875                         5     4.12
154     6     6000 make                   6     5.15 make
155     7     4400                        7   4.2015
156     8     4800                        8     4.55
157     9     6000                        9     5.15
158    10     3600                       10 3.454333
159    11     4400                       11   4.2015
160    12     3000                       12  2.403333
161    13     6000 13-15                 13     5.15 13-15
162    14     4800                       14     4.55
163    15     6000                       15     5.15
164
```

As you see from this solution, the expected value of the problem has risen from $4,200 with no information to $4,416 with the consultant's advice. Thus, on an expected-value basis, you should be willing to pay up to the difference of $216 for the consultant's advice, but no more.

Sensitivity to the Consultant's Accuracy

You can determine how the expected value of the consultant's advice changes as his accuracy in correctly specifying the true state of nature as to whether the gadget will work is allowed to vary. This could be done using the **Probability Distribution** worksheet, just described, to generate a series of prior, marginal, and posterior distributions. However, it is easier and more efficient in this case to construct tables to carry out the Bayesian updating within the decision analysis worksheet itself. The procedure for creating the updating calculations and incorporating the results in the decision analysis computations is described.

The following screen sets up a table in the scratch area to the right of the title screen, in the range [I1..P20], to carry out the Bayesian updating of the prior probabilities. The titles shown in the screen have been simply typed in as shown, and the prior probabilities (0.2 and 0.8) have been entered as shown. The conditional probability that the consultant says Poor if the gadget will fail has been entered in cell K3 as 0.6, and the probability that he says Good if it will fail has been entered in cell L3 as the formula **1-K3**. Similarly, cell L4 contains the probability he says Good if the gadget really will work as 0.7, and cell K4 contains the formula **1-L4**.

The joint probabilities have been calculated by multiplying each prior probability by the corresponding conditional probability, so, for instance, the entry in cell M3 is **+J3*K3** and in N4 is **+J4*L4**. The marginal probabilities of the consultant saying either Poor or Good are found by summing the columns of the corresponding joint probabilities, so cell M6 contains the formula **+M3+M4**, and cell N6 contains **+N3+N4**. Finally, the posterior probabilities are found by dividing each joint probability by the corresponding marginal probability, so, for example, cell O3 contains the formula **+M3/M6**, and P4 contains **+N4/N6**. The others are found in a similar fashion.

	I	J	K	L	M	N	O	P
1			Cond'l(info|state)		Joints		Posteriors	(state|info)
2	states	priors	poor	good	-----------------		poor	good
3	fails	0.2	0.6	0.4	0.12	0.08	0.333	0.125
4	works	0.8	0.3	0.7	0.24	0.56	0.667	0.875
5					-----------------			
6			marginals=>		0.36	0.64		
7								

At this point, the marginal probabilities can be transferred to the decision data area by entering **+N6** in cell D87 and **+M6** in D88. The posteriors are transferred to the decision data area by entering **+P4** into D96 and D99, **+P3** into D97 and D100, **+O4** in D117 and D124, and **+O3** in D118 and D125. PROPS+ then solves the decision problem with the given data.

You can now determine how the expected value of the consultant's advice changes as his accuracy varies. In this case, there are two different types of accuracy involved: how well he correctly identifies the state that the gadget will work (called the *sensitivity* of the advice) and how well he correctly identifies a gadget which will not work (called the *specificity* of the information). The current sensitivity is 0.7 and specificity is 0.6. The value of the consultant's advice depends on both of these parameters, so to examine how sensitive the value is to his accuracy requires ranges for both. This is done using the **/D**ata Table **2** command.

Enter a range of values for the sensitivity in, say, row 8 of the scratch area, as shown in the range [J8..P8]. The **/D**ata **F**ill command is useful here. Now create a similar range of values for the specificity in column I, as shown in the range [I9..I17]. Move the cursor to the upper-left corner cell I8 (currently blank), which will be the location of the function to be evaluated for each possible pair of sensitivity and specificity values. Since we are interested in the expected value of the problem contained in cell C143, enter the formula **+C143** in cell I8. The result is shown in the following screen.

	I	J	K	L	M	N	O	P
7								
8	4416	0.7	0.75	0.8	0.85	0.9	0.95	1
9	0.6							
10	0.65							
11	0.7							
12	0.75							
13	0.8							
14	0.85							
15	0.9							
16	0.95							
17	1							

Now issue the **/D**ata Table **2** command (**/DT2**), and describe the table range as [I8..P17]. The first input variable required by the system is the cell location corresponding to the left-hand side values of the table (the specificity, cell K3 in this case), and the second input variable corresponds to the values along the top of the table (the sensitivity, cell L4 in this case). Then the table appears as follows:

	I	J	K	L	M	N	O	P
7								
8	4444	0.7	0.75	0.8	0.85	0.9	0.95	1
9	0.6	4416	4480	4544	4608	4672	4736	4800
10	0.65	4466	4530	4594	4658	4722	4786	4850
11	0.7	4516	4580	4644	4708	4772	4836	4900
12	0.75	4566	4630	4694	4758	4822	4886	4950
13	0.8	4616	4680	4744	4808	4872	4936	5000
14	0.85	4666	4730	4794	4858	4922	4986	5050
15	0.9	4716	4780	4844	4908	4972	5036	5100
16	0.95	4766	4830	4894	4958	5022	5086	5150
17	1	4816	4880	4944	5008	5072	5136	5200

As you can see, an increase in specificity of 5% yields an increment of $20 in the expected value, and a 5% increase in sensitivity gives a $40 increase. Note here that the assumption in this formulation was that the consultant's advice would be acted on regardless. This would have to be modified if poorer accuracy values were considered.

Features

1. Transient Analysis

- given an initial state, calculates the vector of state probabilities for the specified number of transitions.

- calculates the n-step transition probability matrix.

2. Steady State

- calculates the vector of steady state probabilities.

3. First Passage Time Distribution

- calculates the probability distribution of the first passage time between any two states.

4. Expected First Passage Time

- calculates the expected first passage time from all states to a specified state.

5. Returns

- calculates the expected present value of future returns from each state under discounting.

- calculates the relative rewards of being in each state and the steady state expected return per transition if future returns are not discounted.

Chapter 14. Markov Chains

```
14. Markov Chains
```

```
Transient  Steady_state  1st_pass_time  Mean_1st_pass  Returns  Edit
```

```
State_Vectors   Transition_Matrix
```

> **The Model:**
>
> System is described by
>
> Transition probability matrix $P_{m \times m} = \{p_{ij}\}$ and
>
> Vector of one-step returns $r = \{r_i\}$
>
> where
>
> p_{ij} = the probability that the system makes a transition from state i to state j in one step. Thus $0 \leq p_{ij} \leq 1$ and
>
> $$\sum_j p_{ij} = 1 \text{ for all } i.$$
>
> r_i = the expected return (cost) arising from the next transition, given that the system is in state i.
>
> **Computation:** States are assigned integer values, starting from any value.
>
> **Limitations:** Assumes a finite number of states, discrete time, and time-invariant transition probabilities. The maximum number of states is limited only by the size of the spreadsheet.

A Markov chain describes how a system evolves probabilistically over time. The status of the system at any given time can be described by saying that it is in one of a finite number of *states* $\{S_1, S_2, ..., S_m\}$. We will restrict our attention to a discrete set of observation times $\{t_1, t_2, ...\}$. To describe changes in the system over time, we can specify the probability of making a transition from each possible starting state to each ending state using a one-step transition matrix P. Thus, the element p_{ij} is the probability of making a transition to state j in one step given that the starting state is i. Finally, there may or may not be a cost or reward r_i, which is the expected return during the next transition, given that the system is in state i. PROPS$^+$ provides a variety of tools for analyzing finite-state, discrete-time Markov chains.

Example: A Weather Problem

Imagine you are an ice cream vendor and have noticed that sales are dependent on the weather. For simplicity, you categorize the weather each day as hot, mild, or cool, and you have learned to expect a net income on hot days of $75, on mild of $50, and on cool of $20. Moreover, the weather on any given day appears to be dependent on the weather on the preceding days. The following matrix shows the probability of the following day's weather given the preceding day's.

		Next Day is:		
		Hot	Mild	Cool
Preceding	Hot	.3	.5	.2
Day	Mild	.2	.6	.2
is:	Cool	.1	.4	.5

You might be interested in the following sorts of questions:

1) If today is hot, what is the probability distribution for the weather condition four days from now?

2) In the long run, what is the probability that a randomly selected day will be hot? mild? cool?

3) If it is hot today, what is the probability distribution for the number of days before it is cool?

4) What is the average number of days between a hot day and a cool one?

5) What is your average daily income?

The Markov Chain Spreadsheet

You can answer each of these questions using PROPS+. Begin by accessing the **14. Markov Chains** worksheet from the PROPS+ ACCESS menu. You will see this screen:

```
        A       B        C         D        E        F        G        H
1    ==============================
2               PROPS+                      MARKOV CHAIN SPREADSHEET
3                                         - state probabilities
4            Copyright (C)                  - transient
5            PROPS SYSTEMS                  - steady state
6                                         - 1st passage time distribution
7            02/03/92 04:12 PM            - mean 1st passage times
8    ==============================        - return (cost) evaluation
9
10   Instructions:
11           First define the problem and its size. States are numbered
12           consecutively from lowest to highest and are multiplied by the
13           state increment (usually 1). Returns (costs) need only be
14           entered if desired.
15
16           PROMPT mode when CMD is on. Type response, press [ENTER].
17
18           Alt-M -- Presents user with MENU of possible actions.
19
20                                        Press [ENTER] to begin...
```

When you press [Enter], PROPS⁺ asks you to define the problem size through a sequence of questions. Follow each response by pressing the [Enter] key. Remember, if you make a typing mistake before you press [Enter], you can use the backspace key, or press the [Esc] key and retype your whole response. If you recognize a mistake after pressing [Enter] in this initial set-up portion of the problem, it is best to simply start over using **/FR** to recall the ACCESS worksheet.

In the weather problem, there are three states, which you can number from 1 to 3, with 1 = hot, 2 = mild, and 3 = cool. Then the following responses describe the problem size to PROPS⁺.

	A	B	C	D	E	F	G	H
20								
21		Analyst Name?			Your_name			
22		Problem Name?			weather			
23								
24		States numbered from			1	to	3	
25		Increment for states			1			
26								
27								

PROPS⁺ will now construct the input data area for a problem with these dimensions. In this case, the input data area appears as follows:

	A	B	C	D	E	F	G	H
26								
27		INPUT DATA:						
28								
29		End	1	2	3	Return	Check	
30	Start	+---						
31	1	|	0	0	0	0	ERR	
32	2	|	0	0	0	0	ERR	
33	3	|	0	0	0	0	ERR	
34		*** Warning: Probabilities do not sum to one ***						
35								
36		% Interest/Period		0	==>	Alpha =	1	
37								
38		Fill the above data table with transition probabilities and						
39		return data (if needed).						
40								
41					([Alt M] invokes the command menu)			
42								
43								

At this point, use ordinary spreadsheet methods to enter the data. Using the cursor keys to move the cursor from cell to cell, enter the transition probabilities in the matrix locations corresponding to the start and end state. The "Check" column adds the row probabilities and each entry changes from "ERR" to "ok" when the entries in the row sum to 1. In the "Return" column, enter the expected immediate return (in the example, the expected daily income) given each starting state. You can specify a discount rate for expressing returns as a present value by specifying the % Interest/Period in percent (for example, 10.3% would be entered as 10.3). Then the discount factor Alpha = $1/(1+i)$ is computed automatically. Note that you are in READY mode, so typing errors can be corrected simply by moving the cursor to the cell and retyping the correct entry. Assuming no discounting for the moment, the completed data entry area for our sample problem appears as follows:

```
          A         B         C         D         E         F         G         H
26
27                  INPUT DATA:
28
29                  End         1         2         3    Return    Check
30      Start       +---------------------------------------
31        1         |          0.3       0.5       0.2        75    ok
32        2         |          0.2       0.6       0.2        50    ok
33        3         |          0.1       0.4       0.5        20    ok
34
35
36                  % Interest/Period        0    ==>    Alpha =          1
37
38                  Fill the above data table with transition probabilities and
39                  return data (if needed).
40
41                                            [Alt M] invokes the command menu
42
```

Pressing [Alt M] displays the following menu at the top of the screen, and returns control to PROPS[+].

```
F34:                                                                        MENU
Transient  Steady-State  1st_pass_time  Mean_1st_Pass  Returns  Edit
Transient Analysis (n-stage)
          A         B         C         D         E         F         G         H
26
27                  INPUT DATA:
28
```

Let us examine each of these options in turn.

Transient Analysis

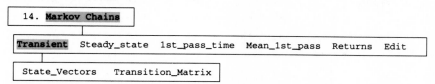

```
14. Markov Chains
```

```
Transient  Steady_state  1st_pass_time  Mean_1st_pass  Returns  Edit
```

```
State_Vectors    Transition_Matrix
```

The Model:

$$\pi(n) = \pi(n-1)P$$
$$= \pi(0)P^n$$

where

$$\pi(n) = \{\pi_1(n), \pi_2(n), \ldots, \pi_m(n)\} \text{ and}$$

$\pi_i(n)$ = the probability of being in state i after n transitions given an initial probability distribution $\pi(0)$

$P^n = \{p_{ij}^{(n)}\}$ = the n-step transition probability matrix

$p_{ij}^{(n)}$ = the probability that the system goes from state i to state j in n transitions

Computations: PROPS$^+$ recursively solves for the state probability vector, $\pi(n)$, or the n-step transition matrix P^n.

Limitations: Problem size is limited only by the spreadsheet size.

Transient analysis of the Markov chain refers to its behavior over a limited horizon; i.e., it describes the probabilities of various states being occupied after only a few transitions. Two questions are immediately interesting: starting from a given state, what is the probability of being in every other state after a given number of transitions, and what is the n-step transition probability matrix for a given number of transitions? PROPS$^+$ provides answers to both of these. Selecting **Transient** from the preceding menu generates the following submenu at the top of the screen:

```
F34:                                                              MENU
State_Vectors  Transition_Matrix
Create probability vectors given the initial state and number of periods
      A         B         C        D        E       F       G       H
```

On selecting **State_Vectors**, you are asked for the initial state and the number of transitions you are interested in. Remember, use the [Enter] key to input data when in PROMPT mode (the CMD indicator is on at the bottom of the screen). The probability distribution for being in each state at each transition up to your value is then determined. In the example, if you wanted the probabilities of being in each state after four transitions if you started in state 1, the following screen appears:

```
          A        B        C        D        E        F        G        H
40
41                 Transient Analysis (given initial state):
42                 =========================================
43
44                 Index of initial state:              1
45
46                 Number of transitions:              4
47
48                          Probability of being in State
49     Transition              1        2        3
50     ---------               -------------------------
51         0                   1        0        0
52         1                  0.3      0.5      0.2
53         2                  0.21     0.53     0.26
54         3                  0.195    0.527    0.278
55         4                  0.1917   0.5249   0.2834
56
```

Thus, for example, starting in state 1, after four transitions (days) the probability that the system has not left, or has returned to, state 1 is 0.1917. In terms of the example, if today is Monday and it is hot, the probability that Friday will be hot is 0.1917, that it will be mild is 0.5249, and that it will be cool is 0.2834. As an example of how to use this distribution, Friday's expected income given a hot Monday can be calculated in the worksheet. Find an empty cell (A56 for example) and use it to multiply the vector of returns in column F, rows 31 to 33, by the vector of probabilities in row 55, columns C, D, and E. This operation yields the following worksheet:

```
A56: +F31*C55+F32*D55+F33*E55                                          READY
```

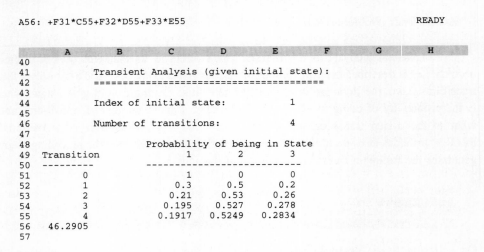

```
          A        B        C        D        E        F        G        H
40
41                 Transient Analysis (given initial state):
42                 =========================================
43
44                 Index of initial state:              1
45
46                 Number of transitions:              4
47
48                          Probability of being in State
49     Transition              1        2        3
50     ---------               -------------------------
51         0                   1        0        0
52         1                  0.3      0.5      0.2
53         2                  0.21     0.53     0.26
54         3                  0.195    0.527    0.278
55         4                  0.1917   0.5249   0.2834
56     46.2905
57
```

Thus, if Monday is hot, Friday's expected income is $46.29.

The second natural question is, what does the n-step transition matrix look like for a specific number of transitions; i.e., what is the probability of passing from any state to any other state in exactly n transitions? To answer this in PROPS⁺, press [Alt M], select **Transient** from the menu, and choose the second option from the submenu, **Transition_Matrix**. PROPS⁺ prompts for the number of transitions you wish. In the example, choosing five transitions produces the following matrices in the worksheet:

	A	B	C	D	E	F	G	H
60								
61		Number of transitions:			5			
62								
63		2-step Transition Matrix						
64		0.21	0.53	0.26				
65		0.2	0.54	0.26				
66		0.16	0.49	0.35				
67								
68		4-step Transition Matrix						
69		0.1917	0.5249	0.2834				
70		0.1916	0.525	0.2834				
71		0.1876	0.5209	0.2915				
72								
73		5-step Transition Matrix						
74		0.19083	0.52415	0.28502				
75		0.19082	0.52416	0.28502				
76		0.18961	0.52294	0.28745				
77								

Intermediate steps in the computation of the final matrix are included for interest. The last matrix provides the probabilities of ending the fifth transition in any state, given an initial state. Thus, for example, the probability of a hot Saturday given a cool Monday is 0.1896. Observe that PROPS⁺ does not erase the earlier results found in the **Transient** option: additional results are added below the current ones in the worksheet. Should you wish to erase these, you can use the spreadsheet **R**ange **E**rase command (**/RE**). Be careful not to accidentally erase other data from your worksheet, however.

Observe in the five-step transition matrix that, as n grows, the values in any element in each column of the matrix seem to be converging to a single value. This demonstrates that as one looks further and further into the future, the state in which the Markov chain began has less and less influence on the probability that the chain will occupy any given future state. Continuing this process indefinitely into the future would give us the "steady state" probabilities for each state, which in PROPS⁺ is calculated using the next menu item, **Steady_State**.

Steady State Analysis

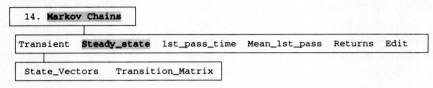

The Model:

$$\text{Solve } \pi = \pi P$$

where

$$\sum_i \pi_i = 1$$

$\pi = (\pi_1, \pi_2, \ldots, \pi_m)$ is a row vector

$\pi_i = $ the steady state probability that the system is in state i

Computation: PROPS⁺ solves the set of linear equations for π.

Limitations: The Markov chain must be a single recurrent chain. If not, PROPS⁺ will show the message: "The above matrix will not invert—no single solution exists." In this case, the steady state solution depends on the starting state and must be analyzed using the Transient option.

The example in the last section showed that as the number of transitions grows, the rows of the transition matrix look more and more alike. As n gets very large, the rows become identical, implying that the probability of being in any given state is independent of the starting state. The steady state probability distribution for a Markov chain is the limit of the n-step transition matrix row values, or in other words is the probability of being in any state after a large number of transitions, regardless of starting state. In the context of the example, this distribution can be thought of as the average proportion of the time spent in each state. To find this distribution using PROPS⁺, leave the previous worksheet in place, call up the menu with [Alt M], and select **Steady_state**. PROPS⁺ immediately computes the steady state probability distribution, as follows:

	A	B	C	D	E	F	G	H
79		Steady-State Analysis:						
80		=====================						
81								
82		State		Prob				
83		1		0.190476				
84		2		0.523809				
85		3		0.285714				

From this table, on the average it is hot 19% of the time, mild 52% of the time, and cool 29% of the time.

First Passage Time Distributions

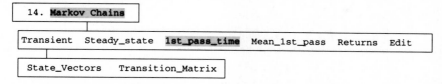

The Model:

$$f_{ij}^{(1)} = p_{ij}$$
$$f_{ij}^{(2)} = p_{ij}^{(2)} - f_{ij}^{(1)} p_{jj}$$
$$f_{ij}^{(n)} = p_{ij}^{(n)} - f_{ij}^{(1)} p_{jj}^{(n-1)} - \ldots f_{ij}^{(n-1)} p_{jj}$$

where

$f_{ij}^{(n)}$ = the probability that the system will arrive in state j for the first time in exactly n transitions, given that it started in state i

$p_{ij}^{(n)}$ = the probability of moving from state i to state j in n transitions (the n-step transition probability)

Computations: PROPS+ solves for $f_{ij}^{(n)}$ recursively.

Limitations: Note that $\sum_n f_{ij}^{(n)} = 1$ only if j is not a transient state and i and j are states in the same recurrent chain.

Often in Markov chains, one is interested in determining the number of transitions, n, required to go from state i to state j for the *first* time. For example, in the weather problem, if today is hot (state 1), how many days (transitions) must you wait until the first cool day (state 3) occurs?

To calculate the first passage time probability distribution, invoke the execution menu with [Alt M] and select **1st_pass_time**. You are then asked for the indices of the states for which you wish the first passage time, and for the number of transitions to be considered (maximum 50). Suppose you are interested in the first passage time distribution between states 1 (hot) and 3 (cool), and wish to know the probabilities that the first passage occurs on transition n for values for n ranging from 1 to 5. The worksheet appears as follows:

	A	B	C	D	E	F	G	H
87								
88		First-Passage Time Distribution:						
89		=================================						
90								
91		Index of starting state			1			
92		Index of ending state			3			
93								
94		Max. number of transitions			5			
95								
96		Trans	Prob					
97		1	0.2					
98		2	0.16					
99		3	0.128					
100		4	0.1024					
101		5	0.08192					

To illustrate one use of this distribution, suppose that today is hot and you are going to take a day off on the next cool day. What is the probability that you will get a day off in the next five days? To answer this question, find an unused cell in the worksheet (say, G101), and sum up the first five values in the distribution in this cell (with the formula **@SUM(C97..C101)**, for example). The result in the cell, 0.67232, is the probability that the first cool day happens on one of the next five days.

Expected First Passage Times

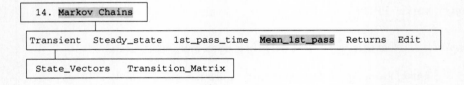

The Model:

$$\mu_{ij} = 1 + \sum_{k \neq j} p_{ik}\mu_{kj} \qquad \text{for all } i$$

where

μ_{ij} = the expected first passage time from state i
to state j

Computation: PROPS⁺ solves the set of linear equations of the model.

Limitations: The model requires a single recurrent Markov chain, and state j may not be a transient state.

The expected first passage time from any given state to any other is the mean of the first passage time distribution, and indicates the expected number of transitions required to reach the ending state from the starting one for the first time. In PROPS⁺, to find the expected first passage time from each state to, say, state 3 (cool), select the option **Mean_1st_Pass** from the menu, and respond to the question asking for the ending state index by typing **3** and then pressing [Enter]. The following screen then appears:

	A	**B**	**C**	**D**	**E**	**F**	**G**	**H**
108								
109		Mean First-Passage Times:						
110		=========================						
111								
112		Index of ending state			3			
113								
114		Start State		Expected FPT				
115		1		5				
116		2		5				
117		3		3.5				
118								
119								

Thus, on the average five days must pass after either a hot day or a mild one before the first cool day will occur, and an average of 3.5 hot or mild days occur between successive cool days. Similar calculations yield the first passage times to the other states, hot and mild.

Analysis of Returns

```
 14.  Markov Chains

Transient  Steady_state  1st_pass_time  Mean_1st_pass  Returns  Edit

State_Vectors   Transition_Matrix
```

The Model:

If $\alpha = 1$: Solve $au + b = r + Pb$

where

a = the steady state expected return for each transition

u = the unit vector (all entries = 1)

$b = \{b_i\}$ = the vector of relative expected values for each state

$r = \{r_i\}$ = the vector of expected immediate returns

P = the probability transition matrix

$\alpha = \dfrac{1}{(1 + i)}$ the discount factor with interest rate i per transition

If $\alpha < 1$: Solve $d = r + \alpha Pd$

where

$d = \{d_i\}$ vector of discounted expected returns over an infinite horizon

Computation: PROPS$^+$ solves the above linear equations. If $\alpha = 1$, b_1 is arbitrarily set to zero.

Limitations: The Markov chain must be recurrent.

A Markov chain may have financial returns associated with each transition. Expressing the time value of money through an interest rate per period, PROPS$^+$ calculates the expected present value of the future income stream from starting in any given state. With no discounting, of course, the expected present value becomes unbounded as the number of transitions becomes large. In this case, PROPS$^+$ calculates the expected return per transition and a relative value of starting in each state. Let us examine the expected returns for the ice cream vendor.

Select the option **Returns** from the Markov chain menu. In the sample problem, with the interest rate set at 0, the screen appears as follows:

	A	B	C	D	E	F	G	H
120		Analysis of Returns:						
121		====================						
122								
123	State		1	2	3			
124	Relative Values		0	-27.7777	-74.6031			
125								
126	Expected return per transition			46.19047				
127								

The average return per transition (per day) is $46.19, and the vender is worse off by an expected amount of $27.78 if the initial day is mild rather than hot, and by $74.60 if the initial day is cool rather than hot. That is, if the first day of the rest of eternity is cool, the vender would be willing to pay up to $74.60 to change the weather to hot (if that were possible).

With a nonzero interest rate, PROPS+ can compute the present value of starting the infinite horizon problem directly. To do so, move up the worksheet to the data input area and change the interest rate (cell D36) from 0 to, say, 20 (that is, $1.00 today is equivalent to $1.20 tomorrow). Calling up the menu with [Alt M] and choosing **Returns** produces the following output at the bottom of the worksheet:

	A	B	C	D	E	F	G	H
129		Analysis of Returns:						
130		====================						
131								
132	State		1	2	3			
133	Present Values		311.5151	284.2424	241.2121			
134								

The present values of starting the infinite Markov chain in each state, on a hot, mild, or cool day, are as shown. You could continue the procedure with different interest rates and graph the returns to show the sensitivity of the discounted present values to the interest rate, using standard spreadsheet methods.

Editing

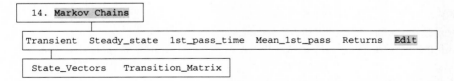

In formulating a problem as a Markov chain, you may discover that you wish to include one or more additional states. The **Edit** feature is included to let you do this easily. For example, in the weather problem, suppose you wish to distinguish between "cool" days and "cool and rainy" days. This means that you wish to add an additional state. To do this using PROPS⁺, press [Alt M] to bring up the menu, and select **Edit**. You will see a warning message, and when you proceed, you will see the following menu:

```
F34:                                                                        EDIT
How many states to add?
```

	A	B	C	D	E	F	G	H

Type in **1**, followed by [Enter], and you will see the following modified data input area:

	A	B	C	D	E	F	G	H
23								
24		States numbered from			1	to	4	
25		Increment for states			1			
26								
27		INPUT DATA:						
28								
29		End	1	2	3	(new)	Return	Check
30	Start	+--						
31	1	|	0.3	0.5	0.2		75	ok
32	2	|	0.2	0.6	0.2		50	ok
33	3	|	0.1	0.4	0.5		20	ok
34	(new)	|						ERR
35		*** Warning: Probabilities do not sum to one ***						
36								
37		% Interest/Period	20	==>	Alpha =	0.833333		
38								
39								
40								
41								

A new state called "(new)" has been added. You are back in spreadsheet mode and can add new data and modify the existing transition probabilities and returns.

We will now consider a number of problems that can be modeled as Markov chains and analyzed using PROPS⁺. These examples are chosen to illustrate the power of PROPS⁺, using the capabilities of the spreadsheet, to construct and solve many interesting types of problems.

Example: Gambler's Ruin

Imagine two players, A and B, gambling for $1 bets by flipping a fair coin. Suppose that their total assets are $m, and they continue to play until one player has $m and the other has none. The state of the system can be described by specifying the assets of one of the players (say, player A). If the system is in state 0, player A has lost everything, whereas if the system state is m, player A has won all $m. The transition probabilities for this chain are all zero except for the following:

$p_{00} = 1$, $p_{mm} = 1$,

$p_{i,i-1} = 0.5$ and $p_{i,i+1} = 0.5$, for i = 1, 2, ..., (m-1).

As an example, suppose the total assets for the two players are $4, and assume player A starts with $2. Also assume no discounting of future assets. Label the states with the integers 0 to 4, corresponding to player A's current asset level. Call up the **14. Markov Chains** worksheet from the ACCESS menu and answer the initial set-up questions (following each response with the [Enter] key) to generate the following worksheet:

	A	B	C	D	E	F	G	H	I
21		Analyst Name?			Your_name				
22		Problem Name?			gambler's ruin				
23									
24		States numbered from			0	to	4		
25		Increment for states			1				
26									
27		INPUT DATA:							
28									
29		End	0	1	2	3	4	Return	Check
30	Start	+--							
31	0	|	0	0	0	0	0	0	ERR
32	1	|	0	0	0	0	0	0	ERR
33	2	|	0	0	0	0	0	0	ERR
34	3	|	0	0	0	0	0	0	ERR
35	4	|	0	0	0	0	0	0	ERR
36		*** Warning: Probabilities do not sum to one ***							
37									
38		% Interest/Perio	0	==>	Alpha =	1			
39									
40		Fill the above data table with transition probabilities and							
41		return data (if needed).							
42									
43					([Alt M] invokes the command menu)				
44									

Entering the transition probability data into the matrix can be done easily using spreadsheet copy commands, such as the 1-2-3 copy (/C) feature. On completion, the worksheet appears as follows:

	A	B	C	D	E	F	G	H	I
27		INPUT DATA:							
28									
29		End	0	1	2	3	4	Return	Check
30	Start	+--							
31	0	|	1	0	0	0	0	0	ok
32	1	|	0.5	0	0.5	0	0	0	ok
33	2	|	0	0.5	0	0.5	0	0	ok
34	3	|	0	0	0.5	0	0.5	0	ok
35	4	|	0	0	0	0	1	0	ok
36									
37									
38		% Interest/Perio	0	==>	Alpha =	1			
39									
40									

Now call up the analysis menu by pressing [Alt M], which displays the master menu at the top of the screen:

```
G36:                                                                      MENU
Transient  Steady_state  1st_pass_time  Mean_1st_pass  Returns  Edit
Transient Analysis (n-stage)
          A         B         C         D         E         F         G         H
20
```

You can determine, for example, the probability distribution of player A's assets during the next ten transitions using the **Transient** option from this menu. Selecting **Transient** displays the following submenu at the top of the screen:

```
G36:                                                                      MENU
State_Vectors  Transition_Matrix
Create probability vectors given the initial state and number of periods
          A         B         C         D         E         F         G         H
20
```

Choosing **State_Vectors** and responding to the prompts "Index of initial state" with **2** and "Number of transitions" with **10** yields the following worksheet:

```
          A         B         C         D         E         F         G         H
42
43                    Transient Analysis (given initial state):
44                    =========================================
45
46                    Index of initial state:          2
47
48                    Number of transitions:          10
49
50                              Probability of being in State
51        Transition              0         1         2         3         4
52        ---------      -------------------------------------------------
53            0                    0         0         1         0         0
54            1                    0       0.5         0       0.5         0
55            2                 0.25         0       0.5         0      0.25
56            3                 0.25      0.25         0      0.25      0.25
57            4                0.375         0      0.25         0     0.375
58            5                0.375     0.125         0     0.125     0.375
59            6               0.4375         0     0.125         0     0.4375
60            7               0.4375    0.0625         0    0.0625     0.4375
61            8              0.46875         0    0.0625         0    0.46875
62            9              0.46875   0.03125         0   0.03125    0.46875
63           10             0.484375         0   0.03125         0   0.484375
64                              ([Alt M] invokes the command menu)
```

To generate the n-step transition matrix, call up the menu with [Alt M] and select **Transient** and **Transition_Matrix** in succession from the menus. If you want the transition matrix after, say, 100 transitions, enter the value **100** for the number of transitions, and PROPS$^+$ constructs the transition matrices corresponding to 2, 4, 8, 16, 32, 64, 96, and finally 100 steps, displaying each. (PROPS$^+$ determines the minimum combination of powers of the transition matrix needed to reach the desired number of transitions.) The following figure shows the beginning and ending portions of this progression:

	A	B	C	D	E	F	G	H
65								
66		Transient Analysis (n-stage Transition Matrix):						
67		===						
68								
69		Number of transitions:			100			
70								
71		2-step Transition Matrix						
72		1	0	0	0	0		
73		0.5	0.25	0	0.25	0		
74		0.25	0	0.5	0	0.25		
75		0	0.25	0	0.25	0.5		
76		0	0	0	0	1		
77								
78		4-step Transition Matrix						
79		1	0	0	0	0		
80		0.625	0.125	0	0.125	0.125		
81		0.375	0	0.25	0	0.375		
82		0.125	0.125	0	0.125	0.625		
83		0	0	0	0	1		
:								
119								
120		100-step Transition Matrix						
121		1	0	0	0	0		
122		0.75	4.4E-16	0	4.4E-16	0.25		
123		0.5	0	8.9E-16	0	0.5		
124		0.25	4.4E-16	0	4.4E-16	0.75		
125		0	0	0	0	1		

You can use the first passage time distribution option from the menu to determine the probability that player A will be bankrupt at any particular transition starting from, say, state 2. Calling up this option and entering **2** as the initial state, **0** as the ending state, and running for ten transitions produces the following entries in the worksheet:

	A	B	C	D	E	F	G	H
127								
128		First-Passage Time Distribution:						
129		=================================						
130								
131		Index of starting state			2			
132		Index of ending state			0			
133								
134		Max. number of transitions			10			
135								
136		Trans	Prob					
137		1	0					
138		2	0.25					
139		3	0					
140		4	0.125					
141		5	0					
142		6	0.0625					
143		7	0					
144		8	0.03125					
145		9	0					
146		10	0.015625					

Thus the probability that player A is bankrupt after two flips is 0.25, after four flips it is 0.125, and so on. Note that the first passage time probabilities do not sum to 1, since this is not a recurrent Markov chain.

Example: Baseball

To demonstrate PROPS[+] with a larger example, one can construct a Markov chain model of a baseball game (as given in Howard[*]). Let us model half of an inning of a baseball game when one team is at bat. Each player is identical, and player performance doesn't vary as the inning progresses, despite earlier strong or weak play. The possible outcomes for a player at bat are shown in the following table:

Outcome	Prob. of Outcome	Batter goes to	Player on first goes to	Player on second goes to	Player on third goes to
Single	.15	1	2	3	Home
Double	.07	2	3	Home	Home
Triple	.05	3	Home	Home	Home
Home run	.03	Home	Home	Home	Home
Base on balls	.10	1	2	3 (if forced)	Home (if forced)
Fly out	.10	Out	1	2	Home (if < 2 outs)
Strike out	.30	Out	1	2	3
Ground out	.10	Out	1	2	Home (if < 2 outs)
Double play	.10	Out	The player nearest first is out.		

Interpretation should be according to common sense. For example, if there is no one on base, hitting a double play is counted simply as making an out.

The state of the system depends on the number of outs and on what the current situation is on the bases. One can identify the possible states using the following convention:

State	Designation	Description
1	(0 000)	no one out, no one on base
2	(0 001)	no one out, one player on first
3	(0 010)	no one out, one player on second
:	:	:
:	(0 111)	no one out, bases are loaded
9	(1 000)	one out, no one on base
:	:	:
25	(3 000)	three outs, and the inning is over

---

[*]R. A. Howard, *Dynamic Programming and Markov Processes* (Cambridge: MIT Press, 1960).

The former table allows computation of the transition probabilities for the 25 states of the problem. Denoting the one-step transition probability from state i to state j as p_{ij} as before, observe that $p_{11} = 0.03$ (a home run is the only way to achieve this, earning 1 run). Likewise, $p_{12} = 0.25$, corresponding to either a single or a base on balls; $p_{13} = 0.07$, a double; $p_{16} = 0.05$, a triple; $p_{19} = 0.60$, the batter is out. The transition probabilities for the other states are calculated similarly.

In baseball, the expected return, or reward, from a batter is the expected number of runs he or she generates. One can then define the reward r_i from a batter as the expected number of runs (rbi's, or "runs batted in") from the next transition, given that the current state of the batter is i. For example,

$r_1 = (.03)(1) = .03$	(no one on base, and a home run is hit)
$r_2 = (.03)(2) + (.05)(1)$	(one player on first, so 2 rbi's if a home run
$\quad = .11$	is hit or 1 rbi if a triple is hit)
$r_3 = (.03)(2) + (.05)(1) + (.07)(1)$	(one player on second, so 2 rbi's for a homer
$\quad = .18$	or 1 rbi for either a double or a triple)

and similarly for r_4 to r_{25}.

To enter this problem into the spreadsheet, assign numbers from 1 to 25 for the possible states of the system as described in the preceding section. Then call up the **14. Markov Chains** worksheet and press [Enter] and respond to the prompts. You will see the following screen:

	A	B	C	D	E	F	G	H
20								
21		Analyst Name?			Your_name			
22		Problem Name?			baseball			
23								
24		States numbered from			1	to	25	
25		Increment for states			1			
26								
27		INPUT DATA:						
28								
29		End	1	2	3	4	5	6
30	Start	+--
31	1	|	0	0	0	0	0	0
32	2	|	0	0	0	0	0	0
33	3	|	0	0	0	0	0	0
34	4	|	0	0	0	0	0	0
35	5	|	0	0	0	0	0	0
36	6	|	0	0	0	0	0	0
37	7	|	0	0	0	0	0	0
38	8	|	0	0	0	0	0	0
39	9	|	0	0	0	0	0	0
40	10	|	0	0	0	0	0	0
41	11	|	0	0	0	0	0	0
42	12	|	0	0	0	0	0	0
43	13	|	0	0	0	0	0	0
44	14	|	0	0	0	0	0	0
45	15	|	0	0	0	0	0	0

	A	B	C	D	E	F	G	H
46	16	|	0	0	0	0	0	0
47	17	|	0	0	0	0	0	0
48	18	|	0	0	0	0	0	0
49	19	|	0	0	0	0	0	0
50	20	|	0	0	0	0	0	0
51	21	|	0	0	0	0	0	0
52	22	|	0	0	0	0	0	0
53	23	|	0	0	0	0	0	0
54	24	|	0	0	0	0	0	0
55	25	|	0	0	0	0	0	0
56	*** Warning: Probabilities do not sum to one ***							
57								
58	% Interest/Period		0	==>	Alpha =	1		
59								
60	Fill the above data table with transition probabilities and							
61	return data (if needed).							

The rest of the input matrix can be viewed by moving the cursor over the range [A27.. AC55]. Now enter the data with normal spreadsheet methods; note that the dashes in column B and row 30 in the input matrix act only as visual separators on the screen, and may be overwritten with other symbols. Here, the four-digit state descriptor is written in column B and in row 30 beside each state number for reference. You can change the width of the columns using the 1-2-3 command **W**orksheet **G**lobal **C**olumn-width (**/WGC**) to make the input data area easier to see. The input matrix is

	A	B	C	D	E	F	G	H	I	J
26										
27	INPUT DATA:									
28										
29		End	1	2	3	4	5	6	7	8
30	Start	+--	0 000	0 001	0 010	0 011	0 100	0 101	0 110	0 111
31	1	0 000	0.03	0.25	0.07	0	0.05	0	0	0
32	2	0 001	0.03	0	0	0.25	0.05	0	0.07	0
33	3	0 010	0.03	0	0.07	0.1	0.05	0.15	0	0
34	4	0 011	0.03	0	0	0	0.05	0	0.07	0.25
35	5	0 100	0.03	0.15	0.07	0	0.05	0.1	0	0
36	6	0 101	0.03	0	0	0.15	0.05	0	0.07	0.1
37	7	0 110	0.03	0	0.07	0	0.05	0.15	0	0.1
38	8	0 111	0.03	0	0	0	0.05	0	0.07	0.25
39	9	1 000	0	0	0	0	0	0	0	0
40	10	1 001	0	0	0	0	0	0	0	0
41	11	1 010	0	0	0	0	0	0	0	0
42	12	1 011	0	0	0	0	0	0	0	0
43	13	1 100	0	0	0	0	0	0	0	0
44	14	1 101	0	0	0	0	0	0	0	0
45	15	1 110	0	0	0	0	0	0	0	0
46	16	1 111	0	0	0	0	0	0	0	0
47	17	2 000	0	0	0	0	0	0	0	0
48	18	2 001	0	0	0	0	0	0	0	0
49	19	2 010	0	0	0	0	0	0	0	0
50	20	2 011	0	0	0	0	0	0	0	0
51	21	2 100	0	0	0	0	0	0	0	0
52	22	2 101	0	0	0	0	0	0	0	0
53	23	2 110	0	0	0	0	0	0	0	0
54	24	2 111	0	0	0	0	0	0	0	0
55	25	3 000	0	0	0	0	0	0	0	0
56										
57										
58		% Interest/Per		0	==>	Alpha =	1			
59										

	K	L	M	N	O	P	Q	R	S	T
28										
29	9	10	11	12	13	14	15	16	17	18
30	1 000	1 001	1 010	1 011	1 100	1 101	1 110	1 111	2 000	2 001
31	0.6	0	0	0	0	0	0	0	0	0
32	0	0.4	0.1	0	0	0	0	0	0.1	0
33	0	0	0.4	0	0.1	0	0	0	0.1	0
34	0	0	0	0.4	0	0	0.1	0	0	0
35	0.2	0	0	0	0.3	0	0	0	0.1	0
36	0	0.1	0.1	0	0	0.3	0	0	0	0
37	0	0	0.1	0	0.1	0	0.3	0	0	0
38	0	0	0	0.1	0	0	0.1	0.3	0	0
39	0.03	0.25	0.07	0	0.05	0	0	0	0.6	0
40	0.03	0	0	0.25	0.05	0	0.07	0	0	0.4
41	0.03	0	0.07	0.1	0.05	0.15	0	0	0	0
42	0.03	0	0	0	0.05	0	0.07	0.25	0	0
43	0.03	0.15	0.07	0	0.05	0.1	0	0	0.2	0
44	0.03	0	0	0.15	0.05	0	0.07	0.1	0	0.1
45	0.03	0	0.07	0	0.05	0.15	0	0.1	0	0
46	0.03	0	0	0	0.05	0	0.07	0.25	0	0
47	0	0	0	0	0	0	0	0	0.03	0.25
48	0	0	0	0	0	0	0	0	0.03	0
49	0	0	0	0	0	0	0	0	0.03	0
50	0	0	0	0	0	0	0	0	0.03	0
51	0	0	0	0	0	0	0	0	0.03	0.15
52	0	0	0	0	0	0	0	0	0.03	0
53	0	0	0	0	0	0	0	0	0.03	0
54	0	0	0	0	0	0	0	0	0.03	0
55	0	0	0	0	0	0	0	0	0	0
56										

	U	V	W	X	Y	Z	AA	AB	AC	AD
28										
29	19	20	21	22	23	24	25	Return	Check	
30	2 010	2 011	2 100	2 101	2 110	2 111	3 000	-------		
31	0	0	0	0	0	0	0	0.03	ok	
32	0	0	0	0	0	0	0	0.11	ok	
33	0	0	0	0	0	0	0	0.18	ok	
34	0.1	0	0	0	0	0	0	0.26	ok	
35	0	0	0	0	0	0	0	0.53	ok	
36	0	0	0.1	0	0	0	0	0.61	ok	
37	0	0	0.1	0	0	0	0	0.68	ok	
38	0	0	0	0	0.1	0	0	0.86	ok	
39	0	0	0	0	0	0	0	0.03	ok	
40	0.1	0	0	0	0	0	0.1	0.11	ok	
41	0.4	0	0.1	0	0	0	0.1	0.18	ok	
42	0	0.4	0	0	0.1	0	0.1	0.26	ok	
43	0	0	0.3	0	0	0	0.1	0.53	ok	
44	0.1	0	0	0.3	0	0	0.1	0.61	ok	
45	0.1	0	0.1	0	0.3	0	0.1	0.68	ok	
46	0	0.1	0	0	0.1	0.3	0.1	0.86	ok	
47	0.07	0	0.05	0	0	0	0.6	0.03	ok	
48	0	0.25	0.05	0	0.07	0	0.6	0.11	ok	
49	0.07	0.1	0.05	0.15	0	0	0.6	0.18	ok	
50	0	0	0.05	0	0.07	0.25	0.6	0.26	ok	
51	0.07	0	0.05	0.1	0	0	0.6	0.33	ok	
52	0	0.15	0.05	0	0.07	0.1	0.6	0.41	ok	
53	0.07	0	0.05	0.15	0	0.1	0.6	0.48	ok	
54	0	0	0.05	0	0.07	0.25	0.6	0.66	ok	
55	0	0	0	0	0	0	1	0	ok	
56										

Interesting questions one might pose include 1) how many batters will get a chance to bat during the inning? 2) what is the probability that n team members come up to bat? 3) what is the expected number of runs for an inning? PROPS⁺ will help to answer these. First let us calculate the first passage time distribution from state 1 (the inning begins) to state 25 (three outs: the inning ends). After the model is run, calculate the cumulative probability distribution in column E by entering the formula **+C72+E71** in cell E72. Copy this formula to the range [E73..E86]. The spreadsheet should look like this:

	A	B	C	D	E	F	G
62							
63		First-Passage Time Distribution:					
64		=================================					
65							
66		Index of starting state			1		
67		Index of ending state			25		
68							
69		Max. number of transitions			15		
70							
71		Trans	Prob		cdf		
72		1	0		0		
73		2	0		0		
74		3	0.2779		0.2779		
75		4	0.263211		0.541111		
76		5	0.190830		0.731941		
77		6	0.120440		0.852381		
78		7	0.069775		0.922157		
79		8	0.038132		0.960289		
80		9	0.019974		0.980264		
81		10	0.010131		0.990396		
82		11	0.005010		0.995407		
83		12	0.002428		0.997835		
84		13	0.001156		0.998992		
85		14	0.000543		0.999535		
86		15	0.000252		0.999788		
87							
88							

From the first passage time distribution, there is no chance the inning will be over after two batters (three outs are necessary to end the inning), a 27.8% chance that only three batters will bat this inning (all three are out), a 26.3% chance that exactly four batters come up to bat. From the cumulative probabilities, we see there is a 98% chance the team will go through the batting order (at least nine at bat).

Let us now calculate the mean first passage time to state 25 from any state. [Alt M] presents the menu, select **Mean_1st_Pass** and you will see the following:

	A	B	C	D	E	F	G	H
88								
89		Mean First-Passage Times:						
90		=========================						
91								
92		Index of ending state			25			
93								
94		Start State		Expected FPT				
95		1		4.752171				
96		2		4.512449				
97		3		4.512449				
98		4		4.512449				
99		5		4.545782				
100		6		4.512449				
101		7		4.512449				
102		8		4.512449				
103		9		3.230555				
104		10		3.063888				
105		11		3.063888				
106		12		3.063888				
107		13		3.063888				
108		14		3.063888				
109		15		3.063888				
110		16		3.063888				
111		17		1.666666				
112		18		1.666666				
113		19		1.666666				
114		20		1.666666				
115		21		1.666666				
116		22		1.666666				
117		23		1.666666				
118		24		1.666666				
119		25		1				
120								
121								

The mean first passage times indicate that starting from state 1 (the inning has just begun), you expect 4.75 batters to come up to bat each inning; if the first player gets to first base (state 2) you expect an additional 4.51 players to come up to bat; the first batter on second and the second batter just coming up to bat gives the same expectation of 4.51. (This looks odd, but is reasonable considering the assumed double- play rule: if there is any player on base and the batter suffers a double play, both the batter and the player *nearest* first are out.)

Finally, to examine the expected number of runs from being in each state, call up the menu again with [Alt M] and select **Returns**. (Recall that the data input (column AB) described the expected number of rbi's from each state transition.) The following entries are created in the worksheet:

	A	B	C	D	E	F	G	H	I	J
122	Analysis of Returns:									
123	====================									
124										
125	State		1	2	3	4	5	6	7	8
126	Relative Value		0	0.4350	0.5352	1.0731	0.7488	1.2556	1.3558	1.9231
127			0.8121	1.2472	1.3474	1.8853	1.5610	2.0678	2.1680	2.7353
128	Expected return per transiti		0							
129										

	K	L	M	N	O	P	Q	R	S	T
122										
123										
124										
125	9	10	11	12	13	14	15	16	17	18
126	-0.356	-0.041	0.0478	0.4228	0.2941	0.6328	0.7218	1.1428	-0.638	-0.472
127	0.4560	0.7709	0.8599	1.2349	1.1062	1.4449	1.5339	1.9549	0.1734	0.3397
128										

	U	V	W	X	Y	Z	AA	AB
122								
123								
124								
125	19	20	21	22	23	24	25	
126	-0.412	-0.222	-0.304	-0.132	-0.072	0.1776	-0.812	
127	0.3994	0.5897	0.5074	0.6797	0.7394	0.9897	0	
128								

In this table, the relative value of being in state 1 is arbitrarily set at 0. Note that the corresponding relative value for state 25, inning ended, is –0.81. Since state 25 means no more runs and state 0 is 0.81 runs better than this, the expected number of runs starting the inning is 0.81, in accordance with Howard's result for this game. In row 127 of the above table, we have added 0.81217 to each relative value. The value in this row is the expected number of runs for the rest of the inning, conditional on being in each state from 19 to 25.

Example: A Hydroelectric Power System

Suppose a hydroelectric power system consists of a single dam on a river. There is a reservoir above the dam that can store up to ten units of water. Modeling the system on a monthly basis, let the state of the system be the reservoir contents at the start of each month. Assume the flow of water into the reservoir from the river ("streamflow") is independent from month to month and follows a Poisson distribution with a mean of ten units of water per month. Suppose that the electric utility has a firm contract to sell power equivalent to ten units of water each month, for $2 per unit. If the utility is unable to supply the full amount, it must pay a penalty of $10 per unit it is short. Finally, if the reservoir is full of water and about to spill, the utility can generate surplus energy with the excess, and sell it for $1 per unit.

You can model this system as a Markov chain and analyze it through PROPS+. Select the **14. Markov Chains** option from the ACCESS menu. The state of the system is the level in the reservoir at the beginning of the month (from 0 to 10 units of water), so set up the data area by numbering the states from 0 to 10 in increments of 1, producing the following worksheet:

```
            A         B          C         D        E         F         G         H
20
21                Analyst Name?             Your_name
22                Problem Name?             hydro-electric
23
24                States numbered from              0       to        10
25                Increment for states             1
26
27                INPUT DATA:
28
29                          End      0        1        2        3        4        5
30        Start            +--------------------------------------------------------
31          0              |         0        0        0        0        0        0
32          1              |         0        0        0        0        0        0
33          2              |         0        0        0        0        0        0
34          3              |         0        0        0        0        0        0
35          4              |         0        0        0        0        0        0
36          5              |         0        0        0        0        0        0
37          6              |         0        0        0        0        0        0
38          7              |         0        0        0        0        0        0
39          8              |         0        0        0        0        0        0
40          9              |         0        0        0        0        0        0
41         10              |         0        0        0        0        0        0
42                *** Warning: Probabilities do not sum to one ***
43
44                % Interest/Period         0      ==>    Alpha =           1
45
46                Fill the above data table with transition probabilities and
47                return data (if needed).
48
49                                             (Alt M invokes the command menu)
```

To complete this table, you will require probability values for the Poisson distribution with a mean of 10 in the worksheet. These values could be constructed directly, or you may use another PROPS[+] worksheet, **12. Probability Distributions**, described in Chapter 12, to generate the probability distribution, including the cumulative distribution, mean, and standard deviation. The spreadsheet commands File eXtract (**/FX**) and File Combine (**/FC**) commands can be used to quickly transfer the probability distribution from the **12. Probability Distribution** worksheet to an unused area of the current sheet. (In all PROPS[+] worksheets, the area to the right of the title page is always kept clear for a scratch working area.) Chapter 1 summarizes the use of these commands. Remember that you can always save any current problem for future analysis by saving the whole current worksheet when in normal spreadsheet READY mode.

Find an empty area in the current worksheet, for example, the range [Q19.. AO23]. Using the **/FX** and **/FC** commands to copy the distribution into this area yields the following screen:

	Q	R	S	T	U	V	W	X	Y
19		Poisson distribution: POISSON-10							
20									
21	Lambda·t	10	| cdf:	0.00004	0.00049	0.00276	0.01033	0.02925	0.06708
22	mean	10	| pdf:	0.00004	0.00045	0.00226	0.00756	0.01891	0.03783
23	std dev	3.16227	| x:	0	1	2	3	4	5

	Z	AA	AB	AC	AD	AE	AF	AG	AH
19									
20									
21	0.13014	0.22022	0.33281	0.45792	0.58303	0.69677	0.79155	0.86446	0.91654
22	0.06305	0.09007	0.11259	0.12511	0.12511	0.11373	0.09478	0.07290	0.05207
23	6	7	8	9	10	11	12	13	14

	AI	AJ	AK	AL	AM	AN	AO	AP
19								
20								
21	0.95125	0.97295	0.98572	0.99281	0.99654	0.99841	0.99930	
22	0.03471	0.02169	0.01276	0.00709	0.00373	0.00186	0.00088	
23	15	16	17	18	19	20	21	

You are now ready to construct entries in the data input matrix. First, note that the worst case is an empty reservoir and 0 streamflow in a month, corresponding to a shortage of ten units of water. On the other hand, the largest volume of water you could experience is 21 units, if the reservoir was full and the highest streamflow occurred. If the ending state is above 10, water will be spilled for the generation of excess power, and the expected value of this can be easily calculated. We will compute the values for intermediate points between these two extremes. To analyze these, construct the following table in an unused portion of the worksheet. In the Markov worksheet, the area to the right of the input matrix is never used, so you could choose the range [Q30..BA41] as a work area. In the following table, copy the Poisson probability density function into row 31 of the spreadsheet, from column S to AN. Then use the spreadsheet Copy command (/C) to replicate the following completed row, offsetting each replication by one cell. (The first pass copies row 31 into row 32, starting the copy in column T. The second copies 31 and 32 into 33 and 34, starting in column U, and so on.)

	Q	R	S	T	U	V	W	X	Y
29									
30			-10	-9	-8	-7	-6	-5	-4
31	0		0.0000	0.0005	0.0023	0.0076	0.0189	0.0378	0.0631
32	1			0.0000	0.0005	0.0023	0.0076	0.0189	0.0378
33	2				0.0000	0.0005	0.0023	0.0076	0.0189
34	3					0.0000	0.0005	0.0023	0.0076
35	4						0.0000	0.0005	0.0023
36	5							0.0000	0.0005
37	6								0.0000
38	7								
39	8								
40	9								
41	10								
42									
43									

	Z	AA	AB	AC	AD	AE	AF	AG	AH
29									
30	-3	-2	-1	0	1	2	3	4	5
31	0.0901	0.1126	0.1251	0.1251	0.1137	0.0948	0.0729	0.0521	0.0347
32	0.0631	0.0901	0.1126	0.1251	0.1251	0.1137	0.0948	0.0729	0.0521
33	0.0378	0.0631	0.0901	0.1126	0.1251	0.1251	0.1137	0.0948	0.0729
34	0.0189	0.0378	0.0631	0.0901	0.1126	0.1251	0.1251	0.1137	0.0948
35	0.0076	0.0189	0.0378	0.0631	0.0901	0.1126	0.1251	0.1251	0.1137
36	0.0023	0.0076	0.0189	0.0378	0.0631	0.0901	0.1126	0.1251	0.1251
37	0.0005	0.0023	0.0076	0.0189	0.0378	0.0631	0.0901	0.1126	0.1251
38	0.0000	0.0005	0.0023	0.0076	0.0189	0.0378	0.0631	0.0901	0.1126
39		0.0000	0.0005	0.0023	0.0076	0.0189	0.0378	0.0631	0.0901
40			0.0000	0.0005	0.0023	0.0076	0.0189	0.0378	0.0631
41				0.0000	0.0005	0.0023	0.0076	0.0189	0.0378
42									
43									

	AI	AJ	AK	AL	AM	AN	AO	AP	AQ
29									
30	6	7	8	9	10	11	12	13	14
31	0.0217	0.0128	0.0071	0.0037	0.0019	0.0009			
32	0.0347	0.0217	0.0128	0.0071	0.0037	0.0019	0.0009		
33	0.0521	0.0347	0.0217	0.0128	0.0071	0.0037	0.0019	0.0009	
34	0.0729	0.0521	0.0347	0.0217	0.0128	0.0071	0.0037	0.0019	0.0009
35	0.0948	0.0729	0.0521	0.0347	0.0217	0.0128	0.0071	0.0037	0.0019
36	0.1137	0.0948	0.0729	0.0521	0.0347	0.0217	0.0128	0.0071	0.0037
37	0.1251	0.1137	0.0948	0.0729	0.0521	0.0347	0.0217	0.0128	0.0071
38	0.1251	0.1251	0.1137	0.0948	0.0729	0.0521	0.0347	0.0217	0.0128
39	0.1126	0.1251	0.1251	0.1137	0.0948	0.0729	0.0521	0.0347	0.0217
40	0.0901	0.1126	0.1251	0.1251	0.1137	0.0948	0.0729	0.0521	0.0347
41	0.0631	0.0901	0.1126	0.1251	0.1251	0.1137	0.0948	0.0729	0.0521
42									
43									

	AR	AS	AT	AU	AV	AW	AX	AY	AZ
29									
30	15	16	17	18	19	20	21		
31									
32									
33									
34									
35	0.0009								
36	0.0019	0.0009							
37	0.0037	0.0019	0.0009						
38	0.0071	0.0037	0.0019	0.0009					
39	0.0128	0.0071	0.0037	0.0019	0.0009				
40	0.0217	0.0128	0.0071	0.0037	0.0019	0.0009			
41	0.0347	0.0217	0.0128	0.0071	0.0037	0.0019	0.0009		
42									
43									

Now, for each initial state of the reservoir on the vertical left axis, you can add up the probabilities of all values less than or equal to zero on the top axis to find the probability that the reservoir is empty at the start of the next month. (Note that here you can set up the function in cell R31 to add the columns from S31 to AC31. Then simply copy this formula into each cell in the range [R32..R41].) For each value on the horizontal axis from 10 up, do a similar sum to find the probability that the reservoir ends the month in the full state, and store the results in, say, the range [AY31..AY41]. Calculate the expected shortages by multiplying the probability row values for each initial state times the horizontal axis value in columns S through AB. Finally, calculate the expected surplus by multiplying each row of probabilities by the horizontal axis value—10 for columns AN through AX; store these in, say, columns AZ and BA. Add titles in rows 29 and 30 of the columns created; the worksheet now contains, in addition to the array on the previous page, the following information:

	Q	R			AY	AZ	BA
28				28			
29		Prob		29	Prob	Exp.	Exp.
30		Empty		30	Full	Shortage	Surplus
31	0	0.583039		31	0.002754	-1.25110	0.000888
32	1	0.457929		32	0.006486	-0.79317	0.003643
33	2	0.332819		33	0.013577	-0.46035	0.010130
34	3	0.220220		34	0.026341	-0.24013	0.023708
35	4	0.130141		35	0.048040	-0.10998	0.050050
36	5	0.067085		36	0.082758	-0.04290	0.098090
37	6	0.029252		37	0.134835	-0.01365	0.180849
38	7	0.010336		38	0.207743	-0.00331	0.315685
39	8	0.002769		39	0.302524	-0.00054	0.523429
40	9	0.000499		40	0.416260	-0.00004	0.825953
41	10	0.000045		41	0.541370	0	1.242214
42				42			

The data in columns R and AY, representing the probability of an empty and full reservoir at the start of the next month for each initial state, can be copied directly into the first and last columns of the input matrix for the Markov chain; i.e., into ranges [C31..C41] and [M31..M41]. **Important note:** In this case you wish to copy only the *values* in the cells and not the *formulas*, so you should use the **Range Value (/RV)** command and not the **Copy** command (/**C**).

In addition, the values between 1 and 9 inclusive on the horizontal axis in the array are the probabilities of ending in each state on the horizontal axis, given that the system began in the state on the vertical axis. Hence, simply copy this range [AD31..AL41] directly into the input matrix, into the range [D31..L41], again using the **Range Value** command (/**RV**) to copy only the values and not the formulas.

Finally, pick a convenient area near the input matrix, say cells [I22..K25], and record some constants in the problem (monthly load, price, surplus unit value, shortage cost) for later analysis. These values can be used in computing the return resulting from each transition in the system (in conjunction with the expected shortage and surplus values for each starting state found earlier). The "Returns" formula entered in cell N31 for the return for starting the month in state 0 is

$$+\$K\$22*\$K\$23+BA31*\$K\$24+AZ31*\$K\$25$$

Using the copy command replicates this formula with appropriate changes for the rest of the "Returns" column, producing the following input area:

	A	B	C	D	E	F	G	H
21								
22		Problem Name?			hydro-electric			
23								
24		States numbered from			0	to	10	
25		Increment for states			1			
26								
27		INPUT DATA:						
28								
29		End	0	1	2	3	4	5
30	Start	+------						
31	0	|	0.583039	0.113736	0.094780	0.072907	0.052077	0.034718
32	1	|	0.457929	0.125110	0.113736	0.094780	0.072907	0.052077
33	2	|	0.332819	0.125110	0.125110	0.113736	0.094780	0.072907
34	3	|	0.220220	0.112599	0.125110	0.125110	0.113736	0.094780
35	4	|	0.130141	0.090079	0.112599	0.125110	0.125110	0.113736
36	5	|	0.067085	0.063055	0.090079	0.112599	0.125110	0.125110
37	6	|	0.029252	0.037833	0.063055	0.090079	0.112599	0.125110
38	7	|	0.010336	0.018916	0.037833	0.063055	0.090079	0.112599
39	8	|	0.002769	0.007566	0.018916	0.037833	0.063055	0.090079
40	9	|	0.000499	0.002269	0.007566	0.018916	0.037833	0.063055
41	10	|	0.000045	0.000453	0.002269	0.007566	0.018916	0.037833

	I	J	K	L	M	N	O
21							
22	Load		10				
23	Price		2				
24	Surplus price		1				
25	Shortage cost		10				
26							
27							
28							
29	6	7	8	9	10	Return	Check
30	------						
31	0.021698	0.012763	0.007091	0.003732	0.002754	7.489885	ok
32	0.034718	0.021698	0.012763	0.007091	0.006486	12.07193	ok
33	0.052077	0.034718	0.021698	0.012763	0.013577	15.40662	ok
34	0.072907	0.052077	0.034718	0.021698	0.026341	17.62240	ok
35	0.094780	0.072907	0.052077	0.034718	0.048040	18.95016	ok
36	0.113736	0.094780	0.072907	0.052077	0.082758	19.66906	ok
37	0.125110	0.113736	0.094780	0.072907	0.134835	20.04434	ok
38	0.125110	0.125110	0.113736	0.094780	0.207743	20.28254	ok
39	0.112599	0.125110	0.125110	0.113736	0.302524	20.51798	ok
40	0.090079	0.112599	0.125110	0.125110	0.416260	20.82549	ok
41	0.063055	0.090079	0.112599	0.125110	0.541370	21.24221	ok

This procedure for creating the data for this problem looks complicated, but in reality demonstrates the power of being in a spreadsheet environment. Very few keystroke operations were required. Doing such a complicated data entry manually would be tedious and very error prone.

At this point, you can use **Steady_State** to find the proportion of time the reservoir is in each state; the **Mean_1st_Pass** option to find, for example, the expected time until the reservoir is empty from each starting state; and the **Returns** option to generate expected income data. The following data is generated by selecting each of these in turn, and responding to the prompts in the obvious way.

	A	B	C	D	E	F
49		Steady-State Analysis:				
50		======================				
51						
52		State		Prob		
53		0		0.202446		
54		1		0.063261		
55		2		0.067749		
56		3		0.070535		
57		4		0.072168		
58		5		0.072930		
59		6		0.072616		
60		7		0.070633		
61		8		0.066372		
62		9		0.059628		
63		10		0.181657		
64						

	A	B	C	D	E	F
66		Mean First-Passage Times:				
67		=========================				
68						
69		Index of ending state			0	
70						
71		Start State		Expected FPT		
72		0		4.880224		
73		1		6.282606		
74		2		7.851111		
75		3		9.490399		
76		4		11.09668		
77		5		12.58177		
78		6		13.88922		
79		7		14.99618		
80		8		15.90356		
81		9		16.62350		
82		10		17.17189		
83						

	A	B	C	D	E	F	G	H
85		Analysis of Returns:						
86		====================						
87								
88	State			0	1	2	3	4	5
89	Relative Values			0	8.362846	16.18865	23.41676	30.00888	35.94729
90								
91	Expected return per transition				16.68022			
92								

	I	J	K	L	M
85					
86					
87					
88	6	7	8	9	10
89	41.22929	45.86187	49.85984	53.24837	56.06793
90					
91					

Observe from the steady state analysis that the reservoir is empty on the average about 20% of the time, full about 18% of the time, and so on. Also, if the reservoir is empty now, it will be empty again in an average of 4.88 months, whereas if it is full, an average of 17.17 months must pass before it is empty. Finally, the Analysis of Returns indicates that you can expect an average income of $16.68 per month from the system, and also shows the relative difference, starting with different reservoir levels.

As an illustration of the power of this system, you could now go back to the input area and alter one of the problem constants to see how the system statistics change. Suppose you were to reduce firm load to 9. Creating a new transition matrix and repeating the analyses above shows a rather startling result: with the lower monthly power requirement on the system, the average income increases to $18.45 and the reservoir is empty only 4.3% of the time. This is because the penalty costs decrease faster than the revenue. Also, by incorporating the constants in the formulas for the returns, you can easily carry out a sensitivity analysis on the value of each of the constants. From this point, you could continue to run the problem with a variety of levels of demand and use standard spreadsheet methods to generate tables and graphs showing the sensitivity of any of the statistics to variations in the parameters.

Features

1. **<u>Deterministic Dynamic Programming</u>**

   - calculates the shortest path through a network.

   - solves any deterministic dynamic programming problem.

   - finds the optimal deterministic inventory and production plans.

2. **<u>Knapsack Problems</u>**

   - calculates the optimal allocation of a resource among competing activities.

   - permits a nonlinear objective function.

   - finds an integer solution.

Chapter 15. Dynamic Programming

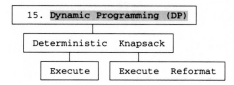

Many decision problems have a form that permits them to be solved in a particular structured manner, called dynamic programming. The principle underlying this method of analysis is to divide the problem into a number of separate small decisions, which are made sequentially. Then, from the solutions for this collection of small problems, one can identify the solution to the original large problem.

This chapter describes two deterministic dynamic programming models. The first, called **Deterministic**, solves any finite-state deterministic dynamic programming problem. This model structures the problem in the form of a shortest (or longest) path through a network. The second model, called **Knapsack**, finds the optimal allocation of a resource among competing activities. This worksheet permits easy entry of data for this common problem. Dynamic programming models involving uncertainty are discussed in the next chapter.

Deterministic Dynamic Programming

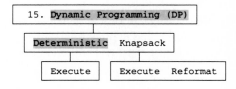

The Model:

$$f_n(x_i) = \min_{x_f} \left[c_n(x_i x_f) + \alpha f_{n-1}(x_f) \right], \qquad n = 1, 2, \ldots, N$$

where

$x_i \in S_n$ = the set of states at the beginning of stage n

$x_f \in S_f$ = the set of states at the end of stage n (the beginning
of stage $n - 1$)

$c_n(x_i, x_f)$ = the cost (reward) when the system evolves
from state x_i to x_f

Computations: Recursively, for each stage $n = 1, 2, \ldots,$ solves for the optimal
action $x_f^*(x_i)$ for each state $x_i \in S_n$, and finds the value $f_n(x_i)$. The
objective can be either to minimize or maximize the sum of costs or
rewards.

Limitations: It is assumed that all $x_f \in S_{n-1}$ are feasible. If this is not the case,
introduce a large penalty to ensure that infeasible x_f are not chosen.

Example: The Stagecoach Problem

To introduce the model, consider the following classic stagecoach problem. Suppose you wish to travel overland by a series of stagecoaches from state 1 to state 10. Although the initial and final points of the journey are fixed, you may route the journey through different states to minimize the cost of the total trip. The available individual stagecoaches between pairs of states and the cost of each are shown in the following table:

to from	2 3 4	to from	5 6 7	to from	8 9	to from	10
1	2 4 3	2	7 5 6	5	1 4	8	3
		3	3 2 4	6	6 3	9	4
		4	4 1 5	7	3 3		

Distance between States

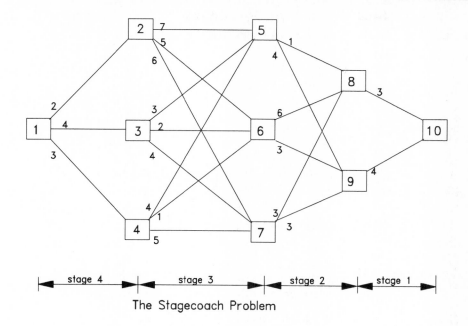

The Stagecoach Problem

To find the lowest-cost ("shortest") path from state 1 to state 10, you can divide any journey into four stages (corresponding to the four stagecoach journeys you must take). For each stage, the beginning state x_i is the state occupied at the start of the stage, and the ending state x_f is the next state number chosen. Dynamic programming solves this problem by starting at the end of the process (your final destination) and working recursively backwards, stage by stage, to the start of the problem (your initial state). In the diagram, the stages are labeled in order from the end, so the stage number represents the number of stages to go until the journey is completed.

The objective is to minimize the total cost of travel from state 1 to state 10. To do so, one can associate with every possible state x_i, which is n stages from the final destination, a number $f_n(x_i)$ equal to the value of the shortest trip from that state to the journey's end. To start the recursion, you can set $f_0(10) = 0$ (called the "terminal value"). Then, at the start of stage n=1, you could be in either state 8 or state 9. From 8, the only choice is to go directly to 10, with a cost of $f_1(8) = 3$. Similarly, from 9, the optimal (and only) choice is to go to 10, and $f_1(9) = 4$.

Now back up one more stage, to n=2. If you are in state 5, you could choose to go to state 8 or 9. Choosing 8 would yield a total cost of $1+f_1(8) = 4$, whereas choosing 9 costs $4+f_1(9) = 8$. Thus the optimal choice from state 5 is "choose 8", and $f_2(5) = 4$.

Following this same procedure for each state at each stage leads eventually to state 1, and you will have identified the optimal path and cost from state 1 to state 10.

To solve this problem using PROPS⁺, retrieve the ACCESS menu. Select **15. Dynamic Programming (DP)** and you will see the following screen:

```
B13: PR [W36]  ' 15.  Dynamic Programming (DP)                          MENU
Deterministic  Knapsack
Deterministic DP Problems
                          A                                B
```

The cursor is resting on **Deterministic**. Press [Enter] to retrieve the worksheet. The following screen appears:

```
          A       B       C       D       E       F       G       H
1
2                  PROPS+              DETERMINISTIC DYNAMIC PROGRAMMING
3                                               SPREADSHEET
4              Copyright (C)          - discrete states
5              PROPS SYSTEMS          - maximize or minimize
6                                     - solves general network
7              03/09/92 03:32 PM         shortest path problem
8           ==============================
9
10  Instructions:
11
12            PROMPT mode when CMD is on. Type response, press [ENTER].
13
14            [Alt M] -- Presents user with MENU of possible actions.
15
16                                           Press [ENTER] to begin...
```

Press [Enter], and you will be prompted in sequence for a problem name, the number of stages in the problem, and the type of objective function: max (the default) or min. Respond to each prompt by typing your answer followed by [Enter]. For the stagecoach problem, the screen should look like this:

```
          A       B       C       D       E       F       G       H
21              Analyst Name?      Your_name
22              Problem Name?      stagecoach
23
24              Number of periods (stages)?        4
25
26              Maximize or Minimize?      min
27
```

PROPS⁺ will set up an input matrix and will request that you assign a number to each of the states and each stage of the problem using the following table:

	A	B	C	D	E	F	G	H
27								
28	STATE IDENTIFICATION: At each period (stage) the initial states are							
29	numbered consecutively, from i to j, i≤j. If i=j there is only one							
30	initial state for that stage. The "end" period specifies the states							
31	at the end of the last period. Fill in the table, giving i and j for							
32	each period.							
33								
34	Start of Period #		1	2	3	4	(end)	
35			---					
36	Number	from (i)						
37		to (j)						
38								

In this table, PROPS⁺ expects sequential numbers for the states within each stage, so that describing the starting and ending state number automatically describes the number of states at the beginning of that stage. Enter each requested value, following each by pressing the [Enter] key (remember, you are in PROMPT mode). Note that for stages with a single state, the i and j entries will have the same value. For the example problem, the screen with the completed input appears as follows:

	A	B	C	D	E	F	G	H
33								
34	Start of Period #		1	2	3	4	(end)	
35			---					
36	Number	from (i)	1	2	5	8	10	
37		to (j)	1	4	7	9	10	
38								

When the table is complete, PROPS⁺ will present you with the following array for entering the immediate objective function impact (reward or cost) involved in passing from each initial state to each final state at each stage. At this point, you are no longer in PROMPT mode, and can use normal spreadsheet commands to complete the data table.

	A	B	C	D	E	F	G	H
40	CONTRIBUTION MATRIX:							
41	Stage 4		Stage 3		Stage 2		Stage 1	
42	+--- Period 1 ----+--- Period 2 ----+--- Period 3 ----+--- Period 4 ---							
43	Trans.	Cost	Trans.	Cost	Trans.	Cost	Trans.	Cost
44								
45			4 to 7	0				
46			4 to 6	0				
47			4 to 5	0				
48			3 to 7	0	7 to 9	0		
49			3 to 6	0	7 to 8	0		
50			3 to 5	0	6 to 9	0		
51	1 to 4	0	2 to 7	0	6 to 8	0		
52	1 to 3	0	2 to 6	0	5 to 9	0	9 to 10	0
53	1 to 2	0	2 to 5	0	5 to 8	0	8 to 10	0
54								
55	Trans.	Cost	Trans.	Cost	Trans.	Cost	Trans.	Cost
56	+--- Period 1 ----+--- Period 2 ----+--- Period 3 ----+--- Period 4 ---							
57	Stage 4		Stage 3		Stage 2		Stage 1	
58								
59	% Interest rate / period =			0	===>	Alpha =	1	

Use the cursor keys to move within the spreadsheet to fill in the costs for the entire CONTRIBUTION MATRIX. If a transition cannot be made between any particular initial state and final state, in minimizing (maximizing) problems you should assign a large cost (small reward) to such a transition to prevent it from being selected. Once you have completed this table by inserting the cost of each transition in place of the 0 cost entries, it appears as follows:

```
          A         B        C         D        E         F         G         H
40  CONTRIBUTION MATRIX:
41       Stage 4             Stage 3           Stage 2             Stage 1
42  +--- Period 1 ----+--- Period 2 ----+--- Period 3 ----+--- Period 4 ----
43  Trans.        Cost  Trans.       Cost  Trans.       Cost  Trans.        Cost
44
45                      4 to 7         5
46                      4 to 6         1
47                      4 to 5         4
48                      3 to 7         4   7 to 9         3
49                      3 to 6         2   7 to 8         3
50                      3 to 5         3   6 to 9         3
51  1 to 4         3    2 to 7         6   6 to 8         6
52  1 to 3         4    2 to 6         5   5 to 9         4   9 to 10         4
53  1 to 2         2    2 to 5         7   5 to 8         1   8 to 10         3
54
55  Trans.        Cost  Trans.       Cost  Trans.       Cost  Trans.        Cost
56  +--- Period 1 ----+--- Period 2 ----+--- Period 3 ----+--- Period 4 ----
57       Stage 4             Stage 3           Stage 2             Stage 1
58
59  % Interest rate / period =        0   ===>     Alpha =         1
```

Leaving the interest rate at 0% (i.e., no discounting), pressing [Alt M] then calls up the execution menu, which appears at the top of the screen as follows:

```
H54:                                                                    MENU
Execute
Execute the DP model (after data has been entered)
          A         B        C         D        E         F         G         H
40   CONTRIBUTION MATRIX:
```

Press [Enter] to solve the dynamic programming model (or press [Esc] to return to the spreadsheet system to make changes). PROPS⁺ solves the problem in the manner discussed earlier, and constructs the following dynamic programming tableaux for each stage. At the conclusion, you are returned to the spreadsheet system so you can use the [PgUp] and [PgDn] keys and the cursor control keys to look over the solution.

```
          A         B        C         D        E         F         G         H
61  STAGE-BY-STAGE ANALYSIS:
62
63            Stage 1: Period 4
64
65  Start             End State Optimal  Optimal
66  State        |         10      End    Value
67              +-------------------------------
68       8       |          3       10        3
69       9       |          4       10        4
70
```

```
          A        B        C        D        E        F        G        H
71
72                Stage 2: Period 3
73
74      Start              End State           Optimal  Optimal
75      State      |           8        9         End    Value
76                 +-------------------------------------
77        5        |           4        8         8        4
78        6        |           9        7         9        7
79        7        |           6        7         8        6
80
81
82                Stage 3: Period 2
83
84      Start              End State                    Optimal  Optimal
85      State      |           5        6         7         End    Value
86                 +------------------------------------------------
87        2        |          11       12        12         5       11
88        3        |           7        9        10         5        7
89        4        |           8        8        11         5        8
90
91
92                Stage 4: Period 1
93
94      Start              End State                    Optimal  Optimal
95      State      |           2        3         4         End    Value
96                 +------------------------------------------------
97        1        |          13       11        11         4       11
98
99
100  SUMMARY OF OPTIMAL PATH: (Note: Other optimal paths may exist)
101    [Traceback will automatically recalculate if initial state is changed.]
102
103           Initial State =          1
104
105                        End
106           Period      State
107           ------------------
108              1          4
109              2          5
110              3          8
111              4         10
112
113        Optimal value =           11
```

In the final summary, PROPS⁺ traces through the dynamic programming tableaux to identify an optimal journey. For the stagecoach problem, the minimum cost is 11 and an optimal route is 1 to 4 to 5 to 8 to 10. If there is more than one optimal path, PROPS⁺ will identify only one of them, and you can find the others by tracing through the tableaux in the worksheet.

At this point the original data is still in the worksheet. You could now return to the data input section and change any problem parameters (path length or interest rate) and re-solve the problem. Changes are made simply by moving the cursor to the item and typing in the new value. When all changes have been made, pressing [Alt M] calls up the execution menu, which here has only one choice (**Execute**). Press [Enter] and PROPS⁺ will solve the revised problem. To store results from successive analyses, the worksheet range [I1..P20] is maintained in all worksheets as a scratch area. In addition, you are free to use empty areas of the worksheet for temporary storage. Sensitivity to assumptions embodied in the problem formulation can be generated and analyzed easily in this fashion, especially by using the spreadsheet Graph utility.

Example: The General Shortest Path Problem

The preceding shortest path problem has a structure that allowed easy identification of stages and possible states at each stage. Now consider the network shown in the following diagram.

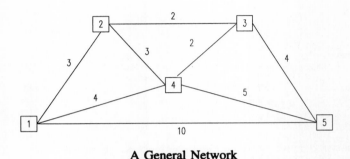

A General Network

This problem does not fit the same pattern as before, since it is possible, for example, to go from 1 directly to 5. To set this problem up as a dynamic program, one must be more subtle in the definition of a "stage". Here, define the stage number n as the number of transits to be made until the end node is reached, and the states are again the node numbers. Suppose you wish to calculate the shortest path from each node to node 5. In stage 1, you will find the shortest path from each state to state 5 in one transit. (In some cases, such as from state 2 to state 5, there will be no possible path of the given length.) Stage 2 will calculate the shortest path from each state to 5 in exactly two transits. Since this may involve remaining at the starting node for the first transit, one can define the cost of a transit from state i to itself as zero. In this example, for this definition you need at most three stages. (In general, the maximum number of stages required is the number of states minus one.)

To solve this problem, access PROPS[+] and select **15. Dynamic Programming (DP)** and **Deterministic** from the successive menus. Enter **3** for the number of stages and **min** for the optimization direction. In the state identification array, let the number of states at the beginning of each stage run from 1 to 4. Insert the (end) state range as 5 to 5. The worksheet will then appear as follows:

	A	B	C	D	E	F	G	H
21		Analyst Name?		Your_name				
22		Problem Name?		general shortest path				
23								
24		Number of periods (stages)?			3			
25								
26		Maximize or Minimize?			min			
27								
28	STATE IDENTIFICATION: At each period (stage) the initial states are							
29		numbered consecutively, from i to j, i≤j. If i=j there is only one						
30		initial state for that stage. The "end" period specifies the states						
31		at the end of the last period. Fill in the table, giving i and j for						
32		each period.						
33								
34	Start of Period #			1	2	3	(end)	
35				---------------------------------				
36	Number	from (i)		1	1	1	5	
37		to (j)		4	4	4	5	
38								
39								
40	CONTRIBUTION MATRIX:							
41		Stage 3		Stage 2		Stage 1		
42	+--- Period 1 ----+--- Period 2 ----+--- Period 3 ----							
43	Trans.		Cost	Trans.	Cost	Trans.	Cost	
44								
45	4 to 4		0	4 to 4	0			
46	4 to 3		0	4 to 3	0			
47	4 to 2		0	4 to 2	0			
48	4 to 1		0	4 to 1	0			
49	3 to 4		0	3 to 4	0			
50	3 to 3		0	3 to 3	0			
51	3 to 2		0	3 to 2	0			
52	3 to 1		0	3 to 1	0			
53	2 to 4		0	2 to 4	0			
54	2 to 3		0	2 to 3	0			
55	2 to 2		0	2 to 2	0			
56	2 to 1		0	2 to 1	0			
57	1 to 4		0	1 to 4	0	4 to 5	0	
58	1 to 3		0	1 to 3	0	3 to 5	0	
59	1 to 2		0	1 to 2	0	2 to 5	0	
60	1 to 1		0	1 to 1	0	1 to 5	0	
61								
62	Trans.		Cost	Trans.	Cost	Trans.	Cost	
63	+--- Period 1 ----+--- Period 2 ----+--- Period 3 ----							
64		Stage 3		Stage 2		Stage 1		
65								
66	% Interest rate / period =			0	===>	Alpha =	1	
67								
68		Fill the above table with the return or cost associated with						
69		each transition. If a transition is infeasible, enter a large						
70		negative number if maximizing (positive if minimizing). Enter						
71		the interest rate (if applicable), then hit [Alt M] for the						
72		command menu.						
73								

You can now enter the cost of each transition. If a transition is not possible, enter a high cost (say 999) for the transition to ensure it will not be selected. You can use the spreadsheet to help you enter data here: simply fill in the costs for period 1 and use the **Copy** command (**/C**) to copy these to period 2. Enter the cost from each state to state 5 in period 3. Your input should appear as follows:

	A	B	C	D	E	F	G	H
40	CONTRIBUTION MATRIX:							
41	Stage 3		Stage 2		Stage 1			
42	+--- Period 1 ----+--- Period 2 ----+--- Period 3 ----							
43	Trans.	Cost	Trans.	Cost	Trans.	Cost		
44								
45	4 to 4	0	4 to 4	0				
46	4 to 3	2	4 to 3	2				
47	4 to 2	3	4 to 2	3				
48	4 to 1	4	4 to 1	4				
49	3 to 4	2	3 to 4	2				
50	3 to 3	0	3 to 3	0				
51	3 to 2	2	3 to 2	2				
52	3 to 1	999	3 to 1	999				
53	2 to 4	3	2 to 4	3				
54	2 to 3	2	2 to 3	2				
55	2 to 2	0	2 to 2	0				
56	2 to 1	3	2 to 1	3				
57	1 to 4	4	1 to 4	4	4 to 5	5		
58	1 to 3	999	1 to 3	999	3 to 5	4		
59	1 to 2	3	1 to 2	3	2 to 5	999		
60	1 to 1	0	1 to 1	0	1 to 5	10		

To run the model, press [Alt M] and select **Execute**. The following tables will be created in the worksheet:

	A	B	C	D	E	F	G	H
68	STAGE-BY-STAGE ANALYSIS:							
69								
70			Stage 1: Period 3					
71								
72	Start		End State	Optimal	Optimal			
73	State	|	5	End	Value			
74		+------------------------------						
75	1	|	10	5	10			
76	2	|	999	5	999			
77	3	|	4	5	4			
78	4	|	5	5	5			
79								
80								
81			Stage 2: Period 2					
82								
83	Start		End State				Optimal	Optimal
84	State	|	1	2	3	4	End	Value
85		+---						
86	1	|	10	1002	1003	9	4	9
87	2	|	13	999	6	8	3	6
88	3	|	1009	1001	4	7	3	4
89	4	|	14	1002	6	5	4	5
90								
91								
92			Stage 3: Period 1					
93								
94	Start		End State				Optimal	Optimal
95	State	|	1	2	3	4	End	Value
96		+---						
97	1	|	9	9	1003	9	1	9
98	2	|	12	6	6	8	3	6
99	3	|	1008	8	4	7	3	4
100	4	|	13	9	6	5	4	5
101								
102								

	A	B	C	D	E	F	G	H
103	SUMMARY OF OPTIMAL PATH: (Note: Other optimal paths may exist)							
104	[Traceback will automatically recalculate if initial state is changed.]							
105								
106		Initial State =		1				
107								
108			End					
109		Period	State					
110		------------------						
111		1	1					
112		2	4					
113		3	5					
114								
115		Optimal value =		9				
116								

From this output, you can see that the shortest path from 1 to 5 has a cost of 9 and involves two actual transitions, from 1 to 4 to 5. If you want to know the shortest path from state 2 to 5, change the initial state in the SUMMARY OF OPTIMAL PATH portion of the worksheet, and you will see this screen:

	A	B	C	D	E	F
106		Initial State =		2		
107						
108			End			
109		Period	State			
110		------------------				
111		1	3			
112		2	3			
113		3	5			
114						
115		Optimal value =		6		
116						

Thus the minimum cost from 2 to 5 is 6, following transition path 2 to 3 to 5 (remaining at 3 for one transition).

Because of this automatic recalculation, you can set up a table of values showing the value of the shortest path from each initial state to state 5. Using the **Data Fill** command (**/DF**) to create values in column A and the **Data Table 1** (**/DT1**) command (see page 17) to construct the corresponding costs in column B, with appropriate titles, the table appears as follows:

	A	B	C	D	E	F
116						
117	Initial	min cost				
118	State	to state 5				
119		6				
120	1	9				
121	2	6				
122	3	4				
123	4	5				
124						

The Knapsack Problem

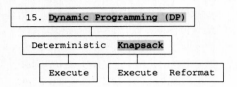

The Model:

$$\max \sum_i r_i(x_i) \qquad \text{(or min)}$$

subject to

$$\sum_i a_i x_i \leq b \qquad \text{for scalar } b$$

$$x_i \geq 0 \text{ and integer} \qquad \text{for } i = 1, 2, \ldots, N$$

Computation: Solved by dynamic programming using the recursive formula

$$f_n(S_n) = \max_{x_n \geq 0,\ \text{integer}} \left[r_n(x_n) + f_{n-1}(S_{n-1}) \right], \quad n = 1, 2, \ldots, N$$

where

$$S_{n-1} = S_n - a_n x_n \qquad S_N = b \qquad f_0(S_0) = 0$$

Limitations: Problem must be scaled so that a_i and b are integral.

The knapsack problem is a special form of a deterministic problem that seeks optimal integral values for a set of decision variables, subject to a single resource constraint. A convenient metaphor for the problem is to imagine you have a set of N types of objects and you want to know how many, x_i, of each type of object i to place in a knapsack which can hold a maximum weight of b, to maximize or minimize some objective. The value of including x_i items of type i is given by the function $r_i(x_i)$, which may be any linear or nonlinear function. Which combination of items maximizes the sum of the values of all the items?

To solve the problem using dynamic programming, assume that the consideration of each item in turn represents a stage and the state is the quantity of resource left to allocate to the remaining items. You could solve this problem using the same model as in the previous section. However, due to its special structure and the frequency with which this type of problem arises, PROPS⁺ has a separate routine for this type of problem.

Example: A Camping Problem

You are preparing a knapsack for a camp, and are choosing how many pairs of trousers, shirts, and socks to pack. Each pair of trousers takes up four cubic units, each shirt two units, and each pair of socks one unit. Your knapsack will hold 12 units. Your value for trousers is 20 for the first pair, 15 for the second, and 10 for the third. Shirts are valued at 12 for the first, 8 for the second, 4 for the third, 2 for the fourth and nothing for any more. Socks are worth 2 for each pair up to four pairs, and 1 for each pair thereafter. (You can't have too many clean dry socks.) What clothes should you pack?

In this problem, the scarce resource to be allocated is knapsack volume, and the decision variable is how many of each item to place in the sack. Consideration of each successive item will correspond to a stage, and the state of the system at stage n will be the remaining unused volume in the sack with n items left to allocate.

To solve this problem using PROPS$^+$, select **15. Dynamic Programming (DP)** from the ACCESS menu. You will see the following menu at the top of the screen:

```
B19:                                                               MENU
Deterministic  Knapsack
Deterministic DP Problems
        A         B         C         D         E         F         G         H
```

Select **Knapsack** from this menu, and the following initial screen for the knapsack worksheet will appear:

```
          A         B         C         D         E         F         G         H
1    ==============================
2              PROPS+                    KNAPSACK PROBLEM SPREADSHEET
3                                        - dynamic programming
4            Copyright (C)               - nonlinear costs/benefits
5            PROPS SYSTEMS               - integer solution
6                                        - maximize or minimize
7            09/26/92 10:25 AM
8    ==============================
9
10   Instructions:
11
12            max/min  Sum[r(x_i)]        [sums are from 1 to N]
13            s.t. Sum[(a_i)(x_i)] ≤ b    [x_i ≥ 0, a_i & x_i both integer]
14
15            PROMPT mode when CMD is on.  Type response, press [Enter].
16
17            [Alt M] -- Presents user with MENU of possible actions.
18
19                                             Press [Enter] to begin...
20
```

Pressing [Enter] generates a series of prompts for the problem name, the number of items, and the value of the resource constraint. Respond to these, following each response, by pressing the [Enter] key. PROPS⁺ then sets up a table for you to fill in to identify each item and describe its resource consumption, as shown in the following screen:

	A	B	C	D	E	F	G	H
21		Analyst Name?			Your_name			
22		Problem Name?			knap-1			
23								
24		Max or Min?			max			
25								
26		Number of items (N)			3			
27								
28		Resource constraint (b)			12			
29								
30		Item Number (i)		1	2	3		
31		Item Name						
32		Resource Use (a_i)						
33								
34								

Enter values into this table, pressing [Enter] after each value (you are still in PROMPT mode). Observe that entering the resource use coefficient causes PROPS⁺ to calculate immediately the maximum permissible quantity of each item if it alone were chosen.

	A	B	C	D	E	F	G
28		Resource constraint (b)			12		
29							
30		Item Number (i)		1	2	3	
31		Item Name		trousers	shirts	socks	
32		Resource Use (a_i)		4	2	1	
33		Max. Quantity		3	6	12	
34							
35							

When the last item is described, PROPS⁺ sets up a table for the description of the total objective function contributions for different levels of each item. In this table, you are requested to fill in the total contribution of each possible level of each item that would be feasible under the resource constraint b (that is, enter objective function values for every item at every level from 0 to the maximum quantity, which PROPS⁺ previously computed). In this example, the completed table appears as follows:

```
            A       B       C       D       E       F       G       H
36                OBJECTIVE FUNCTION    Item
37                                        1       2       3
38                                +---------------------------------
39   Quantity         0        |        0       0       0
40                     1        |       20      12       2
41                     2        |       35      20       4
42                     3        |       45      24       6
43                     4        |        0      26       8
44                     5        |        0      26       9
45                     6        |        0      26      10
46                     7        |        0       0      11
47                     8        |        0       0      12
48                     9        |        0       0      13
49                    10        |        0       0      14
50                    11        |        0       0      15
51                    12        |        0       0      16
52
53
54                Fill in the above table with the value of each (feasible)
55                quantity of the various items. Then hit [Alt M] for the
56                command menu.
```

Once this table is complete, [Alt M] calls up the following menu:

```
F71:                                                                      MENU
Execute   Reformat
Execute the DP model (after data has been entered)
            A       B       C       D       E       F       G       H
```

Press [Enter] and PROPS⁺ solves the problem. (Press [Esc] if you do not wish to proceed. You will return to the READY mode in the spreadsheet system.) PROPS⁺ then calculates the dynamic programming tableaux for each stage, which show entries for every possible starting state (available storage volume) for every corresponding feasible decision variable value at that stage. At the bottom, PROPS⁺ displays an optimal solution and objective function value. Other optimal solutions may exist, which you can identify by tracing the optimal sequence back through the tableaux.

```
        A    B   C   D   E    F   G    H       I       J      K
54   STAGE-BY-STAGE ANALYSIS:
55
56       Allocating Item #1 (Stage 1)
57
58       Start     Actions              Optimal Optimal    End
59       State  |  0   1    2    3  Action  Value   State
60              +---------------------------------------------
61         0    |  0   NA   NA   NA     0       0       0
62         1    |  0   NA   NA   NA     0       0       1
63         2    |  0   NA   NA   NA     0       0       2
64         3    |  0   NA   NA   NA     0       0       3
65         4    |  0   20   NA   NA     1      20       0
66         5    |  0   20   NA   NA     1      20       1
67         6    |  0   20   NA   NA     1      20       2
68         7    |  0   20   NA   NA     1      20       3
69         8    |  0   20   35   NA     2      35       0
70         9    |  0   20   35   NA     2      35       1
71        10    |  0   20   35   NA     2      35       2
72        11    |  0   20   35   NA     2      35       3
73        12    |  0   20   35   45     3      45       0
```

```
        A    B    C    D    E    F    G    H    I    J    K    L    M

75
76      Allocating Item #2 (Stage 2)
77
78      Start      Actions                                   OptimalOptimal   End
79      State  |   0    1    2    3    4    5    6 Action  Value  State
80             +----------------------------------------------------------
81        0    |   0   NA   NA   NA   NA   NA   NA     0      0      0
82        1    |   0   NA   NA   NA   NA   NA   NA     0      0      1
83        2    |   0   12   NA   NA   NA   NA   NA     1     12      0
84        3    |   0   12   NA   NA   NA   NA   NA     1     12      1
85        4    |  20   12   20   NA   NA   NA   NA     0     20      4
86        5    |  20   12   20   NA   NA   NA   NA     0     20      5
87        6    |  20   32   20   24   NA   NA   NA     1     32      4
88        7    |  20   32   20   24   NA   NA   NA     1     32      5
89        8    |  35   32   40   24   26   NA   NA     2     40      4
90        9    |  35   32   40   24   26   NA   NA     2     40      5
91       10    |  35   47   40   44   26   26   NA     1     47      8
92       11    |  35   47   40   44   26   26   NA     1     47      9
93       12    |  45   47   55   44   46   26   26     2     55      8
94
```

```
 A  B  C  D     E     F     G     H     I     J     K     L     M     N     O     P  Q         R

96   Allocating Item #3 (Stage 3)
97
98   Start Actions                                                            Optimal Optimal
99   State   0    1    2    3    4    5    6    7    8    9   10   11   12 Action  Value
100  -----------------------------------------------------------------------------------------
101   12 |  55   49   51   46   48   41   42   31   32   25   26   15   16     0       55
```

```
         A         B         C         D         E         F         G         H

103
104 OPTIMAL ALLOCATION: (Note: Other optimal allocations may exist)
105
106        Value of Optimal Policy =        55
107
108        Item    Amount
109        -----------------
110          1        2
111          2        2
112          3        0
```

The optimal solution is to pack two trousers and two shirts (apparently you *can* have too many socks!). You can change the data for the problem and re-solve. For example, suppose that after looking at the above solution, you decide that the first pair of socks is worth 5, the second worth 4, the third worth 3, the fourth 2, and each pair thereafter worth 1. If you make these changes to the values of socks in the OBJECTIVE FUNCTION table and press [Alt M] and select **Execute** to rerun the model, you will see the following output:

```
         A         B         C         D         E         F         G         H

103
104 OPTIMAL ALLOCATION: (Note: Other optimal allocations may exist)
105
106        Value of Optimal Policy =        56
107
108        Item    Amount
109        -----------------
110          1        2
111          2        1
112          3        2
```

Now the optimal solution is to pack two trousers, one shirt, and two pairs of socks. If you wish to add new items or change the available resource (12 volume units), then the number of stages or states has changed and the formulation must be restructured. As an example, suppose that you want to consider whether or not to include a rain jacket. It is bulky and takes up 6 units, but has an estimated value of 10 for the first one (additional jackets are worth 0). To make this change, move the cursor to cell E26 and change the number of items to 4. Press [Alt M] and select **Reformat** from the menu. You will see the following screen:

	A	B	C	D	E	F	G
21		Analyst Name?			Your_name		
22		Problem Name?			knap-1		
23							
24		Max or Min?			max		
25							
26		Number of items (N)			4		
27							
28		Resource constraint (b)			12		
29							
30		Item Number (i)		1	2	3	4
31		Item Name	trousers	shirts	socks		
32		Resource Use (a_i)		4	2	1	
33		Max. Quantity		3	6	12	
34							

PROPS$^+$ prompts for the name and resource used by each item. Previous values can be selected by pressing [Enter]. In this example, press [Enter] six times to include the previous data, and then type in **raincoat** and **6**. You will see the following screen:

	A	B	C	D	E	F	G	H
36		OBJECTIVE FUNCTION		Item				
37				1	2	3	4	
38			+---					
39	Quantity	0	|	0	0	0		
40		1	|	20	12	5		
41		2	|	35	20	9		
42		3	|	45	24	12		
43		4	|	0	26	14		
44		5	|	0	26	15		
45		6	|	0	26	16		
46		7	|	0	0	17		
47		8	|	0	0	18		
48		9	|	0	0	19		
49		10	|	0	0	20		
50		11	|	0	0	21		
51		12	|	0	0	22		
52								

Note that the old data is preserved, and you need only enter the objective function data for the new item (number 4). Enter the values **0** and **10** and then **0**'s in column G. To run this model, press [Alt M] and select **Execute**. (The optimal solution does not change in this case.)

Features

1. **<u>Stochastic Dynamic Programming</u>**

   - calculates the optimal set of sequential decisions under probabilistic transition laws.

2. **<u>Markov Programming</u>**

   - uses policy evaluation and iteration to solve for the optimal steady state decision policy.

3. **<u>Optimal Probabilistic Inventory Model</u>**

   - calculates the optimal periodic review (s,S) policy.

   - uses stochastic dynamic programming to find a solution.

   - permits both buying and selling of inventory, for problems of the cash balance management type.

Chapter 16. Stochastic Dynamic Programming

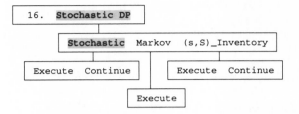

The Model:

$$f_n(i) = \max_{k \in D} \left[r_i^k + \alpha \sum_{j=1}^{S} p_{ij}^k f_{n-1}(j) \right] \quad n = 1, 2, \ldots, N$$

where
  $i, j \in S$ is the set of possible states
  $k \in D$ is the set of possible actions

  $p_{ij}^k = $ probability that the system changes from state i to state j if action k is taken

  $r_i^k = $ the expected immediate return if in state i and action k is taken

  $f_n(i) = $ the expected value of being in state i at the start of stage n if an optimal sequence of actions is followed to the end

  $f_0(i) = $ terminal value of ending in state i
  $\alpha = $ the discount factor

Computations: Recursively solves for the optimal action k for each stage n and value $f_n(i)$ for each state i. Finds either minimizing or maximizing solutions.

Limitations: Assumes time (stage) invariance, with the same set of states and actions available in each period. Time-varying problems can be solved as a sequence of interrelated time-invariant problems.

Many real-world problems involve sequential decision making under uncertainty. Whether to buy, sell, or continue to hold shares in a company given uncertainty in future prices is such a problem; what trading rule maximizes expected earnings? What is the optimal level of corporate research and development or advertising for a firm, given the uncertain nature of the future returns from these activities? Stochastic dynamic programming answers these sorts of questions by finding the optimal period-by-period decision rules. To see how PROPS⁺ solves these problems, consider the following simple example.

Example: An Investment Problem

Suppose you have $1,000 to invest. You can choose to invest $1,000 in either investment A or investment B at the beginning of each of the next three years. Both investments are for one year and have uncertain returns. With A, you either lose your money entirely or get back $2,000. With B, there is a chance that you merely get back your $1,000 or you may get back $2,000. The following table describes the probability of each of these occurrences.

Investment	Amount Returned	Probability
A	$0 $2,000	0.4 0.6
B	$1,000 $2,000	0.9 0.1

In any year, assume your maximum investment is $1,000 (the rest of the money remains idle). You cannot borrow. What investment policy maximizes your expected fortune at the end of three years?

Let the state variable in the problem be your current wealth, and let each stage correspond to one year. Observe that since you can only invest $1,000 at most in any year, your maximum possible fortune at the end of three years is $4,000, but it could be as low as $0. Thus you can label the five possible states as 0, 1, 2, 3, 4. The possible actions are "Buy A" (action 1) or "Buy B" (action 2). You can ignore the "Do Nothing" option since you would always at least buy B, as it has no downside risk. The following table describes the probability of making the transition from each state to each other state in any year under each action:

Action 1		Ending State 0	1	2	3	4		Action 2		Ending State 0	1	2	3	4
	0	1	0	0	0	0			0	1	0	0	0	0
Starting	1	.4	0	.6	0	0		Starting	1	0	.9	.1	0	0
State	2	0	.4	0	.6	0		State	2	0	0	.9	.1	0
	3	0	0	.4	0	.6			3	0	0	0	.9	.1

There is no return in each period apart from the transition to a different state.

The Stochastic Dynamic Programming Worksheet

To solve this problem in PROPS⁺, select **16. Stochastic DP** from the PROPS⁺ main ACCESS menu. You will see the following menu:

```
B14: PR [W36] ' 16.  Stochastic DP                                    MENU
Stochastic  Markov  (s,S)_Inventory
Stochastic DP Problems
       A         B         C         D         E         F         G         H
```

Press [Enter] to select **Stochastic**, and you will see the following screen:

```
          A         B         C         D         E         F         G         H
1     ==============================
2                 PROPS+                    PROBABILISTIC DYNAMIC PROGRAMMING
3                                                     SPREADSHEET
4              Copyright (C)               - discrete state
5              PROPS SYSTEMS               - time invariant
6                                          - finite horizon
7              09/26/92 11:15 AM
8     ==============================
9
10    Instructions:
11
12            States and actions are numbered consecutively from lowest to
13            highest.  Assume the same number of actions for each state.
14            There must be at least 2 states and 2 actions.
15
16            PROMPT mode when CMD is on.  Type response, press [Enter].
17
18            [Alt M] -- Presents user with MENU of possible actions.
19
20                                             Press [Enter] to begin...
```

Pressing [Enter] sets up the following series of prompts. Respond to each as shown, following each response (i.e., *each* state number and *each* action number) by pressing [Enter], since you are in PROMPT mode.

```
          A         B         C         D         E         F         G         H
21              Analyst Name?    Your_name
22              Problem Name?    invest
23
24              States numbered from          0        to        4
25              Actions numbered from         1        to        2
26
27              Maximizing or Minimizing?  max
28
29
```

After you enter the direction of optimization (max), PROPS⁺ sets up the following matrix for you to fill in to describe the problem:

	A	B	C	D	E	F	G	H	I
29		INPUT DATA							
30	State	Action		Ending state				Return	Check
31	i	k	0	1	2	3	4	r	
32									
33	0	1	0	0	0	0	0	0	ERR
34		2	0	0	0	0	0	0	ERR
35	1	1	0	0	0	0	0	0	ERR
36		2	0	0	0	0	0	0	ERR
37	2	1	0	0	0	0	0	0	ERR
38		2	0	0	0	0	0	0	ERR
39	3	1	0	0	0	0	0	0	ERR
40		2	0	0	0	0	0	0	ERR
41	4	1	0	0	0	0	0	0	ERR
42		2	0	0	0	0	0	0	ERR
43		*** Warning: Probabilities do not sum to one ***							
44									
45		% Interest Rate per period		0	===>		Alpha	1	
46									
47		How many STAGES?		1					
49		State							
50		0	1	2	3	4			
51	f(0)	0	0	0	0	0			
52									
53		Fill the INPUT DATA table with state transition probabilities							
54		and the expected returns or costs. If an action is not							
55		feasible use a large penalty cost (or large negative return)							
56		to eliminate it.							
57									
58		Before execution set NUMBER OF STAGES and TERMINAL VALUES f(0).							
59									
60		When finished entering data, hit [Alt M] for the command menu.							
61									

At this point, you are back in the spreadsheet environment and you can use spreadsheet commands to help complete the data table. For example, the Copy command (/C) is very useful when data is repeated at different places in the input array. You can also define parameters in an empty area of the spreadsheet (for example, in the range [I1..P20]) and use formulas or functions to define the input data. This has the great advantage of automatically updating the input data table when parameter values are changed.

Entering the values for this problem results in the following worksheet. Note that the (immediate) returns for each stage are 0, and the terminal reward function f(0) is just the total fortune you own at the end of the planning period, and is determined by the state you are in (e.g., state 2 means $2,000). Also note that there are three stages in the problem, since you are planning over a three-year investment horizon. Assume no discounting in this problem, so the interest rate is left at 0.

	A	B	C	D	E	F	G	H	I
29		INPUT DATA							
30	State	Action		Ending state				Return	Check
31	i	k	0	1	2	3	4	r	
32		---							
33	0	1	1	0	0	0	0	0	ok
34		2	1	0	0	0	0	0	ok
35	1	1	0.4	0	0.6	0	0	0	ok
36		2	0	0.9	0.1	0	0	0	ok
37	2	1	0	0.4	0	0.6	0	0	ok
38		2	0	0	0.9	0.1	0	0	ok
39	3	1	0	0	0.4	0	0.6	0	ok
40		2	0	0	0	0.9	0.1	0	ok
41	4	1	0	0	0	0	1	0	ok
42		2	0	0	0	0	1	0	ok
43									
44									
45		% Interest Rate per peri			0	===>	Alpha	1	
46									
47		How many STAGES?		3					
48									
49		State							
50		0	1	2	3	4			
51	f(0)	0	1000	2000	3000	4000			

Press [Alt M] to reveal the following menu:

```
F49:                                                                    MENU
Execute   Continue
Execute the DP model (after data has been entered)
        A       B       C       D       E       F       G       H       I
```

The **Execute** command solves the model for the specified number of stages. (**Continue** permits you to increase the number of stages in the problem, with possible modifications to the INPUT DATA.) Pressing [Enter] to select **Execute** yields the following dynamic programming tableaux:

	A	B	C	D	E	F	G	H
53	STAGE-BY-STAGE ANALYSIS:							
54								
55		Stage 1						
56								
57	State	0	1	2	3	4		
58	f(n)	0	1200	2200	3200	4000		
59	decision	1	1	1	1	1		
60								
61								
62		Stage 2						
63								
64	State	0	1	2	3	4		
65	f(n)	0	1320	2400	3280	4000		
66	decision	1	1	1	1	1		
67								
68								
69		Stage 3						
70								
71	State	0	1	2	3	4		
72	f(n)	0	1440	2496	3360	4000		
73	decision	1	1	1	1	1		
74								

Stage 1 describes the optimal values and actions if one stage (one year) remains until the end of the horizon, stage 2 has two years to go, and stage 3 is at the beginning of the three-year horizon. The values in the "f(n)" rows are the expected returns if you start in each state, while the values in the "decision" rows are the optimal actions for each state. In this problem, the optimal action to maximize the expected value after three years is 1 (buy A) for each state.

This analysis takes no account of the difference in variance in results from the two actions. An alternative objective might be to maximize rewards subject to the penalty that ending with $1,000 after three years is worth 0. To solve this problem, you can modify the earlier input by assigning a terminal value of 0 to ending the planning period in state 1. Making this change in cell C51, the terminal rewards appear as follows:

	A	B	C	D	E	F	G
49		State					
50		0	1	2	3	4	
51	f(0)	0	0	2000	3000	4000	
52							

Call up the menu with [Alt M] and select **Execute**; the problem solution appears:

	A	B	C	D	E	F	G	H
53	STAGE-BY-STAGE ANALYSIS:							
54								
55		Stage 1						
56								
57	State	0	1	2	3	4		
58	f(n)	0	1200	2100	3200	4000		
59	decision	1	1	2	1	1		
60								
61								
62		Stage 2						
63								
64	State	0	1	2	3	4		
65	f(n)	0	1290	2400	3280	4000		
66	decision	1	2	1	2	1		
67								
68								
69		Stage 3						
70								
71	State	0	1	2	3	4		
72	f(n)	0	1440	2488	3360	4000		
73	decision	1	1	2	1	1		

Here, with one year to go, if you had $1,000 left (stage 1, state 1), you would choose "Buy A" since that maximizes your chances of ending up with at least $2,000. If you had $2,000, however, you would choose "Buy B" to avoid the possibility of ending at $1,000. Similarly, if you had $3,000 left, "Buy A" is indicated since you will certainly have at least $2,000, and this choice maximizes your expected value.

If you start with $1,000, then at the beginning of stage 3 (the first year of investment) you should choose the riskier "Buy A" for an expected terminal value of $1,440 (excluding any terminal value of ending in state 1). If you have $2,000 at this point, you should choose the conservative investment "B", for an expectation of $2,488. With $3,000 at this point, you should gamble and choose "A". Although counter-intuitive, this strategy is optimal for this problem.

Example: The Toymaker Problem[*]

A toymaker is involved in the novelty toy business. She may be in one of two states: state 1, the toy is in favor with the public; or state 2, the toy is out of favor. Suppose she is in state 1. During the next month she will earn six units. If she does nothing to promote her toy, there is a 50% chance of remaining in state 1 at the end of the month and a 50% chance of a transition to state 2. On the other hand, when in state 1 the toymaker can advertise at a cost of two units, and can thereby change the probabilities to 0.8 for remaining in state 1 and 0.2 for a change to state 2.

If she is in state 2 and undertakes no new research and development, she will incur a loss of three units and has a probability of 0.6 of remaining in state 2 and of 0.4 of a fortuitous change to state 1. If she carries out R&D at a cost of two units, these probabilities change to 0.3 for remaining in state 2 and 0.7 for a switch to state 1. These data are summarized in the table below.

State i	Action d	Prob $(x_t=1)$ given d	Prob $(x_t=2)$ given d	Expected Immediate Return $r(x_i, d)$
1	1. No Promo 2. Promotion	0.5 0.8	0.5 0.2	6 units 4 "
2	1. No R&D 2. R&D	0.4 0.7	0.6 0.3	-3 units -5 "

Transition Probabilities and Rewards for the Toymaker

Assuming that the toymaker wishes to maximize expected returns over some planning horizon, PROPS[+] can solve her problem. Suppose she starts with a planning horizon of four months. At the end of the last month in the planning horizon, there is no terminal value for being in either state. Then select **16. Stochastic DP** from the PROPS[+] ACCESS menu and **Stochastic** from the submenu. Press [Enter] to initiate the program and respond to each of the questions when prompted, ending each response by pressing [Enter]. The worksheet appears as follows:

---

[*]From R. A. Howard, *Dynamic Programming and Markov Processes* (Cambridge: MIT Press, 1960).

	A	B	C	D	E	F	G
21		Analyst Name?		Your_name			
22		Problem Name?		toymaker			
23							
24		States numbered from			1	to	2
25		Actions numbered from			1	to	2
26							
27		Maximizing or Minimizing? max					

Following the entry of the response to the "Maximizing or Minimizing?" prompt, PROPS⁺ creates the following data area for you to complete:

	A	B	C	D	E	F	G
29		INPUT DATA					
30	State	Action		Ending state	Return	Check	
31	i	k	1	2	r		
32	--						
33	1	1	0	0	0	ERR	
34		2	0	0	0	ERR	
35	2	1	0	0	0	ERR	
36		2	0	0	0	ERR	
37		*** Warning: Probabilities do not sum to one ***					
38							
39		% Interest Rate per period			0	===>	Alpha
40							
41		How many STAGES?		1			
42							
43		State					
44		1	2				
45	f(0)	0	0				
46							
47		Fill the INPUT DATA table with state transition probabilities					
48		and the expected returns or costs. If an action is not					
49		feasible use a large penalty cost (or large negative return)					
50		to eliminate it.					
51							
52		Before execution set NUMBER OF STAGES and TERMINAL VALUES f(0).					
53							
54		When finished entering data, hit [Alt M] for the command menu.					

Enter the data for this problem in the INPUT DATA. The worksheet appears:

	A	B	C	D	E	F	G
29		INPUT DATA					
30	State	Action		Ending state	Return	Check	
31	i	k	1	2	r		
32	--						
33	1	1	0.5	0.5	6	ok	
34		2	0.8	0.2	4	ok	
35	2	1	0.4	0.6	-3	ok	
36		2	0.7	0.3	-5	ok	
37							
38							
39		% Interest Rate per period			0	===>	Alpha
40							
41		How many STAGES?		4			
42							
43		State					
44		1	2				
45	f(0)	0	0				
46							

Noting that you have changed the number of stages to 4 (corresponding to four months), press [Alt M] to call up the following menu:

```
D48:                                                              MENU
Execute   Continue
Execute the DP model (after data has been entered)
        A         B         C         D         E         F         G         H
```

From this menu, select **Execute** by pressing [Enter]. PROPS⁺ then creates the following stage-by-stage solution in the worksheet:

```
        A         B         C         D         E         F         G
47  STAGE-BY-STAGE ANALYSIS:
48
49                Stage 1
50
51      State         1         2
52      f(n)          6        -3
53  decision          1         1
54
55
56                Stage 2
57
58      State         1         2
59      f(n)        8.2      -1.7
60  decision          2         2
61
62
63                Stage 3
64
65      State         1         2
66      f(n)      10.22      0.23
67  decision          2         2
68
69
70                Stage 4
71
72      State         1         2
73      f(n)     12.222     2.223
74  decision          2         2
75
```

The optimal policy is, in state 1 always advertise unless in the final month (stage 1), and in state 2 always carry out R&D unless in the final month. You could now, if desired, extend the analysis by re-solving the problem over a longer planning horizon (say, eight months). To do so, alter the number of stages to 8. Press [Alt M] and select the **Continue** option from this menu (move the cursor to **Continue** and press [Enter]). PROPS⁺ then continues the analysis of stages 5 through 8, recognizing that the first four stages have already been solved. The STAGE-BY-STAGE ANALYSIS is simply extended to the new horizon limit.

Example: A Stock Trading Problem

Suppose a certain stock price fluctuates monthly among the prices $30, $31, and $32 according to the following probability distributions:

```
Price Next Month:    $30      $31      $32

    Current  $30  │  .8       .2        0   │
    Price    $31  │  .25      .25      .5   │
             $32  │   0       .75      .25  │
```

Imagine that you can hold at most one unit of the stock, so that in each month, if you own the stock, the only decisions are "hold the stock" (pass) or "sell"; whereas if you don't own it, the only decisions are "do nothing" (pass) or "buy." You can label the pass option in either case as Action 1 and the buy or sell option as Action 2, knowing from the ownership position what this means.

With this problem structure, it is natural to identify a stage as the passage of a month. The state of the system will be the current price of the stock together with an indicator of ownership. Letting 0 stand for "no stock owned" and 1 for "stock owned", if the current price is, say, $30 and you own the stock, this state would be represented as (30,1). The return is immediate revenue if you take that action (e.g., if you sell when the stock is at 30, return is +30; if you buy, it is –30). With these definitions, you can describe the possible transitions between the various states depending on the actions chosen, as indicated in the following table.

#	State	Action	(30,0)	(30,1)	(31,0)	(31,1)	(32,0)	(32,1)	Return
1	(30,0)	1 pass	.8		.2				0
		2 buy		.8		.2			–30
2	(30,1)	1 pass		.8		.2			0
		2 sell	.8		.2				+30
3	(31,0)	1 pass	.25		.25		.5		0
		2 buy		.25		.25		.5	–31
4	(31,1)	1 pass		.25		.25		.5	0
		2 sell	.25		.25		.5		+31
5	(32,0)	1 pass			.75		.25		0
		2 sell				.75		.25	–32
6	(32,1)	1 pass				.75		.25	0
		2 sell			.75		.25		+32

Using the state numbering system indicated in the table, and assuming that at the end of the planning horizon the stock will be sold at the prevailing price at the time, you can solve the problem for, say, four months with no discounting.

Select **16. Stochastic DP** from the main ACCESS menu and **Stochastic** from the submenu to retrieve the probabilistic dynamic programming spreadsheet. Press [Enter] and answer the question sequence, numbering the states from 1 to 6 and the actions from 1 to 2. Then complete the INPUT DATA table as shown below.

	A	B	C	D	E	F	G	H	I	J
21		Analyst Name? Your_name								
22		Problem Name? stock trading								
23										
24		States numbered from			1	to	6			
25		Actions numbered from			1	to	2			
26										
27		Maximizing or Minimize		max						
28										
29		INPUT DATA								
30	State	Action		Ending state					Return	Check
31	i	k	1	2	3	4	5	6	r	
32										
33	1	1	0.8	0	0.2	0	0	0	0	ok
34		2	0	0.8	0	0.2	0	0	-30	ok
35	2	1	0	0.8	0	0.2	0	0	0	ok
36		2	0.8	0	0.2	0	0	0	30	ok
37	3	1	0.25	0	0.25	0	0.5	0	0	ok
38		2	0	0.25	0	0.25	0	0.5	-31	ok
39	4	1	0	0.25	0	0.25	0	0.5	0	ok
40		2	0.25	0	0.25	0	0.5	0	31	ok
41	5	1	0	0	0.75	0	0.25	0	0	ok
42		2	0	0	0	0.75	0	0.25	-32	ok
43	6	1	0	0	0	0.75	0	0.25	0	ok
44		2	0	0	0.75	0	0.25	0	32	ok
45										
46										
47		% Interest Rate per period				0	===>	Alpha	1	
48										
49		How many STAGE		4						
50										
51		State								
52			1	2	3	4	5	6		
53	f(0)		0	30	0	31	0	32		
54										

In this input, you have requested a model run of four stages. If you wish to extend this horizon later, you can increase the number of stages and use the **Continue** option from the menu produced by pressing [Alt M]. This facilitates the good modeling practice of running for a small number of stages to ensure that the problem is appropriately captured in the model before continuing the model for longer periods. Executing the model for four stages yields the following tables:

	A	B	C	D	E	F	G	H
55	STAGE-BY-STAGE ANALYSIS:							
56								
57		Stage 1						
58								
59	State	1	2	3	4	5	6	
60	f(n)	0.2	30.2	0.25	31.25	0	32	
61	decision	2	1	2	1	1	2	
62								
63								
64		Stage 2						
65								
66	State	1	2	3	4	5	6	
67	f(n)	0.41	30.41	0.3625	31.362	0.1875	32.187	
68	decision	2	1	2	1	1	2	
69								
70								
71		Stage 3						
72								
73	State	1	2	3	4	5	6	
74	f(n)	0.6005	30.600	0.5368	31.536	0.3187	32.318	
75	decision	2	1	2	1	1	2	
76								
77								
78		Stage 4						
79								
80	State	1	2	3	4	5	6	
81	f(n)	0.7877	30.787	0.6937	31.693	0.4823	32.482	
82	decision	2	1	2	1	1	2	
83								

The optimal policy, which is the same for each stage, is "buy the stock at $30 or $31 if you do not already own it, and sell the stock at $32 if you do." Note that the optimal values f(n) at Stage 4 are the optimal values (for a four-period horizon) associated with each state. Thus, if the stock is currently selling at $30, you expect to earn $0.79 over the next four periods. If it is now at $31, you expect to earn $0.69, and at $32 you expect earnings of $0.48. To see this, note that even if the stock is at $32 and you would not currently buy it at that price, over the four-period horizon the stock price may decline, presenting an opportunity for purchase and sale with a positive expected return of $0.48.

It might be interesting to examine the effect of discounting on this optimal policy. Suppose, for example, you have solved the problem as just shown and wish to see how the solution changes if you discount at, say, 0.8 percent per month (or about 10 percent per year). To do this, move the cursor up to the interest rate portion of the worksheet and enter 0.8 as the "% Interest Rate per period". The discount factor Alpha, which measures the present value of $1 received in the next period, automatically adjusts to 0.992063. Leaving the rest of the input data as it is, press [Alt M] and select **Execute** from the menu; PROPS⁺ recalculates the optimal decisions with this new set of input data, yielding the following screen:

	A	B	C	D	E	F	G	H	I
46									
47	% Interest Rate per period				0.8	===>	Alpha 0.9920		
48									
49	How many STAGE			4					
::									
::									
55	STAGE-BY-STAGE ANALYSIS:								
56									
57	Stage 1								
58									
59	State	1	2	3	4	5	6		
60	f(n)	0	30	0.0019	31.001	0	32		
61	decision	1	2	2	1	1	2		
62									
63									
64	Stage 2								
65									
66	State	1	2	3	4	5	6		
67	f(n)	0.0003	30.000	0.0024	31.002	0.0014	32.001		
68	decision	1	2	2	1	1	2		
69									
70									
71	Stage 3								
72									
73	State	1	2	3	4	5	6		
74	f(n)	0.0008	30.000	0.0034	31.003	0.0022	32.002		
75	decision	1	2	2	1	1	2		
76									
77									
78	Stage 4								
79									
80	State	1	2	3	4	5	6		
81	f(n)	0.0013	30.001	0.0041	31.004	0.0030	32.003		
82	decision	1	2	2	1	1	2		
83									

With an interest cost of 0.8 percent per month, the optimal policy changes when the stock is priced at $30. At this price, don't buy the stock if you don't own it, and sell it if you do. Since there is a small likelihood of a price increase, you are better off not holding the stock because of the opportunity cost of 0.8 percent of $30, or $0.24, per month. In this revised problem, f(n) is now the present value of expected trades over the four-period horizon.

You could now easily continue the analysis, parametrically examining the impact of the discount rate on the investment policy. PROPS⁺ readily permits sensitivity analysis on critical problem parameters.

The next example illustrates another powerful feature of PROPS⁺: input data can be defined with respect to variables established elsewhere in the worksheet.

Example: A Parking Problem

Imagine you are going to a theater that is located midway along a one-way street. You wish to park as close as you can to the theater to minimize your walk, but as it is approaching show time, you cannot go down the street more than once. Numbering the parking spaces in terms of their distance from the theater and labeling the parking space in front of the theater as 0, the street appears as follows:

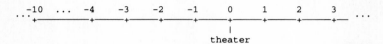

Suppose you are traveling down the street from left to right. As you proceed down the street and encounter an empty parking space, you must decide whether to park there or pass the space in hopes of finding another one closer to the theater. Of course, once you have passed it, you can never return to the space since the street is one way.

Note that if you ever reach the theater, you will park at the next available spot. The issue is how far from the theater in the direction marked by negative numbers in the sketch should you accept a free space if one is there? (This is an example of what is called an "optimal stopping problem.")

The policy will clearly depend on the probability that, if an empty space is passed up, another will be available closer to the theater. Suppose that the probability that any given space is empty is p and that each parking space is equally likely to be empty. Then, once you have driven as far as the theater (should this happen), the expected distance to walk in numbers of parking spaces is given by

$$f_0(0) = 0(p) + 1(1-p)(p) + 2(1-p)^2(p) + 3(1-p)^3(p) + \dots$$

$$= (1-p)/p$$

There are different ways to formulate this problem using dynamic programming. One of these is to define the state of the system as the number of the parking space you are opposite if you haven't yet parked (which could be $-10,-9,-8,\dots,-1,0$), or 1 if you have parked. If you reach state 0 in an unparked condition, you will take the next parking place that is available, and you know the expected cost of this occurrence from the equation. State 1 is a trapping state, denoting that the search is over. With these definitions, the probability transition matrix for each action in the problem appears as follows:

Start State	Action	Ending State								Expected Return
		-10	-9	-8	-2	-1	0	1	
-10	1. continue	1							0
	2. try to park	1-p						p	-10p
-9	1. continue		1						0
	2. try to park		1-p					p	-9p
:	:			:					:
-2	1. continue				1				0
	2. try to park				1-p			p	-2p
-1	1. continue					1			0
	2. try to park					1-p	p		-p
0	1. continue						1		0
	2. try to park						1		0
1	Done						1		0

In this formulation, if you try to park given an initial state of, say, -10, there is a probability p that the space is free, so the immediate "reward" is a walk of 10. The expected immediate reward is thus $-10p$. If the space is not free, you automatically move to state -9 (with probability $[1-p]$).

Suppose the probability that a space is empty, p, is 0.1. To enter this problem in PROPS[+], select menu item **16. Stochastic DP** from the ACCESS menu, and set up the data area as in the following worksheet. Here, an empty cell in the worksheet, G29, has been set up to store the value for p of 0.1 (with a descriptive tag in F29). The entries in the INPUT DATA table are functions of this cell; e.g., cell D34 contains the formula **+1–$G$29**, cell N34 contains **+$G$29**, and cell O34 contains **+10*$G$29**. The entry in cell L65 corresponding to the terminal value is **+(1–$G$29)/$G$29**. Use the Copy command (**/C**) to copy these formulas to fill in the data, as shown in the following two screen images:

```
      A    B    C    D    E    F    G    H    I    J    K    L    M    N    O    P    Q
21              Analyst Your_name
22              Problem parking
23
24              States numbe-10  to    1
25              Actions numb  0  to    1
26
27              Maximizing or Min   min
28
```

	A	B	C	D	E	F	G	H	I	J	K	L	M	N	O	P	Q
29		INPUT DATA			p= 0.1												
30	Stat	Acti			Ending	state										Cost	Check
31	i	k	-10	-9	-8	-7	-6	-5	-4	-3	-2	-1	0	1	c		

#	i	k	-10	-9	-8	-7	-6	-5	-4	-3	-2	-1	0	1	c	Check
33	-10	0	0	1	0	0	0	0	0	0	0	0	0	0	0	ok
34		1	0	0.9	0	0	0	0	0	0	0	0	0	0.1	1	ok
35	-9	0	0	0	1	0	0	0	0	0	0	0	0	0	0	ok
36		1	0	0	0.9	0	0	0	0	0	0	0	0	0.1	0.9	ok
37	-8	0	0	0	0	1	0	0	0	0	0	0	0	0	0	ok
38		1	0	0	0	0.9	0	0	0	0	0	0	0	0.1	0.8	ok
39	-7	0	0	0	0	0	1	0	0	0	0	0	0	0	0	ok
40		1	0	0	0	0	0.9	0	0	0	0	0	0	0.1	0.7	ok
41	-6	0	0	0	0	0	0	1	0	0	0	0	0	0	0	ok
42		1	0	0	0	0	0	0.9	0	0	0	0	0	0.1	0.6	ok
43	-5	0	0	0	0	0	0	0	1	0	0	0	0	0	0	ok
44		1	0	0	0	0	0	0	0.9	0	0	0	0	0.1	0.5	ok
45	-4	0	0	0	0	0	0	0	0	1	0	0	0	0	0	ok
46		1	0	0	0	0	0	0	0	0.9	0	0	0	0.1	0.4	ok
47	-3	0	0	0	0	0	0	0	0	0	1	0	0	0	0	ok
48		1	0	0	0	0	0	0	0	0	0.9	0	0	0.1	0.3	ok
49	-2	0	0	0	0	0	0	0	0	0	0	1	0	0	0	ok
50		1	0	0	0	0	0	0	0	0	0	0.9	0	0.1	0.2	ok
51	-1	0	0	0	0	0	0	0	0	0	0	0	1	0	0	ok
52		1	0	0	0	0	0	0	0	0	0	0	0.9	0.1	0.1	ok
53	0	0	0	0	0	0	0	0	0	0	0	0	1	0	0	ok
54		1	0	0	0	0	0	0	0	0	0	0	1	0	0	ok
55	1	0	0	0	0	0	0	0	0	0	0	0	0	1	0	ok
56		1	0	0	0	0	0	0	0	0	0	0	0	1	0	ok

```
59      % Interest Rate  0 ===>Alph  1

61      How many Stages 10

63      State
64      -10  -9  -8  -7  -6  -5  -4  -3  -2  -1   0   1
65 f(0)   0   0   0   0   0   0   0   0   0   0   9   0
```

Call up the menu with [Alt M] and press [Enter] to select **Execute**, and PROPS⁺ solves the problem. Here we present the first and last solution steps.

	A	B	C	D	E	F	G	H	I	J	K	L	M	N
67	STAGE-BY-STAGE	ANALYSIS:												
69		Stage 1												
71	State	-10	-9	-8	-7	-6	-5	-4	-3	-2	-1	0	1	
72	f(n)	0	0	0	0	0	0	0	0	0	8.2	9	0	
73	decis	0	0	0	0	0	0	0	0	0	1	0	0	
76		Stage 2												
78	State	-10	-9	-8	-7	-6	-5	-4	-3	-2	-1	0	1	
79	f(n)	0	0	0	0	0	0	0	0	7.58	8.2	9	0	
80	decis	0	0	0	0	0	0	0	0	1	1	0	0	

	A	B	C	D	E	F	G	H	I	J	K	L	M	N
124														
125		Stage 9												
126														
127	State	-10	-9	-8	-7	-6	-5	-4	-3	-2	-1	0	1	
128	f(n)	0	6.56	6.56	6.56	6.56	6.62	6.80	7.12	7.58	8.2	9	0	
129	decis	0	0	0	0	1	1	1	1	1	1	0	0	
130														
131														
132		Stage 10												
133														
134	State	-10	-9	-8	-7	-6	-5	-4	-3	-2	-1	0	1	
135	f(n)	6.56	6.56	6.56	6.56	6.56	6.62	6.80	7.12	7.58	8.2	9	0	
136	decis	0	0	0	0	1	1	1	1	1	1	0	0	
137														

The optimal solution (Stage 10) is to pass up any available spaces until the parking spot six spaces from the theater. If any subsequent space is free, take it immediately. The expected distance to walk (in number of parking space lengths) is shown in the solution output as f(n) and is 6.5659 if you are six spaces from the theater. As you continue and are still not parked, this figure increases.

You now could return to the data area and alter the value for p in G29 to, say, 0.2. Note that the values in the INPUT DATA table immediately change to reflect this new value, but that you must call up the menu again and select **Execute** to find the new solution with this revised p value. As p is varied, storing the solution f(n) and decision values in an unused area of the worksheet (e.g., in the range [I1..P40]) will permit subsequent analysis of the sensitivity of the solution to varying the parameter p.

Markov Programming

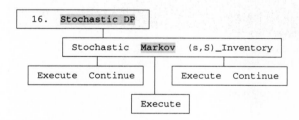

The Model:

Policy Evaluation: letting $P = \left[p_{ij}^k \right]$ and $r = \left[r_i^k \right]$, solve

$$au + b = r + Pb \qquad\qquad \text{if } \alpha = 1$$
$$d = r + \alpha Pd \qquad\qquad \text{if } \alpha < 1$$

Policy Improvement: for each state i, find k to

$$\max \left[r_i^k + \sum_{j=1}^{S} p_{ij}^k b_j \right] \qquad\qquad \text{if } \alpha = 1$$

$$\max \left[r_i^k + \alpha \sum_{j=1}^{S} p_{ij}^k d_j \right] \qquad\qquad \text{if } \alpha < 1$$

where

$i, j \in S$ is the set of possible states

$k \in D$ is the set of possible actions

p_{ij}^k = the probability that the system goes from state i to state j if action k is taken

r_i^k = the expected immediate return if in state i and action k is taken

a = steady-state expected return per transition

u = unit vector, all values = 1

b = vector of relative state values ($b_1 = 0$)

d = vector of present values for each state

α = discount factor

Computation: Step 0: choose an initial policy
   Step 1: evaluate the policy
   Step 2: policy improvement: if no improvement, stop;
            otherwise find a new policy and return to Step 1

Limitations: Each transition probability matrix P must represent a recurrent Markov chain.

Markov programming is a procedure for finding the steady state or infinite-horizon policy in a stochastic dynamic programming problem. The method consists of the selection of an initial trial policy, an evaluation step to determine the long-run value of that policy, and a policy improvement step that tries to find a better policy. The policy evaluation and improvement steps are repeated until the optimal steady state policy is found. Each iteration of this process guarantees a strict improvement in the policy.

Example: The Gardener Problem

A gardener's annual crop can be in one of three states: good, fair, or poor. In each state she can choose one of two actions: do nothing or fertilize. Fertilizing costs two units. Suppose her profits from the garden each season are as follows. If she chooses to do nothing, profits are r(1) = (10, 4, 0). If she chooses to fertilize, however, profits are r(2) = (8, 2, −2). On the other hand, if she chooses to do nothing, the probabilities of transition from each current state to each possible state next year are

$$p_{ij}^1 = \begin{bmatrix} .2 & .5 & .3 \\ 0 & .5 & .5 \\ 0 & 0 & 1 \end{bmatrix}$$

If she chooses to fertilize, the transition matrix is

$$p_{ij}^2 = \begin{bmatrix} .3 & .6 & .1 \\ .2 & .6 & .2 \\ .1 & .5 & .4 \end{bmatrix}$$

The gardener has an opportunity cost of capital of 10% per annum. What is her optimal fertilization policy to maximize the expected present value of the future profit stream?

To solve the problem using PROPS⁺, select **16. Stochastic DP** from the ACCESS menu and **Markov** from the menu of stochastic dynamic programming options. You will see this screen:

```
         A         B         C         D        E          F          G          H
1    ==============================
2              PROPS+                      MARKOV PROGRAMMING SPREADSHEET
3                                          - dynamic programming
4              Copyright (C)               - policy iteration method
5              PROPS SYSTEMS               - optimal steady-state policy
6                                          - discrete state, probabilistic
7              09/26/92 12:39 PM           - time invariant
8    ==============================
9
10   Instructions:
11           States and actions are numbered consecutively from lowest to
12           highest.  Assumes the same number of actions for each state.
13           There must be at least two states and two actions.
14
15           PROMPT mode when CMD is on.  Type response, press [Enter].
16
17           [Alt M] -- Presents user with MENU of possible actions.
18
19                                          Press [Enter] to begin...
20
```

Press [Enter] and respond to the following series of questions, pressing [Enter] after each response, to describe the numbers of states and actions in this question.

	A	B	C	D	E	F	G	H
21		Analyst Name?		Your_name				
22		Problem Name?		gardener				
23								
24		States numbered from			1	to	3	
25		Actions numbered from			1	to	2	
26								
27		Maximize or minimize?			max			

Using these values, PROPS+ creates an input matrix for the transition matrix and returns for each action in each state, as follows:

	A	B	C	D	E	F	G	H
29		INPUT DATA						
30	State	Action		Ending state		Return	Check	
31	i	k	1	2	3	r	sum	
32	---	---	---	---	---	---	---	---
33	1	1	0	0	0	0	ERR	
34		2	0	0	0	0	ERR	
35	2	1	0	0	0	0	ERR	
36		2	0	0	0	0	ERR	
37	3	1	0	0	0	0	ERR	
38		2	0	0	0	0	ERR	
39		*** Warning: Probabilities do not sum to one. ***						
40								
41		% Interest/Period		0	==>	Alpha =		1
42								
43		INITIAL POLICY:						
44	State	1	2	3				
45	Action	1	1	1				
46								
47		Fill the INPUT DATA table with state transition probabilities						
48		and the expected returns or costs. If an action is not feasible						
49		use a large penalty cost (or large negative return) to						
50		eliminate it. When finished hit [Alt M] for the command menu.						

Inserting the values from the problem into this matrix yields this worksheet:

	A	B	C	D	E	F	G	H
29		INPUT DATA						
30	State	Action		Ending state		Return	Check	
31	i	k	1	2	3	r	sum	
32	---	---	---	---	---	---	---	---
33	1	1	0.2	0.5	0.3	10	ok	
34		2	0.3	0.6	0.1	8	ok	
35	2	1	0	0.5	0.5	4	ok	
36		2	0.2	0.6	0.2	2	ok	
37	3	1	0	0	1	0	ok	
38		2	0.1	0.5	0.4	-2	ok	
39								
40								
41		% Interest/Period		10	==>	Alpha =	0.909090	
42								
43		INITIAL POLICY:						
44	State	1	2	3				
45	Action	1	1	1				

The initial policy defaults to the first (lowest numbered) action in each state, as shown in rows 43 to 45. Note that the "Check sum" column entry changes from "ERR" to "ok" when the probabilities in the row sum to 1, and the warning message disappears. Using [Alt M] to call up the menu (which in this case only has one choice, **Execute**), the model is solved and you see the following entries in the worksheet:

	A	B	C	D	E	F
43		INITIAL POLICY:				
44	State	1	2	3		
45	Action	1	1	1		
46	Rel Val	16.29629	7.333333	0		
47						
48		Iteration 1				
49	State	1	2	3		
50	Policy	2	2	2		
51	Rel Val	32.13483	24.96629	19.28089		
52						
53		Iteration 2				
54	State	1	2	3		
55	Policy	1	2	2		
56	Rel Val	33	25.52	19.8		
57						
58		Iteration 3				
59	State	1	2	3		
60	Policy	1	2	2		

Since the policy repeats from Iteration 2 to Iteration 3, you have found the optimal policy: choose action 1 (do nothing) in state 1 (good crop), and choose action 2 (fertilize) in states 2 or 3 (fair or poor crop). Starting in each state, the expected present value of the future income stream is $33.00, $25.52, and $19.80 respectively, if an optimal policy is followed thenceforth.

Example: A Machine Replacement Problem

Suppose that a certain machine is required on an ongoing basis, and must be replaced from time to time. Older machines cost more to maintain and are more likely to fail, but this must be balanced against the cash flows involved in the purchase of a new machine.

A new machine costs $1,100. The following table describes, for each machine age, the annual maintenance cost, trade-in value toward the purchase of a new machine, and the probability that a machine starting the period at each age will fail during the next period, necessitating replacement. Assume that failure takes place at the beginning of the period, so a failure with replacement finishes the period with a one-year-old machine.

Machine Age	Annual Maintenance Cost	Trade-in Value	Probability of Failure
0	$0	–	0
1	$100	$600	.1
2	$110	$500	.2
3	$140	$350	.3
4	$170	$200	.4
5	$210	$100	.5
6	$260	$ 50	1.0

What replacement policy minimizes the expected average cost of operating the machine, assuming no discounting of cash flows? Note, for example, that non-replacement of a one-year-old machine has expected maintenance costs of 0.9 ($100) and an expected replacement cost due to failure of 0.1 ($1,100). (This is the replacement cost with no trade-in, since the machine has failed.) Thus the expected cost of not replacing a one-year-old machine is $200. Replacing a one-year-old machine costs ($1,100 – $600), or $500, and you finish the year with another one-year-old machine.

Assuming you would never replace a brand new machine, the possible states are 1 to 6, corresponding to the age of the machine at the start of the year. Possible actions are 0: do not replace the machine, or 1: replace it. Load the **Markov** spreadsheet, and respond to the PROPS⁺ prompts to generate the INPUT DATA table. Fill in the transition probabilities. To calculate the costs, the cost data can be entered in a blank area of the worksheet to the right of the input data matrix, as shown. Then a formula can be used to compute the costs of each action. In cell I33, for example, put **0.9*K33+0.1*$G$29**, and in cell I34 put **$G$29–L33**. This facilitates later sensitivity analysis.

	A	B	C	D	E	F	G	H	I	J	K	L
21		Analyst Name		Your_name								
22		Problem Name		machine replacement								
23												
24		States numbered from			1	to	6					
25		Actions numbered from			0	to	1					
26												
27		Maximize or minimize			min							
28												
29		INPUT DATA				new cost	1100					
30	State	Action		Ending state					Cost	Check	op	trade
31	i	k	1	2	3	4	5	6	c	sum	cost	value
32	----	----	----	----	----	----	----	----	----	----	----	----
33	1	0	0.1	0.9	0	0	0	0	200	ok	100	600
34		1	1	0	0	0	0	0	500	ok		
35	2	0	0.2	0	0.8	0	0	0	308	ok	110	500
36		1	1	0	0	0	0	0	600	ok		
37	3	0	0.3	0	0	0.7	0	0	428	ok	140	350
38		1	1	0	0	0	0	0	750	ok		
39	4	0	0.4	0	0	0	0.6	0	542	ok	170	200
40		1	1	0	0	0	0	0	900	ok		

	A	B	C	D	E	F	G	H	I	J	K	L
41	5	0	0.5	0	0	0	0	0.5	655	ok	210	100
42		1	1	0	0	0	0	0	1000	ok		
43	6	0	1	0	0	0	0	0	1100	ok	260	50
44		1	1	0	0	0	0	0	1050	ok		
45												
46												
47		% Interest/P	0	==>	Alpha	1					
48												
49		INITIAL POLICY:										
50	State	1	2	3	4	5	6					
51	Action	0	0	0	0	0	0					

Pressing [Alt M] and [Enter] executes the model, yielding the following solution:

	A	B	C	D	E	F	G	H
49		INITIAL POLICY:						
50	State	1	2	3	4	5	6	
51	Action	0	0	0	0	0	0	
52	Rel Val	0	219.7003	386.7883	509.3123	608.4045	702.2696	
53	=> Expected cost per transition =			397.7303				
54								
55		Iteration 1						
56	State	1	2	3	4	5	6	
57	Policy	0	1	1	1	1	1	
58	Rel Val	0	210.5263	360.5263	510.5263	610.5263	660.5263	
59	=> Expected cost per transition =			389.4736				
60								
61		Iteration 2						
62	State	1	2	3	4	5	6	
63	Policy	0	0	1	1	0	1	
64	Rel Val	0	209.1603	361.7557	511.7557	597.6335	661.7557	
65	=> Expected cost per transition =			388.2442				
66								
67		Iteration 3						
68	State	1	2	3	4	5	6	
69	Policy	0	0	1	1	0	1	

Interestingly, as seen in Iteration 3, the optimal policy is to hold on to a machine one or two years old, sell a three- or four-year-old one, retain a five-year-old one, and sell a six-year-old machine. The annual expected cash outflow is $388.24 with this policy. A two-year-old machine on average costs $209.16 more than a one-year-old machine, while a three-year-old one costs an average of $361.76 more than a one-year-old one.

Example: Blackjack

Blackjack is a two-person card game in which, in the common version, a dealer takes one card from a 52-card deck and places it face down in front of herself. The player is then dealt one card face down and one face up, but can ask for as many cards as he wants. His objective is to get as close to a card value sum of 21 as possible, without going over 21. (Aces count as either 1 or 11, as the player chooses. Face cards count 10.) If the player goes over 21 ("breaks"), the dealer wins automatically. When the player stops taking cards, the dealer does the same thing but follows the standard casino rule that if the dealer's sum is less than or equal to 16, she takes a card. A sum of 17 to 21 means the dealer stops taking cards. The player wins if the dealer's sum exceeds 21. Assume that ties mean no one wins.

Assume that the deck is shuffled before each card or that a large number of decks are used (as happens in casinos). What is the optimal policy for the player?

You can compute the possible occurrences when the dealer plays and their likelihoods using a simulation technique, with results as shown in the following table. A simulation model for this problem was demonstrated in Chapter 11 on page 207. (A Markov model could be used to calculate the exact probabilities.) A particular run of the simulation model gave the following estimates for the dealer's outcome.

Dealer outcome	Probability
Break	0.2841
17	0.1435
18	0.1402
19	0.1338
20	0.1783
21	0.1199
	1.0000

Ignoring game variations such as doubling down or splitting, the player will always take a card with a total of 11 or less (since breaking is impossible from this level). Thus the interesting states of the player's hand are sums of 12 through 21, plus additional states: 22 corresponding to a break by the player, and 23 corresponding to "player stands with what he has, and it is now the dealer's turn".

Let k=0 represent the action of "standing" by the player: taking no more cards and letting the dealer play. Then for all states i, $p^0_{i,23} = 1$. The other action, k=1, is "take a card". Ignoring slight variations from having already seen those cards in his hand, the player's probability of getting one of $\{1,2,3,...,$or $9\}$ is 1/13, and of getting 10 is 4/13 (the ten card plus the three face cards in each suit). Hence, if the current state i = 12, and action k=1 is selected, then $p^1_{12,j} = 1/13$, for j=13,14,...,21; and $p^1_{12,22} = 4/13$. The probability of other possible transitions are calculated similarly.

The player realizes an expected return only when he stands. Assuming a bet size of 1, for each state, the expected return is

r^0_i = (1)(probability of win) - (1)(probability of loss)

Thus, for example,

r^0_{12} = (.2841) - (1 - .2841) = -.4318
r^0_{18} = (.2841 + .1435) - (.1338 + .1783 + .1199) = -.0044 since no one wins on ties

The PROPS⁺ input for this problem is as follows. The returns for each state and action pair are computed as just illustrated, by means of formulas using the dealer probability distribution, which have been inserted in a convenient blank area to the right of the opening PROPS⁺ prompts (in columns J and K, rows 10 to 17). The returns for the action corresponding to "standing," taking no more cards, are computed by calculating the difference between the probability that the player wins the hand and the probability that the dealer wins and multiplying the result by the bid size, which is 1 in this example. If the player breaks, of course, his return is −1.

	A	B	C	D	E	F	G	H	I	J	K	L	M	N	O
20									dealer						
21		Analyst		petersen					hand prob.						
22		Problem		blackjack					brk	0.28					
23									17	0.14					
24		States number		12	to		23		18	0.14					
25		Actions numbe		0	to		1		19	0.13					
26									20	0.17					
27		Maximize or max							21	0.11					
28															
29		INPUT DATA													
30	StatAct		Ending state												Return
31	i	k	12	13	14	15	16	17	18	19	20	21	22	23	r
32	---	---	---	---	---	---	---	---	---	---	---	---	---	---	---
33	12	0	0	0	0	0	0	0	0	0	0	0	0	1	−0.431
34		1	0	0.07	0.07	0.07	0.07	0.07	0.07	0.07	0.07	0.07	0.30	0	0
35	13	0	0	0	0	0	0	0	0	0	0	0	0	1	−0.431
36		1	0	0	0.07	0.07	0.07	0.07	0.07	0.07	0.07	0.07	0.38	0	0
37	14	0	0	0	0	0	0	0	0	0	0	0	0	1	−0.431
38		1	0	0	0	0.07	0.07	0.07	0.07	0.07	0.07	0.07	0.46	0	0
39	15	0	0	0	0	0	0	0	0	0	0	0	0	1	−0.431
40		1	0	0	0	0	0.07	0.07	0.07	0.07	0.07	0.07	0.53	0	0
41	16	0	0	0	0	0	0	0	0	0	0	0	0	1	−0.431
42		1	0	0	0	0	0	0.07	0.07	0.07	0.07	0.07	0.61	0	0
43	17	0	0	0	0	0	0	0	0	0	0	0	0	1	−0.288
44		1	0	0	0	0	0	0	0.07	0.07	0.07	0.07	0.69	0	0
45	18	0	0	0	0	0	0	0	0	0	0	0	0	1	−0.004
46		1	0	0	0	0	0	0	0	0.07	0.07	0.07	0.76	0	0
47	19	0	0	0	0	0	0	0	0	0	0	0	0	1	0.2696
48		1	0	0	0	0	0	0	0	0	0.07	0.07	0.84	0	0
49	20	0	0	0	0	0	0	0	0	0	0	0	0	1	0.5817
50		1	0	0	0	0	0	0	0	0	0	0.07	0.92	0	0
51	21	0	0	0	0	0	0	0	0	0	0	0	0	1	0.8799
52		1	0	0	0	0	0	0	0	0	0	0	1	0	0
53	22	0	0	0	0	0	0	0	0	0	0	0	0	1	−1
54		1	0	0	0	0	0	0	0	0	0	0	0	1	−1
55	23	0	0	0	0	0	0	0	0	0	0	0	0	1	0
56		1	0	0	0	0	0	0	0	0	0	0	0	1	0
57															
58															
59		% Intere		0	==>	Alpha	1								
60															
61		INITIAL POLICY:													
62	State12		13	14	15	16	17	18	19	20	21	22	23		
63	Acti 0		0	0	0	0	0	0	0	0	0	0			
64															

Press [Alt M] to call up the menu, and press [Enter] to select **Execute**; PROPS⁺ computes the following solution:

	A	B	C	D	E	F	G	H	I	J	K	L	M	N
58														
59		% Interest		0	==>	Alpha		1						
60														
61		INITIAL POLICY:												
62	State	12	13	14	15	16	17	18	19	20	21	22	23	
63	Actio	0	0	0	0	0	0	0	0	0	0	0	0	
64	Rel V	0	0	0	0	0	0.14	0.42	0.70	1.01	1.31	-0.5	0.43	
65	=> Expected return p				0									
66														
67		Iteration 1												
68	State	12	13	14	15	16	17	18	19	20	21	22	23	
69	Polic	1	1	1	0	0	0	0	0	0	0	0	0	
70	Rel V	0	-0.0	-0.0	-0.1	-0.1	0.03	0.31	0.59	0.90	1.20	-0.6	0.32	
71	=> Expected return p				0									
72														
73		Iteration 2												
74	State	12	13	14	15	16	17	18	19	20	21	22	23	
75	Polic	1	1	1	0	0	0	0	0	0	0	0	0	

The optimal strategy is for the player to take a card when he holds 12, 13, or 14, and to stand on all other hands. PROPS⁺ reports an expected return of 0, which follows since state 23 is a trapping state with an assigned return of zero. It is the *relative* values of the states that are of interest here. The PROPS⁺ solution procedure arbitrarily sets the relative value, b_i, of the first state in the list (i=12) at zero and calculates the remainder relative to this level. However, you know that the value of being in state 22 (player breaks) is –1, so you can construct a new relative value vector by subtracting $(1 - b_{22}) = 0.324$ from each of the b_i values to obtain a new relative value. The new values are shown below (to only 1 or 2 decimal places, so the entire table can be seen).

	A	B	C	D	E	F	G	H	I	J	K	L	M	N
77														
78	State	12	13	14	15	16	17	18	19	20	21	22	23	
79	new	-0.3	-0.3	-0.4	-0.4	-0.4	-0.2	-0.0	0.26	0.58	0.87	-1	0	

As this table shows, if the player has a hand with a sum of 12, he expects to lose $.324 ("new value" for State 12 in cell B79, to three decimal places). If he did not take a card, but "stood" with 12, the INPUT DATA table shows that his expected loss is $.431. If the player has 20, he will stand and expect to win $0.5817 (cell J79).

We leave it for the reader to consider modifying the model to incorporate other provisions of the casino version of this game. That is, you might want to include options like splitting (permitting the player to start two new hands with each member of a pair dealt as the first two cards) or doubling down (doubling the bet, but only receiving one more card). In this example, the probabilities of results for a dealer following standard casino rules were found using simulation. If the dealer's first card is shown, then simulation can again be used to generate the conditional distribution of the dealer's ending hand given the first card. You could then solve the dynamic problem for each, giving an optimal strategy conditional on the dealer's first card.

Optimal Probabilistic Inventory

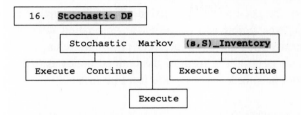

The Model:

$$f_n(x_n) = \min_y E_w[c(z) + L(y) + \alpha f_{n-1}(x_{n-1})], \qquad n = 1, 2, \ldots$$

where

n = stage number (periods to end of horizon)

x_n = stock on hand at start of stage

$f_n(x_n)$ = expected optimal value function

y = order-up-to quantity

$z = y - x_n$, the quantity ordered

$$x_{n-1} = \begin{cases} y - w, & \text{with backlogging} \\ \max(0, y - w) & \text{with no backlogging} \end{cases}$$

$c(z)$ = ordering cost function:

$$= \begin{cases} K_1 + cz, & z > 0 \quad \text{(buy)} \\ 0, & z = 0 \quad \text{(do nothing)} \\ K_2 + cz, & z < 0 \quad \text{(sell)} \end{cases}$$

$L(y)$ = expected holding plus shortage cost:

$$= \int_0^y h(y - w)\theta(w)dw + \int_y^\infty [p(w - y) + u]\theta(w)dw$$

$\theta(w)$ = the demand probability distribution

α = the discount factor

$h(.), p(.)$ are the holding and shortage cost functions

u is the fixed cost on shortage

Computation: The optimal policy is assumed to be (s, S). At each stage, PROPS+ finds the optimal action if a transaction is made, and then for each state compares the cost of making the optimal transaction to the cost of no transaction, and selects the minimum.

Limitations: If the fixed stockout penalty u > 0, the optimal policy may not be (s, S).

Stochastic dynamic programming is used to calculate the optimal inventory policy. The model allows a probabilistic demand for the good within each period, and permits buying and selling of units of the good during the period. (The selling option is useful for solving cash management type problems.) Stockout, or unsatisfied demand during a period, involves a fixed penalty should a stockout occur plus a unit charge for each unit of inventory short during the period. The form of the optimal policy is (s,S); that is, if the inventory level drops below s, order to bring the level up to S.

The simplest assumption with respect to demand is that it is stationary over time, so that the demand probability distribution remains invariant from period to period. PROPS⁺ assumes a stationary demand; however, the following nonstationary demand example shows how to modify the approach for such problems.

In the problem setup, PROPS⁺ requests the possible values that the inventory level can assume during the planning horizon (the state space, in dynamic programming terms). For problems with a large number of possible values of inventory level, PROPS⁺ provides for aggregation through specification of an increment size. Thus, for example, if demand could range from, say, 0 to 100 each period, we might wish to allow possible inventory values from perhaps –50 to +200. Even though PROPS⁺ will handle this size of problem directly, it would entail a lot of typing and solution time. It would be better in this case to consider demand in units of, for example, 10, meaning that there would be 11 demand values and 35 state values. Even though this is an approximation of the "real" problem, it is probably accurate enough for most practical problems. (The sensitivity can easily be tested using the inventory model described on page 143).

Example: The Widget Problem Revisited

Let us return to the widget problem used in the inventory examples in Chapter 8, page 136. (Seeing the same problem in the different models demonstrates the advantages and limitations of each model.) Assume that the inventory is reviewed at the end of every second week. Demand during the two-week period is given by the following distribution:

Demand	5	10	15	20	25	30	35
Probability	.05	.1	.2	.3	.2	.1	.05

(This is the same distribution used in the probabilistic EOQ model with an arbitrary demand distribution.) The fixed cost of placing an order is $40, the annual holding cost is $14 (including the cost of capital at 12%), and the cost of a shortage is $10 per unit short, when a shortage occurs.

Begin with the PROPS[+] ACCESS worksheet menu; select **16. Stochastic DP** and **(s,S)_Inventory** from the successive menus. The following screen will appear:

```
        A       B       C       D       E       F       G       H
1    ==============================
2              PROPS+              OPTIMAL (s,S) INVENTORY POLICY
3                                       SPREADSHEET
4           Copyright (C)          - periodic review
5           PROPS SYSTEMS          - probabilistic demand
6                                  - buy or sell option
7         03/10/92 03:38 PM        - stochastic dynamic programming
8    ==============================     solution
9
10   Instructions:
11
12           There must be at least 2 states and 2 points in the demand
13           distribution. In addition, the zero state must be included in
14           the state space.
15
16           PROMPT mode when CMD is on. Type response, press [ENTER].
17
18           [Alt M] -- Presents user with MENU of possible actions.
19
20                                       Press [ENTER] to begin...
```

After providing an analyst and problem name when requested, following each with [Enter], you are prompted for indices for states and demands. These indices can be any numbers, but the range must include all of the integer values needed to represent the problem. Finally, you are asked for the increment. In this problem, a reasonable state space for the problem is the range from about –15 to +100, or an index range of –3 to +20, with an increment of 5. The states of the demand distribution are indexed from 1 to 7 with an increment of 5. Following entry of the data, the worksheet layout is completed by PROPS[+] and now appears as follows:

```
        A       B       C       D       E       F       G       H       I
21           Analyst Name?          Your_name
22           Problem Name?          probabilistic inventory
23
24           States indexed from        -3      to      20
25           Demands indexed from        1      to       7
26
27           Increment for Demands/States       5
28
29           DEMAND P.D.F.:  * WARNING: Probabilities do not sum to one *
30   Demand      5      10      15      20      25      30      35
31   Prob(D)     0       0       0       0       0       0       0
32
33   % Annual Interest rate       0   ==>   Alpha =      1
34
35   Backlogs allowed      y      Maximum Order size      99999
36   Can buy AND sell      n
37                                Holding Cost/item/year       0
38   Fixed Cost-Buy      0        Shortage Cost per unit       0
39   Fixed Cost-Sell     0        Fixed Cost per shortage      0
40   Order Cost/unit     0        # of review_periods/yr       1
41
42                                How many STAGES?       1
```

```
     A         B        C        D        E        F        G        H        I
43           TERMINAL VALUES:
44   State     -15      -10      -5       0        5        10       15       20
45   f(0)       0        0        0       0        0        0        0        0
46
47           Enter data values (where applicable) and then use [Alt M]
48           to call up the commands menu.
```

At this point, enter the problem data by moving the cursor from field to field and typing in the required numbers. For now, leave the number of stages at the default value of 1. The worksheet then appears as follows:

```
     A         B        C        D        E        F        G        H        I
29           DEMAND P.D.F.:
30   Demand     5        10       15       20       25       30       35
31   Prob(D)   0.05     0.1      0.2      0.3      0.2      0.1      0.05
32
33   % Annual Interest rate         0    ==>    Alpha =        1
34
35   Backlogs allowed        y          Maximum Order size      99999
36   Can buy AND sell        n
37                                      Holding Cost/item/year     14
38   Fixed Cost-Buy         40          Shortage Cost per unit     10
39   Fixed Cost-Sell         0          Fixed Cost per shortage     0
40   Order Cost/unit         0          # of review_periods/yr     26
41
42                                      How many STAGES?            1
43           TERMINAL VALUES:
44   State     -15      -10      -5       0        5        10       15       20
45   f(0)       0        0        0       0        0        0        0        0
```

Now press [Alt M], and the top of the screen displays:

```
H48:                                                                              MENU
Execute   Continue
Execute the DP model (after data has been entered)
     A         B        C        D        E        F        G        H        I
```

Leave the cursor at **Execute** and press [Enter]. PROPS$^+$ produces the following screen:

```
     A    B    C    D    E    F    G    H    I    J    K    L    M    N
50
51        Stage 1
52   (s,S)  20   30
53   State -15  -10  -5    0    5   10   15   20   25   30   35   40   45
54   F(I)  48.0 48.0 48.0 48.0 48.0 48.0 48.0 28.9 13.2 8.01 8.07 10.7 13.4
55   D_hat  45   40   35   30   25   20   15    0    0    0    0    0    0
```

You have solved the first stage of the dynamic programming model. The optimal one-period inventory policy calls for reordering when inventory drops below 20 (s), and ordering enough to raise the inventory to 30 (S). The F(I) values on the output give the present value of the future expected costs from entering each stage in the indicated state, and the D_hat values give the optimal decision implementing the policy for each possible entering state. Note that PROPS$^+$ requires considerable computation time to solve for the optimal policy, so that beginning with a single-stage analysis is useful for ensuring that the data is correct and you are obtaining reasonable results. (Details of the computations performed by PROPS⁺ are retained in the worksheet to the right of the Stage 1 table. These may be useful in validating your model.)

You can now continue the computation by changing the number of stages to 10. Having done so, press [Alt M] to call up the command menu and select the option **Continue**. PROPS⁺ will then continue the computation up to stage 10, placing the results for each stage sequentially in the worksheet. The last two stages follow.

	A	B	C	D	E	F	G	H	I	J	K	L	M	N
100		Stage 9												
101	(s,S)	20	70											
102	State	-15	-10	-5	0	5	10	15	20	25	30	35	40	45
103	F(I)	290.	290.	290.	290.	290.	290.	290.	288.	272.	266.	264.	262.	258.
104	D_hat	85	80	75	70	65	60	55	0	0	0	0	0	0
105														
106		Stage 10												
107	(s,S)	20	70											
108	State	-15	-10	-5	0	5	10	15	20	25	30	35	40	45
109	F(I)	322.	322.	322.	322.	322.	322.	322.	319.	303.	297.	294.	293.	289.
110	D_hat	85	80	75	70	65	60	55	0	0	0	0	0	0

At stage 10, which is the beginning of the 10-period planning horizon, the optimal policy is "Order if inventory is less than or equal to 15 (s=20), ordering enough to bring inventory up to 70; otherwise, do nothing".

The optimal policy calls for an order of at least 55 widgets each time an order is placed, and the cost of the 10-period (20-week) policy starting with no inventory is $322.52 (in F(0) for stage 10). Compare these results with the probabilistic EOQ model from Chapter 8, page 145, and note that the reorder point is lower in this case. The EOQ model selects the reorder point so that the marginal holding cost is equal to the marginal penalty cost, whereas this model also includes the value of ending each stage at a different inventory level. The values of the ending inventory are given by the function F(I), plotted below. (The function is k-convex, as inventory theory suggests.)

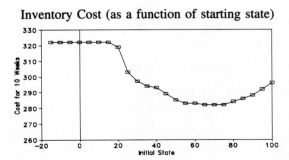

Inventory Cost (as a function of starting state)

If you wish to examine the optimal policy over a longer planning horizon, you can move the cursor to the "How many STAGES?" field and increase the current value of 10 to some larger number. Then access the menu with [Alt M], select the **Continue** option, and PROPS⁺ will continue from where the previous analysis ended.

This model can be formulated in a number of different ways. Above, we have only included the variable cost components of the fixed ordering cost, the holding, and the penalty costs. Since demand is satisfied (possibly after being backlogged), the cost of the widgets is constant over all policies. The cost of capital tied up in inventory was included in the holding cost. Discounting could be included to reflect the time value of money, but would have little effect in a two-week review period.

An alternate formulation could include the item cost of $100 per widget ordered, reduce the holding cost to $2 per unit per year (just the warehousing portion of cost), and include discounting. Here, since the widget cost itself is very high compared to the other costs, care must be taken to include all possible states in the description of the state space. Otherwise, this cost will dominate the others, and the solution will tend not to order inventory beyond the minimal amount required. Since shortages as great as 35 are possible, in this case the state space must range from –35 to +100. The terminal value can be left at zero (assuming inventory held at the end of the planning horizon is scrapped), or we could let the terminal value be $f(x) = -100x$, the value (negative cost) of the widgets in inventory. (If $x < 0$, this becomes a positive cost since the backlogged widgets must still be purchased.) For a reasonably long horizon (say, 10 periods) each of these formulations will result in the same policy for the first year. Only as the end of the horizon is approached will the policy differ markedly due to the different assumptions about terminal values.

In formulating a model, remember that if the unit cost c is included and the interest rate is positive, the holding cost h should only include direct costs and not the cost of capital invested in inventory.

In the rest of this chapter, we will develop a number of examples to show the power of the PROPS⁺ inventory models.

Example: The News Vendor Problem

A news vendor wants to know the optimal number of papers to order each day. She pays 20 cents for each paper, which she sells for 30 cents. She knows that each day she will sell between six and ten papers with equal likelihood. Papers not sold in a day are worthless.

You can use the optimal probabilistic inventory model to solve her problem. First, you must convert from a profit-maximizing problem to the equivalent cost-minimization problem, the form of the standard inventory model.

Profit is the margin per paper sold ($.10) less the opportunity cost of each paper unsold at the end of the day ($.30). Maximizing the profit is the same as minimizing the value of (–profit). Then, in the form of a standard inventory problem, the cost is –$.10 (the negative of the profit margin) and the holding cost is +$.30 (the negative of the opportunity loss). The model is a one-period model with terminal value of inventory equal to zero (unsold papers are worthless).

From the ACCESS worksheet menu, select **16. Stochastic DP** and **(s,S)_Inventory** from the successive menus. After providing a problem name when prompted, define the state index from 0 to 10 (the maximum number of papers that could be sold) and the demand index from 6 to 10, with an increment of one paper. Then the worksheet constructed by PROPS+ appears as follows:

```
       A         B        C       D        E        F        G        H        I
21              Analyst Name?             Your_name
22              Problem Name?             news vendor
23
24              States indexed from        0       to       10
25              Demands indexed from       6       to       10
26
27              Increment for Demands/States        1
28
29              DEMAND P.D.F.:   * WARNING: Probabilities do not sum to one *
30   Demand        6         7       8        9       10
31   Prob(D)       0         0       0        0        0
32
33   % Annual Interest rate       0    ==>    Alpha =        1
34
35   Backlogs allowed       y           Maximum Order size        99999
36   Can buy AND sell       n
37                                      Holding Cost/item/year         0
38   Fixed Cost-Buy        0            Shortage Cost per unit         0
39   Fixed Cost-Sell       0            Fixed Cost per shortage        0
40   Order Cost/unit       0            # of review_periods/yr         1
41
42                                      How many STAGES?        1
43              TERMINAL VALUES:
44   State       0         1       2        3       4        5        6        7
45   f(0)        0         0       0        0       0        0        0        0
46
47              Enter data values (where applicable) and then use [Alt M]
48              to call up the commands menu.
```

Enter the probabilities of 0.2 for each demand from 6 to 10 and set the ordering cost c = –10 cents and the holding cost h = 30 cents. (It does not matter if backlogs are allowed since there are no penalty costs.) Leave the number of stages at 1, press [Alt M], and select **Execute** to run the model. The following worksheet is created:

	A	B	C	D	E	F	G	H	I
29		DEMAND P.D.F.:							
30	Demand	6	7	8	9	10			
31	Prob(D)	0.2	0.2	0.2	0.2	0.2			
32									
33	% Annual Interest rate			0	==>	Alpha =		1	
34									
35	Backlogs allowed		y		Maximum Order size			99999	
36	Can buy AND sell		n						
37					Holding Cost/item/year			30	
38	Fixed Cost-Buy		0		Shortage Cost per unit			0	
39	Fixed Cost-Sell		0		Fixed Cost per shortage			0	
40	Order Cost/unit		-10		# of review_periods/yr			1	
41									
42						How many STAGES?		1	
43		TERMINAL VALUES:							
44	State	0	1	2	3	4	5	6	7	8	9	10
45	f(0)	0	0	0	0	0	0	0	0	0	0	0
46									
47		Enter data values (where applicable) and then use [Alt M]							
48		to call up the commands menu.							
49									
50									
51		Stage 1							
52	(s,S)	7	7						
53	State	0	1	2	3	4	5	6	7	8	9	10
54	F(I)	-64	-54	-44	-34	-24	-14	-4	6	18	36	60
55	D_hat	7	6	5	4	3	2	1	0	0	0	0
56									

The optimal action and corresponding cost (–profit) can be determined from the Stage 1 table values for a state of 0 (the stock at the beginning of each day). The optimal order is seven papers, and from the formula you can calculate that the daily expected profit is $.64.

Nonstationary Demand Problems

Problems that have a nonstationary demand distribution can also be easily solved in PROPS[+] by solving a sequence of one-stage problems. To do so, enter the probability distribution for the demand during the last period before the end of the horizon, and solve the problem for one stage. When this is complete, replace the probability distribution with that for the second-last period, set "How many STAGES?" to 2 and **Continue**. Repeat this for the rest of the stages, in each case solving a one-stage problem. The following seasonal inventory problem illustrates this procedure.

Suppose there are two demand distributions, one that applies in the summer and the other in the winter:

	Demand	0	30	60	90
Probability Distribution	Summer	.4	.3	.2	.1
	Winter	.1	.2	.3	.4

Assume no backlogging, so stockouts mean lost sales. Suppose the fixed cost of placing an order is $50, the annual cost of holding an item in inventory is $5, and the cost of a shortage (including lost contribution to profits) is $20.

To solve this problem, access PROPS+ and select **16. Stochastic DP** and **(s,S)_Inventory** from the successive menus. Since there is no backlogging allowed, let the state space range from 0 to 180 in increments of 30. Thus the state space index runs from 0 to 6, and the demand is indexed from 0 to 3. With this data entered, the worksheet appears as follows:

	A	B	C	D	E	F	G	H	I
21		Analyst Name?			Your_name				
22		Problem Name?			seasonal demand				
23									
24		States indexed from			0	to	6		
25		Demands indexed from			0	to	3		
26									
27		Increment for Demands/States				30			
28									
29			DEMAND P.D.F.:		* WARNING: Probabilities do not sum to one *				
30	Demand		0	30	60	90			
31	Prob(D)		0	0	0	0			
32									
33	% Annual Interest rate				0	==>	Alpha =	1	
34									
35	Backlogs allowed		y		Maximum Order size			99999	
36	Can buy AND sell		n						
37					Holding Cost/item/year			0	
38	Fixed Cost-Buy		0		Shortage Cost per unit			0	
39	Fixed Cost-Sell		0		Fixed Cost per shortage			0	
40	Order Cost/unit		0		# of review_periods/yr			1	
41									
42						How many STAGES?		1	
43			TERMINAL VALUES:						
44	State		0	30	60	90	120	150	180
45	f(0)		0	0	0	0	0	0	0
46									
47			Enter data values (where applicable) and then use [Alt M]						
48			to call up the commands menu.						
49									

In a blank area to the right of the demand distribution, store both summer and winter demand distributions so they can be copied into the DEMAND PDF when needed. Copying in the summer distribution and entering the rest of the data yields the following worksheet:

	A	B	C	D	E	F	G	H	I	J
29		DEMAND P.D.F.:								
30	Demand	0	30	60	90 summer		0.4	0.3	0.2	0.1
31	Prob(D)	0.4	0.3	0.2	0.1 winter		0.1	0.2	0.3	0.4
32										
33	% Annual Interest rate			0	==>	Alpha =	1			
34										
35	Backlogs allowed		y		Maximum Order size			99999		
36	Can buy AND sell		n							
37					Holding Cost/item/year			5		
38	Fixed Cost-Buy		50		Shortage Cost per unit			20		
39	Fixed Cost-Sell		0		Fixed Cost per shortage			0		
40	Order Cost/unit		0		# of review_periods/yr			2		
41										
42					How many STAGES?			1		
43		TERMINAL VALUES:								
44	State	0	30	60	90	120	150	180		
45	f(0)	0	0	0	0	0	0	0		

Press [Alt M] and select **Execute**, producing this output:

	A	B	C	D	E	F	G	H	I
51		Stage 1 summer							
52	(s,S)	60	60						
53	State I	0	30	60	90	120	150	180	
54	F(I)	192.5	192.5	142.5	150	225	300	375	
55	D_hat	60	30	0	0	0	0	0	

This output is read in the same way as before, with the optimal values for the (s,S) policy given for each stage, and the optimal cost function F(I) and inventory ordering decision D_hat listed for each state at each stage. Copy the winter demand distribution into [B31..E31], and set the number of stages to **2**. Press [Alt M] and select **Continue** to calculate the next stage of the model. This yields the following output:

	A	B	C	D	E	F	G	H	I
58		Stage 2 winter							
59	(s,S)	60	90						
60	State I	0	30	60	90	120	150	180	
61	F(I)	360.5	360.5	315	310.5	407.75	531.75	675	
62	D_hat	90	60	0	0	0	0	0	

This procedure is repeated as long as necessary. Continuing for two seasons yields:

	A	B	C	D	E	F	G	H	I
65		Stage 3 summer							
66	(s,S)	60	90						
67	State I	0	30	60	90	120	150	180	
68	F(I)	526.85	526.85	484.8	476.85	580.3	728.625	917.125	
69	D_hat	90	60	0	0	0	0	0	
70									
71									
72		Stage 4 winter							
73	(s,S)	60	90						
74	State I	0	30	60	90	120	150	180	
75	F(I)	694.235	694.235	652.53	644.235	749.82	909.39	1124.18	
76	D_hat	90	60	0	0	0	0	0	
77									

Observe that for this cost-minimizing problem, the policy is the same for both periods. If the inventory level is 60 or less, order up to 90. The costs are quite different each season.

Example: A Plant Expansion Problem

Suppose you are considering the expansion of a heating plant for a firm. The present plant capacity will just meet the current peak demand rate of 100 million BTU's per hour. (BTU, or British Thermal Unit, is the amount of heat required to raise one pound of water one degree Fahrenheit.) The annual growth in peak demand is random, and is believed to obey the following probability distribution:

Peak Demand Growth (Million BTU/hr)	-5	0	5	10	15	20
Probability	.1	.15	.2	.25	.2	.1

Growth in peak demand is statistically independent from year to year. Expansion of heating plants involves marked economies of scale—the per-unit cost of larger plants is smaller. In particular, suppose that the unit cost (UC) per 1,000 BTU/hr of new capacity is approximated by the relationship

$$UC = 10 + 100/Q$$

where UC is measured in dollars and Q is the size of the new plant in millions of BTU/hr.

The total cost in thousands of dollars for a plant of size Q will be UC×Q = 100 + 10Q if Q > 0, and 0 if Q = 0. Note that this form of equation corresponds to the fixed setup plus linear cost of the inventory model.

To formulate the problem you need a way to specify the state of the system. One way might be to specify two state variables, the current installed plant capacity and the current demand. However, some reflection should convince you that a sufficient description of the system is the difference between these variables, or the excess peak load capacity. When the plant is expanded, you are buying excess capacity, which is then drawn down by demand growth.

Assume that decisions to expand the capacity are made annually, and that one year is required to construct and install new capacity. Assume a 15% cost of capital. Finally, assume that the cost of a shortage in capacity is $50,000 per million BTU/hr short (we must purchase from elsewhere). The optimal plant expansion policy will be of the (s,S) form: if excess capacity drops to s, build enough capacity to raise it to S; the PROPS⁺ optimal inventory model will calculate the parameters of this policy.

To enter the problem into PROPS⁺, note that a convenient increment is 5 million BTU/hr. A reasonable level for the state variable (excess peak load capacity) is from –20 million BTU/hr to +60 million BTU/hr. That is, –20 million is the largest possible shortage, and an excess capacity of +60 million will satisfy the expected growth in demand for the next 7.5 years. (A quick way to estimate the range of the state space is to use the PROPS⁺ EOQ model.) Calling up the **(s,S)_Inventory** spreadsheet, we can set up the data area with the following sequence of inputs to the PROPS⁺ prompts:

	A	B	C	D	E	F	G	H
21		Analyst Name?			Your_name			
22		Problem Name?			plant expansion			
23								
24		States indexed from			-4	to	12	
25		Demands indexed from			-1	to	4	
26								
27		Increment for Demands/States				5		
28								

and then complete the data input area using normal spreadsheet cell input methods, as follows:

	A	B	C	D	E	F	G	H	I
29		DEMAND P.D.F.:							
30	Demand	-5	0	5	10	15	20		
31	Prob(D)	0.1	0.15	0.2	0.25	0.2	0.1		
32									
33	% Annual Interest rate			15	==>	Alpha = 0.86956			
34									
35	Backlogs allowed		y		Maximum Order size			99999	
36	Can buy AND sell		n						
37					Holding Cost/item/year			0	
38	Fixed Cost-Buy		100		Shortage Cost per unit			50	
39	Fixed Cost-Sell		0		Fixed Cost per shortage			0	
40	Order Cost/unit		10		# of review_periods/yr			1	
41									
42					How many STAGES?			10	
43		TERMINAL VALUES:							
44	State	-20	-15	-10	-5	0	5	10	15
45	f(0)	0	0	0	0	0	0	0	0
46									

To solve the model, call up the menu with [Alt M] and select **Execute** by pressing [Enter]. PROPS⁺ shows the solutions for each stage. The results for stages 1, 2, 9, and 10 are shown in the following figure:

	A	B	C	D	E	F	G	H	I	J	K	L	M	N	O	P	Q
51		Stage 1															
52	(s,S)	10	15														
53	State	-20	-15	-10	-5	0	5	10	15	20	25	30	35	40	45	50	55
54	F(I)	475	425	375	325	275	225	100	25	0	0	0	0	0	0	0	0
55	D_hat	35	30	25	20	15	10	0	0	0	0	0	0	0	0	0	0
56																	
57																		
58		Stage 2																
59	(s,S)	15	20														
60	State	-20	-15	-10	-5	0	5	10	15	20	25	30	35	40	45	50	55
61	F(I)	589.	539.	489	439	389	339	289	170	89.	42.	13.	2.1	0	0	0	0
62	D_hat	40	35	30	25	20	15	10	0	0	0	0	0	0	0	0	0
63																	

	A	B	C	D	E	F	G	H	I	J	K	L	M	N	O	P	Q
99																		
100		Stage 9																
101	(s,S)	15	40														
102	State	-20	-15	-10	-5	0	5	10	15	20	25	30	35	40	45	50	55
103	F(I)	1030	980.	930	880	830	780	730	640	559	500	439	381	330	283	240	200
104	D_hat	60	55	50	45	40	35	30	0	0	0	0	0	0	0	0	0
105																		
106		Stage 10																
107	(s,S)	15	40														
108	State	-20	-15	-10	-5	0	5	10	15	20	25	30	35	40	45	50	55
109	F(I)	1065	1015	965	915	865	815	765	674	594	534	474	416	365	318	274	234
110	D_hat	60	55	50	45	40	35	30	0	0	0	0	0	0	0	0	0
111																		

With a 10-year horizon and zero terminal inventory values, the optimal policy is to expand capacity when the excess capacity drops to 10 million BTU/hr or less (s=15), and bring the excess capacity up to 40 million BTU/hr. If the current excess capacity is zero, then the present value of costs over the 10-year horizon is $865,000. Note that the values of the discounted future costs neglect any demand beyond the end of the planning horizon—a common problem in finite-horizon models. Assigning terminal values to the ending states can rectify this problem.

Example: A Coal Inventory Problem

The heating plant in the previous plant expansion problem is coal-fired. Coal is brought in by marine barge each summer and stockpiled for use during the rest of the year. Management wishes to find an annual inventory policy for the coal pile.

Assume that the peak demand for heat in any year is 108 million BTU/hr. The average load on the plant is 0.5 of the peak load, but the total heat required in any year is a random variable that can be approximated by a normal distribution with a standard deviation equal to 0.3 of the mean. Suppose the effective BTU content of coal is 10 million BTU/ton. The cost of coal brought in by barge is $90/ton. The current contract with the shipping company allows up to 50,000 tons of coal to be carried each year. If a shortage develops, however, coal can be brought in by rail at $150/ton; any amount can be brought in this way. Assume the cost of capital is 15%.

At the peak demand of 108 million BTU/hr, the plant uses 10.8 tons of coal per hour. The average coal consumption is therefore 5.4 tons/hr (that is, 0.5 of peak consumption). Since a year has 8,760 hours, the annual average demand is 47,304 tons of coal. The standard deviation of the distribution of annual consumption is thus, by the earlier assumption, $(0.30)(47,304) = 14,191$ tons. You can generate the normal distribution for coal demand using the PROPS$^+$ probability distribution worksheet as follows. (A complete description of this worksheet is provided in Chapter 12.) To begin, select **12. Probability Distributions** from the main PROPS$^+$ ACCESS menu. You will see the header for this worksheet. Press [Alt M] and select **Distributions, Continuous**, and then **Normal** from the successive menus. PROPS$^+$ asks for a name for the distribution, of up to 14 characters. Here you might call the distribution "COAL". PROPS$^+$ then successively asks for the mean and standard deviation of the distribution, in sequence:

```
        A         B         C         D         E         F         G         H
20                Normal distribution: COAL
21
22      mean      47304
23   std dev      14191
24                                   4731
25                          Start x at?
26
```

PROPS$^+$ then requests information about how you wish to represent the sample space for this distribution (PROPS$^+$ constructs discrete approximations for continuous distributions—assume discrete increments of 10,000 tons in this example). PROPS$^+$ begins by asking for a starting, or lowest, random variable value (with a default value equal to the mean minus three standard deviations, or 4731 here). You might choose a start value of, say, 10,000 tons. A request for the upper value follows, with a default of the mean plus three standard deviations:

```
        A         B         C         D         E         F         G         H
20                Normal distribution: COAL
21
22      mean      47304
23   std dev      14191
24                                   89877
25                          Stop x at?
26
```

You might choose 90,000 tons here. Finally, PROPS$^+$ asks if you wish to specify the size of the interval or the number of intervals in the discretization with this menu:

```
D24:                                                                          MENU
Interval   Samples
You specify the interval ("step"), I calculate the number of sample points
        A         B         C         D         E         F         G         H
```

Select **Interval** and respond to the question "How Big?" with 10000. PROPS[+] then constructs the normal distribution in the worksheet as follows:

	A	B	C	D	E	F	G	H	I	J	K	L
20		Normal distribution: COAL										
21												
22	mean 47304		cdf	0.004	0.027	0.111	0.303	0.575	0.814	0.945	0.989	0.998
23	std de14191		pdf	0.000	0.000	0.000	0.000	0.000	0.000	0.000	0.000	0.000
24			x	10000	20000	30000	40000	50000	60000	70000	80000	90000
25			z	-2.62	-1.92	-1.21	-0.51	0.189	0.894	1.599	2.303	3.008
26	Note: "pdf" is the value of f(x) at x											
27												

Note that this is a discrete approximation to a continuous random variable. The pdf values are the relative likelihood of each x. An approximation for the probability distribution for x can be constructed by normalizing these pdf values so that they sum to 1. (Alternatively, you could generate the distribution at the midpoints of each interval (15 to 85) and use the difference in successive cdf values for the corresponding probabilities.) To use the first method, add the values of the pdf into, say, cell M23, as follows:

M23: @SUM(C23..L23)

	J	K	L	M	N	O
20						
21						
22	0.945127	0.989377	0.998683			
23	0.000007	0.000001	0.000000	0.000099		
24	70000	80000	90000			
25	1.599323	2.303995	3.008667			

Using the spreadsheet **Copy** command (**/C**), you can recreate the variable values in row 24, in cells [D28..L28], and set up the function **+D23/$M$23** in cell D29 as follows:

D29: +D23/$M$23   READY

	A	B	C	D	E	F	G	H
20		Normal distribution: COAL						
21								
22	mean	47304		cdf:	0.004294	0.027182	0.111342	0.303395	0.575344
23	std dev	14191		pdf:	0.000000	0.000004	0.000013	0.000024	0.000027
24				x:	10000	20000	30000	40000	50000
25				z:	-2.62870	-1.92403	-1.21936	-0.51469	0.189979
26	Note: "pdf" is the value of f(x) at x							
27								
28				10000	20000	30000	40000	50000
29				0.008892				

Finally, using the copy command to replicate this formula in the range [D29..L29] yields the following results:

	A	B	C	D	E	F	G	H	I	J	K	L
20		Normal distribution: COAL										
21												
22	mean 47304		cdf0.004	0.027	0.111	0.303	0.575	0.814	0.945	0.989	0.998	
23	std de14191		pdf0.000	0.000	0.000	0.000	0.000	0.000	0.000	0.000	0.000	
24			x10000	20000	30000	40000	50000	60000	70000	80000	90000	
25			z-2.62	-1.92	-1.21	-0.51	0.189	0.894	1.599	2.303	3.008	
26		Note: "pdf" is the value of f(x) at x										
27												
28			10000	20000	30000	40000	50000	60000	70000	80000	90000	
29			0.008	0.044	0.133	0.246	0.276	0.188	0.078	0.019	0.003	
30												

You can then use the spreadsheet **File eXtract command (/FX)** to transfer these values to another spreadsheet.

Now, to solve the coal inventory problem, call up the **(s,S)_Inventory** worksheet as before, though now the increment is 10000, the states indexed from, say, 0 to 8, and the demands indexed from 1 to 9. Once PROPS$^+$ sets up the demand pdf, we can use the **File Combine command (/FC)** to retrieve the normal distribution we just constructed, provide the remaining problem parameters, and solve the problem for, say, six stages. The worksheet appears as follows:

	A	B	C	D	E	F	G	H	I	J
21		Analyst Name?			Your_name					
22		Problem Name?			coal inventory					
23										
24		States indexed from			0	to	8			
25		Demands indexed from			1	to	9			
26										
27		Increment for Demands/States 10000								
28										
29		DEMAND P.D.F.:								
30	Demand	10000	20000	30000	40000	50000	60000	70000	80000	90000
31	Prob(D)	0.0088	0.0442	0.1338	0.2466	0.2765	0.1886	0.0783	0.0198	0.0030
32										
33	% Annual Interest rat		15	==>	Alpha =0.8695					
34										
35	Backlogs allowed?		y		Maximum Order size			99999		
36	Can buy AND sell?		n							
37					Holding Cost/item/year			0		
38	Fixed Cost-Buy K1		0		Shortage Cost per unit			150		
39	Fixed Cost-Sell K2		0		Fixed Cost per shortage			0		
40	Order Cost/unit c		90		# of review_periods/year			1		
41										
42					How many STAGE		6			
43		TERMINAL VALUES:								
44	State	0	10000	20000	30000	40000	50000	60000	70000	80000
45	f(0)	0	0	0	0	0	0	0	0	0
46										
47										

Call up the menu with [Alt M] and select **Execute**; PROPS$^+$ generates the following worksheet entries:

	A	B	C	D	E	F	G	H
75		Stage 5						
76	(s,S)	60000	60000					
77	State I	0	10000	20000	30000	40000	50000	60000
78	F(I)	17678947	16778947	15878947	14978947	14078947	13178947	12278947
79	D_hat	60000	50000	40000	30000	20000	10000	0
80								
81		Stage 6						
82	(s,S)	60000	60000					
83	State I	0	10000	20000	30000	40000	50000	60000
84	F(I)	19873745	18973745	18073745	17173745	16273745	15373745	14473745
85	D_hat	· 60000	50000	40000	30000	20000	10000	0

The optimal policy is to order enough coal to bring the pile up to 60,000 tons annually.

Example: A Cash Management Problem

This example illustrates a two-sided inventory control problem. At the beginning of each working day, a firm determines its current balance of cash for making transactions during the day. If it has excess cash, it invests in short-term securities to earn interest on the cash. If it is short, however, it sells short-term securities to raise the cash level. Transactions occur instantaneously, and the short-term interest rate is 12%, with the fixed cost of each transaction being $50. If the cash balance becomes negative at some point during the day, an emergency transaction to make up the shortfall is made at a fixed cost of $300. This emergency transaction cost is a fixed shortage cost.

Suppose the net demand for cash each day is normally distributed with a mean of $0 and a standard deviation of $40,000. That is, there may be either a net inflow or a net outflow of cash on any given day. We would like to find the cash management policy to minimize costs. That is, if all the cash needs are met, we wish to minimize the transaction costs plus the cost of holding cash. The cost of holding $1.00 in cash for a year is $.12, the short-term interest rate. The transaction cost when buying cash (selling securities) is $K_1 = \$50$, and when selling cash (buying securities) is $K_2 = \$50$. If the cash balance drops below zero during the day (stockout), then the emergency cost u = $300 is incurred and the cash balance is brought to zero (i.e., enough securities are sold to reach this level).

Following the same techniques as in the previous example, you can generate the required normal distribution for cash demand using the **12. Probability Distribution** worksheet in PROPS⁺ assuming discrete increments of, say, $20,000. In the same fashion as the previous example, we can insert this distribution into the **Inventory** worksheet when required, using the **File eXtract** and **File Combine** spread-sheet commands (**/FX**) and (**/FC**).

Assume a five-day planning horizon. To solve the cash management problem in PROPS⁺, call up the optimal probabilistic inventory worksheet in the same fashion as the last example and fill in the values for this problem. This generates the following worksheet. Note especially that the default y on "Backlogs allowed?" has been changed to n, and the buy and sell option has been changed from n to y.

	A	B	C	D	E	F	G	H	I
21		Analyst Name?			Your_name				
22		Problem Name?			cash management				
23									
24		States indexed from			0	to	12		
25		Demands indexed from			-6	to	6		
26									
27		Increment for Demands/States				20000			
28									
29		DEMAND P.D.F.:							
30	Demand	-120000	-100000	-80000	-60000	-40000	-20000	0	20000
31	Prob(D)	0.00221	0.00877	0.02702	0.06482	0.12110	0.17621	0.19967	0.17621
32									
33	% Annual Interest rate			0	==>	Alpha =	1		
34									
35	Backlogs allowed		n		Maximum Order size			99999	
36	Can buy AND sell		y						
37					Holding Cost/item/year			0.12	
38	Fixed Cost-Buy		50		Shortage Cost per unit			0	
39	Fixed Cost-Sell		50		Fixed Cost per shortage			300	
40	Order Cost/unit		0		# of review_periods/yr			365	
41									
42						How many STAGES?		5	
43		TERMINAL VALUES:							
44	State	0	20000	40000	60000	80000	100000	120000	140000
45	f(0)	0	0	0	0	0	0	0	0

Pressing [Alt M] and selecting **Execute** from the menu generates the following solution:

	A	B	C	D	E	F	G	H	I	J	K
51		Stage 1									
52	(s,S)		80000								
53	State	0	20000	40000	60000	80000	100000	120000	140000	160000	180000
54	F(I)	79.69	76.25	45.02	31.47	29.69	33.56	39.45	46.03	52.60	59.18
55	D_hat	80000	0	0	0	0	0	0	0	0	0
56											

	A	B	C	D	E	F	G	H	I	J	K
74											
75		Stage 5									
76	(s,S)		80000								
77	State	0	20000	40000	60000	80000	100000	120000	140000	160000	180000
78	F(I)	254.8	254.8	232.2	211.0	204.8	208.9	219.4	233.3	247.6	254.8
79	D_hat	80000	60000	0	0	0	0	0	0	0	-100000

From the solution, you see that with one day to go until the end of the horizon, the optimal decision is only raise the cash balance if it is 0, and if so raise it to $80,000. Never buy securities. With more than one day to go, the policy settles down to "raise the balance to $80,000 if it is less than or equal to $20,000; reduce the balance to $80,000 if it is greater than or equal to $180,000; otherwise do nothing." (The actual policy is found directly from the "D_hat" row.) You might find it interesting to explore how the cash management policy changes as the mean demand is varied from positive to negative values.

Index

License Agreement

IMPORTANT: READ THIS LICENSE AGREEMENT CAREFULLY BEFORE OPENING THIS PACKAGE. BY OPENING THE PACKAGE, YOU ACCEPT THE TERMS OF THIS AGREEMENT.

REFUND

If you don't wish to follow the terms of this license agreement, you may obtain a full refund by returning this package with your receipt to your Authorized Dealer within ten (10) days provided you have not opened the sealed disk package. Your right to return this product for a refund for this reason expires on the eleventh day after purchase.

Addison-Wesley Publishing Company, Inc. ("Addison-Wesley") has authorized distribution of this copy of the Software to you pursuant to a license from Props Systems ("PS") and retains ownership of this copy of the Software. PS retains ownership of the Software itself. This copy is *licensed* to you for use under the following conditions:

DEFINITIONS

The term "Software" as used in this agreement means the computer programs contained in the disks in this package, together with any updates subsequently supplied by Addison-Wesley.

The term "Software Copies" means the actual copies of all or any portion of the Software, including backups, updates, merged or partial copies permitted hereunder or subsequently supplied by Addison-Wesley.

The term "Related Materials" means all of the printed materials provided in this package or later supplied by Addison-Wesley for use with the Software.

PERMITTED USES

You may:

- Use this software only for educational purposes.
- Load into RAM and use the Software on a single terminal or a single workstation of a computer (or its replacement).
- Install the Software onto a permanent storage device (a hard disk).
- Make and maintain up to three back-up copies provided they are used only for back-up purposes, and you keep possession of the backups. In addition, all the information appearing on the original disk labels (including the copyright notice) must be copied onto the back-up labels.

This license gives you certain limited rights to use the Software, Software Copies, and Related Materials. You do not become the owner of, and Addison-Wesley and PS (according to their respective interests) retain title to, all the Software, Software Copies, and Related Materials. In addition, you agree to use reasonable efforts to protect the Software from unauthorized use, reproduction, distribution, or publication.

All rights not specifically granted in this license are reserved by Addison-Wesley and PS.

USES NOT PERMITTED

You may not:

- Use this software for any purposes other than educational purposes.
- Make copies of the Software, except as permitted above.
- Make copies of the Related Materials.
- Use the Software in a network or multiple user arrangement unless you pay for and obtain a separate licensed Software package for each terminal or workstation from which the Software will actually be accessed.
- Rent, lease, sub-license, time-share, lend, or transfer the Software, Software Copies, Related Materials, or your rights under this license except that transfers may be made with Addison-Wesley's prior written authorization.
- Alter, decompile, disassemble, or reverse engineer the Software or make any attempt to unlock or bypass the initialization system used on the initialized disks.
- Remove or obscure the PS or Addison-Wesley copyright and trademark notices.
- Use the Software, Software Copies, or Related materials outside the United States and Canada.

DURATION

This agreement is effective from the day you open the sealed disk pouch. Your license continues for fifty years or until you return to Addison-Wesley the original disks and any back-up copies, whichever comes first.

If you breach this agreement, we can terminate this license upon notifying you in writing. You will be required to return all Software Copies and Related Materials. We can also enforce our other legal rights.

GENERAL

This agreement represents our entire understanding and agreement regarding the Software, Software Copies, and Related Materials and supersedes any prior purchase order, communications, advertising, or representations.

This license may only be modified in a written amendment signed by an authorized Addison-Wesley officer. If any provision of this agreement shall be unlawful, void, or for any reason enforceable, it shall be deemed severable from, and shall in no way affect the validity or enforceability of, the remaining provisions of this agreement. This agreement will be governed by Massachusetts law.

You acknowledge that you have read every provision of this contract.

Addison-Wesley and PS retain all rights not expressly granted. Nothing in this agreement constitutes a waiver of Addison-Wesley's or PS's rights under the U.S. copyright laws or any other federal or state law.

Should you have any questions concerning this agreement, you may contact Addison-Wesley by writing to Addison-Wesley Publishing Company, Inc., Business and Economics, Jacob Way, Reading, MA 01867.